PERSPECTIVES ON COGNITIVE SCIENCE

PERSPECTIVES ON COGNITIVE SCIENCE

edited by

Donald A. Norman

ABLEX PUBLISHING CORPORATION
NORWOOD, NEW JERSEY

LAWRENCE ERLBAUM ASSOCIATES
HILLSDALE, NEW JERSEY

Library of Congress Cataloging in Publication Data
Main entry under title:

Perspectives on cognitive science.

  Papers presented at the 1st annual meeting of the
Cognitive Science Society, La Jolla, Calif., Aug. 1979.
  Includes bibliographies and index.
  1. Cognition—Congresses. 2. Cognition—Research—
Congresses. I. Norman, Donald A. II. Cognitive
Science Society (U.S.)
BF311.P37   153.4   80-21343
ISBN 0-89391-071-6

ABLEX Publishing Corporation
355 Chestnut Street
Norwood, New Jersey 07648

Contents

Preface   v

1   What Is Cognitive Science?   1
        Donald A. Norman

2   Cognitive Science: The Newest Science
        of the Artificial   13
        Herbert A. Simon

3   Neurological Knowledge and Complex Behaviors   27
        Norman Geschwind

4   Physical Symbol Systems   37
        Allen Newell

5   K-Lines: A Theory of Memory   87
        Marvin Minsky

6   Language and Memory   105
        Roger C. Schank

7   Mental Models in Cognitive Science   147
        P. N. Johnson-Laird

8   The Metaphorical Structure
        of the Human Conceptual System   193
        George Lakoff and Mark Johnson

                                                                                iii

9   The Intentionality of Intention and Action   207
        John R. Searle

10 What Does It Mean to Understand Language?   231
        Terry Winograd

11 Twelve Issues for Cognitive Science   265
        Donald A. Norman

        Author Index   297

        Subject Index   301

Preface

It was to be the "defining meeting," the meeting where many of those concerned with the birth of Cognitive Science could record its origins, speak of its hopes, and chart its course. We knew these aspirations to be unrealistic, but did not let that knowledge deter us. The speakers at the conference—the contributors to this volume—all work within the sibling disciplines that comprise Cognitive Science. All were charged with the task of presenting broad, overview statements of their views, statements that would last beyond the year of the conference and that would help set the definition of the field, statements that would prove useful in the initial stages of the discipline and that would provide examples of what we are, what we wish to become, and even what we should not be.

This book is the result of that conference. Here, in ten very different statements, the ten invited speakers present their views of the science. All were urged to present papers that ranged beyond the immediate concerns of the field, to express some of the hopes, aspirations, and critical issues that face the development of a cognitive science. They were urged to be substantive as well, not simply to present lofty aims and ideals, but to demonstrate how they have approached the issues of the field. The different contributors responded to these urgings in different ways. Some thought it best to provide general overviews of the science, or of their philosophy of approach. Others presented substantive pieces of research or deep analyses of a key issue, illustrating the science by deed. All styles of papers were encouraged. Each author, though, was urged to make the paper intelligible even to the nonspecialist, if not in substance, then at least in spirit. Thus, papers on one's current pet project can be of lasting value if they demonstrate the philosophy of approach used in tackling the problem, if they reveal the doubts, the false steps, and the history by which the current state was reached, and then state one's current working hypotheses about the problem. In this way, the research papers complement the more broadly stated position papers. The one provides a statement of what Cognitive Science could be, the other provides a demonstration of the science in progress.

The task of selecting speakers was complex, all the more so because we were pleasantly pleased to discover that there were more candidates than could possibly be accommodated in a single conference. Accordingly, we aimed for some breadth, for a balance of positions. The "we" who helped organize the conference include the members of the Program in Cognitive Science at the University of California, San Diego, and in particular, my co-directors of the program: George Mandler and David Rumelhart. The procedure we followed was to select a balanced, representative group of speakers from among those disciplines and people in Cognitive Science. The list of candidate speakers (and symposia topics and organizers) was refined through continual assessment with the help of the people who were then Visiting Scholars in the Program: Robert Buhr, Larry Carleton, Geoffrey Hinton, Edwin Hutchins, Ian Moar, and Leonard Talmy. Many other people across the country aided in the selection process, through lengthy telephone calls, letters, and computer mail networks. Several of those invited could not attend, due to prior commitments or other conflicts. With each acceptance or declination of an invitation, we reassessed the entire list of invitees, making whatever changes seemed necessary to preserve the balance. In the end, we felt that nearly all important directions in Cognitive Science were represented. One of the major omissions occurred because none of the (three) people invited from what might be called the "MIT school of linguistics" was able to attend.

This was not the first conference on Cognitive Science. There are numerous candidates for this title, with perhaps the most authoritative claims attached to a spate of conferences on Artificial Intelligence, on Thought Processes, on Cybernetics, and on Information Theory, all held in 1956. However, now is the time when the name "Cognitive Science" is attached to the varied activities of its proponents. There is a journal by that name, and a society: the journal started in 1977, the society born during the planning stages of this conference. The journal, the society, the conference—each deciding to adopt the other two as their official vehicles. The result is that this conference also serves as the first official (and annual) conference of the Cognitive Science Society and the journal which is the official publication of the society.

This book provides ten perspectives on Cognitive Science, each viewing a different set of topics, each presented in a different style. Taken together, the set of papers provides far-ranging, broad coverage of the wide variety of disciplines and approaches within Cognitive Science. The papers presented here do not serve as the formal definition of the field: that task is probably not possible. But they do serve to illustrate many of the foundations, many of the hopes and aspirations of the workers, and something of the variety of style and point of view that characterizes the research. The book does not provide a single definition: it provides ten perspectives for viewing the emerging discipline of Cognitive Science.

Acknowledgments

The Program in Cognitive Science at UCSD and many of the expenses of the conference were supported by a grant from the Alfred P. Sloan Foundation. I thank Kenneth Klivington of the Sloan Foundation for his support of the program and the conference. I also thank the many people across the country—too numerous to list—who helped in the selection of the conference, who served as the organizers for the six state-of-the-art symposia, and those who participated in the symposia themselves. Thank you all.

DONALD A. NORMAN
Program in Cognitive Science
Center for Human Information Processing
University of California, San Diego
La Jolla, California

PERSPECTIVES ON COGNITIVE SCIENCE

1

What Is
Cognitive Science?

DONALD A. NORMAN

Department of Psychology
and
Program in Cognitive Science
Center for Human Information Processing
University of California, San Diego

Cognitive Science is a new discipline, created from a merger of interests among those pursuing the study of cognition from different points of view. The critical aspect of Cognitive Science is the search for understanding of cognition, be it real or abstract, human or machine. The goal is to understand the principles of intelligent, cognitive behavior. The hope is that this will lead to better understanding of the human mind, of teaching and learning, of mental abilities, and of the development of intelligent devices that can augment human capabilities in important and constructive ways.

The chapters in this book address these issues by their contents, by the variety of their different approaches, and by the breadth of the questions they pose, the methods they apply. But the chapters will not provide an answer. Indeed, they may add to the confusion. What is Cognitive Science? Why is it needed?

We lack a science of cognition: a science of the mind, of intelligence, of thought, a science concerned with knowledge and its uses. True, numerous disciplines have been concerned with these matters, but not in any complete fashion. The study of cognition requires a broad base, and full understanding will require more than the tools from a single existing discipline. Human cognition exists within the context of the person, the society, the culture. To understand the human requires understanding of these different issues and the ways in which interactions among them shape the cognitive processes. The hardware of the human is the brain, the province of the neurosciences, setting limits on what can be done, constraints on how. The philosopher has worried about different issues, about mind, thought, intention, memory, acts and beliefs. The psychologist has been concerned with both brain and functional mechanisms of mind, with the operations of the cognitive processing systems, with language, perception, emotions, with maturation of the infant, and with the nature of social interactions.

1

The society and the culture color our actions as much as do brain structures. Here the cognitive anthropologist and sociologist play important roles. The tasks and the environment exert strong constraints upon actions. Human artifacts become essential elements of human cognition—writing, reading, communication technology, social groups, the computer as a tool for cognition. Even the innocent metaphors of language convey hints (or more strongly, entailments) as to the underlying belief structures. Interpretation of a current event depends upon history, which is based upon culture. If we create artificial intelligences, will they not be subject to the same constraints? If they attempt to mimic human intelligence, they must thereby share the same cultural and social knowledge. If they exist by themselves, as artificial intelligences, to be truly creative and communicative, must they not develop their own background and culture? And they will be strongly constrained by their environments, by the tasks given to them, by the sensory and motor organs with which they are provided, as well as by the more obvious constraints offered by their processing mechanisms and algorithms. To understand cognitive processes is to understand all these different contributing factors.

There are other aspects of the science. I personally have need for new insights into intelligent mechanisms. As a psychologist, I want to understand the mechanisms of mind–the human mind. As a cognitive scientist, my goal is somewhat different. Here I no longer restrict myself to the study of the human. Now, my goal is to understand cognition in the general and in the abstract. For this purpose, I care not whether the cognition is of something natural or artificial, human or non-human, real or hypothetical. How can I understand human cognition until I understand the range of cognitive mechanisms and functions? I need to know the possible theoretical approaches, the range of possibilities. Then, and only then, can I distinguish among the possibilities, to know the strengths and weaknesses of each, to determine which best characterizes human thought and cognition. As a cognitive psychologist, I need a Cognitive Science. Today, the general theoretical structure of Cognitive Science does not exist. It should.

Why a new discipline? Why not continue within the existing sciences? The answer lies within the sociology and politics of Science. At the moment, each individual worker within Cognitive Science suffers the problem of not fitting within any given scientific area. I believe that important issues of the nature of cognition can only be addressed by the developments of new methods of procedure, new methodology, new experimental techniques, new theory. But the existing disciplines come with existing constraints and existing beliefs about the primacy of their own individual methods and interests. Even where there is agreement about the importance of a particular issue, often there is no agreement about where such an issue should fit within the normal academic departmental structures. The relevant members of each discipline might agree that the work is important and useful, but that it is simply not central enough a part of their discipline. In such cases how can a researcher progress? How can a graduate student expect to get a thesis approved? How can the student then get a job? How can a young faculty member get tenure within an established discipline? The only answer seems to be that there should be a discipline with a common focus on knowledge, but encouraging diverse methodologies.

Hence Cognitive Science: a field that can concentrate on understanding knowledge and cognitive processes, free of the concerns of the individual sciences.

TEN PERSPECTIVES ON COGNITIVE SCIENCE

What do the chapters in this book offer toward an understanding of Cognitive Science? They provide eloquent summaries of the varied viewpoints of the authors, but how do they fit together? On the surface they appear to disagree with one another as much as they agree. Their goals conflict and contradict. And some seem simply orthogonal to the issues, or at least to the issues raised by the others. How do these chapters provide insight into the study of cognition?

The central theme of the book is the role of computation and symbol manipulation in cognition. To some, the very essence of a cognitive system is that of a symbol processing system. The human and the computer are indeed very different beasts, goes their argument, but they share in common the ability to create, manipulate, and process abstract symbols. This is what gives intellectual power to humans, to animals, to artificial devices. How do the ten chapters treat this issue? That the human is a symbol processing system is discussed most explicitly in the two chapters by Simon and Newell. But the basic assumption is used by almost all the others, sometimes explicitly, sometimes implicitly. The use does not mean agreement. Indeed, the minor theme of the book is a criticism of the ubiquitous acceptance of symbol processing systems as the model of human and animal cognition. This criticism is voiced most strenuously by Geschwind and Winograd. Lakoff & Johnson and Searle seemed not to address these issues at all, but nonetheless, the arguments they posed were designed to give difficulties to the contemporary beliefs in symbol processing mechanisms. In my contribution—the last chapter of the book—I straddle both sides of the argument, saying yes, we are symbol processors, but we are more.

What is the argument about symbol processing? What is a symbol? Central to the definition is that a symbol ''symbolizes'' something, a symbol stands for something else. This provides a basis for the problem of representation, and then of processing, for the assumption carries with it the implication that cognitive processes operate through the manipulation, transformation, and combination of internal symbols that represent experiences, meanings, perceptions, and actions. In his chapter on ''Physical Symbol Systems, Newell quoted Whitehead: I repeat that quotation here:

> The human mind is functioning symbolically when some components of its experience elicit consciousness, beliefs, emotions, and usages reflecting other components of its experience. The former set of components are the "symbols," and the latter set constitute the "meaning" of the symbols. The organic functioning whereby there is transition from the symbol to the meaning will be called "symbolic reference." (Whitehead, 1927, pp. 7–8)

Why is there disagreement over this issue? The difficulty seems to be that symbol systems imply discrete, purposeful representation. Must all cognitive processes by symbolic processes?

Consider a simple organism—a moth—so constructed that the relative rate at which the two wings beat is affected by the relative difference in light intensity arriving at the two eyes. When light arrives at the left eye, it increases the neural signal sent to the right wing and decreases the neural signal sent to the left wing. The result is to speed up the beating of the wings that are away from the light, to slow down the beating of the wings that are toward the light, and to cause the moth to fly toward lights, circling as it does. The observer says that the moth is attracted to the light, that it "likes light." But where is the intentionality of the moth? Where the likes and dislikes? Where is the symbol system of the moth? Is this an intelligent system?

The moth is not a good prototype for a cognitive system but the questions that its mechanisms raise are important. How much of the complex behavior of people is built up of specialized subsystems, much as those of the moth, systems that do not have discrete symbols upon which to do formal operations? In "wired-in" systems such as these, the intentionality and purpose are revealed only in the evolutionary history that gave rise to the system in the first place, but not present in the system in any explicit form, other than that of the existence of the system itself.

Geschwind raised this issue explicitly in his chapter when he discusses innate, wired-in mechanisms. Some cats that have been raised so as never to have seen a rat, Geschwind reminded us, will attack a rat upon first exposure, attacking in the same manner as an animal in the wild, not just attacking, but biting the rat precisely in the proper region of the neck (and from the proper angle) so as to kill it. These are specific, wired-in mechanisms of some complexity, involving aspects of perception, rat anatomy, and skilled motor actions. But the program is apt to exist in the cat in the same manner that the program for flying toward a light exists in the moth. Is this symbol processing?

What are the classes of mechanism that qualify as symbol processors? It is possible to argue that almost any mechanism that is used to guide action has a symbolic component. In the moth, the rate of firing of the neurons symbolizes the intensity and location of the light. This representation is interpreted by the muscle system. Is the system of the moth a symbol processing system? It is possible to view the human as consisting to a large part of specialized mechanisms, prewired to work in certain ways. These mechanisms are similar in spirit to that of the moth. The system is put together to respond directly: the system state reflects the condition of its variables. In this system it is not easy to identify the stages of processing, cognition, and decision so favored by contemporary theorists of human processing. Rather, the system just operates to do "what is needed to be done." But what does it mean to do "what is needed?" The identification of a signal with a "variable" of the system suggests symbol processing.

So too with the cat. The attack of the cat is not just a complex reflex. "After all," says Geschwind,[1] "the cognitive system is really what is embodied in the genes and is inherited. It is, if you will, a racial memory. It thus embodies a useful strategy which has been learned in the past and simply does not have to be learned again. At least in the case of the cat I presume that he has very subjective sensations and intentions. He will, for example, go around a barrier to attack the rat. This is no more surprising than the human's felt emotions and intentions to all of the inherited stimuli to which we have inherited responses."

I prefer to bypass this debate, to argue that a major component of Cognitive Science is the specification of the rules and mechanism by which cognitive systems operate. This definition admits the importance of physical symbol processing, but also allows variety in the choice of specification of cognitive functions. By this definition, the study of the specialized mechanisms of cognitive functioning, of the rules of language, of biological principles relevant to cognition, or of physical symbol processing systems are all fundamental to the science.

A second theme of the book concerns the ways in which human and animal cognition are shaped by the environment and by the biology. Part of the issue is the biological structures that result from evolution, part is the system of human artifacts that have been created by us through our various cultures, and that strongly influence our knowledge, beliefs, and cognitions. Simon emphasized the relativity of behavior to the environment. We are really studying sociology, he said. Cognitive systems are adaptive, they "are what they are from being ground between the nether millstone of their physiology or hardware, as the case may be, and the upper millstone of a complex environment in which they exist. Systems that are adaptive may equally well be described as 'artificial,' for as environments change, they can be expected to change too, as though they were deliberately designed to fit those environments" (Simon, 1980, abstract). Natural intelligence is actually artificial: life did not always exist. All intelligences, said Simon, are symbol systems, built on the same basic processes. Computers are built in the image of their maker: the human. Evolution is an important process, but without goals (unless it be the ability to survive till reproduction). The result is the infinite shaping of an animal species for a particular ecological niche. The shaping works upon both the animal and the environment: change either one and there is no longer a match. We humans also have been shaped to fit our environment. But we have also shaped the environment; we have made the environment into our tool. The environment has become as much a part of our computational apparatus as our brains. Through human

[1]Letter from Geschwind, May 20, 1980.

changes of the environment, through the invention of new technologies, we have substantially enriched our computational powers.

The chapter by Geschwind makes similar points. We are specialized creatures. The brain is a complex device, bathed in fluids, communicating with itself and with the body through chemicals, liquids, electrical impulses. There are specialized systems interacting in interesting ways. Is the brain the ideal cognitive device? Probably not, said Geschwind. And why do we say "the brain?" Is there only one model of brain? The brain exists as the result of compromises with biology and evolution, compromises that have probably traded superior design in one area for inferior design in another. "Simon has said," said Geschwind, "that when we think we are studying properties of the nervous system we may really be studying the effects of past history. A little reflection, however, shows that the opposite situation may be equally frequent—when we thought we were studying the effects of experience we were really studying the properties of the nervous system." One model of the human mind is of a powerful, general purpose symbol processing system. Another model is that of a collection of specialized systems, each designed for a particular function, each with built-in "knowledge," each honed and shaped over millions of years to do its job, constrained by the biological, ecological, evolutionary forces that it encounters.

Geschwind argued for the importance of knowledge of neurological systems for the understanding of mind. We have specific wired-in functions. We are complex creatures. Neurological mechanisms are more complex than we realize. The study of disordered cognitive functioning from brain diseases is a powerful way to test cognitive theories. Geschwind's plea is an important one, although often overlooked in the general course of contemporary Cognitive Science. Geschwind was invited to participate precisely for this reason: it would be folly to ignore our biological bases.

Newell argued convincingly that no matter the hardware, intelligent cognition implies a symbol processing system. It is important to examine such systems in great depth, to examine the fundamental properties of their operation, the primitives from which any cognitive system must be built. A physical symbol system is one that is realizable, a system that deals with the symbols and reference. The physical symbol system is ground for the figure of processing.

Newell provides us with important constraints of symbol processing systems. I believe his point is essential, for I agree with him and Simon that at the core of Cognitive Science must be a symbol processing system. The chapter is of special importance because prior to this, we did not have a clear and definite statement of what was meant or implied by physical symbol systems. The chapter provides a definitive statement of the position, complete with examination of the basic primitive command structure of symbol processing devices, of the issues of real time processing constraints, of the implications of the need for diversity and specialization of human processing systems. Many of the objections to the view of the human as a symbol processing system will find both support and refutation in this chapter. Unfortunately, the chapter will not settle the issues, but they will allow them to be stated more precisely, they will allow the debates to proceed more constructively, with agreement as to the fundamental issues that are being questioned. Newell is right to emphasize the importance of understanding the primitives of a physical symbol system, for issues of representation and processing form the basis of Cognitive Science.

Minsky continues the discussion about mechanism, but in a novel way. In a sense, what Minsky is attempting is to devise a new principle of processing architecture by taking seriously the constraints that neurological development of the brain must place upon its physical structure, and then asking how those physical constraints will affect the information processing structures: bridging the gap between Geschwind and Newell. His presentation at the conference was lucidly incomprehensible. Minsky explained why; some of the important issues necessary for understanding his concepts were explained in other papers that he had written, papers that we had not read. But alas, Minsky told us, he himself did not understand those other papers either. Why the difficulty? Because they are difficult problems. After all, would you rather a scientific theory be correct or would you rather it be intelligible? Minsky's chapter reflects the struggles to shape a new direction of theorizing, a fundamentally different approach to the study of memory and the nature of the processing mechanism.

How could the brain have evolved to be a physical symbol system? The question raises important issues about brain architecture. In earlier papers Minsky worried about the passing of arguments (Minsky, 1977, 1979). In the chapter in this book, Minsky postulates a new form of organization of knowledge, into nodes, lines, and pyramids. The goal is no less than reconceptualization of the problems of memory, starting with the function of memory function, of mental states, and of mental agencies. Who is the ''I'' that does one thing or another in the head. When someone says ''I just had a brilliant idea'' what is that ''I?'' Minsky says it isn't ''I'' it is a ''we''—agents—a collective we as opposed to the classical I, to Freud's ego. This allows talk of societies of agents, of minds within minds. The concepts of mental state and partial mental state get interpreted in terms of ''subsets of the states of the parts of the mind.'' Minsky is advocating a complete change in our way of thinking about processing. The arguments are not complete and so the chapter is suggestive, not definitive. Do not expect it to be easy to understand.

Clearly there is more to the study of Cognitive Science than the study of processing structures, of whatever sort. Some content is required, some way of making use of the processing structures, whatever their nature. The chapters by Schank and Johnson-Laird start the discussion of these issues. Schank is worried about memory, but in ways quite unlike that of Minsky. Well, he said, I needed to understand memory in order to understand understanding. Psychologists weren't telling me anything useful about memory—all they said was that it was there, and that maybe there were two of them. So if the psychologists won't talk about memory in the way that is useful for learning about how it is used in things like language understanding, then I will have to act like a psychologist.

Schank's chapter is of interest for more than his analysis of memory structures. He also provides us with some insights into his general approach to the study of language. Schank starts by analyzing his earlier work, explaining how he began his endeavor, why he is studying the issues that he is. His tact is to identify the important issues, to attempt to categorize human behavior relevant to those issued, then to devise a scheme for accounting for the majority of the phenomena. No matter that the scheme is simplified over what must be the important thing is whether the ideas work, whether they can be realized in a programmable system. The chapter demonstrates that Schank does not believe his theories nearly as much as do some of his readers. Each new theory is a step toward further understanding, nothing more. Scripts are found to be faulty, so they are modified. This paper proposes a new level of memory organization, one that is bound to lead to much discussion and controversy: MOPs and TOPs. But before you judge them, remember their real purpose: they are current approximations, useful if they work in illuminating and describing phenomena of memory.

Another aspect of Schank's work that becomes clear from the chapter is that it is based upon examination of psychological phenomena—not by doing experiments, as the psychologists would do, but as an observer of human behavior with a good feel for what are important phenomena and what are not. Schank is a classifier: having identified a phenomenon, the next step is to categorize its various manifestations. Then, each separate category can be examined, and solved. Divide a hard problem into manageable subparts; a well-known scientific strategy.

Johnson-Laird poses a different set of problems. How do humans reason? What is the status of the models of the reasoning process? What is the status of the model provided by the logicians: the theory of syllogistic inference? Johnson-Laird argues that this view flies in the face of psychological evidence. Models of inference are going to need a more intimate connection between our understanding of the world and our logical thought processes. Indeed, he said, we do not necessarily reason through logic, but rather through example, through the development of mental models.

Allen Newell, standing up from the audience after the talk by Johnson-Laird, complained. "Look," he told Johnson-Laird, "I'm confused. You deny we use logical inference, yet the brain machinery that evaluates the experiential models must itself use logical inferences to do the evaluation of the model. Isn't that a contradiction?"

I believe both Johnson-Laird and Newell are correct. This is really a problem of the specification of level. At the level of brain, the brain stuff follows physical-chemical-biological rules of operation. The rules followed by the mind stuff is determined by the functional interaction of its component mechanisms and of its representation. Upon this substrate of processing machinery lies the contents of mind, wherein the "I/we" of internal cognition models the environment based upon experiences. We solve some problems by modeling them according to our mental models of the world, of space, time, and object: so says Johnson-Laird. Our problem solving will then mirror the laws we have deduced of the world, as interpreted through the limits of working memory and human processing. These models need not be accurate reflections of the world; they need not even be consistent with themselves. If this "experiential" reasoning fails to follow "logical" reasoning, the failure implies nothing about the machinery of mind, only about the contents.

Johnson-Laird has commented upon this discussion.[2]

> "I sense that Newell and I may be misunderstanding rather than disagreeing. . . . The word 'logical' has an unfortunate ambiguity. On the one hand, it can mean reasoning according to some system of logic. On the other hand, it can merely mean making inferences that are logical, i.e., valid. I suspect that my interchange with Allen Newell was a mutual misunderstanding because of the ambiguity. My claim is that people can make logical (valid) inferences without employing any sort of mental logic. All that they possess to guide them is the fundamental semantic principle of valid inference; i.e., an inference is valid if there is no way of interpreting the premises so that they are inconsistent with the conclusion. What logic is, is a system of principles (axioms, rules of inference, inferential schemata or what have you) that is intended to provide a machine for making valid inference. And what I am saying is that, in general, we possess no such machine. That is why Aristotle decided to invent logic. He knew that we often erred, but because he, in common with most people, possessed the fundamental semantic principle, he was capable of making valid deductions—an essential prerequisite for anyone who wishes to construct a system of logic."

Johnson-Laird's contribution can be seen as building upon several of the issues of the book. His work uses symbol processing structures and a person's experiences within a cultural environment to perform thought and reason by means of internal models of those experiences. The work, therefore, merges several of the apparently conflicting view of the human as a symbol processor, working according to what appear to be non-logical principles.

Lakoff & Johnson argue that one's internal, mental models are reflected in speech. We talk in models, in metaphors. The metaphors are subtle, but they have strong entailments. Think of ideas as children of the creators—"he conceived a brilliant theory," "Cognitive Psychology is still in its infancy," "This concept is the brainchild of . . . "—and you automatically bring a large set of concepts to the understanding of "idea." Moreover, the entailments of one metaphor may not be consistent with those of another: contrast the metaphor of ideas as children with those of ideas as plants, or products, commodities, resources, money, cutting instruments, food, or fashions. Each metaphor brings a new set of perspectives upon the concept, each illuminates the concept differently: ideas (as cutting instruments) can "cut to the heart of the matter" but these ideas are made, not born, as would be idea as child. Johnson-Laird and Lakoff & Johnson are saying similar things: knowledge as model, as analogy and metaphor to other knowledge. But Lakoff & Johnson say more. They were concerned with the power of the hidden entailments of metaphor to trap the user into believing more than was explicitly stated. Their chapter concludes with this statement: "If Cognitive Science is to be concerned with human understanding in its full richness and not merely those phenomena that fit the MIND IS MACHINE

---

[2]Letter from Johnson-Laird, May 20, 1980.

metaphor, then it may have to sacrifice metaphorical consistency in the service of fuller understanding.''

It is not enough to talk of mechanism and of thought. There are a number of critical issues so far absent from the analysis of cognitive functioning. One is the role of intention. Intelligent animals have intentions that they attempt to fulfill. But the notion of "intention" is a complex one, involving consideration of a number of deep philosophical issues of the relationship between intention and action. Searle tells us of action and intention, and of memory and of perception, and of the relationship and philosophical underpinnings of these concepts. The chapter gets technical, introducing philosophical argument. Intention is a state of consciousness. It is not the same as behavior. What is intention? When can we say that we have done what we intended to do? In the process of examining these issues, Searle draws a parallel between the intentionality of visual perception and the intentionality of intentional action which then gives rise to analysis of the parallelisms among seeing something, remembering that something, prior intention to action, and action. The result is both an increase in our understanding of intention and action and also some views of how a philosopher of cognition approaches the job.

The two final chapters of the book re-examine the basis of Cognitive Science. Winograd does this by reconsideration of his own work in relationship to a growing realization of the incompleteness of work in that tradition, specially as measured against a view of knowledge and understanding as always being determined relativistically. The chapter raises issues: that is its goal, the raising of questions about the nature of understanding. Winograd examines the very foundations of his earlier work on language understanding. Is representation needed? What are the basic assumptions that one brings to bear in the development of a processing model of language? Taking part of his background from the Hermeneutic tradition within philosophy, Winograd argues for a new view of the understanding process. The path is a complex one and the goal not fully formulated. The issues, however, are critical to the success of Cognitive Science. They get at the essence of natural reasoning and the natural understanding.

In the concluding chapter of the book I address the many different issues that comprise Cognitive Science. I identify twelve major issues that have attracted my attention. These twelve are neither independent of one another nor equal in importance. And I make no claim that they cover all that is important in the study of cognition. I do claim, however, that these twelve are among a core of issues among which we must progress if our field is to have substance.

I believe in the value of multiple philosophies, multiple viewpoints, and multiple approaches to common issues. I believe the virtue of Cognitive Science is that it brings together heretofore disparate disciplines to work on common themes. My reason for discussing these twelve issues is the hope that I can focus some efforts upon common problems. I discuss these issues primarily from my own perspective, a perspective that is primarily that of a psychologist interested in the workings of the mind. Alternate points of view are possible, welcome and necessary. Some alternatives are provided in the other chapters of this book.

In the treatment of the twelve topics, I provide varying amounts of discussion based upon my own knowledge and understandings of the issues and the current state of work on that set of problems. Each issue, however, is a whole topic that must be addressed from all directions: neurological, psychological, sociological, cultural, philosophical, linguistic.

Much is missing from this volume. There are important fields that have not been represented, important points of view that are absent. Several obvious gaps exist. There is no statement about anthropology, about evolution, about development. Can we learn from studies of animal intelligence? Even from within the disciplines that have been covered, the book contains only one or two views, sometimes not the dominant view of that discipline. The strength of the book is in its diversity as the contributors approach a common theme: the study of cognition. There is no lack of opportunities for each proponent of any particular view to be heard. But there are few opportunities for the proponents of differing points of view to speak with one another, or to address a common audience. The strength of this book lies in the success with which the contributors succeed at that task. This book should be approached in the spirit of the search for understanding of a most complex topic: the understanding of cognition.

2

Cognitive Science: The Newest Science of the Artificial*

HERBERT A. SIMON

Carnegie-Mellon University

We are assembled here to take part in the christening of a domain of scientific inquiry that is to be called Cognitive Science. It is not often that a christening is postponed for as many years as this one has been, for even with a conservative reckoning of birthdates, cognitive science has been for some time old enough to vote. There is substantial evidence that the infant was born no later than 1956.

This christening ceremony, then, does not seek to create a new discipline, but to provide a channel for recognizing and handling a set of common concerns among cognitive psychologists, researchers in artificial intelligence, linguists, philosophers, and others seeking to understand the human mind. Understanding the human mind is indeed a venerable goal of cogitation and research. A history of that endeavor must begin no later than with Aristotle.

If that is so, why do I mention the year 1956? That year is important because it signaled a new approach to understanding the human mind, a new scientific paradigm, that today we call the information processing paradigm. In 1956 George A. Miller published an information processing account of the limited capacity of short-term memory (Miller, 1956); Chomsky published one of his first analyses of the formal properties of transformational grammars (Chomsky, 1956); Bruner, Goodnow, and Austin, in their *A Study of Thinking* (1956), introduced strategies as mediating constructs in cognitive theory; and Allen Newell and I published a description of the *Logic Theorist*, the first computer program that solved problems in imitation of humans by heuristic search (Newell & Simon, 1956). A busy year, 1956.

If I may take 1956, then, as the year of the birth of cognitive science—of

*This research was supported by Research Grant MH-07722 from the National Institute of Mental Health, and by a grant from the Alfred E. Sloan Foundation.

the analysis of the human mind in terms of information process—the ensuing years have witnessed its steady and moderately rapid growth. The growth is evident whether measured in terms of the research effort going into the field, in terms of the production of new knowledge about mind, or in terms of the acceptance of the information processing approach by the scientific disciplines on which it impinges.

The growth of cognitive science generated new journals in several of these disciplines, when the existing journals were too crowded or too stodgy, or both, to accept the new contributions. *Artificial Intelligence* and *Cognitive Psychology* are just two of these new channels of communication. But they, and others like them, were largely confined to their separate disciplines, and only with the establishment of *Cognitive Science*, about three years ago, was a channel created that cut squarely across the disciplinary boundaries.

THE STUDY OF INTELLIGENT SYSTEMS

But already my characterization of cognitive science has been too narrow. I have been speaking of the understanding of the human mind as its research goal. Historically, that is perhaps not wholly inaccurate. Until quite recently, the idea of intelligence has always been associated closely with brains and minds, and especially with the human mind. But programs of research in artificial intelligence and in the computer simulation of human thinking have taught us how to construct intelligent systems that are not human, and how to abstract the requisites and earmarks of intelligence from the "hardware" of the brains and electronic boxes that exhibit it.

Hence, I think that most of us today would prefer to define cognitive science as the domain of inquiry that seeks to understand intelligent systems and the nature of intelligence. We have learned that intelligence is not a matter of substance—whether protoplasm or glass and wire—but of the forms that substance takes and the processes it undergoes. At the root of intelligence are symbols, with their denotative power and their susceptibility to manipulation. And symbols can be manufactured of almost anything that can be arranged and patterned and combined. Intelligence is mind implemented by any patternable kind of matter.

I will not elaborate on the topic of symbol structures and their manipulation as the core of intelligence, for that theme will be developed by my colleague, Allen Newell, at a later session of this conference.[1] But in everything that follows, I will simply assume this basis for intelligent behavior, and will turn, instead, to a different aspect of the intelligent systems known to us—their malleability and adaptability, and hence, their fundamental artificiality.

[1] For an initial statement of this point of view, see Newell and Simon, 1976.

MALLEABILITY AND ADAPTATION

Intelligent systems exhibit their intelligence by achieving goals (e.g., meeting their needs for survival) in the face of different and changing environments. Intelligent behavior is adaptive, hence must take on strikingly different forms when the environments are correspondingly different. Intelligent systems are what they are from being ground between the nether millstone of their physiology or hardware, which sets inner limits on their adaptation, and the upper millstone of a complex environment, which places demands on them for change.

Systems that are adaptive may equally well be described as "artificial," for as environments change, they must change too, as though they were deliberately designed to fit those environments (as indeed they sometimes are) (Simon, 1969). The task of empirical science is to discover and verify invariants in the phenomena under study. The artificiality of information processing systems creates a subtle problem in defining empirical invariants for them. For observed regularities are very likely invariant only within a limited range of variation in their environments, and any accurate statement of the laws of such systems must contain reference to their relativity to environmental features.

It is common experience in experimental psychology, for example, to discover that we are studying sociology—the effects of the past histories of our subjects—when we think we are studying physiology—the effects of properties of the human nervous system. Similarly, business cycle economists are only now becoming aware of the extent to which the parameters of the system they are studying are dependent on the experiences of a population with economic events over the previous generation (Simon, 1979a).

Finding invariants, then, in artificial phenomena is not an easy task. But that is no counsel of despair for cognitive science. Absolute invariance is very rare in nature, unless it be in the structure of space-time or in the hypothesized elementary particles for which the physicists long so ardently. Biology deals with the laws of systems that have only come into existence in the later stages of the history of our solar system; and if life exists elsewhere in the universe, as we are assured on probabilistic grounds that it must, biologists have no assurance that the basic regularities they observe in life on Earth will also hold for living forms in other galaxies.

What we are searching for are relative invariants: regularities that hold over considerable stretches of time and ranges of systems. What is invariant in adaptive systems will depend on the time intervals during which we observe them. There are at least three time scales of relevance to such systems, corresponding to three different forms of adaptation.

On the shortest time scale, intelligent—hence adaptive—systems continually change their behavior in the course of solving each problem situation they encounter. Hence a prime characteristic of heuristic search, the more so the more successful the search, is that the system gradually takes on the form and behavior that is requisite to adapt it to the environment in which it finds itself.

On a somewhat longer time scale, intelligent systems make adaptations that are preserved and remain available for meeting new situations successfully. They learn. There are many forms that this semi-permanent adaptation can take, and correspondingly many forms of learning. One important form is the accumulation of information in memories and the acquisition of access routes for retrieving it. Learning provides an enormous source for variation in system behavior, hence makes more difficult the search for the elusive invariants.

On the longest time scale, intelligent systems evolve. Their evolution may be Darwinian, by mutation and natural selection in the organismic case. It may equally well be social, through discovery of new knowledge and strategies and their transmission from one system to another. This transmitted inheritance, whether biological or social or both, will also cause a progressive change in system behavior, and will consequently narrow the domain of invariance.

In view of all of these capacities for adaptation, for learning, and for evolutionary change, what room is left for a general science of cognition? What are the invariants we are searching for? We must seek them in the inner and outer environments that bound the adaptive processes. We must ask whether there are any basic characteristics we should expect to be held in common among diverse forms of intelligent "hardware," and we must ask if there are any characteristics that complex problem environments hold in common.

THE INNER ENVIRONMENT

Our understanding of the invariants associated with the inner environments of intelligent systems is limited to those with which we have experience. From one standpoint, the range of such systems is limited: living organisms and computers. All living organisms make use of essentially the same protoplasmic material, but exhibit a wide variety of organizations. All of the computers that have been built in the course of the short history of that species exhibit remarkable similarity of organization, but have been assembled from a most diverse set of alternative component materials. Hence, over these two classes of intelligent systems, we do encounter a considerable diversity of both organization and material substrate.

In the comments that follow, I will focus on human intelligence and computer intelligence. For some purposes, I will broaden the range to include social insects and human organizations. I do not think the picture would be changed greatly if we looked at other forms of intelligence.

Both classes of systems are symbol systems. They achieve their intelligence by symbolizing external and internal situations and events, and by manipulating those symbols. They all employ about the same basic symbol-manipulating processes. Perhaps that particular invariance arose because computers were made (unintentionally) in the image of man. But no one has yet succeeded in inventing an intelligent system that employs exotic symbol-manipulating processes, and so perhaps the invariance goes deeper than imitation.

None of the systems exhibits a large amount of parallelism in its operation. This assertion is, of course, controversial in the case of human intelligence, and I will not undertake to defend it in detail here (although I firmly believe it to be true and amply confirmed by evidence).[2] In the case of computers, we have apparent counterexamples in such systems as ILLIAC-IV, but the difficulties of programming such parallel computers for all but very special tasks are notorious.

We may conjecture that the real reason for the predominance of seriality in process is that it is very difficult to organize parallel computational systems that require precise coordination of the computations being made simultaneously by the different components. These difficulties defeat human programmers, and apparently they also defeat learning and evolutionary processes.

Where processing is basically serial, all of the relatively labile inputs and outputs of the basic processes can be handled in a working memory of limited size. In the human system, this working memory produces the familiar phenomena of attentional focus. In computer systems, we do not need to be correspondingly limited, unless we wish to be, but roughly similar architectures emerge from the tradeoff between high-speed but costly (hence small) memory components, and low-speed but cheap (hence large) components.

The need for a tradeoff too between flexible adaptation to the environment and coherent attention to goals also seems to point toward mechanisms for attentional focus. Hence, when intelligence is implemented by production systems, a portion of memory is generally designated as working memory or as the "activated" portion of memory in which the condition sides of the productions must be satisfied. We certainly have not learned to design intelligent systems that can take everything (in their memories and in their environments) into account at once; and perhaps nature has not learned to design such systems either. In this case, here is one of the invariants we may seek to characterize and understand.

But am I not ignoring the whole current trend toward multiprocessors, which are the very quintessence of parallelism? And am I not ignoring also those venerable parallel systems, human organizations and ant colonies? I think the apparent contradiction here can be resolved. I spoke above of the difficulty of organizing systems "that require precise coordination of the computations being made simultaneously by the different components." The secret of the human organization and the ant colony is that they do not require coordination of high precision among the individual human employees or the individual ants.

---

[2]From my assertion about the rarity of parallelism, I must exempt, of course, the sensory organs, which clearly are parallel devices. But once feature extraction has been achieved, even recognition processes can be realized readily in real time by serial discrimination nets. What appears to be parallel in central processing (e.g. talking while driving) is almost certainly time sharing in a serial system. See Simon (1979b), Chapter 2.3.

Thought processes can be measured in milliseconds, seconds, or minutes. Coordination of behavior among members of human organizations does not require transmission of information from one to another at millisecond rates, and usually not even with a precision of seconds or minutes. I suppose the limits of such precision are tested in athletic teams, but even in this case the information transmitted from one team member to another is very small compared with the rate at which information is processed in each individual head.

Of course if the members of an organization are engaged in independent tasks, or if the needs for coordination are modest, nothing prevents their operating in parallel. All of the numerous examples of parallelism we see in nature seem to conform to this general principle: the rate of inter-component interaction is small compared with the rate of intra-component interaction. Systems having this property are called nearly-decomposable systems, and their near-decomposability has a number of interesting theoretical consequences (Simon, 1969, Chapter 4; Courtois, 1977).

I will predict that as we proceed with the design of ever larger and more complex multiprocessors, their architecture will exhibit with ever greater clarity the property of near decomposability and the quasi-hierarchical structure that goes with it.[3] This will happen independently of whether the designers of these multiprocessors turn to the lessons of human organization (and ant colonies) for design ideas, or whether they ignore the literatures that record this experience and reinvent the wheel.

Perhaps these remarks suffice to give some idea of the nature of the invariants we may hope to discover in the inner environments of intelligent systems. As can be seen from my examples, the invariants are of a relatively abstract kind, and tend to impose constraints on the possible organizations of intelligent systems rather than upon their material substrates. Intelligent systems, it would appear, will necessarily be symbol systems, their high-frequency components will be serial in operation with attentional focus, and the more complex systems will be hierarchic and nearly decomposable.

THE OUTER ENVIRONMENT

The second source of invariance in intelligent systems derives from common characteristics of the environments to which they must adapt, and in which their behavior takes place. Again, since these environments are of such diverse sorts, the invariants will be of a highly abstract nature.

The environments we are concerned with, those that demand the exercise

---

[3]I use hierarchy here in the same sense as in Simon (1969), Chapter 4, not to refer to pyramidal control structure but to describe a modular (nearly decomposable) structure that is "layered" according to the frequencies and temporal precisions of the interactions among modules, among their submodules, and so on. A system with a highly "democratic" control structure can be hierarchic in this sense.

of intelligence, are problem environments. They do not present obvious paths to the attainment of a system's goals. Frequently, though not always, problem environments contain large, sometimes immense, numbers of alternatives, only a small fraction of which satisfy the goal requirements.

The principal mechanism of intelligence that we have observed (in people or computers) operating in problem environments is heuristic search. The "search" part of the heuristic search process is obvious enough. What are more subtle are the heuristic devices that enable an intelligent system to carry on searches with great selectivity by (1) using information stored in memory to choose more promising over less promising paths, and (2) extracting from the problem environment new information about regularities in its structure that can similarly guide the search. Since we have acquired a considerable knowledge and a considerable literature about heuristic search over the past quarter century, I will not expand upon this topic here (a standard reference is Nilsson, 1971).

Before leaving the topic of the outer environment, however, I should like to call attention to the critical importance of the interface between that environment and the intelligent system: the sensory and motor organs that the latter possesses. This interface presents what is in many ways the most delicate problem in the design of an adaptive system, for it must meet the requirements of both the outer and the inner environments—must, in fact, communicate between them. It is probably no accident that our progress has been much slower in designing effective sensors or effectors, or imitating the corresponding human organs, than in understanding and imitating those intelligent processes that can go on inside the human head or the black box.

LEARNING

The idea that intelligent systems are highly adaptive and flexible in their behavior could well lead to the notion that their invariants are to be found, not in their behavior or the structures responsible for performance, but in the longer-run mechanisms that bring about the adaptation—their learning mechanisms.

As a matter of fact, learning was a very popular topic in the early history of artificial intelligence research, and an almost dominating topic in cognitive psychology during the period from World War I to the middle 1950s. The historical reasons are not entirely obvious in either case, and we must be careful not to assume that the reason suggested in the previous paragraph was the important one in giving learning its prominence in these two fields.

With respect to artificial intelligence, it is my impression that many workers held the view that it was easier to induce a system to organize itself from scratch, by exposing it to an appropriate sequence of training experiences, than it was to provide it with the knowledge it would need for expert performance. There was perhaps also a borrowing of attitudes from psychology, where learning was then viewed as the core of the subject, and where Hebb and others were considering how nerve nets might organize themselves.[4] Finally, there was probably the desire to avoid the charge, commonly directed toward artificial intelligence systems, that the intelligence was really in the programmer, and not in the system at all. If the programmer only provided a potential for learning, and not the program for the finished performance, then this accusation could not stand.

Whatever the reason, many investigators in the early years followed the learning route, and I think it fair to say that they largely failed. All of the expert systems that have been produced up to the present time have been given directly all or most of the knowledge and the problem-solving strategies on which their expertness rests.

We should be careful not to extrapolate the research experience of the past two decades to the research programs for the next two. Over the past five years there have been many signs of a revival of the learning enterprise, but with a viewpoint quite different from the original nerve net or simple reinforcement paradigms. Systems like METADENDRAL (Buchanan & Mitchell, 1977), which induce their own theories, or like Lenat's AM, which acquire new concepts that help them, in turn, to discover still others, are certainly learning systems. So is UNDERSTAND (Hayes & Simon, 1974), which generates, and then uses, problem representations; Langley's (1979) BACON, that induces scientific laws from data using recursive procedures; Neves' (1978) program that learns skills by analysing worked-out textbook examples; and many others.

What is characteristic of the new generation of learning programs is that most of them are basically problem-solving programs, capable of undertaking heuristic search with a reasonable armory of methods like generate-and-test and means-ends analysis. They do not start out in anything like the barebones fashion of the earlier generation of self-organizing systems.

Let me now turn back to psychology's preoccupation with learning during the period that just preceded the information processing revolution. I suggested earlier that the motivation for this preoccupation might have been the concern that only learning parameters could be invariants in an artificial system. A review of the writings of the most prominent investigators does not support this hypothesis. I can find only a weak hint of it in the first edition of Hilgard's *Theories of Learning* (1948), and no hints at all in the books of Hull, Watson, or Thorndike.

The historical reasons appear to be quite different. In the first place, there was an applied motivation. An understanding of learning was key to an understanding of the educational process. This motivation was quite clear in the work of John Dewey, of Thorndike and others. But even stronger than the urge of relevance to education was a philosophical goal that ties the learning research back to the earliest concerns of psychology.

Psychology had its birth, of course, in philosophy. And the philosophical question that led most directly to a psychological one was the epistemological

---

[4]For an important early example of work developing this point of view, see Rochester, Holland, Haibt, and Duda, 1956; and for a basic critique of the approach, see Minsky, 1963, Section III.

question: How can we know the world outside ourselves, and how can the mind store knowledge about that world? It is a quite easy and direct step from asking how we know the world to asking how we acquire that knowledge—how we learn (as well as the closely related question of how we perceive). It would seem plausible that this epistemological concern accounts for psychology's preoccupation with learning during a period when psychology was relatively unconcerned about application, sometimes almost belligerently so.

I would now like to leave these historical questions and point to what almost amounts to a contradiction in the return to an interest in learning that I asserted has been taking place in the past five years. If most of our progress in understanding expert skills (both in psychology and artificial intelligence) has been gained by studying and constructing expert performance systems, why are we now turning back to an "empty box" approach?

Part of the answer has already been suggested. The new learning systems do not much resemble those of two decades ago. They start out with a much more complex and sophisticated system than did the earlier nerve-net and perception approaches. Therefore, we have reason to hope that they can climb higher on the ladder of skill, and we already have experience that supports that hope.

A second part of the answer is that we now have a vastly better picture than we had earlier of the goal of the learning: of the expert performance systems that the learner is seeking to attain. We know a great deal about how expert knowledge is stored in associative, list-structure memories, and how this knowledge can be organized for effective access.

A third part of the answer is that most of our expert performance systems are now constructed as production systems, and we have clearer ideas of the mechanisms needed to enable a production system to bootstrap itself (adaptive production systems (Waterman, 1975)) than we ever did for systems organized as hierarchic structures of closed subroutines.

I am not predicting that we are soon going to abandon our current emphasis, in psychology and artificial intelligence, on understanding performance systems in favor of studying learning. Much less am I urging that we do this. But as the manpower available for research in cognitive science continues to grow, there probably are hands and heads enough to go forward on both fronts.

In our study of performance, however, we must not imagine invariants where there are none. Since intelligent systems are programmable, we must expect to find different systems (even of the same species) using quite different strategies to perform the same task. I am not aware that any theorems have been proved about the uniqueness of good, or even best, strategies. Thus, we must expect to find strategy differences not only between systems at different skill levels, but even between experts.

Hence, research on the performance of adaptive systems must take on a taxonomic, and even a sociological aspect. We have a great deal to learn about the variety of strategies, and we should neither disdain nor shirk the painstaking, sometimes pedestrian, tasks of describing that variety. That substrate of description is as necessary to us as the taxonomic substrate has been to modern biology. Within the domains of cognitive science, perhaps only the linguists (and to some extent, the developmental psychologists) have had a tradition of detailed description instead of a tradition of experimentation in search of generally valid truths.

As for the sociological aspect, performance programs are in considerable part the product of social learning, and we must not expect the performance programs of the twentieth century to be identical with those of the nineteenth, or the tenth, or the first. The prospect of far-ranging changes in human cognitive programs again reintroduces important philosophical problems that have received only modest attention in psychological research. In what respects is the mind of the Greek citizen the same as or different from the mind of modern man? Is thinking in an African village the same process as thinking on a mechanized farm? Experimental material is available for studying the latter kind of question, if not the former, and a little such research has been done. But as we begin to take more seriously the proposition that human cognitive programs are determined as much by social and historical forces as by neurology, our research emphases will surely shift.

NORMATIVE AND POSITIVE SCIENCES

In artificial sciences, the positive (descriptive) and the normative are never far apart. Thus, in economics, the "principle of rationality" is sometimes asserted as a descriptive invariant, sometimes as advice to decision makers. The business firm is assumed to act so as to maximize its profits, and theories of how the economy works are erected on this assumption of maximization. On the other hand, specialists in operations research, bringing to bear the sharp tools of linear programming, integer programming, queuing theory, and the like, offer to help business firms maximize profits where they are not so doing.

Similarly, in psychology, the view that intelligent systems are adaptive, can learn, and evolve does not prevent us from studying them in order to discover how to improve their learning or problem-solving powers. The feeling of contradiction between the positive and normative views is less acute in psychology than in economics precisely because in the former field we only rarely assume that adaptation or learning or evolution maximizes something and therefore is not open to improvement.

The recent emergence of sociobiology, with its claim that fitness arguments can be used to explain, and even predict, how things are, threatens to introduce new confusion in the relation between the positive and the normative. I will have more to say about that in the next section of this paper.

Linguistics, too, has suffered its confusions between descriptive and normative attitudes toward its subject. I do not refer so much to the old-fashioned dictionary maker's notion that his task was to prescribe "correct" usage, but to the more modern idea of a language sharply defined in terms of "competence" and "grammaticality." There is a continuing danger that focus upon an ideal competence that resides in some kind of Platonic heaven (or a Cartesian one) will impose normative constraints on the study of actual language behavior.

I am not arguing against the desirability of normative science in any of these domains, but simply against a confusion of the normative with the positive—of what ought to be with what is. Artificial intelligence, in particular, certainly addresses itself to normative goals, and ought to. It is interested, in its applied aspects, not only in understanding intelligence but in improving it. Perhaps we need to recognize this explicitly by speaking of cognitive engineering as well as cognitive science. If we do, however, I hope that the two ventures will keep in the closest relation with each other, as they have done through the past quarter century. The dangers of confusing the normative with the positive are slight compared with the losses that would be suffered from isolating the science from its engineering applications.

EVOLUTION AND OPTIMIZATION

I want to return now to the topic of evolutionary theory, especially in its contemporary incarnation as sociobiology (Wilson, 1975). Economists, in particular, are seizing upon evolutionary arguments to expand their domain from strictly economic phenomena to the whole domain of individual and social behavior (Simon, 1979a).

The slogan, of course, of evolutionary theory is "survival of the fittest," certainly a claim of optimization. It is important to examine what this means, and can mean, in the world as we know it. "Survival of the fittest" refers to the outcome of the competition among species seeking to occupy particular ecological niches. In the simplest form of the theory, there can be at least as many surviving, fit species as there are niches—that is, an enormous number. Moreover, the niches themselves are not determined by some inflexible, invariant environment, but are defined in considerable measure by the whole constellation of organisms themselves. There can be no lice without hairy heads for them to inhabit, nor animals without plants. Hence, it is not obvious what optimization problem, if any, is being solved by the process of evolution. At most, the occupancy of each niche is being locally "optimized" relative to the entire configuration of niches.

Two formal developments, the theory of games and linear programming theory, give us important insights into the difficulties of using optimization assumptions to predict the behavior of complex systems. From the theory of games we learn that in competitive situations it may be impossible to define what we mean by an optimum in an unambiguous way, much less to guarantee that unique optimal solutions of the game exist. From linear programming, we learn that very strong conditions must be met by a system (e.g., linearity of the criterion function, convexity of the feasibility space) to guarantee that local maxima will be global maxima, and that when these conditions are not met, it is very difficult—in fact, usually impossible—to devise algorithms that will discover global optima within the limits of a reasonable computational effort.

For these reasons, cognitive science is likely to remain a science of systems that satisfice—that find tolerable solutions for their problems—rather than a science of systems that optomize—that adapt perfectly to their environments. But to understand satisficing intelligence, it is necessary to understand the process through which that intelligence is exercised. It is not enough simply to infer what the intelligent behavior "must" be from the description of the environment and the conditions of optimization. But I will not elaborate this argument further, for I expect that most cognitive scientists in this audience would not disagree with it.

CONCLUSION

It might have been necessary a decade ago to argue for the commonality of the information processes that are employed by such disparate systems as computers and human nervous systems. The evidence for that commonality is now overwhelming, and the remaining questions about the boundaries of cognitive science have more to do with whether there also exist nontrivial commonalities with information processing in genetic systems than with whether men and machines both think. Wherever the boundary is drawn, there exists today a science of intelligent systems that extends beyond the limits of any single species.

Intelligence is closely related with adaptivity—with problem-solving, learning, and evolution. A science of intelligent systems has to be a science of adaptive systems, with all that entails for the difficulty of finding genuine invariants. Cognitive science is a science of the artificial. It is concerned with phenomena that could be otherwise than they are—and which will be altered continually as they adapt to the demands of their environments.

So long as we do not confuse adaptability with the ability to attain optimal solutions, cognitive science will be a basically empirical science. Inference from optimality conditions will play a modest role in helping us to discover how things are. Most of our knowledge will have to come from extensive painstaking observation of the vast variety of intelligent systems that exist in the world, the equally vast variety of programs that these systems acquire and employ, and from formal theories—mainly in the form of computer programs—induced from that body of observation.

REFERENCES

Bruner, J. S., Goodnow, J. J., & Austin, G. A. *A study of thinking*. New York: Wiley, 1956.
Buchanan, B. G., & Mitchell, T. M. Model-directed learning of production rules. Presented at the Workshop on Pattern-directed inference Systems, Honolulu, Hawaii, May 1977.

Chomsky, N. Three models of the description of language. Proceedings of a Symposium on Information Theory. *IRE Transactions on Information Theory*, Sept. 1956, IT-2(*3*), 113–124.

Courtois, P. J. *Decomposability: Queueing and computer system applications*. New York: Academic Press, 1977.

Hayes, J. R., & Simon, H. A. Understanding written problem instructions. In L. W. Gregg (Ed.), *Knowledge and cognition*. Hillsdale, NJ: Lawrence Erlbaum Associates, 1974.

Hilgard, E., & Bower, G. H. *Theories of learning* (4th ed.). Englewood Cliffs, NJ: Prentice-Hall, 1975.

Langley, P. Rediscovering physics with BACON.3. *Proceedings of the 6th IJCAI–Tokyo, 1979, 1*, 505–507.

Miller, G. A. The magical number seven. *Psychological Review*, 1956, *63*, 81.

Minsky, M. Steps toward artificial intelligence. In E. A. Feigenbaum & J. Feldman (Eds.), *Computers and thought*. New York: McGraw-Hill, 1963.

Neves, D. A computer program that learns algebraic procedures by examining examples and by working test problems in a textbook. *Proceedings of the 2nd CSCSI Conference*—Toronto, 1978, 191–195.

Newell, A., & Simon, H. A. Computer science as empirical inquiry: Symbols and search. *Communications of the ACM*, March 1976, *19*, 111–126.

Newell, A., & Simon, H. A. The logic theory machine. *IRE Transactions on Information Theory*, Sept. 1956, IT-2(*3*), 61–79.

Nilsson, N. J. *Problem solving methods in artificial intelligence*. New York: McGraw-Hill, 1971.

Rochester, N., Holland, J. H., Haibt, L. H., & Duda, W. L. Test on a cell assembly theory of the action of the brain, using a large digital computer. *IRE Transactions on Information Theory*, 1956, IT-2(*3*), 80–93.

Simon, H. A. Rational decision making in business organizations. *American Economic Review*, Sept. 1979, *69*, 493–513.

Simon, H. A. *Models of thought*. New Haven: Yale University Press, 1979b.

Simon, H. A. *The sciences of the artificial*. Cambridge, MA: M.I.T. Press, 1969.

Waterman, D. A. Adaptive production systems. *Proceedings of the 4th IJCAI*—Tbilisi, Georgia, USSR, 1975, *1*:296–303.

Wilson, E. O. *Sociobiology: The new synthesis*. Cambridge, MA: Belknap Press of Harvard University, 1975.

3

Neurological Knowledge and Complex Behaviors

Harvard Medical School
Massachusetts Institute of Technology

In the months preceding this conference I made a point of asking many of my colleagues for their concept of Cognitive Science. The answers I received were, as one might well expect, remarkably varied, even from some who identified themselves as cognitive scientists. Some argued that it was a new field, whereas one respondent insisted that although he could not define it, the area could not be new since, whatever it was, Helmholtz *must* have practiced it. I soon realized, however, and this realization was, so to speak, punctuated by Professor Simon's elegant opening address, that the novelty of the field was irrelevant. What was important was the novelty of the growing realization that numerous apparently disparate disciplines shared certain concerns in common.

I was equally interested in the response to my second question: If Cognitive Science existed, what did knowledge of the workings of the brain have to do with it? Again the answers were varied. Reading the proceedings of this symposium one finds a similar range of views. There were some who thought that the brain was totally irrelevant, or, worse yet, that the study of nervous mechanisms could only add naive conclusions to befuddle the unwary. Flowers are made of chemicals, but biochemistry exists perfectly happily with the barest nod to floriculture. The brain may be a machine designed for cognitive functions but is hardly the place to study basic principles.

There are, by contrast, others who consciously or otherwise place the brain at the very center of the field. Some would say that ideal cognitive systems are indeed realized—or realizable—in the brain. Others, more extreme, would argue that Cognitive Science will in the end be nothing more than the end product of neurophysiology.

I will, on reflection, accept none of these extreme views, not out of a desire to compromise or from some notion of tolerant intellectual liberalism or distaste

27

for controversy, but simply because none of these arguments convinces me. I hope to make my position clear in the following pages.

If I may borrow from Herbert Simon's presentation, let us accept that Cognitive Science is, above all, a field which concerns itself with strategies of adaptation, particularly to varying and unexpected environmental circumstances.

The realization that the conceptual structure cuts across so many areas should perhaps make us all realize that inspiration may come from areas that appear at first glance to be totally remote. This new society is concerned with psychology, mathematics, computer science, linguistics, philosophy, the social sciences, and, of course, the neurological sciences. But before I deal with the possible role of neurological studies in this hybrid field, let me point out at least two biological fields whose data and theories may in fact have important lessons for Cognitive Science and its concern with systems that can adapt to changes in the environment, and in particular to unexpected changes. How does one design a system to do this? Perhaps the most dramatic example of this type of design is embodied in the immunological systems of the body. How is it that these systems adapt with the most remarkably subtle strategies to environmental alterations that could apparently have never entered into the design of these systems, e.g., immune responses to recently invented chemical structures? There are indeed highly individual responses to thousands of such antigenic substances synthesized only in the past few years. Conversely, many infectious agents, particularly the so-called slow viruses, maintain their infectivity only by ingenious mechanisms which depend precisely on the environments to which they have been subjected. Indeed, immunologists have called attention to the formal similarity of learning and immunological mechanisms.

Another field in which equally remarkable adaptive mechanisms are at play is that of genetics and more broadly the whole process of evolution. Indeed, the existence of genetic codes (I use the plural since we now know that there is no universal code) itself reveals the importance of symbolic systems in biology.

Yet, having pointed out that many biological systems embody cognitive scientific principles, let me hasten to add that I doubt that "*the* brain" is the ideal cognitive device. Indeed, when we say "*the*" brain we imply that there is *only one* model. But we know that brains differ and that some may be far more effective adaptive models than others. Indeed, the problem is further complicated by the fact that some brains adapt well to a certain group of environmental changes but poorly to another group, whereas in other brains the reverse situation may hold. One might even consider the evolution of the brain as a slow progress toward an ideal but nonexistent device.

Why is the brain not ideal? We can only guess. In some instances better paradigms for cognitive tasks have simply never been "wired into" the system by appropriate mutations. But even when superior paradigms are available, not all brains may contain them. The reason for this is probably dependent in major part on the fact that there are many constraints on the brain. It is limited in size at birth by the requirement that it should not exceed the maximum possible diameter of the birth canal. It is limited in final size because it already uses a quarter of the cardiac output. I also suspect that even at its current size not all areas can operate maximally since this would involve increases of blood flow beyond the capacity of the heart in a subject using the rest of his body actively.

The compromises that are made presumably trade superior design in one area for inferior design (one that has too few nerve cells even with the best principles) in another. This distribution of inborn potentials for talent will differ from brain to brain.

If this is true then the brain may be the *best* device in existence (even this is probably not true in all areas), but it is not the *ideal* device. There is no reason why better devices cannot and will not be built as this field advances. Furthermore, as Duncan Luce has pointed out there is no reason to assume that the best man-made devices will be similar in design to the best human brains, any more than an airplane's flight is similar to a bird's.

If that is so, then why should the cognitive scientist study the brain and not just the mind? The answer is given away in the very structure of the question. Most cognitive scientists are strongly interested in the human mind, i.e., precisely in the output of a particular accidental device. The field has not yet become a purely mathematical one, but continues to find its major inspiration in behavior. The brain may not be the ideal device, but it is almost certainly at this moment far and away the greatest single reservoir of such adaptive mechanisms. The device comes equipped with hundreds of built-in clever devices designed to maintain certain invariants. Thus, despite a wide range of environmental states, body temperature, food intake, and blood pressure are remarkably constant. Body weight is normally held within an astonishingly narrow range, despite the fact that the machine has no built-in method of directly ascertaining its own weight. Yet these adjustments are only the beginning: It has a remarkable capacity to learn, to store knowledge of changes in the environment, to store knowledge of changes in the strategies followed by others, and to acquire new strategies. Evolution has been a highly effective, if slow, strategy for the development of adaptive cognitive devices, and most of the best ones extant are being carried around in human heads. We are still the best machines for pattern recognition, classification, and for the very talent of design of clever devices.

Despite all this, the position of neural science in relation to cognition remains an uneasy one. Indeed, in this very symposium it is very sparsely represented. And whereas one of the original possible state-of-the-art symposia was to be in the neurosciences, this did not materialize. Some will say that this is because neural science has not delivered the goods. Thus the pioneering attempts of McCulloch and Pitts to correlate detailed neural circuitry with function did not succeed although the more modest attempts of Lettvin and Maturana and Hubel and Wiesel are dramatic examples that such correlates are possible. Our knowledge of the circuitry of mammalian brains is extensive, but astonishingly imprecise in the small details. To make this clear let me point out that there is not a single neuron in the central nervous system of any *mammal* whose connections are fully specified, although such neurons are known in some invertebrates. Despite this fact, the neural sciences and Cognitive Science will perforce be partners. In my view, many of the problems of interfacing the neural sciences with the cognitive sciences are more sociological than scientific, i.e., professional xenophobia and infatuation with one's own discipline are the greatest barriers to adaptation. The average neurological researcher is not likely to be enamored of philosophy, discursive thinking, psychological analysis, or computer models. Conversely, many nonneural cognitive scientists are uncomfortable with the data obtained with the microelectrode from a few neurons or from the derangements in cognitive strategy which follow damage to the nervous system.

Let me now turn to a few hopefully more precise indications of how neurological knowledge can contribute to this growing field. Let me briefly indicate an area remote from my own field of major study—that of the study of behavior in relatively simple invertebrate nervous systems. I heard John von Neumann in one of his last lectures point out that there existed invertebrates whose nervous systems contained far fewer units than were present in the primitive calculating machines (as they were still called) of that period. Yet, von Neumann added, these primitive animals were in his view far more complex than these calculating devices, more complex in that he thought it would take more axioms to describe their behavior. Von Neumann's message was clear: There are design principles in these simple nervous systems which will enormously expand our capacities to understand adaptive complexity.

The advantage of these simple systems is obvious. They contain small numbers of nerve cells; and furthermore the complete connectivity of many of these cells can be specified and the adaptive intenuity of many of these organisms is often striking. The possibilities for breeding of genetic variants opens the possibility of experimental tests of theories of mechanisms of strategies of adaptation. At this moment this field may appear to be far from the major concerns of cognitive science, but my prediction is that it will increasingly be found to be surprisingly relevant.

Let me now turn to some areas nearer to my own central interests. Simon has said in his presentation that when we think we are studying the properties of the nervous system we really may be studying the effects of past history. A little reflection, however, shows that the opposite situation has been equally frequent—when we thought we were studying the effects of experience we were really studying the properties of the nervous system. The adult chimpanzee usually responds to the sight of a snake with fear. The interpretation that immediately comes to mind is that this fear was instilled during development. Yet Hebb showed many years ago that a baby chimpanzee responds with the same brisk fear to his first sight of a snake.

It would in fact be surprising if it were not the case that the brain had many built-in properties. The need for many built-in systems is one of the lessons that the history of the attempts to build intelligent devices, which Simon has so elegantly summarized, has taught cognitive scientists: Any system which has to learn everything it needs is simply too slow and inefficient. The acquisition of motor skills is an excellent example. Children may take years to tie their shoe laces and even the novice in surgery often takes a remarkably long time to learn to tie knots in sutures. There are, by contrast, complex motor patterns like those of walking that are primarily inborn and are acquired at high speed. In fact, the maturation of an inborn process is often mistaken for learning.

Furthermore, there are some experiments that appear to show learning effects which are, in fact, not really present. Consider the following: Two sets of kittens are raised in the laboratory. In one group the right and left eyes are patched on alternate days so that at no time is the use of both eyes permitted. These animals are compared to controls without eye patches. At six months it is found that in the first group of animals there are few cells in the visual cortex which respond to binocular stimulation, while in the control group there are many. The apparently obvious conclusion is that the animal who has had binocular stimulation has acquired binocular vision. The elegant experiments of Hubel and Wiesel reveal a different sequence. Cells which respond to binocular stimulation are present in the newborn animal. They are *lost* only if binocular stimulation is not supplied over the following months.

There is of course an experiental effect, but it is the *loss* of a built-in program, rather than the acquisition of a new one. But in some cases it is clear that even the apparent loss of a built-in program is illusory. Consider what happens when for the first time a rat is put into the cage of a cat raised in the laboratory. If the cat has in the past seen rats attacked by other cats, he will almost invariably attack. What happens, however, if the cat has never seen a rat (and has of course never seen one attacked)? As shown by several experiments (e.g., Kuo, 1930; Yerkes & Bloomfield, 1910), about half of the cats do not attack. The remainder, however, do attack. Furthermore, the attack is not random. The cats will, in fact, attack in the same manner as the animal in the wild. They will bite at the neck or turn the rat over so as to bite at the throat.

It is clear therefore that built-in systems for attack are present in the cat, or at least in many cats. There are at least three interpretations as to why certain cats do not attack. The first is that these animals do not have built-in systems and would therefore have had to learn to attack. The second is that innate systems for attack were present but were lost as a result of lack of early experience. The third is that the built-in programs are present but inaccessible. As we will now see the third interpretation is probably the correct one.

John Flynn of the Yale Medical School has published a dramatic series of experiments on cats who do not attack spontaneously (e.g., Wasman & Flynn, 1962). The animal, with a rat in its cage, receives stimulation through electrodes implanted in the brain. In most locations this stimulation is without effect. If, however, the electrode is in certain locations, e.g., the lateral hypothalamus, the cat will attack. The manner of attack is again similar to that of the wild animal. The attack is specific in its goal, so that the cat does not attack small objects placed in the cage. Furthermore, although a dead stuffed rat is attacked, the attack is less persistent than on a live animal.

These experiments show that the innate program for attack is still present in these animals. In addition, there must be innate perceptual programs which contain models of the anatomy of a rat which determine the specificity not only of the object of attack, but of portions of that object.

We must conclude that there are elaborate preprogrammed systems of analysis and action which can be modified or triggered by experience. Furthermore, even the capacity to learn itself reflects specializations of neural organization: Whether or not the chimpanzee has language, it is clear that the human learns it better.

The ability to learn is probably not a general one. Instead, there exists systems which have a specialized capacity to learn certain kinds of material. Thus Maureen Dennis of Toronto has studied children with the Sturge-Weber syndrome, a congenital disturbance of the cortex of one side of the brain. Several such children have undergone the total removal of this abnormal cortex from one side of the brain because of uncontrollable seizures. Since these children have all had brain lesions existing from before birth they tolerate these operations very well, and the types of gross language disorders seen in adults do not occur. Yet even in these cases with very early lesions, Dennis has shown clearly that those who have undergone left decortication employ different strategies in certain linguistic tasks from those of children with early right decortications whose strategies are much closer to those of normal controls.

As I have already indicated, we do not yet have detailed knowledge of neural circuits involved in complex adaptive behaviors. I will, however, list certain general principles illustrated by specific examples. Most of these are based on information from the study of humans who have suffered delimited lesions to their nervous system and been well studied, although some of these principles are based on experimentation in nonhuman animals.

1. As already noted, *there exist specialized systems for the learning of many behaviors that at first might appear to be purely cultural.* Thus we have known for over 100 years that there are specialized systems for language. We also know that there are systems which deal with recognition of special stimuli, e.g., faces (i.e., systems which are specialized and not designed for the recognition of other types of visual pattern), and for the expression and recognition of emotion.

2. *There is no evidence for the existence of any all-purpose computer.* Instead, there seems to be a multiplicity of systems for highly special tasks, e.g.,

the systems for facial recognition appear to be separate from those for other visual recognition tasks. Systems for the recognition and production of music appear to be separate from those for language. There is, at present, no good evidence—although counter-evidence is perhaps equally weak—for the existence of a generalized logical deductive capacity.

3. *There are many surprising dissociations,* some of which have already been indicated. There are many others. Thus Japanese patients with reading difficulties acquired as the result of delimited brain damage typically have more difficulty comprehending words written in the apparently simpler syllabary system (*kana*) than in the more elaborate logographic (or ideographic) system (*kanji*) (Sasanuma & Fujimura, 1971). In some Europeans with reading difficulties the category of written words that is best preserved is that of names of public buildings such as *bank*, *restaurant*, or *post office*. It is obvious in this case that there is some remarkable interaction between damage to the hardware and past experience. In this case it appears as if the patient has learned to read words which are attached to their referents (e.g., the words ''bank'' or ''hotel'' are usually on the appropriate buildings) in a different or additional way from those which are not (e.g., ''telephone,'' ''plate,'' ''if'').

4. The study of the nervous system enables one to formulate more precise mechanisms for *the role of emotion in cognitive functions*. I cannot elaborate this in detail here, but I would first point out that the portions of the brain involved in memory functions, e.g., the hippocampus, amygdala, mammillary bodies, etc., are all portions of the limbic system which is clearly involved in emotional activities. Furthermore, MacDonnell and Flynn's (1966) work on aggression in cats again shows that stimulation of specific limbic structures ''sets'' the animal for increased receptiveness to certain inputs and preparedness for certain outputs. One of the striking effects of many brain lesions is the alteration of these emotional components while rational, calculating functioning may be spared.

5. *Some behaviors can probably be understood poorly or not at all if the neural substrate is not considered.* Thus patients with certain lesions (who suffer from what are called *apraxic* disorders) will show certain remarkable dissociations (Geschwind, 1975). They will fail to carry out certain verbal commands which they understand, whereas they succeed in carrying out others. These patients will fail to salute, to pretend to use a hammer, or throw a ball. They will also fail to pretend how to blow out a match or suck through a straw. On the other hand, they will successfully carry out commands to move the eyes, to stand, to walk, bow, or turn. How do we account for the successful ability to carry out certain movements to verbal command while others fail? Let me point out briefly that the commands for movement which succeed do *not* differ from those which fail in linguistic structure, age of acquisition, or in any measure of complexity. The movements which succeed are those which are mediated by motor systems in the brain other than the contralateral pyramidal system. In other words, there are cognitive systems the understanding of which may depend on knowledge of the specific pattern of realization in the ''hardware'' of the nervous system.

6. The *most complex* cognitive systems in most brains may be those which deal with *attentional* processes. Simon has stressed the serial features of attention, but I would stress that the parallel features are equally important. An attentional system functions properly only if it combines a central focus with a continuous survey of what is not at the center. The work of Broadbent has illustrated this very well.

Let me now describe some other properties of brains that must be kept in mind by the cognitive scientist who is studying human behavior.

1. There is a tendency to ask "What is *the* strategy by which a cognitive problem is solved?" But since we know that brains differ from each other in structure, it is very likely that the strategies for solution of certain problems differ from person to person. Thus patients in whom the corpus callosum is congenitally absent show a marked increase in the size of the anterior commissure. We also know that the brains of left-handers differ on the average from those of right-handers. Thus left-handers have, on the average, less anatomical asymmetry in the brain than right-handers (Galaburda et al., 1978).

2. It is furthermore conceivable that the presence of certain innate cognitive strategies in a brain may prevent that brain from employing other strategies which might be optimal for other problems. This is a situation that evolutionary theory would lead us to expect with considerable frequency. It is even conceivable that disorders such as childhood dyslexia may in some cases be the result of the high development of certain perceptual strategies at the expense of others.

3. Any theory about a cognitive strategy will probably have certain implications as to the particular modes or breakdown that might be expected after brain lesions. This in turn implies that study of disordered cognitive function from brain disease may be a valuable way to test cognitive theories.

Let me close with a prediction—and a plea. I believe that the neurological sciences and the study of syndromes of delimited neurological damage will have a continuing major effect on the future development of Cognitive Science. It is well worth recalling that the profound effect of neurology on psychology which has occurred in the past quarter century was not expected by the majority of psychologists. But this influence will not be unilateral. Indeed, I will not be surprised if the influence of cognitive science on the neurological sciences is not greater than the reverse.

Let me now state my plea that the practitioners of both fields take each other seriously. I state this not as the customary exhortation to cooperate, but as the result of the knowledge that the failure not merely to take account of certain neurological data, but even their active suppression, led to the dramatic neglect of important cognitive findings. Thus many of the effects of the destruction of the corpus callosum were elaborately described and well understood theoretically before the First World War. Their neglect was the direct result of the influence of major figures in the history of cognitive psychology such as Karl Lashley, Henry Head, and Kurt Goldstein (Geschwind, 1964). It is tragic that it took until the 1960s to correct this gross error. It would not be fitting for a science whose object is the study of adaptive cognitive strategies to make an equally maladaptive error.

REFERENCES

Galaburda, A. M., LeMay, M., Kemper, T. L., & Geschwind, N. Right-left asymmetries in the brain. *Science*, 1978, *199*, 852–856.

Geschwind, N. The paradoxical position of Kurt Goldstein in the history of aphasia. *Cortex,* 1964, *1*, 214–224.

Geschwind, N. The apraxias: Neural mechanisms of disorders of learned movement. *American Scientist*, 1975, *63*, 188–195.

Kuo, Z. Y. The genesis of the cat's response to the rat. *Comp. Psychol.*, 1930, *11*, 1–35.

MacDonnell, M. F., & Flynn, J. P. Control of sensory fields by stimulation of hypothalamus. *Science*, 1966, *152*, 1406–1408.

Sasanuma, S., & Fujimura, O. An analysis of writing errors in Japanese aphasic patients: Kanji versus kana words. *Cortex*, 1971, *8*, 265–282.

Wasman, M., & Flynn, J. P. Directed attack elicited from hypothalamus. *Arch. Neurol.*, 1962, *6* 220–227.

Yerkes, R. M., & Bloomfield, D. Do kittens instinctively kill mice? *Psychol. Bull.*, 1910, *7*, 253–263.

4

Physical Symbol Systems*

ALLEN NEWELL

Carnegie-Mellon University

1. INTRODUCTION

The enterprise to understand the nature of mind and intelligence has been with us for a long time. It belongs not to us alone, who are gathered at this conference, nor even to science alone. It is one of the truly great mysteries and the weight of scholarship devoted to it over the centuries seems on occasion so oppressively large as to deny the possibility of fundamental progress, not to speak of solution.

Yet for almost a quarter century now, experimental psychology, linguistics, and artificial intelligence have been engaged in a joint attack on this mystery that is fueled by a common core of highly novel theoretical ideas, experimental techniques, and methodological approaches. Though retaining our separate disciplinary identities, we have strongly influenced each other throughout this period. Others have been involved in this new attack, though not so centrally—

*This research was sponsored by the Defense Advanced Research Projects Agency (DOD), ARPA Order No. 3597, Monitored by the Air Force Avionics Laboratory Under Contract F33615-78-C-1551.

The views and conclusions contained in this document are those of the author and should not be interpreted as representing the official policies, either expressed or implied, of the Defense Advanced Research Projects Agency, or the U.S. Government.

Herb Simon would be a co-author of this paper, except that he is giving his own paper at this conference. The key ideas are entirely joint, as the references indicate. In addition, I am grateful to Greg Harris, John McDermott, Zenon Pylysyhn, and Mike Rychener for detailed comments on an earlier draft.

additional parts of computer science and psychology, and parts of philosophy, neurophysiology, and anthropology.

Our communality continues to increase. In consequence, we are engaged in an attempt to bind our joint enterprise even more tightly by a common umbrella name, *Cognitive Science*, a new society, and a new series of conferences devoted to the common theme—the outward and institutional signs of inward and conceptual progress. On such an occasion, attempts to increase our basis of mutual understanding seem to be called for.

In my own estimation (Newell & Simon, 1976), the most fundamental contribution so far of artificial intelligence and computer science to this joint enterprise has been the notion of a *physical symbol system*. This concept of a broad class of systems that is capable of having and manipulating symbols, yet is also realizable within our physical universe, has emerged from our growing experience and analysis of the computer and how to program it to perform intellectual and perceptual tasks. The notion of symbol that it defines is internal to this concept of a system. Thus, it is a hypothesis that these symbols are in fact the same symbols that we humans have and use everyday of our lives. Stated another way, the hypothesis is that humans are instances of physical symbol systems, and, by virtue of this, mind enters into the physical universe.

In my own view this hypothesis sets the terms on which we search for a scientific theory of mind. What we all seek are the further specifications of physical symbol systems that constitute the human mind or that constitute systems of powerful and efficient intelligence. The physical symbol system is to our enterprise what the theory of evolution is to all biology, the cell doctrine to cellular biology, the notion of germs to the scientific concept of disease, the notion of tectonic plates to structural geology.

The concept of a physical symbol system is familiar in some fashion to everyone engaged in Cognitive Science—familiar, yet perhaps not fully appreciated. For one thing, this concept has not followed the usual path of scientific creation, where development occurs entirely within the scientific attempt to understand a given phenomenon. It was not put forward at any point in time as a new striking hypothesis about the mind, to be confirmed or disconfirmed. Rather, it has evolved through a much more circuitous root. Its early history lies within the formalization of logic, where the emphasis was precisely on separating formal aspects from psychological aspects. Its mediate history lies within the development of general purpose digital computers, being thereby embedded in the instrumental, the industrial, the commercial and the artificial—hardly the breeding ground for a theory to cover what is most sublime in human thought. The resulting ambivalence no doubt accounts in part for a widespread proclivity to emphasize the role of the *computer metaphor* rather than a *theory of information processing*.

The notion of symbol permeates thinking about mind, well beyond attempts at scientific understanding. Philosophy, linguistics, literature, the arts—all have independent and extensive concerns that focus on human symbols and symbolic activity. Think only of Cassirier or Langer or Whitehead in philosophy. Consider semantics, concerned directly with the relation between linguistic symbols and what they denote, or Jung, in a part of psychology remote from experimentation and tight theory. These are vast realms of scholarship, by any reckoning.

I cannot touch these realms today in any adequate way. Perhaps, I can let one quote from Whitehead stand for them all:

> After this preliminary explanation we must start with a definition of symbolism: The human mind is functioning symbolically when some components of its experience elicit consciousness, beliefs, emotions, and usages, respecting other components of its experience. The former set of components are the "symbols", and the later set constitute the "meaning" of the symbols. The organic functioning whereby there is transition from the symbol to the meaning will be called "symbolic reference". (1927, pp. 7–8)

This statement, from over fifty years ago, has much to recommend it. Let it serve as a reminder that the understanding of symbols and symbolism is by no means brand new. Yet the thread through computer science and artificial intelligence has made a distinctive contribution to discovering the nature of human symbols. Indeed, in my view the contribution has been decisive.

The notion of a physical symbol system has been emerging throughout the quarter century of our joint enterprise—always important, always recognized, but always slightly out of focus as the decisive scientific hypothesis that it has now emerged to be.

For instance, recall the rhetoric of the fifties, where we insisted that computers were *symbol manipulation machines* and not just *number manipulation machines*. The mathematicians and engineers then responsible for computers insisted that computers only processed *numbers*—that the great thing was that instructions could be translated into numbers. On the contrary, we argued, the great thing was that computers could take instructions and it was incidental, though useful, that they dealt with numbers. It was the same fundamental point about symbols, but our aim was to revise opinions about the computer, not about the nature of mind.

Another instance is our ambivalence toward list processing languages. Historically, these have been critically important in abstracting the concept of symbol processing, and we have certainly recognized them as carriers of theoretical notions. Yet we have also seen them as *nothing but* programming languages, i.e., as nothing but tools. The reason why AI programming continues to be done almost exclusively in list processing languages is sought in terms of ease of programming, interactive style and what not. That Lisp is a close approximation to a pure symbol system is often not accorded the weight it deserves.

Yet a third instance can be taken from our own work. When we laid out the notion of physical symbol system in our book on human problem solving (Newell & Simon, 1972), we did this as an act of preparation, not as the main point. We focussed the theory on how people solved problems, given that they were symbol manipulation systems. Even when, a little later, we chose to focus on the physical symbol system hypothesis per se (Newell & Simon, 1976), it was in the context of receiving an award and thus we described it as a conceptual advance that had already transpired.

A fourth and final instance is the way information processing systems are presented in cognitive psychology. Even in the best informed presentations (e.g., Clark & Clark, 1977; Lindsay & Norman, 1977; Rumelhart, 1977) there is little emphasis on symbolic functioning per se. When concern is expressed about the adequacy of information processing notions for psychology (e.g., Neisser, 1976), the role of symbolic functioning is not addressed. There are some very recent exceptions to this picture (Lachman, Lachman, & Butterfield, 1979). But some of these (Allport, 1979; Palmer, 1978) seem to view such developments as rather new, whereas I see them as having been the taproot of the success in Artificial Intelligence right from the start almost twenty-five years ago.

In sum, it seems to me, a suitable topic for this conference is to attempt, systematically but plainly, to lay out again the nature of physical symbol systems. All this will be in some ways familiar, but I hope far from useless. Restatement of fundamentals is an important exercise. Indeed, I can take my text from Richard Feynman. He is speaking of Fermi's law of optics, but it applies generally:

> Now in the further development of science, we want more than just a formula. First we have an observation, then we have numbers that we measure, then have a law which summarizes all the numbers. But the real *glory* of science is that we can find a way of thinking such that the law is *evident*. (1963, p. 26)

Physical symbol systems are becoming for us simply *evident*. But they are our *glory*, and it is fitting that we should understand them with a piercing clarity.

And so, if you cannot stand what I say here as science, then take it as celebration.

1.1 Constraints on Mind

Let me provide a general frame for the paper. The phenomena of mind have arisen from a complex of aspects of the physical universe, localized strikingly (though possibly not exclusively) in us humans. We scientists, trying to discern the physical nature of mind, can cast these aspects as a conjunction of constraints on the nature of mind-like systems. Then our discovery problem is that of finding a system structure that satisfies all these constraints. In trying to make that discovery, we can use any tactics we wish. The constraints themselves are simply desiderata and have no privileged status.

There is no magic list of constraints that we can feel sure about. Their choice and formulation is as much a step in the discovery process as solving the constraint satisfaction problem after positing them. However, it is easy to list some candidate constraints that would find general acknowledgement. Figure 1 presents a baker's dozen.

These constraints are far from precisely defined. Operationalizing the notion of self-awareness poses difficult problems, however critical it seems as a requirement. Even what constitutes the brain is open, moving over the last thirty years from an essentially neural view to one that includes macromolecular mechanisms as well. Not all the constraints are necessarily distinct. Conceivably, human symbolic behavior and linguistic behavior could be the same, as could development and learning. Not all constraints are necessarily independent. To be a neural system implies being a physical system, though there can be reasons to consider the more general constraint separately. Some of the constraints are familiar back to Aristotle, others are recent additions. Who would have thought to add the concern with robustness under error if computers and their programs had not exhibited the sort of brittle, ungraceful degradation that we have all come to know so well.

What seems clear is that, when we finally come to know the nature of mind in humans, it will be seen to satisfy all of these constraints (and others that I have neglected to list). And when we finally come to know the nature of intelligence generally, it will be seen how its variety arises from a release from some of these constraints.

Our difficulty, as scientists, is that we cannot solve for systems that satisfy

1. Behave as an (almost) arbitrary function of the environment (universality).
2. Operate in real time.
3. Exhibit rational, i.e., effective adaptive behavior.
4. Use vast amounts of knowledge about the environment.
5. Behave robustly in the face of error, the unexpected, and the unknown.
6. Use symbols (and abstractions).
7. Use (natural) language.
8. Exhibit self-awareness and a sense of self.
9. Learn from its environment.
10. Acquire its capabilities through development.
11. Arise through evolution.
12. Be realizable within the brain as a physical system.
13. Be realizable as a physical system.

Figure 1. Constraints on Mind.

such simultaneous constraints. Indeed, we cannot usually do better than to generate on one constraint and test on the others. Thus, particular constraints are taken by various groups of scientists as the frame within which to search for the nature of mind. One thinks of Ashby (1956) and his formulation in terms of general differential equation systems, which is to say, basically physically realizable systems. Or the endeavor of those working in the fifties on self-organizing systems to work within neuron-like systems (Yovits & Cameron, 1960; Yovits, Jacobi, & Goldstein, 1962). Or the emergence of a sociobiology that works primarily from evolutionary arguments (Wilson, 1975). And, of course, both the neurophysiologists and the linguists essentially work from within their respective disciplines, which correspond to constraints in our list. Artificial intelligence works from within the digital computer—sometimes, it seems, even from within Lisp. However, the computer is not one of these constraints, though strongly associated with the first item, and my purpose is not to identify particular constraints with particular disciplines. The constraints are conceptual aspects of the nature of the human mind, and they must all be taken into account in the final analysis, whatever the starting point.

Which constraint forms a preferred basis from which to conduct the search for the nature of mind? Most important, a constraint must provide a *constructive* definition of a class of systems. Otherwise, search within it cannot occur, because it will not be possible to generate candidates whose properties can then be explored. Several of the constraints have real difficulty here—development and learning, robustness, real-time operation. For instance, we simply have no characterization of all systems that show development; all we can do is pose a system described within some other class and ask about its developmental characteristics. The constraint of development must remain primarily a test, not a generator. On the other hand some constraints, such as using language, do very well. The formalisms for grammars provide potent generative bases.

The strength of a constraint, or its distinctiveness with respect to mind, also weighs in the balance, however difficult the assessment of such a characteristic. For example, one real problem with the evolution constraint is that we know it gives rise to an immense diversity of systems (organisms). It is not clear how to get it to generate systems that are shaped at all to mind-like behavior. Again, linguistics has fared much better in this regard. For linguistics has appeared, until recently, to be distinctively and uniquely human. As a last example, one major argument against the universal machines of logic and computer science has always been that universality had been purchased at the price of total inefficiency, and a class which relied on such an aspect seemed irrelevant to real systems.

But such considerations are only preferences. Our joint scientific enterprise demands that substantial groups of scientists focus on all these constraints and their various combinations. It demands that new constraints be discovered and added to the list, to provide new ways from which to seek the true nature of mind.

My focus on physical symbol systems in this paper certainly amounts to an argument for taking one particular class of systems as the base—as the generator—for the search for mind. This class appears to satisfy jointly at least two of the constraints in the list—*universality* and *symbolic behavior*—and to give good evidence of being able to be shaped to satisfy other constraints as well, while still remaining usefully generative. But, as the discussion should make clear, this is just an argument over scientific tactics—over the right way to go about untying the great puzzle knot that is the mind. On the matter of scientific substance, we need to understand all we can about all the aspects represented in these constraints.

1.2. Plan

Let me preview what I intend to do, so as to be as plain and straightforward as possible.

To present the notion of a physical symbol system, I introduce a specific example system. This permits a concrete discussion of the key property of universality, the first constraint on our list. With this concept in hand, I generalize the example system to the class of all physical symbol systems. This makes it evident that systems that satisfy the constraint of universality also are capable of a form of symbolic behavior. The Physical Symbol System Hypothesis states in essence that this form of symbolic behavior is all there is; in particular, that it includes human symbolic behavior. I turn briefly to the question of system levels, which allows the placement of the symbol level within the larger frame of physical systems. With all these elements on the table, I then discuss some issues that are important to understanding the notion of physical symbol system and the hypothesis, and their roles in cognitive science.

So far I have been careful always to refer to a *physical* symbol system, in order to emphasize two facts. First, such a system is realizable in our physical universe. Second, its notion of symbol is *a priori* distinct from the notion of symbol that has arisen in describing directly human linguistic, artistic and social activities. Having been clear about both of these, we can drop the adjective, except when required to emphasize these two points.

As already stated, the fundamental notion of a physical symbol system presented here is not novel scientifically. Even the formulation presented does not differ in any important way from some earlier attempts (Newell & Simon, 1972; Newell & Simon, 1976). I am engaged in restatement and explication. The details and the tactics of the formulation are new and I hope thereby to make matters exceptionally clear and to highlight some important features of such systems. Still, it does not follow that the notion of physical symbol system and the particular hypothesis about it are accepted by all, or accepted in exactly the form that is given here.

2. SS: A PARADIGMATIC SYMBOL SYSTEM

Figure 2 lays out our example symbol system schematically. We will call it SS (Symbol System) for short. It is a machine which exists in an environment consisting of *objects*, distributed in a space of *locations*. We can imagine the objects having some sort of structure and dynamics, and doing their individual and interactive thing in this space.

SS consists of a *memory*, a set of *operators*, a *control*, an *input*, and an *output*. Its inputs are the objects in certain locations; its outputs are the modification or creation of the objects in certain (usually different) locations. Its external behavior, then, consists of the outputs it produces as a function of its inputs. The larger system of environment plus SS forms a closed system, since the output objects either become or affect later input objects. SS's internal state consists of the state of its memory and the state of the control; and its internal behavior consists of the variation in this internal state over time.

The memory is composed of a set of *symbol structures*, $\{E_1, E_2, \ldots E_m\}$, which vary in number and content over time. The term *expression* is used interchangeably with *symbol structure*. To define the symbol structures there is given a set of abstract *symbols*, $\{S_1, S_2, \ldots S_n\}$. Each symbol structure is of a given *type* and has some number of distinguished *roles*, $\{R_1, R_2, \ldots\}$. Each role contains a symbol, so if we take the type as understood implicitly and the roles as the successive positions on the paper, we could write an expression as:

$$(S_1 \; S_2, \ldots S_n)$$

If we wanted to show the roles and the type explicitly we could write:

$$(\text{Type: T } R_1{:}S_1 \; R_2{:}S_2, \ldots R_n{:}S_n)$$

The roles (and their number) are determined by the *type*, of which there can be a large variety. The same symbol, e.g., S_k, can occupy more than one role in a structure and can occur in more than one structure. By the *content* of an expression is meant simply the symbols associated with the roles of the expression.

SS has ten operators, each shown as a separate box in the figure. Each operator is a machine that takes one or more symbols as input and produces as output some symbol (plus possibly other effects) as a result. The behavior that occurs when an operator and its inputs combine is called an *operation*. The details of the behavior of the system come from these operations, which we will go over in a moment.

SS: EXAMPLE SYMBOL SYSTEM

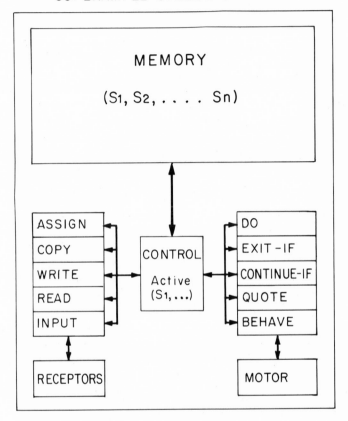

MEMORY

(S1, S2, ... Sn)

ASSIGN

COPY

WRITE

READ

INPUT

CONTROL

Active

(S1,...)

DO

EXIT-IF

CONTINUE-IF

QUOTE

BEHAVE

RECEPTORS

MOTOR

Figure 2. Structure of SS, a Paradigmatic Symbol System.

The behavior of the system is governed by the control. This is also a machine; its inputs include the operators: It has access to their inputs and outputs and can evoke them. It also has as an input the symbol for a single expression, which is called the *active* expression. The behavior of the control consists of the continual *interpretation* of whatever expression is active. If this specifies an operation to be performed, then the control will bring the input symbols to the input locations of the indicated operator and then evoke the operator to produce the result, i.e., it will effect the combining of data and operators. The control also determines which expression shall become active next, so that the behavior of the total system runs on indefinitely. We will describe the control in detail after discussing the operators.

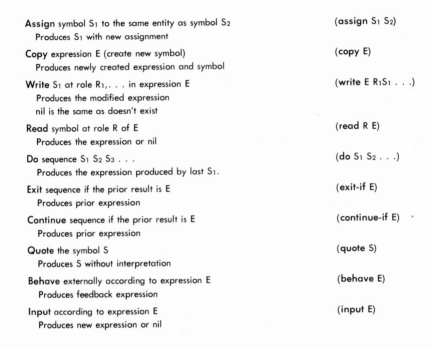

Assign symbol S_1 to the same entity as symbol S_2	(**assign** S_1 S_2)
Produces S_1 with new assignment	
Copy expression E (create new symbol)	(**copy** E)
Produces newly created expression and symbol	
Write S_1 at role R_1,. . . in expression E	(**write** E R_1S_1 . . .)
Produces the modified expression	
nil is the same as doesn't exist	
Read symbol at role R of E	(**read** R E)
Produces the expression or nil	
Do sequence S_1 S_2 S_3 . . .	(**do** S_1 S_2 . . .)
Produces the expression produced by last S_1.	
Exit sequence if the prior result is E	(**exit-if** E)
Produces prior expression	
Continue sequence if the prior result is E	(**continue-if** E)
Produces prior expression	
Quote the symbol S	(**quote** S)
Produces S without interpretation	
Behave externally according to expression E	(**behave** E)
Produces feedback expression	
Input according to expression E	(**input** E)
Produces new expression or nil	

Figure 3. Operators of SS.

Figure 3 lists the operations of SS. There exists a type of symbol structure, which we will call a *program*, which has roles corresponding to an operator and the inputs appropriate to that operator. These program expressions are shown in the figure at the right.

Assign a symbol. This establishes a basic relationship between a symbol and the entity to which it is assigned, which we call *access*. While it lasts (i.e., until the assignment is changed) any machine (i.e., the ten operators and the control) that has access to an occurrence of this symbol in an expression has access to the assigned entity. If a machine has access to an expression, then it can obtain the symbols in the various roles of the expression and it can change the symbols in these roles. Symbols can be **assigned** to entities other than expressions, namely, to operators and roles. Access to an operator implies access to its inputs, outputs, and evocation mechanism. Access to a role of a given type implies access to the symbol at that role for any expression of the given type and access to write a new symbol at that role.

Copy expression. This adds expressions and symbols to the system. The new expression is an exact replica of the input expression, i.e., the same type and the same symbols in each role. A new symbol is created along with the new expression (a necessity for gaining access to the expression).

Write an expression. This creates expressions of any specified content. It does not create a new expression (**copy** does that), but modifies its input expression. What to **write** is specified by giving the roles and the new symbols that are to occupy these roles. **Write** permits several symbols to be written with a single operation; it could as well have permitted only one. For example, given a type with roles R₁, R₂, etc., in order, and given an expression (X Y Z), [**write** (X Y Z) R₁ A R₃ C] produces a modified expression (A Y C).

Write establishes a symbol at a given role whether or not there was a symbol at that role before, and independent of what symbols exist at other roles. **Writing** nil at a role effectively deletes it.

Read the symbol at a specific role. This obtains the symbols that comprise an expression, given that the expression has been obtained. It is possible that no symbol exists for a given role; in this case **read** produces the symbol nil. (Thus it can be seen why **writing** nil at a role effectively deletes it.)

Do sequence. This makes the system do arbitrary actions, by specifying that it do one thing after another. There are an unlimited number of input roles, one for each element in the sequence. The last expression produced during such a sequence is taken to be the result of the sequence. All the expressions produced by earlier items in the sequence are ignored. Of course, actions may have taken place along the way (often referred to as side effects), e.g., assignment of symbols.

Exit-if and **Continue-if**. The system behaves conditionally by continuing or exiting (terminating) the execution of a sequence. A conditional operator tests if the expression produced at the immediately preceding step of the sequence is the same as its input expression. It then takes a specific control action. For example, [**do** . . . A (**exit-if** A) . . .] would exit, i.e., would not complete the rest of the sequence. If symbols A and B designate different expressions, then [**do** . . . B (**continue-if** A) . . .] would also exit. The output of the operator is the expression tested, which then becomes the output of the sequence if there is termination.

Quote a symbol. The control automatically interprets every expression that becomes active. This operator permits it to not interpret a given expression, but to treat its symbol as the final result.

Behave externally. There exists some collection of external behaviors controllable by SS. Symbol structures of some type exist that instruct the organs that produce this external behavior. It will be enough to have an operator that evokes these expressions. Execution of the operator will produce some expression that provides feedback about the successful accomplishment (or failure) of the external operation.

Input from environment. Inputs from the external environment enter the system by means of newly created expressions that come to reside in the memory. These inputs occur when the **input** operator is evoked; there may be different channels and styles of input, so that **input** takes an expression as input to specify this. The input expressions are processed when **input** is evoked, since the resulting expression is interpreted by the control, though presumably the new expressions are not of type program, but some type related to describing the external environment.

Interpret the active expression:

   If it is not a program:
     Then the result is the expression itself.

   If it is a program:
     Interpret the symbol of each role for that role;
     Then execute the operator on its inputs;
     Then the result of the operation is the result.

Interpret the result:

   If it is a new expression:
     Then interpret it for the same role.

   If it is not a new expression:
     Then use as symbol for role.

Figure 4. Operation of SS's Control.

The operation of the control is shown in Figure 4. The control continuously interprets the active expression. The result of each interpretation is ultimately a symbol, though other actions (i.e., side effects) may have occurred during the act of interpretation, which are also properly part of the interpretation.

Control interprets the active expression by first determining whether it is a program symbol structure. Thus the control can sense a structure's type. If it is not a program, then the result of the interpretation is just the symbol itself (i.e., the symbol is treated as data).

If the active expression is a program, then the control proceeds to execute the operation specified by the program. However, the actual symbols in the program at the roles for the operator and its inputs must themselves be interpreted. For these symbols might not be the operator and inputs, respectively, but programs whose interpretations are these symbols. Thus, the control interprets each symbol in the program until it finally obtains the actual symbols to be used for the operator and the inputs. Then, it can actually get the operation performed by sending the input symbols to the appropriate operator, evoking it, and getting back the result that the operator produces.

Control then interprets the result (as arrived at through either of the routes above). If it is a new expression, then it proceeds to interpret it. If it is not new, then it finally has obtained the symbol.

The control has the necessary internal machinery to interpret each operator or input symbol in a program until it obtains the symbol finally to be used for each role in the program. This will be the one that is finally not a program type of structure. The control remembers the pending interpretations and the results produced so far that are still waiting to be used. The normal way to realize all this in current technology is with a pushdown stack of contexts; but all that is specified here is end result of interpretation, not how it is to be accomplished.

We now have an essentially complete description of one particular symbol system. To generate a concrete (and particular) behavioral trajectory, it is only necessary to provide an *initial* condition, consisting of the set of initial expressions in the memory and the initial active expression. The system behaves in interaction with the environment, but this is accounted for entirely by the operation of the **input** and **behave** operators. The operation of these two operators depends on the total environment in which the system is embedded. They would normally be given by definite mechanisms in the external structure of the system and the environment, along with a set of laws of behavior for the environment that would close the loop between output and input. From a formal viewpoint the operation of these two operators can just be taken as given, providing in effect a *boundary* condition for the internal behavior of the system.

This type of a machine is certainly familiar to almost everyone in Cognitive Science, at least in outline. The virtue of SS over others that might be even more familiar is that it is designed to aid understanding the essential features of symbols and symbolic behavior. There are no irrelevant details of SS's structure. Each operator (and also the control) embodies a generalized function that is important to understanding symbolic systems.

The expository virtues of SS aside, it remains a garden variety, Lisp-ish sort of beast.

3. UNIVERSALITY

That our example symbol system is garden variety does not keep it from being a variety of a very remarkable genus. Symbol systems form a class—it is a class that is characterized by the property of *universality*. We must understand this remarkable property before we can generalize appropriately from our paradigmatic symbol system to a characterization of the entire class.

Central to universality is flexibility of behavior. However, it is not enough just to produce any output behavior; the behavior must be *responsive* to the inputs. Thus, a universal machine is one that can produce an arbitrary input–output function; that is, that can produce any dependence of output on input.

Such a property is desirable for an adaptive, intelligent system which must cope with environments whose demands are not known at the time the system is designed. Indeed, this property heads the constraints in Figure 1. Being able to produce *any* behavior in response to a situation is neither absolutely necessary nor hardly sufficient for success. But the more flexibility the better; and if behavior is too unresponsive, the system will fail against its environment. Almost all purposive behavior shows intricate dependence on the environment, i.e., shows the flexible construction of novel input-output functions—an animal circling its prey, a person in conversation with another, a player choosing a chess move, a student solving a physics exercise, a shopper bargaining with a seller, and on and on. This was the classic insight of Cybernetics—systems appeared *purposive* when their behavior was dependent on the environment so as to attain (or maintain) a relationship; and *feedback* was necessary to obtain this dependence with a changing environment. The formulation here separates the ability to produce the dependence (universality) from the way such a ability can be used to produce purposiveness, the latter residing in the rationality constraint in Figure 1.

The property of universality cannot be quite so simply defined. Four difficulties, in particular, must be dealt with.

The first difficulty is the most obvious. Any machine is a prisoner of its input and output domains. SS, our example system, presents an abstract machine-centered view, so that the external world is pretty much what is seen by the machine. But this is deceptive. Machines live in the real world and have only a limited contact with it. Any machine, no matter how universal, that has no ears (so to speak) will not hear; that has no wings, will not fly. Thus universality will be relative to the input and output channels. Such a consideration is alleviated in theoretical discussions by the simple expedient of considering only abstract inputs and outputs. It can be alleviated in the real world by providing transducers that encode from one input–output channel to another. Thus, being able to produce any function between two given domains permits inducing any function between two other domains if the domains are hooked up appropriately.[1] But this interface limit must always be remembered.

The second difficulty is also obvious. In the physical world there are limits—limits to the speed of components, to spatial and energy sensitivity, to material available for memory, to reliability of operation, to name just the more obvious. To state a tautology: No system can behave beyond its physical limits. Thus, the universality of any system must be taken relative to such physical implementation limits.

The third difficulty is more serious. A machine is defined to be a system that has a specific determined behavior as a function of its input. By definition, therefore, it is not possible for a single machine to obtain even *two* different behaviors, much less any behavior. The solution adopted is to decompose the input into two parts (or aspects): one part (the *instruction*) being taken to determine which input-output function is to be exhibited by the second part (the *input-proper*) along with the output. This decomposition can be done in any fashion—for instance, by a separate input channel or by time (input prior to a starting signal being instruction, afterward being input-proper). This seems like an innocent arrangement, especially since the input-proper may still be as open as desired (e.g., all future behavior). However, it constitutes a genuine limitation on the structure of the system. For instance, the instruction must have enough capacity to specify all of the alternative functions. (If the instruction to a machine consists only of the setting of a single binary toggle switch, then the machine

---

[1]The internal domains must have enough elements to permit discrimination of the elements of the external domains, a condition which Ashby (1956) called the *Law of requisite variety*.

cannot exhibit three different input-output behaviors.) Most important, the basic decomposition into two parts has far-reaching consequences—it guarantees the existence of symbols.

The fourth difficulty is the most serious of all. There appears to be no way that a universal machine can behave literally according to *any* input–output function, if the time over which the behavior is to occur is indefinitely extended (e.g., the entire future after some period of instruction). This is the import of the discovery of *noncomputable* functions, which is an important chapter in the theory of computing machines (Brainerd & Landweber, 1974; Minsky, 1967). The difficulty is fundamentally that there are too many functions—too many ways to have to instruct a machine to behave.

This can be appreciated directly by noting that each instruction to the machine, no matter how complex, is simply a way of naming a behavior. Thus, a machine cannot produce more distinct behaviors than it can have distinct instructions. Let the number of possible instructions be K. The number of behaviors is the number of input–output functions, so if there are M possible inputs and N possible outputs, then the number of behaviors is N^M (i.e., the assignment of one of the N possible outputs for each of the M inputs). Thus, K instructions must label N^M behaviors. If K, M, and N are all in the same range, then N^M is going to be *very* much bigger than K. Now, as time is permitted to extend indefinitely into the future, all three possibilities (K, M, and N) will grow to become countably infinite. But, although K (the number of instructions) grows to be countably infinite, N^M (the number of functions to be labeled) grows much faster to become uncountably infinite. In sum, there simply are not enough possible instructions to cover all the functions that must be named.

If all possible functions cannot be attained, then some way must be found to describe which can and which cannot. Therein lies a further difficulty. Suppose a descriptive scheme of some sort is used, in order to say that a given machine can realize functions of certain descriptions and not functions of other descriptions. What do we know then about the functions that are not describable by the given scheme? We have confounded the properties of the descriptive scheme with the properties of the machine. Indeed, the suspicion might arise that a connection exists between descriptive schemes and machines, so that this difficulty is part and parcel of the main problem itself.

The solution has been to take the notion of a machine itself as the keystone. Direct description of behavior is abandoned, and in its place is put *the behavior producted by such and such a machine*. For any class of machines, defined by some way of describing its operational structure, a machine of that class is defined to be universal if it can behave like any machine of the class. This puts simulation at the center of the stage; for to show a given input–output behavior is to simulate a machine that shows that input–output behavior. The instructional input to the machine must now be some means of describing any arbitrary machine of the given class. The machine whose universality is being demonstrated must take that input and behave identically to the machine described by its input, i.e., it must simulate the given machine.

The notion of universality thus arrived at is *relative*, referring only to the given class of machines. Universal machines could exist for classes of machines, all right, but the input–output functions encompassed by the whole class could still be very limited. Such a universal machine would be a big frog in a small pond of functions.

The next step is to attempt to formulate very large classes of machines, by means of general notions of mechanism, in order to encompass as wide a range of input–output functions as possible. (The input and output domains are always taken to be intertranslatable, so the relevant issue is the functional dependence of output on input, not the character of the inputs and outputs taken separately.) Another important chapter in the theory of computing (Brainerd & Landweber, 1974; Minsky, 1967) has shown that all attempts to do this lead to classes of machines that are equivalent in that they encompass in toto exactly the same set of input–output functions. In effect, there is a single large frog pond of functions no matter what species of frogs (types of machines) is used. But the frog pond is just a pond; it is not the whole ocean of all possible functions.

That there exists a most general formulation of machine and that it leads to a unique set of input–output functions has come to be called *Church's thesis* after Alonzo Church, the logician who first put forth this claim with respect to one specific formulation (recursive functions) (Church, 1936). Church's statement is called a *thesis* because it is not susceptible fo formal proof, only to the accumulation of evidence. For the claim is about ways to formalize something about the real world, i.e., the notion of machine or determinate physical mechanism. Self-evidently, formal proof applies only after formalization. The most striking evidence has been the existence of different maximal classes of machines, derived from quite different formulations of the notion of machine or procedure, each of which turns out to be capable of producing exactly this same maximal set of functions.

A large zoo of different formulations of maximal classes of machines is known by now—Turing machines, recursive functions, Post canonical systems, Markov algorithms, all varieties of general purpose digital computers, most programming languages (viewed as specifications for a machine). As a single neutral name, these classes are interchangebly called the *effectively computable procedures* and the functions that can be attained by the machines are called the *computable* functions.

These maximal classes contain universal machines, i.e., machines that, if properly instructed through part of their input, can behave like any other machine in the maximal class. But then they can produce all the input-output functions that can be produced by any machine, however defined (i.e., in any other maximal class). It is these machines that are usually referred to as universal machines. From now on this is what we shall mean by *universal*. The proofs of the existence of these universal machines are also part of this early great chapter in the theory of logic and computers.

SS, our paradigmatic symbol system, is universal. Thus, it has as much flexibility as it is possible to obtain. It is useful to show that SS is universal. It is easy to do and its demonstration will make the notion transparent and keep it from accruing any mystery. Having the demonstration will also provide us with an example of a program in SS, which will clarify any confusing points in its definition. We will also be able to use this demonstration to support several points about general symbol systems when we examine them in the next section.

To show that SS is universal, all we need to show is that it can simulate any member of a class of machines already known to be a maximal class. Let us choose the class of Turing machines: It is simple, classical, and everyone knows that it is a formulation of a maximal class.

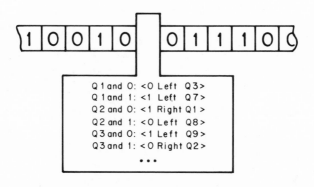

T3: [content:0   left:T2   right:T4]

Q2: [if-0:[content:1   move:right   next:Q1]
      if-1:[content:0   move:left   next:Q8]]

TM: [do
         [do [read content T] [continue-if 0] [assign A [read if-0 S]]]
         [do [read content T] [continue-if 1] [assign A [read if-1 S]]]
         [write T content [read content A]]
         [assign T [read [read move A] T]]
         [assign S [read next A]]
         TM]

Figure 5. Simulation of Arbitrary Turing Machine by SS.

At the top, Figure 5 shows a classical one-tape Turing machine. There is a single unending tape, with each cell holding a 0 or a 1. There is a control, which has a single reading head at a given cell of the tape. The control is in one of a finite set of states, Q1, Q2 . . . ,Qn. For the control to be in a particular state implies it will do the following things:

It will read the symbol on the tape, i.e., detect whether it is 0 or 1.

It will write a symbol on the tape, either a 0 or 1 (as determined by the state and the symbol read).

It will move the tape head one square, either to the left or the right (as determined by the state and the symbol read).

It will change itself to be in a new state (as determined by the state and the symbol read).

Instead of going to a new state, the machine may come to a halt.

Nothing is said about what sorts of physical arrangements are used to create the set of states for a given Turing machine and make it behave in the way specified. But we can write down for each state what it *will* do, and we have done this in Figure 5 for a couple of states (Q1, Q2, etc.) For each state we have two entries, depending on whether the tape cell has a 0 or a 1: the symbol to be written on the tape (either a 0 or a 1); whether to move left or right; and the state to go to. If a special next state, *halt*, is given, the machine halts.

Any machine built to behave this way is a Turing machine. Turing machines differ only in the number of states they have and in what happens at each state, within the limits described above. However, the class of all Turing machines is very large—by using enough states (and it may take a very large number) the input–output behavior of *any* physical mechanism can be approximated as closely as required. It is one of these maximal class of machines, even though a Turing machine's moment by moment behavior seems very restricted.

The bottom of Figure 5 gives the program in SS that simulates an arbitrary Turing machine. The Turing machine itself must be represented. This is done entirely within the memory of SS, rather than in terms of the external input and output interfaces of SS. For any reasonable **input** and **behave** operators this extra translation would be straightforward. The representation uses three types of symbol structures, one for the tape cell and the other two for the state of the Turing machine control. The tape cell has three roles: *Content* holds the tape-symbol, either 0 or 1; *left* holds the symbol for the tape cell to the left; and *right* holds the symbol for the tape cell to the right. The Turing machine state *has* two roles: *if-0* to hold the specifications for what to do if the tape cell holds 0; and *if-1* for what to do if the tape holds 1. Each specification (the third symbol structure type) has three roles: *Content* holds the tape-symbol to be written, either 0 or 1; *move* holds the direction to move the tape, either *left* or *right*; and *next* holds the symbol for the next state to go to.

There is a single program expression, called TM, which accomplishes the simulation. TM consists of **doing** a sequence of six subprograms, each of which accomplishes one step of the basic definition. There is a symbol T for the current tape cell under the head, a symbol S for the current state of the Turing machine control, and a symbol A for the actions specified by the state (which will be different depending on the tape symbol). The program is shown as a single nested expression with many subexpressions. This is simply for convenience of reading; it does not indicate any additional properties of SS. Complex subexpressions are constructed entirely through the use of assignment. In each case what occurs in an expression is a symbol, which is assigned to the subexpression. Thus, the actual representation of TM is:

TM: [**do** TM1 TM2 TM3 TM4 TM5 TM]

TM1: [**do** TM11 TM12 TM13]

TM11: [**read** content T]

TM12: [**continue-if** 0]

TM13: [**assign** A TM131]

TM131: [**read** if-0 S]

TM2: . . .

And so on through the whole expression.

Let us take up the steps of TM in order.

1. The first step reads the symbol on the tape and if it is 0 assigns the symbol A to be the actions specified in case 0 occurs, i.e., the substructure at if-0.
2. The second step similarly assigns A to be the actions specified at if-1, if 1 is the tape symbol. (Only one of the two possible assignments to A will occur, since they are mutually exclusive.)
3. The third step writes the symbol specified via A into the tape-cell. This is a simple transfer of a symbol; it even occupies the same role in both structures, i.e., content.
4. The fourth step moves the tape left or right by using the symbol specified via A as the role symbol to extract the left or right link from the tape-cell.
5. The fifth step is to assign S to be the next state as specified via A.
6. The sixth and final step is to do TM again, which repeats the entire interpretation, now on the changed values of T and S.

This demonstration of universality is transparent, because the universality of some given system (here, Turing machines) has already been established, and the system itself (here, SS) has reasonable properties as a programming system.

Of course, it is necessary that the program be correct. In fact, two bugs exist in the present version. One arises because we didn't take care of halting. This requires more conventions: The Turing machine halts if the symbol *halt* occurs for the next state; then TM should exit and return to whatever program executed it, with the current tape cell (T) as output. The other bug arises because

the tape for a Turing machine is of indefinite extent, while the representation of
the tape in SS necessarily consists of only a finite number of symbol structures,
one for each cell. It is necessary for the simulation to extend the tape in either
direction, if it runs off an end. Again, by convention, the symbol *tape-end*
occurring in a tape cell at either *left* or *right* will indicate the end of the tape.

```
TM-Exec: [do TM T]
TM: [do
        [do [read content T] [continue-if 0] [assign A [read if-0 S]]]
        [do [read content T] [continue-if 1] [assign A [read if-1 S]]]
        [write T content [read content A]]
        [assign T [do [read [read move A] T]
                      [continue-if tape-end]
                      [assign New-T [copy T]]
                      [write New-T content 0 [read [read move A] other ] T]
                      [write T [read move A] New-T]
                      New-T]]
    [assign S [read next A]]
    [exit-if halt]
    TM]
other: [right:left left:right]
```

Figure 6. Correct Simulation of Arbitrary Turing Machine by SS.

Just for completeness, a correct version of the program appears in Figure 6.
To correct the first bug, a top level program TM-Exec is defined, which simply
executes TM and, when it is done, outputs T. Correspondingly, TM now tests if
the new S is halt and exits if it is. For the other bug, TM senses whether the next
tape cell is the symbol tape-end and, if so, extends the tape. This occurs en
passant within the expression for moving the tape, [**assign** T [**read** [**read** move
A] T]], by performing the regular operation within a **do**-sequence where it can
continue if tape-end is found. It then creates a new tape cell (calling it New-T)
and links it up in the several ways necessary. It ends by handing the new cell (as
New-T) to the **assign** operator, just as if that cell had been found initially.

4. GENERAL SYMBOL SYSTEMS

We can now describe the essential nature of a (physical) symbol system. We start
with a definition:

> *Symbol systems* are the same as *universal machines*.

It may seem strange to *define* symbol systems to be universal machines.
One would think that symbol systems should be defined to be that class of

systems that *has* symbols according to some abstract characterization. Then it would be a fundamental theoretical result that symbol systems are universal. However this way is not open to us, without a certain amount of scientific legerdemain. The fact is that we do not have an independent notion of a symbol system that is precise enough to counterpoise to a universal machine, and thus subsequently to prove their equivalence. Instead, we have *discovered* that universal machines always contain within them a particular notion of symbol and symbolic behavior, and that this notion provides us for the first time with an adequate abstract characterization of what a symbol system should be. Thus, tautalogically, this notion of symbol system, which we have here called *physical symbol system*, is universal.

Does not SS, the machine we have just defined, provide a paradigmatic example that could be suitably generalized to define the class of symbol systems? True, SS was put together precisely to bring out the essential properties of symbols. Alas (for such an enterprise), SS and all its kindred have emerged simply as *reformulations* of the concept of universal machines. Historically, we are genuinely in the position of discoverers, not inventers. For analytic purposes we can certainly now propose axiomatic formulations of symbol systems and prove their equivalence to universal machines. But I prefer an exposition that emphasizes the dependence, rather than the independence, of the notion of (physical) symbol system on the notion of universal machines.

Thus, our situation is one of defining a symbol system to be a universal machine, and then taking as a hypothesis that this notion of symbol system will prove adequate to all of the symbolic activity this physical universe of ours can exhibit, and in particular all the symbolic activities of the human mind. In regard to our list of constraints of mind in Figure 1, two seemingly separate constraints (universality and using symbols) have been satisfied by a single class of systems.

We can now proceed to the essential nature of symbols and symbolic behavior in universal systems and to their generality. Note, however, that universal machines provide a peculiar situation with respect to what is essential. Every universal machine exhibits in some form all the properties of any universal machine. To be sure, differences exist among universal machines—in primitive structure, in processing times, in sensitivities, and in processing reliabilities. Though important—even critical—for some aspects of the phenomena of mind, these differences are not critical for the nature of symbols. Thus, when we focus on certain properties, we are providing an emphasis, rather than separating what cannot in truth be separated.

We start with a discussion of designation and interpretation. Then we go through the operators of SS. Though defined as specific operators for a specific machine, each corresponds to a general functional capability. Each operator thus raises the question of the necessity of this functional capability to a symbol system and also of the forms that it can take in alternative implementations while still accomplishing the essential function.

4.1. Designation

The most fundamental concept for a symbol system is that which gives symbols their symbolic character, i.e., which lets them stand for some entity. We call this concept *designation*, though we might have used any of several other terms, e.g., *reference*, *denotation*, *naming*, *standing for*, *aboutness*, or even *symbolization* or *meaning*. The variations in these terms, in either their common or philosophic usage, is not critical for us. Our concept is wholly defined within the structure of a symbol system. This one notion (in the context of the rest of a symbol system) must ultimately do service for the full range of symbolic functioning.

Let us have a definition:

> *Designation:* An entity X designates an entity Y relative to a process P, if, when P takes X as input, its behavior depends on Y.

There are two keys to this definition. First, the concept is grounded in the behavior of a process. Thus, the implications of designation will depend on the nature of this process. Second, there is action at a distance: The process behaves as if inputs, remote from those in it in fact has, effect it. This is the symbolic aspect, that having X (the symbol) is tantamount to having Y (the thing designated) for the purposes of process P.

The symbols in SS satisfy this definition of designation. There are a set of processes (the operators and the control) to which symbols can be input, and when so input the processes behave as a function, not of the symbols themselves, but of what the symbols have been assigned to—what, therefore, they designate.

The question of what symbolization implies in SS can only be worked out by understanding the nature of these processes, which can now be called *symbolic processes*. That these processes taken together are sufficient for attaining universality states the biggest implication. That this universality is attained only because of the existence of symbols provides the conceptual knot that makes the notion deep.

In SS, the second aspect of the definition is provided by the mechanism of *access*, which is part of the primitive structure of SS. It provides remote connections of specific character, as spelled out in describing **assign**. This specification is generated by enumerating for each of the ten operators plus the control the precise access needed to carry out their specified operations. Exactly these and no other forms of access are needed. This access is needed to exactly three types of entities: symbol structures, operators, and roles in symbol structures. Thus, *access* is no homunculus, providing that this finite set of primitive properties can be realized in physical mechanisms. We already know, through our experience with digital computers, that this is not only possible but eminently practical.

The great magic comes because this limited capability for accessing supports a general capability for designation. The set of processes must be expanded to include programs, and their inputs must be taken to include expressions. Then, for any entity (whether in the external world or in the memory), if an expression can be created at time T that is dependent on the entity in some way, processes can exist in the symbol system that, at some later Time T', take that expression as input and, behaving according to the recorded structure, behave in a way dependent on the entity. Hence these expressions designate the entity.

An important transitive law is illustrated in this, in which if X designates Y and Y designates Z, then X designates Z. In the case in point, there is first the acquisition which, through access to the actual external structure, creates a structure in the memory of the system that depends on this external entity; then the preservation of that memory structure through time yields a memory structure at some later time that still depends on the object; finally, the access associated with the internal symbol makes that structure available to a process, which then behaves accordingly, impressing it on still another entity and instantiating the relation of designation.

Because of the universality of symbol systems, the scope of this capability for designation is wide open and hardly yet explored. To repeat an earlier remark, the power of a designatory capability depends entirely on the symbolic processes to which it is coupled. If these processes are restricted enough, the total system may be able to accomplish little; if they are universal, then the total system may be able to do all that is required in human symbolization.

This general symbolic capability that extends out into the external world depends on the capability for acquiring expressions in the memory that record features of the external world. This in turn depends on the **input** and **behave** operators, whose details have not been described, but which limit access to the external world in some fashion. Such limits do not affect the capability of the symbol system to designate arbitrary entities, though they might limit the extent to which such capabilities could be utilized by a given system.

Designation is at the heart of universality. For one machine to behave as an arbitrary other machine, it must have symbols that designate that other. Once the input of the to-be-universal machine is separated into two parts, one of which is an instruction about something outside the machine (to wit, the other machine), there is no way out from generating some symbolic capability. That this symbolic capability should be general enough to encompass all notions of symbolic action derives (if indeed it is true) from the scope of what was to be symbolized, namely any input–output function. But the kernel of the notion of symbols arrived by the single act of getting a machine to act like something other than what it is.

A distinctive feature of SS is taking the general capability for symbols and access as central. Most formalizations of the notion of universal machine (all but those such as Lisp that stem from the work in artificial intelligence) take as central a more primitive capability for accessing, reflecting an interest in showing how universality can be build up by a machine. For instance, the Turing machine has symbols for the states of the control. These have the property of access, but are fixed and unchangeable—symbols cannot be created or reassigned. They do not provide the indefinitely extendable symbol system that is required for universality, but only some of the machinery for it. The indefinitely extendable symbol system is constructed as an addressing scheme on the (indefinitely extendable) tape. The construction is made possible by the tape movement operators, which provide the primitive accessing capability.

The underlying physical mechanism for obtaining access is some sort of switching mechanism that opens up a path between the process and the thing accessed. There are a wide variety of such switching mechanisms, but they are closely related to *search*. If the medium is recalcitrant, e.g., the Turing machine tape, the symbol system is implemented through a linear search of the tape and a match of a finite set of tape-symbols that serves to address the expression accessed. In more perspicuous media, i.e., a preorganized addressing switch for a random access memory, the implementation takes features from the symbol token (the address) and uses them to construct a direct path to the requisite location.

The usual formulations of universal machines also tend to use the term *symbol* for the alphabet of distinctive patterns that can occur in the memory medium (e.g., the 0 and 1 tape symbols for our Turing machine). As defined, these entities are not symbols in the sense of our symbol system. They satisfy only part of the requirements for a symbol, namely being the tokens in expressions. It is of course possible to give them full symbolic character by programming an accessing mechanism that gets from them to some data structure. Table look-up mechanisms provide one scheme. Actually, the alphabet of such symbols is usually quite small (e.g., only two for our version of a Turing machine), so they operate more like letters, i.e., the elements out of which a genuine set of symbols can be constructed.

4.2. Interpretation

The term *interpretation* is taken here in the narrow sense it has acquired in computer science:

> *Interpretation:* The act of accepting as input an expression that designates a process and then performing that process.

All the behavioral flexibility of universal machines comes from their ability to create expressions for their own behavior and then produce that behavior. Interpretation is the necessary basic mechanism to make this possible. The general designatory capabilities of symbol systems underly the ability to create the designating expressions in the first place. Although little can be said about exact boundaries, some *interior milieu* must exist within which the symbol system can freely and successfully interpret expressions. Given this, obtaining other performances according to specification can be compromised in various ways, e.g., by error, by indirect and shared control, or whatever.

The symbols that designate operators are absolutely essential, and no quantity of symbols for expressions or roles can substitute for them. These are the symbols that have an external semantics wired into them—which finally solve Tolman's problem of how his rats, lost in thought in their cognitive maps, could ever behave. The number of such symbols can be shrunk by various encodings and parametrizations, but it cannot vanish. Equally (and more likely for real systems), the number can be much larger and the decomposition can be radically different than for SS.

The control exhibits a basic tripartite decomposition of the total processes of the machine, which can be indicated by *(control + (operators + data))*. Behavior is composed by one part, the control, continually bringing together two other parts, the operators and the data, to produces a sequence of behavior increments (i.e., the operation formed by the application of the operator to the data). This will be recognized as familiar from every computer, programming language, and mathematical system.[2] This structure can be taken as an essential organizational feature of all symbolic systems.

This organization implies a requirement for *working memory* in the control to hold the symbols for the operator and data as they are selected and brought together. Our description of SS in Figure 2 shows only the place for the active symbol and for the input and output symbols for the operators. This is the tip of the iceberg; perusal of Figure 4 shows that additional working memory is needed. What memory will vary with the type of universal machine, but some is always implied by the act of decomposition. Thus working memory is an invariant feature of symbol systems.

However, many things about the control of SS are not invariant at all over different types of universal symbol systems. One must be careful to treat SS as a frame for describing *functional* capabilities, abstracting away from many of its structural features. Three examples of this are:

SS's control requires an unbounded amount of memory (essentially a pushdown stack) because the nesting of programs can be indefinitely extended. This is inessential, though it makes for simplicity. Normally control is a fixed machine with fixed memory; and regular memory (which is unbounded) is used according to some memory management strategy to handle excessive embedding.

SS has a serial control, i.e., a single control stream. This is inessential, though it also makes for simplicity. There may be multiple control streams of all sorts. The **input** and **behave** operators may both be evoked and operate in parallel. There may be multiple controls, a few or many, functionally specialized or all equivalent, and interconnected in a variety of ways. The parallel units may themselves be universal machines, or limited controllers, or only operators. Under some conditions the resulting processing aggregate is not universal, under many it is.

SS is a totally reliable system, nothing in its organization reflecting that its operators,

---

[2]Mathematics exhibits the application of operator to data, i.e., function to argument, while leaving the control indeterminate, i.e., in the hands of the mathematician.

control or memory could be erroful. This is inessential, though it again makes for simplicity. As was noted earlier, universality is always relative to physical limits, of which reliability is one. Once fundamental components are taken as having probabilities of failure, then ultimate performance is necessarily probabilistic. If failure probabilities are significant, the system organization can include counteracting features, such as checking, redundant processing, and redundant memory codes. Up to a point universality can be maintained as a practical matter; at some point it is lost.

All of these complexities are important in themselves, and some of them lie behind other constraints in Figure 1. They do not seem of the essence in understanding the nature of symbolic capability.

4.3. Assign: Creating Designations

The function of the **assign** operator is to create a relation of access, hence of designation, between a symbol and an entity. It is, of course, limited to the access relations supported by the underlying machinery of SS: between SS's symbols and SS's expressions, roles, and operators.

Assign implies several important properties:

At any time, a symbol designates a single entity.
Many symbols can designate the same entity.
A symbol may be used to designate any entity.

SS provides absolute and uniform adherence to these properties, but this is not necessary. For instance, from SS's simulation of a Turing machine, it can be seen that the requirements for multiple assignment and reassignment of a symbol to an arbitrary entity are needed only for the small set of working symbols used in the TM program (T, S, and A). All the other symbols (content, **do**, TM, . . .) can have fixed assignments. From this, the more general capability can be built up—which is what programming the simulation demonstrates.

The situation here generally applies. Small amounts of the requisite capabilities can be parlayed into the full-flecged capability. The minimal conditions are rarely interesting from a theoretical view, though successful elimination of an entire functional capability can be revealing. Minimal basic capabilities often imply gross inefficiencies and unreliabilities. Typical is the additional level of interpretation, if simulation is used to recover the additional capabilities (as in our example). Thus, symbol systems that satisfy additional constraints of Figure 1 are likely to satisfy pervasively such properties as those above.

It is often observed that the symbols of formal systems are totally abstract, whereas symbols as used by humans often have information encoded into the symbol itself, i.e., that is not arbitrary what a symbol is used for. The word for not being happy is "unhappy," in which some knowledge about what the word designates is available from an analysis of the word itself. In plane geometry small letters (a, b, . . .) are sides of triangles and capital letters (A, B, . . .) are their opposite angles. In general, the use (and usefulness) of *encoded names* has no bearing on the basic nature of symbol systems. Encoded names can be taken to be abstract symbols with bound expressions that provide the information in the encoded name. Thus, one expression has been granted a preferred access status. Though the assignment of symbols to entities has been limited, this will have an effect only if no freely assignable symbols remain as part of the system.

4.4 Copy: Creating New Memory

By applying **copy** whenever needed, SS obtains both an unbounded supply of expressions (hence of memory) and of symbols. That **copy** creates a copy is unessential, although by doing so it accomplishes a sequence of **reads** and **writes**. The essential aspect is obtaining the new expression and the new symbol. Neither can be dispensed with.

One of the few necessary conditions known for universal machines is:

A universal machine must have an unbounded memory.

The classical machine hierarchy of finite state machines, pushdown automata, linear bounded automata and Turing machines, expresses the gradation of capability with limitations in memory (Hopcroft & Ullman, 1969). Though essential, the condition of unboundedness is of little import, since what counts is the structure of the system. In all cases, the structure of the unbounded memory must eventually become uniform. Ultimately, SS has just a supply of undifferentiated *stuff* out of which to build expressions; the Turing machine has just a supply of undifferentiated tape cells. Thus, for every machine with unbounded memory, there are machines with identical structure, but bounded memory, that behave in an identical fashion on all environments (or problems) below a certain size or complexity.

The unimportance of actual unboundedness should not be taken to imply the unimportance of large memory. The experience in AI is everlastingly for larger effective memories (i.e., memories with adequately rapid access). A key element in list processing was the creation of dynamic memory, which effectively removed the memory limit problem from the operation of the system, while, of course, not removing it absolutely (i.e., available space eventually runs out). It is no accident that humans appear to have unbounded long-term memory. Thus, rather than talk about memory being actually unbounded, we will talk about it being *open*, which is to say available up to some point, which then bounds the performance, both qualitatively and quantitatively. *Limited*, in opposition to open, will imply that the limit is not only finite, but small enough to force concern. Correspondingly, *universal* can be taken to require only sufficiently open memory, not unbounded memory.

Symbols themselves are not memory; only expressions are. Though in SS symbols and expressions come into existence together, they are independent and could have separate **create** operators. Many symbols may be assigned to a single expression and many expressions may have the same symbol (over time) or may be unsymbolized and be accessible through other means. Symbols are the patterns in the symbol structure that permit accessing mechanisms to operate. Having an open number of symbols, but only a limited amount of memory, is not sufficient for a universal machine. On the other hand, with only a limited set of symbols, but an open supply of expressions, it is possible to create an open set of symbols. The use of a limited alphabet to create words is paradigmatic. However, just the anatomy of alphabets and words does not reveal the key issue, which is the construction of an accessing mechanism that makes the words behave like symbols, i.e., designate.

SS actually has an open supply of expressions of each type (and exactly what types exist was not specified). As might be expected, only a single source of openness is needed, providing it is not peculiarly tucked away, as in a pushdown stack. Further, SS's definition does not specify whether expressions themselves are limited or whether some of them can be open. This is again an unessential issue, as long as at least one open source is available for construction of whatever facilities are needed. The creation of an open structure type, the *list*, out of an open set of expressions of a limited structure type, the *pair* consisting of a *symbol* and a *link*, is paradigmatic. Though conceptually simple, such a construction was a major step in creating appropriate symbol systems.

4.5 Write: Creating Arbitrary Expressions

Another obvious, but important, necessary capability of a universal machine is:

> A universal machine must be able to create expressions of arbitrary character.

SS does this through a single uniform operator, **write**, though there are indefinitely many complex and indirect ways of attaining the result. To be unable to create an expression, by any means at all, would imply a failure to be universal (e.g., to simulate a machine that did produce that expression as an output).

In the usual way of specifying universal machines, particular representations are used for the expressions, e.g., the Turing tape or Lisp lists. Much of the idiosyncracy of such systems arises from the need to encode all structures of interest into this fixed structure. SS has remained general on this score, admitting only a basic capability for having expressions with distinct roles. Thus, we simply defined a new data type for each entity we needed to discuss,—programs, tape cells, and machine states.

It is unclear how to state the fundamental capability provided by expressions, but easy enough to exhibit it in simple and paradigmatic form. It is not enough to have only symbols. Expressions permit more than one symbol to be brought together in a way that is not determined wholly by the symbols, but provides additional structure, hence discriminability. This is what SS has in the roles—actually, in the association from the role symbol to its content symbol. There are an indefinite number of ways to provide such added structure to yield symbol expressions.

In SS's scheme, the symbols for roles are *relative* symbols. They differ in this respect from the symbols for expressions or operators, which are *absolute*. Given the symbol *move*, which designates the role in the tape-cell of the Turing machine, the process that takes roles as input, namely, **write** and **read**, can access the appropriate location in any tape-cell expression. Thus, role symbols are functions of one input (the expression), and akin to operators. These relative role symbols can be replaced by absolute symbols that uniquely designate the locations in particular expressions, though an additional operator is required to obtain these location symbols. This is the standard recourse in common programming languages, which provide *addresses* of list cells and array cells. Thus, all symbols can be absolute, with all context dependence relegated to a limited set of operators.

4.6. Read: Obtaining Symbols in Expressions

Read is the companion process to **write**, each being necessary to make the other useful. **Read** only obtains what was put into expressions by **write** at an earlier time; and a **write** operation whose result is never **read** subsequently might as well not have happened.[3]

The **read-write** coupling emphasises another necessary principle of symbol systems:

Memory must be stable.

Though much less investigated than the question of amount of memory, this principle is of the same character. In so far as memory is unreliable, the ability of the symbol system to deliver a given input-output function is jeopardized. Such a limitation does not destroy the functional character of a symbol system; it only modulates it. Of course, different systems behave differently under unreliability, and systems can be designed to mitigate the effects of unreliability. Such considerations are outside the bounds of the paper (though they show up as one of the constraints in Figure 1).

In SS the reading operator was defined in the classical way, namely, a local operator whose scope was a given expression. This provides no global access to the memory. Indeed, SS is totally dependent on the initial data structures to

---

[3]This is too strong: The read operator is not the only process that reads expressions; control at least reads programs; and if the expression might have been read but wasn't because of a contingency in the environment, then the write operator still would have been useful, analogous to insurance that is never cashed.

provide linkages around the memory. A more global accessing operator could also be given:

> **Find** the expression that matches roles   (**find** R_1 S_1 . . .)
> Produces the expression or nil

In SS, attention must be paid to constructing access links to the new expressions created by **copy**; this is usually done by virtue of their symbols occurring in other expressions that are being built. Given other processing organizations, such as ones with parallel activity, then a **find** operation would be necessary, since the access links could not exist for **read** to suffice as a retrieval mechanism.

Such a global operator cannot as it stands replace the local one, since it identifies expressions by content, not by role in some other expression. However, versions can be created to combine both functions.

4.7 Do: Integrating and Compositing Action

To be able to describe behavior in expressions, the behavior must be decomposed, whether for a description indirectly as a machine that generates the behavior, or any other type of description. All such decompositions involve both primitives and combining schemes. For SS, doing a sequence of operations is the combining operation. It reflects directly a necessary requirement on decomposition:

> Universal machines must be able to determine the future independent of the past.

Looked at in terms of a prespecified input–output function, it is only necessary that the future beyond the point of instruction be open. But if new instructional input is permitted at any time (the realistic version of the flexibility constraint), then any commitment for the entire future can be a genuine restriction of flexibility. Instruction following such a commitment might require its undoing.

Other forms of decomposition exist besides the pure *time-slice* scheme used by SS (and also by existing digital computers and programming languages), in which each operator specifies completely what happens in the next time increment, leaving complete freedom of specification beyond. For instance, the commitments of the past could decay in some way, rather than cease abruptly; the future action, although still free to be anything, could be taken from a different base line in some way. Little is known about such alternative decompositions in terms of providing universal instructable behavior.

Do as an operator can be eliminated, because its essential function is also performed by the control. Interpreting the arguments of an operator prior to executing that operator (which corresponds to function composition) provides the essentials of a time decomposition. Thus, the function would still be provided, even though the **do** operator itself were eliminated.

4.8 Exit-if and Continue-if: Converting Symbols to Behavior

One of the most characteristic features of programming languages is the existence of conditional operators, the **in-then-else** of Algol-like languages, the **branch on zero** of machine languages, or the **conditional expression** of Lisp. These operators seem to contain the essence of making a decision. Beside embodying the notion of data dependence in pure form, they also are unique in embodying the conversion from symbols to behavior. They would appear to be a functional requirement for universality. They do not seem so much deeply implicated in the concept of symbols itself, but rather associated with the system that operates with symbols.

However, it has been known since the earliest formulations of universal machines that such conditionals are not uniquely required. The requirement is to be able to compose all functions, and many other primitive functions provide the essential combinative services. For example, the minimum function is often used. It can be seen that taking the minimum of a set of elements effects a selection, thus making a decision. But the minimum function has no special symbol-to-behavior character; it has the same form as any other function.

Thus, conditionals are a convenience in SS. They can be dispensed with and the same work done by **assign, copy, write, read** and **do**. A simple way to show this is to write the simulation of the Turing Machines without using the conditionals. The universality of SS is shown by this program; hence the universality can be attained by whatever limited means are sufficient to accomplish this simulation. Figure 7 shows this simulation without the conditional. This corre-

```
TM-Exec: [do [assign [quote Next-step] [quote TM]] TM T]
TM: [do
        [assign 0 [read if-0 S]]
        [assign 1 [read if-1 S]]
        [assign A [read content T]]
        [write T content [read content A]]
        [assign T [read [read move A] T ]]
        [assign S [read next A]]
        Next-step]
tape-end: [do
        [assign New-T [copy T]]
        [write New-T content 0 [read [read move A] other ] T]
        [write T [read move A] New-T]
        New-T]
other: [right:left left:right]
halt: [assign [quote Next-step] nil]
```

Figure 7. Elimination of Conditional Operators from Simulation of Turing Machine.

sponds to the completely correct simulation of Figure 6, so that all places where conditionals originally occurred are covered.

It is instructive to understand the basic device in Figure 7. Conditionality is the dependence of behavior on data. The data in the simulation are symbols. Hence, each possible data symbol can be assigned whatever is to be the case if that data symbol is encountered. The symbol that actually occurs and is accessed brings with it the behavior to be taken.

There are three places where conditionals must be removed. The first is taking appropriate action, depending on 0 or 1. For this, 0 is assigned the action specifications for 0, and 1 the action specifications for 1. Then accessing the symbol that actually occurs in the tape cell, via (**read** content T), obtains the action specification as a function of the occurring state. This is assigned to the temporary working symbol, A, and the program can proceed as before.

The second place is sensing the end of the tape. Here, the symbol tape-end is assigned to be the program that extends the tape. Due to the recursive interpretation of control, accessing tape-end leads to the interpretation of this program, which then fixes up the tape en passant. Thus, the main program, TM, never has to deal with the problem explicitly.

The third place is exiting on halt. This is a little tricky, because a symbol (halt) must be converted to a permanent change of behavior (exiting the infinite loop of TM). The final step of TM, which is the recursive step to repeat TM, is made into a variable symbol, Next-step. This is assigned to be TM in TM-Exec, so that if nothing changes this symbol, TM, will be repeated, just as before. The symbol halt is assigned to a program that assigns Next-step to be nil. Thus, if halt is encountered, this program is executed, making TM into a straight-line program, which will then exit. It is necessary to use **quote** in the **assignments** of program symbols (Next-step and TM), or they would be executed inadvertently.

This style of programming illustrates an important relativity of view. From the perspective of the program there is no choice and no decision; it simply puts one foot in front of the other so to speak. From the perspective of the outside observer a choice is being made dependent on the data. The views are reconciled when it is seen that the program is constructing its own path, laying down each next step just in front of itself, like a stepping-stone, and then stepping onto it.

4.9 Quote: Treating Processes as Data

All universal systems contain a distinction between operators and data (i.e., arguments). To create its own procedures, a system must distinguish some expressions as data at one time (when creating or modifying them) and as program at another time (when interpreting them). This is a genuine contextual effect, since the expression is to be same in either case. This is only a binary distinction, and it can be achieved in many ways: by having a program memory as distinct from a data memory, with a transfer operation to activate the program; by marking the program so the control will not interpret it and then removing the mark to activate it; by having an **execute** operator that only interprets under deliberate command; or by having a **quote** operator that inhibits interpretation on command. For SS, since its control cycle is to interpret everything, the **quote** command is the natural choice.

However, as Figure 5 again shows by producing the simulation without the use of **quote**, this operator does not imply an additional primitive functional requirement. What Figure 5 actually shows is that if a symbol system is willing to operate in indirect simulation mode, the distinctions can be introduced by data conventions. This is because the control of the system now becomes programmable.[4]

4.10. Behave and Input: Interacting with the External World

Behave and **input** have played a muted role in the exposition of SS, only because the emphasis has been on the basic functional requirements for symbolization and for universality. These capabilities must exist in some interior system, and thus can be illustrated there, without involving the interaction with the external world.

Behave and **input** imply an extension of the basic access mechanism, beyond the operators, roles and expressions, as described above. The symbols that are operands in **behave** must access in some way the effector mechanisms. These symbols can be viewed simply as additional operators which haven't been specified because there was no need to. **Input**, on the other hand, requires its output symbols to reflect an invariant relation to the state of the external environment (via states of the receptor mechanism). The invariance doesn't have to be perfect; it can even change over time (though not too rapidly). But without some reliable transduction from external structure to symbols, the symbol system will not be able to produce reliable functional dependence on the external environment.

General symbol systems include unlimited elaborations on **behave** and **input**. In particular, versions of these operators need not link to a genuine external world, but simply to other components of the total system that provide additional computational devices. These may be integral to the actual operation of the system in practice. Such additional facilities do not destroy the capability for symbolic action. The only requirement is that they be symbolizable, i.e., have symbols that evoke them and symbols that reflect their behavior.

4.11. Symbol Systems Imply Universality

The notion of universality has been expressed to reveal how it contains a notion

---

[4]The quotes can likewise be removed from Figure 7 by rewriting the TM program so it is a nonprogram data structure that is interpreted by an SS program.

of symbol and symbol system. Though at the beginning of the section I claimed it was inappropriate to act as if we had an independent characterization of symbol system; it is now certainly useful to extract from the current formulation what a symbol system might be, independent of the notion of universality. For instance, this might lead to interesting variants of symbol systems that are not universal in some important way (i.e., in some way other than physical limits).

Consider the following generalized characterization of the notions involved in physical symbol systems:

Symbols as abstract types that express the identity of multiple tokens.

Expressions as structures containing symbol tokens.

Designation as a relation between a symbol and the entities it symbolizes.

Interpretation as realizing the designations of expressions.

Operations of assigning symbols, and copying, reading, and writing expressions.

These notions all seem fundamental to symbolic functioning. It is difficult to envision a notion of symbol that does not embody some version of these capabilities, and perhaps much more besides. These notions are too vague to actually define symbolic functioning. For instance, the statement about designation does not describe the properties of the relation, e.g., between the word "cat" and the animal cat. The statement about interpretation leaves entirely open what symbolic activity is actually about—it could easily hide a homunculus. Still, these might form the thematic kernel from which to precipitate independent characterizations of symbols.

In particular, there exists an instantiation of these notions that regains the formulation of a physical symbol system. The chief additional ingredient (abstracted away in generating the list above) is a notion of symbolic *processing*. Designation is given a primitive basis primarily in the accessing of other expressions. Interpretation is given a formulation involving only expressions that designate symbolic processing. Assigning, copying, reading, and writing are taken as specific processing functions; in particular, reading is taken only as the ability to obtain constituent symbols. These particularities would no doubt be included in some fashion in any instantiation of the general notion of symbols stated above. However, the instantiation for physical symbol systems is still highly special, and much is missing: designation of external entities, wider ranges of interpretive activity, and so on.

Yet, as we have seen, this process-oriented instantiation of these notions is by itself sufficient to produce universality. No embedding of the symbol system into a larger processing system with other capabilities is required, though sufficient freedom from physical limitations (i.e., sufficient memory, reliability, etc.) must exist. In the preceding discussion, the operations of **exit-if**, **continue-if**,

do, **quote**, and **find** were shown to be collectively unnecessary to achieve universality. Thus, the operations that appear inherently involved in symbolic processing (**assign**, **copy**, **read**, **write**, and **interpret**) are collectively sufficient to produce universality. No augmentation with any nonsymbolic processing machinery is required. Although the argument was carried through on a particular system, SS, it applies generally to the functional capabilities themselves.

A novel feature of physical symbol systems is the approach to symbolic function, not just by processing, but by *internal* symbolic processing. The primitive symbolic capabilities are defined on the symbolic processing system itself, not on any external processing or behaving system. The prototype symbolic relation is that of access from a symbol to an expression, not that of naming an external object. Thus, it is an implication of the formulation, not part of its definition, that the appropriate designatory relations can be obtained to external objects (via chains of designation). Because of this, the exact scope of that designatory capability is left open, implicit in the ramifications of universality.

Thus, we are lead finally to the following hypothesis:

Any reasonable symbol system is universal (relative to physical limitations).

It is important to distinguish symbol systems that are computationally limited because of physical constraints or limited programs and data from symbol systems that fall short of providing universality because of structural limitations. The hypothesis refers to the latter.

Despite this hypothesis, one might still want to formulate a notion of symbol system that was not also universal, even though it would be limited. One general path might be to deny the process base. But this seems unfruitful, since symbol systems must ultimately be used by processing systems, and this path simply keeps the processing implications off stage. The addition of a processing base would very likely simply convey universality. Another possibility is to consider systems with many symbol systems, each ranging over severely limited domains with limited intercommunication. These could violate some aspects of assignment, so that genuinely limited systems might emerge. But, in general, looking for a more limited conception of symbolic system, in order to get something conceptually independent of universality, does not seem particularly rewarding. This seems especially the case in trying to understand the human mind, which surely exhibits extreme flexibility even though it must cope with some stringent physical limitations.

5. THE PHYSICAL SYMBOL SYSTEM HYPOTHESIS

Having finally made clear the nature of a physical symbol system, the major hypothesis can be stated explicitly (Newell & Simon, 1976):

Physical Symbol System Hypothesis: The necessary and sufficient condition for a physical system to exhibit general intelligent action is that it be a physical symbol system.

Necessary means that any physical system that exhibits general intelligence will be an instance of a physical symbol system.

Sufficient means that any physical symbol system can be organized further to exhibit general intelligent action.

General intelligent action means the same scope of intelligence seen in human action: that in real situations behavior appropriate to the ends of the system and adaptive to the demands of the environment can occur, within some physical limits.

The hypothesis takes as given the identity of symbol systems and universal systems, and asserts their connection to rationality, a concept which did not enter into their formulation. The hypothesis implicitly asserts that physical symbol systems cover human symbol systems, since general intelligence includes human intelligence. It can be taken as also asserting the essential role of human symbols in human rational behavior, if that cannot be taken for granted.

The hypothesis implies that symbol systems are the appropriate class within which to seek the phenomena of mind. However, it does not mention *mind* explicitly, but rather the notion of general intelligent action. It thereby implicitly takes general intelligence to be the key to the phenomena of mind. Given the democracy of the constraints in Figure 1, this may seem a little presumptuous. If so, it is not a presumption that makes a substantial difference in the short term. The systems that satisfy all of the constraints will undoubtedly be a highly distinctive subclass of those that satisfy only the three involved in the hypothesis—universality, symbols, and rationality. This distinctiveness could well include phenomena of mind that would make the total class appear quite unmind-like. That possibility does not affect the tactical issue of approaching the phenomena of mind via this class of systems.

The statement of necessity is straightforward. A general intelligent system, whatever additional structures and processes it may have, will contain a physical symbol system. It will be possible to find what serves as symbols and as expressions; and to identify what processes provide the functions that we have enumerated and discussed. The variability of realization discussed in the next section may make these structures and processes far from obvious, but they will exist.

The statement of sufficiency requires a little care. A universal system always contains the potential for being any other system, if so instructed. Thus, a universal system can become a generally intelligent system. But it need not be one. Furthermore, instructability does not imply any ability at self-instruction, so that there may be no way to transform such a system into one that is generally intelligent, i.e., no external agent with the capability to successfully instruct it need be available. Given the nature of universality, this sufficient condition does not have much bite; it is the necessary condition which carries the strong implications.

The notion of general intelligence can only be informally circumscribed, since it refers to an empirical phenomenon. However, the intent is clear—to cover whatever will come to be called intelligent action as our understanding of the phenomenon increases. The term *general* excludes systems that operate only in circumscribed domains. If the domain is narrow enough, considerable intellectual power may be possible from systems that are not physical symbol systems. Thus, a specific enumeration algorithm for chess that achieved master level, but was realized directly in hardware in a way that avoided the full capabilities of a symbol system, would not provide a counterexample to the hypothesis. General intelligence implies that within some broad limits anything can become a task. It would suffice to ask if the given narrow algorithm could also accept other novel tasks; and on this it would, per hypothesis, fail.

All real systems are limited: To be generally intelligent does not imply the ability to solve or even formulate all problems. We have used the phrase *physical limits* to indicate the effects of underlying limits to speed, memory size, reliability, sensitivity, etc. The existence of such limits implies the possibility of quibbles in assessing the hypothesis, if the limits are so stringent as to deny a system any reasonable scope for positive performance. The formulation above does not attempt to be precise enough to deal with such quibbles.

5.1. Why Might the Hypothesis Hold?

That the hypothesis refers to rationality, rather than more generally to phenomena of mind, is not just a rhetorical preference. The hypothesis is based on the empirical evidence of the last twenty years in artificial intelligence. That evidence specifically relates to rational goal-directed behavior, and not to the other constraints (though some evidence exists touching one or two others). Thus, the hypothesis really must be cast in this narrower form.

It is important to understand that the hypothesis is empirical and rests on this body of experience. Artificial intelligence has made immense progress in developing machines that perceive, reason, solve problems, and do symbolic tasks. Furthermore, this has involved the deliberate use of symbol systems, as witnessed in the development and exploitation of list processing. This use of symbolic computation distinguishes artificial intelligence from most other enterprises within computer science (though not all). These advances far outstrip what has been accomplished by other attempts to build intelligent mechanisms, such as the work in building robots driven directly by circuits, the work in neural nets, or the engineering attempts at pattern recognition using direct circuitry and analogue computation.[5] There is no space in this paper to review the evidence for this, which covers the development of an entire field over almost a quarter century. Reverence to the most recent textbooks will have to suffice (Nilsson, 1980; Winston, 1977).

Given our present understanding of intelligent programs, an analysis can be made of why symbol systems play a necessary role in general intelligent action. Again, there is no space to do more than outline this analysis here. There seem to be three main points.

1. A general intelligent system must somehow embody aspects of what is to be attained prior to attainment of it, i.e., it must have *goals*. Symbols that designate the situation to be attained (including that it is to be attained, under what conditions, etc.) appear to be the only candidate for doing this. It might seem an alternative to build goal-orientation into the structure of the system at design time (as is often done in programs that have a single fixed task, such as playing a game). However, this does not suffice for a general intelligence facing an indefinite sequence of novel and sufficiently diverse goal situations.
2. A general intelligent system must somehow consider candidate states of affairs (and partial states) for the solutions of these goals (leading to the familiar search trees). Symbols in a symbol system appear to be the only way to designate these, especially as the diversity and novelty of the states and partial states increase without bound.
3. An intelligent system must fashion its responses to the demands of the task environment. As the diversity of tasks expand, i.e., as the intelligence becomes general, there would seem to be no way to avoid a flexibility sufficient to imply universality and hence symbols.

The backbone of the above argument is: (1) rationality demands designation of potential situations; (2) symbol systems provide it; (3) only symbol systems can provide it when sufficient novelty and diversity of task are permitted. This latter aspect is analogous to standard arguments in linguistics concerning the implications of generation of novel sentences.

6. REALIZATIONS AND SYSTEM LEVELS

Symbol systems, as described, are abstract. We now need to consider their realization in our physical universe. The key to this is our experience with the construction of digital computers. That current digital technology involves a hierarchy of levels is well known and appreciated. However, it is part of the story of symbol systems and needs to be recounted briefly.

A standard set of levels has emerged as digital computers have been developed. These levels are levels of *description*, since it is always the same physical system that is being described. Each level consists of characteristic

[5]The term *direct* is used as a shorthand to indicate that the systems do not use digital computers as a major component.

components that can be connected together in characteristic fashion to form systems that process a characteristic medium. The different descriptions form a sequence of levels, because the components, connections and media of one level, are defined in terms of systems at the next lower level.

The bottom-most level starts with the description of the physical devices in electronic terms. It is usually called the *device* level. Above this is the *circuit* level, which consists of electrical currents and voltages, traveling in wires. Above that is the *logic* level, in which there occur registers containing bits, with transfer paths between them and various logical functions occurring when bits pass through functional units. Operation here is entirely parallel, as it is at all lower levels. The next level is the *program* level which contains data structures, symbols (or variables), addresses, and programs. Operation is sequential, consisting of control streams produced by interpreters, though concurrent control streams may exist. This is the level of the symbol system as it occurs in digital computers. Above the programming level is the level of gross anatomy, the so-called *PMS (Processor-Memory-Switch)* level. Here there is simply a medium, called data or information, which flows along channels called links and switches and is held and processed by units called memories, processors, controls, and transducers. It is the level at which you order a computer system from the manufacturer.

Each of these levels provides a complete description of a system, i.e., one in which the present state of the machine plus the laws of behavior of the system (at that level) determine the entire trajectory of the system through time.[6]

Although apparently only a way of describing the physical world, each level in fact constitutes a *technology*. That is, any description of a system can be realized physically, because physical techniques exist for creating the required components and assembling them according to the description. Circuits of any description can be built; so also logic circuits, and programs with any data types and routines. At the PMS level, computer configurations can be ordered with various combinations of memory boxes, disks, and terminals. And so on. (Limits do exist to the realizability of arbitrary descriptions, e.g., the number of nested expressions in a programming language or the fanout in a logic circuit technology; these complicate, but do not destroy, the technological character of a level.) Thus, these levels of description do not exist just in the eye of the beholder, but have a reality in this combinative characteristic in the real world. The levels are not arbitrary and cannot be created at will, just by an act of analysis. On the other hand, there is no persuasive analysis yet that says this particular set of levels is necessary or unique and could not be replaced by a quite different set.

From the prior discussion of symbol systems we should be prepared for the existence of an indefinitely wide variety of symbol systems. Such variety stems from all the different forms of operators, controls, memories, and symbol-

---

[6]The top level (PMS) is often an exception, for behavioral laws are not usually formulated for it.

structures that still add up to universal symbolic capability. The logic level structure that creates a particular symbol system is called the *architecture*. Thus, there is an indefinite variety of architectures. Indeed, they are so diverse that we have no reasonable characterizations of the class of all architectures.

What we had no right to expect is the immense variety of physical ways to realize any fixed symbol system. What the generations of digital technology have demonstrated is that an indefinitely wide array of physical phenomena can be used to develop a digital technology to produce a logical level of essentially identical character. If evidence must be quoted for this, it comes in the form of the *architecture family*, achieved first by IBM in the mid-sixties with System/360 and now provided by most manufacturers, whereby many implementations exist for a given architecture, trading cost for speed and memory capacity. Programs that run on one implementation also run on the other. Furthermore, these implementations are not all planned for in advance, but as brand new technologies gradually come into existence at the device level, new implementations of the existing architecture are created.

Thus the picture that emerges is a series of levels of technology, with a many-many mapping between levels—each level giving rise to an immense diversity of systems at the next higher level, and each system at a given level being realizable by an immense diversity of organizations at the next lower level.

That humans are physical symbols systems implies that there exists a physical architecture that supports that symbol system. The relatively gross facts about the nervous system reveal some natural candidates for the levels of organization at which technologies do exist. The neural level surely constitutes a technology. So also does the macromolecular level (in fact, several technologies may exist there). It is possible to be mistaken about the levels, given the potentiality at the macromolecular level, as seen, for instance, in the immune system. But such uncertainty does not destroy the essential picture:

> There must exist a neural organization that is an architecture—i.e., that supports a symbol structure.

Furthermore, the immense diversity of lower level technologies that can lead to an architecture certainly enhances the chance that a biological based architecture could have evolved.

This is a genuine prediction on the structure of the nervous system and should ultimately inform the attempt to understand how the nervous system functions. It does not appear to have done so, though from time to time the suggestion has even been made directly (Newell, 1962). In fact, I know of no discussion of the issue in the neuroscience literature.

The reasons for this lack of attention by the neurosciences lie beyond the present paper. Some of the considerations are evident in Geschwind's paper at this conference (Geschwind, 1980), where emphasis is placed on the special-purpose computational systems that seem to be available in the organism, even to doubting that any general purpose mechanisms exist. As the present exposition should make clear, the requirement for universal symbolic functioning is not incompatible with extensive special-purpose computational structure. It implies neither that everything must be done through programming a small set of primitive facilities nor that the symbol system occur as an isolated component. To take SS (or similar examples of formally defined universal systems) as implying such properties fails to appreciate the actual functional requirements they express.

The levels structure of physical implementation, and our experience with it for digital technologies, leads to understanding how one level can be *sealed off* from its lower level during normal operation. This is the phenomenon of not being able to identify *under normal conditions* the technology in which a computer is implemented, if access is available only to the behavior at the symbolic level. This sealing off produces an effect in which the symbolic behavior (and essentially rational behavior) becomes relatively independent of the underlying technology. Applied to the human organism, this produces a physical basis for the apparent irrelevance of the neural level to intelligent behavior. The neural system is not in fact irrelevant—its operation supports the symbolic level. But it does so in a way that normally hides most of its properties, realizing instead a symbol system with properties of its own.

The phrase *under normal conditions* is essential to the above characterization. Errors of all sorts that occur at lower levels typically propagate through to higher levels (here, the symbolic level) and produce behavior that is revealing of the underlying structures. Likewise, simply forcing a system against the physical limits of its behavior reveals details of the underlying technologies. Given a stop watch, the freedom to specify the tasks to be performed on a computer, and a system that is not designed to deceive, much can be learned of the lower levels of implementation. Similarly, if the system uses large subsystems of special computational character, these too may reveal themselves.

This entire story of technological system levels, and the many-many relationship of systems on the symbol level to architectures that support it, is an important part of the current knowledge about symbol systems. Like the link to rational behavior (as expressed in the basic hypothesis), it is primarily empirically based.

7. DISCUSSION

With the basic story now before us, a few issues can be touched on to make sure that the notion of symbol system and the hypothesis are correctly understood.

7.1. Knowledge and Representation

Two terms intimately related to symbolic behavior have not appeared in the discussion so far: *representation* and *knowledge*. Both have rather clear meanings within the concept of physical symbol system, especially in the practice of artificial intelligence. However, formal theories of these concepts are relatively chaotic, with little agreement yet. Still, it is useful to indicate the sense of these notions, albeit briefly.

Representation is simply another term to refer to a structure that designates:

> X *represents* Y if X designates aspects of Y, i.e., if there exist symbol processes that can take X as input and behave as if they had access to some aspects of Y.

The qualitification to aspects of Y, rather than just Y, simply reflects language usage in which X can be said to represent a complex object Y without being faithful (i.e., designating) all aspects of Y.

Representation is sometimes formulated in terms of a mapping from aspects of Y to aspects of X. Implicit in this formulation is that something can be done with X, i.e., that processes exist that can detect the aspects of X that are images of aspects of Y. Hence the whole forms a designatory chain.

Representation is also sometimes formulated in terms of a data structure with its associated *proper* operations. This view emphasizes the coupling of the static structure (what is often simply called *the* representation) and the processing that defines what can be encoded into the structure, what can be retrieved from it and what transformations it can undergo with defined changes in what is represented. This view suppresses the function of the memory structure (i.e., what it represents) in favor of the essential mechanics, but it comes to exactly the same thing as the formulation in terms of designation.

The term representation focuses attention on the image of the distal object in the symbolic structure which represents it. The analysis of universality and symbols, as presented here, focuses on the adequacy of constructing functions from the distal object to the behavior of the system, which works through the representations as an intermediate structure. Such a presentation leaves undeveloped the structure of descriptive schemes, with the corresponding questions of efficiency and usefulness. We saw a reason for this in the initial formulation of universality, where it was important to avoid confounding the limitations of descriptive schemes for possible functions with what functions could actually be produced by a machine.

Existing work, mostly stemming from the analysis of formal logic, confirms that the class of systems described here (i.e., universal symbol systems) is also the class of systems with general powers of representation or (equivalently) description. The representational range of all first order predicate calculi is the same and corresponds to universal systems (when one asks what functions can be described in the logic). An important chapter in logic was the demonstration that set theory, perhaps the most useful descriptive scheme developed in mathematics, was formulable in first order logic, thus becoming simply another alternative descriptive scheme, not one capable of describing a different range of entities and situations. Higher order logics (which progressively remove restrictions on the domains of variables in logical formula) do not extend the expressive range. Modal notions, such as *possibility* and *necessity*, long handled axiomatically in a way that made their relationship to standard logic (hence universal symbol systems) obscure, now appear to have an appropriate formulation within what is called *possible world semantics* (Hintikka, 1975; Kripke, 1972), which again brings them back within standard logic. The continuous functions that naturally occur in the world (hence, must be represented) are produced by systems of limited energy. Hence, they must be of limited frequency (i.e., limited *bandwidth*) and have, by the so-called *sampling theorem*, adequate finite discrete representations.

The above rapid transit through some basic theoretical results on representation is meant to indicate only two things: First, some general things are known about representation; and second, representation is intimately tied to symbol systems. Much more is known in empirical and practical ways about representation, especially from investigations of artificial intelligence systems. However, no adequate theory of representation exists for questions of efficiency, efficacy, and design—the level at which most interesting issues arise.

Knowledge is the other term that has not figured as prominently in our discussion as might have been expected. It is a competence-like notion whose nature can be indicated by the slogan formula:

$$\text{Representation} = \text{Knowledge} + \text{Access}$$

Given a representation, making use of it requires processing to produce other symbolic expressions (or behavior). Although it is possible for a symbolic structure to yield only a small finite number of new expressions, in general there can be an unbounded number. Consider what can be obtained from a chess position, or from the axioms of group theory, or from a visual scene. Further, to obtain most of these new expressions requires varying amounts of processing. Thus, it is theoretically useful to separate analytically the set of potential expressions that a representation can yield from the process of extracting them, i.e., the access to them. Knowledge is this abstract set of all possible derived expressions.

This notion, which corresponds to the set of all implications of a set of propositions, has a history in philosophy as a candidate for the definition of knowledge. It has seemed unsatisfactory because a person could hardly be said to know all the implications of a set of propositions. However, its position within an explicit processing theory presents quite a different situation. Here, having knowledge is distinguished from having it available for any particular use, and in a principled way that depends on the details of the processing system. This formulation in fact corresponds to the actual use of the term in artificial intelligence, where it is necessary to talk about what is available in a data structure that could be extracted by more or different processing.

7.2. Obstacles to Consideration

The basic results we have been reviewing have been with us for twenty years in one guise or another. Some attitudes about them have grown up that are obstacles to their correct interpretation. These are worth mentioning, at least briefly:

The Turing Tar Pit. The phrase is Alan Perlis'.[7] The view is that all distinctions vanish when considering systems simply as universal machines (i.e., as Turing machines), since all systems become equivalent. Therefore, general results about universality cannot be of interest to any real questions. On the contrary, the question of interest here is precisely what structure provides flexibility. The discovery that such flexibility requires symbols is a real one. The Turing Tar Pit only traps the unwary who already live within the world of universal symbol systems, which of course computer scientists do.

The computer as tool kit. The universality of the digital computer means it can be used to simulate and build models for any system of interest, from chemical processing plants to traffic control to human cognition. Therefore, its role and significance are no different for cognitive science than for any other science or engineering. On the contrary, it is the structure of the digital computer itself (and the theoretical analysis of it) that reveals the nature of symbolic systems. When the computer, as a general purpose tool, is used to simulate models of mind, these are models of symbol systems (though of different architectures than that of the computer being used as tool).

The requirement for unbounded memory. Universality implies unbounded memory. All real systems only have bounded memory. Therefore, the property of universality cannot be relevant to the understanding of intelligent mechanisms. On the contrary, as we emphasized earlier, the structural requirements for universality are not dependent on unbounded memory, only whether the absolute maximal class of input–output functions can be realized. Symbol systems are still required if universality is demanded over any sufficiently large and diverse class of functions.

The ignoring of processing time. Universality requires no restraint on processing time. Indeed, simulations run indefinitely slower than what they simulate. But time and resource limits are of the essence of intelligent action. Therefore, universality results are of little interest in understanding intelligence. On the contrary, the requirement for symbol systems remains with the additon of physical limits, such as real time (or reliability, sensitivity, . . .). The objection confuses necessary and sufficient conditions. The real question is what is the subclass of symbol systems that also satisfies the real time constraint. This is sufficiently important to the general argument of this paper that we take it up below in more detail.

The requirement for experimental identification. An experimental science of behavior can only be concerned with what it can identify by experimental operations. Universal machines (and various general representations) mimic each other and are indistinguishable experimentally. Therefore, they are not of interest to psychology. On the contrary, if humans have this chameleon-like character (which it appears they do), then it is the basic task of psychology to discover ways to discern it

---

[7]Some readers may be unacquainted with the famous Tar Pits of La Brea, California, which trapped and sucked down innumerable prehistoric animals without distinction—large and small, fierce and meek.

experimentally, however difficult. Without downplaying these difficulties, the objection overstates the lack of identifiability in the large (i.e., in the face of sufficiently wide and diverse contexts and varieties of measurement).

The uniform nature of symbol systems. General symbol systems imply a homogeneous set of symbols, in which everything is done by uniform mechanisms. But physiology and anatomy show clearly that the nervous system is filled with computational systems of immense specialization (and evolution affirms that this is how it would be). Therefore, humans (and other animals) cannot have symbol systems. On the contrary, this objection inducts the wrong attributes from existing computer architectures. The functional properties we have summarized are what is important. These can be realized in an immense diversity of schemes, including ones that are highly parallel and full of special mechanisms.

The discrete nature of symbols. Symbol systems are ultimately just a collection of bits—of yes's and no's. Such a discrete representation cannot possibly do justice to the nature of phenomenal experience, which is continuous and indefinitely rich. On the contrary, there is good reason not to trust the intuition about the relation of phenomenal reality and discreteness. On the side of constructed systems, speech and vision recognition systems begin to show adequate ways in which continuous environments can be dealt with. On the side of the human, the discrete cellular nature of biological systems (and below that of molecular structure) gives pause on the anatomical side; as does the sampled-data character of the visual system on the behavioral side. However, nothing to speak of is known about "continuous" symbol systems, i.e., systems whose symbols have some sort of continuous topology.

The computer metaphor. The computer is a metaphor for the mind. Many metaphors are always possible. In particular, new technologies always provide new ways to view man. Therefore, this metaphor too will pass, to be replaced by a metaphor from the next technology. On the contrary, though it is surely possible and sometimes fruitful to use the computer metaphorically to think about mind, the present development is that of a scientific theory of mind, not different in its methodological characteristics from scientific theories in other sciences. There has been an attempt in the philosophical literature to take *metaphor* as a metaphor for all theory and science (Black, 1962), a view well represented by Lakoff (1980) at this conference. Like all metaphors, it has its kernel of truth. But the sign is wrong. The more metaphorical, the less scientific. Again, the more metaphors the better, but the more comprehensive the theory of a single phenomenon, the better. *Computational metaphor* does not seem a happy phrase, except as a rhetorical device to distance theoretical ideas flowing from the computer and keep them from being taken seriously as science.

7.3. The Real-Time Constraint

A brief discussion of the constraint that processing occurs in real time may serve to clarify the role of symbol systems in the total endeavor to understand the phenomena of mind.

No doubt, living in real time shapes the nature of mind, and in more ways than we can imagine at present. For instance, it produces the existential dilemma that gives rise to search as a pervasive feature of all intelligent activity. Limited processing resources per unit time continually must be committed *now* without further ado—the opportunity to spend *this now* already slipping past. Imperfect present knowledge always produces imperfect commitments, which leads to (still imperfect) corrective action, which cascades to produce combinatorial search.

As noted earlier, such considerations do not remove the need for symbols. Intelligent activity in real time cannot be purchased by foregoing symbols. Rather, those symbol systems that can perform adequately in real time become the focus of interest in the search for a theory of mind. How would one seek to discover such a class? One way—though only one—is to work within the class of symbol systems to find architectures and algorithms that are responsive to the constraints of real time.

An example is the intensive explorations into the nature of multiprocessing systems. This is being fueled much more generally by computer science interests, driven by the advances in technology which provide increasingly less expensive processing power. The range of such explorations is extremely broad, currently, and much of it appears remote from the interests of cognitive science. All of it assumes that the total systems will be general purpose computers (though with interesting twists of efficiency and specialization). It will add up eventually to a thorough understanding of the space, time, and organization trade-offs that characterize computers that operate under severe time constraints.

Another example, somewhat closer to home, are the so called *production systems* (Waterman & Hayes-Roth, 1978), which consist of a (possibly very large) set of condition-action rules, with continuous parallel recognition of which rules are satisfied in the present environment and selection of one (or a few) of the satisfied rules for action execution. There are several reasons for being interested in such systems (Newell, 1973; Newell, 1979). However, a prime one is that they are responsive to the real-time constraint. The parallel recognition brings to bear, at least potentially, all of the knowledge in the system on the present moment when a decision must be made. Such systems are also universal symbol systems. They would have done as well as SS for illustrating the nature of symbols, save for the confusion engendered by their also exhibiting aspects responsive to other constraints.

The point of both examples (and others that could have been given) is not the particular contributions they might make individually. Rather, they illustrate the ability to explore classes of systems that are responsive to additional constraints by developing subclasses of architectures within the class of universal symbol systems. That the space of all universal symbol systems contains vast regions of systems inappropriate to some of the other conditions of mind-like systems is irrelevant. More precisely, it is irrelevant if the larger class is a suitable base for further analysis and exploration—which is exactly what current experience in computer science attests.

8. CONCLUSION

Let us return to our general problem of discovering the nature of mind, and the decomposition of that problem into a dozen constraints (Figure 1). We now have a class of systems that embodies two of the constraints: universality and symbolic behavior. Furthermore, this is a *generative* class. It is possible to construct systems which are automatically within the class. Thus this class can be used to explore systems that satisfy yet other constraints. Indeed, that is exactly the twenty-five-year history of artificial intelligence—an explosion of exploration, all operating from within the class of systems that were automatically universal and symbolic. The generative character comes through clearly in this history as the initial versions of digital computers were shaped via the development of list-processing to also bring their general symbolic character to the fore.

This class of universal–symbolic systems is now tied to a third constraint, rationality. That is what the Physical Symbol System Hypothesis says. Unfortunately, the nature of rational action is not yet well enough understood to yield general generative formulations, to permit exploring other constraints within a constructive framework that automatically satisfies the rationality constraint (as well as the universality and symbolic behavior constraints). Major attempts in artificial intelligence still start from basic symbolic capability and posit their own idiosyncratic processing organization for attaining rational behavior. However, some parts of the puzzle are already clear, such as the notion of goal and goal hierarchies, and the concept of heuristic (i.e., knowledge controlled) search. Thus, we may not be too far away from the emergence of an accepted generative class of systems that are universal-symbol and also rational. The excitement that rippled through the artificial intelligence world at the beginning of the seventies when the so-called planning languages first came on the scene (Hewitt, 1971; Rulifson, Derksen, & Waldinger, 1972) stemmed in large part because it seemed that this step had been taken. We didn't quite make it then, but experience keeps accumulating.

This phenomenon continues: Discovering that it is possible to shape new subclasses that satisfy additional constraints on our list. We discussed briefly the real-time constraint. We did not discuss, but could have, progress with respect to a few of the other constraints (though by no means all), e.g., linguistics or vast knowledge—not just general progress, but progress in shaping a generative class of systems that automatically by construction satisfies the constraint.

I end by emphasizing this evolution of generative classes of systems that satisfy successively more constraints in our list, because it can stand as a final bit of evidence that we are on the right track—that symbol systems provide us with the laws of qualitative structure within which we should be working to make fundamental progress on the problem of mind. It is one more sign, coupled with the rich web of concepts illustrated in the prior pages, of the scientific fruitfulness of the notion of a physical symbol system.

Francis Crick, in his Danz lectures *Of Molecules and Men*, discusses the problem of how life could have arisen:

[This] really is the major problem in biology. How did this complexity arise?

The great news is that we know the answer to this question, at least in outline. I call it news because it is regrettably possible in very many parts of the world to spend three years at a university and take a university degree and still be largely ignorant of the answer to this, our most fundamental problem. The answer was given over a hundred years ago by Charles Darwin and also by A. R. Wallace. Natural selection, Darwin argued, provides an "automatic" mechanism by which a complex organism can survive and increase in both number and complexity. (1966, p. 7)

For us in Cognitive Science, the major problem is how it is possible for mind to exist in this physical universe. The great news, I say, is that we know, at least in outline, how this might be. I call it news because, though the answer has been with us for over twenty years, it seems to be not to be widely recognized. True, the answer was discovered indirectly while developing a technological instrument; and key steps in its evolution occurred while pursuing other scientific goals. Still, there remains no reason not to face this discovery, which has happened to us collectively.

REFERENCES

Allport, D. A. Conscious and unconscious cognition: A computational metaphor for the mechanism of attention and integration. In Nilsson, L. G. (Ed.), *Perspectives on Memory Research,* Hillsdale, N.J.: Erlbaum, 1979.

Ashby, W. R. *Introduction to cybernetics.* New York: Wiley, 1956.

Black, M. *Metaphors and models.* Ithaca, NY: Cornell University, 1962.

Brainerd, W. S., & Landweber, L. H. *Theory of computation.* New York: Wiley, 1974.

Church, A. An unsolvable problem of elementary number theory. *The American Journal of Mathematics,* 1936, *58,* 345–363.

Clark, H., & Clark, E. *The Psychology of language: An introduction to psycholinguistics.* New York: Harcourt, Brace, Jovanovich, 1977.

Crick, F. *Of molecules and men.* Seattle, WA: University of Washington Press, 1966.

Feynman, R. P., Leighton, R. B., & Sands, M. *The Feynman lectures in physics.* New York: Addison Wesley, 1963.

Geschwind, N. Neurological knowledge and complex behaviors. This volume.

Hewitt, C. *Description and Theoretical Analysis (using Schemata) of Planner: A language for proving theorems and manipulating models in a robot.* PhD thesis, MIT, January, 1971.

Hintikka, J. *The Intentions of intentionality and other new models for modality.* Dordrecht, Holland: Reidel, 1975.

Hopcroft, J. E., & Ullman, J. D. *Formal languages and their relation to automata.* Reading, MA: Addison-Wesley, 1969.

Kripke, S. Semantical analysis of modal logic II. In Addision, J. W., Henkin, L. & Tarski, A. (Ed.), *The Theory of Models,* Amsterdam: North Holland, 1972.

Lachman, R., Lachman, J. L., & Butterfield, E. C. *Cognitive psychology and information processing: An introduction.* Hillsdale, NJ: Erlbaum, 1979.

Lakoff, G. Toward an experientialist philosophy: The case from literal metaphor. In Norman, D. A. (Ed.), *La Jolla Conference on Cognitive Science.* Program in Cognitive Science, UCSD, 1979.

Lindsay, P. H., & Norman, D. A. *Human information processing: An introduction to psychology.* 2nd Ed. New York: Academic, 1977.

Minsky, M. *Computation: finite and infinite machines.* Englewood Cliffs, NJ: Prentice-Hall, 1967.

Neisser, U. *Cognition and reality.* San Francisco: Freeman, 1976.

Newell, A. Discussion of the session on integration in information in the nervous system. In *Proceedings of the International Union of Physiological Sciences, III,* International Union of Physiological Sciences, 1962.

Newell, A. Production systems: Models of control structures. In W. C. Chase, (Ed.), *Visual information processing,* New York: Academic, 1973.

Newell, A. Harpy, production systems and human cognition. In R. Cole, (Ed.), *Perception and Production of Fluent Speech,* Hillsdale, N.J.: Erlbaum, 1980.

Newell, A., & Simon, H. A. *Human problem solving.* Englewood Cliffs, NJ: Prentice-Hall, 1972.

Newell, A. & Simon, H. A. Computer science as empirical inquiry: Symbols and search. *Communications of the ACM,* 1976, *19*(3), 113–126.

Nilsson, N. *Principles of artificial intelligence.* Palo Alto, CA: Tioga, 1980.

Palmer, S. E. Fundamental aspects of cognitive representation. In Rosch, E. & Lloyd, B. B. (Ed.), *Cognition and Categorization,* Hillsdale, N.J.: Erlbaum, 1978.

Rulifson, J. F., Derksen, J. A.; & Waldinger, R. J. *QA4: A procedural calculus for intuitive reasoning.* Technical Report 73, Artificial Intelligence Center, Stanford Research Institute, 1972.

Rumelhart, D. E. *Introduction to human information processing.* New York: Wiley, 1977.

Waterman, D. A., & Hayes-Roth, F. (Eds.). *Pattern directed inference systems.* New York: Academic, 1978.

Whitehead. *Symbolism: Its meaning and effect.* New York: Macmillan, 1927.

Wilson, E. O. *Sociobiology: The new synthesis.* Cambridge, MA: Harvard University Press, 1975.

Winston, P. *Artificial intelligence.* Reading, MA: Addison-Wesley, 1977.

Yovits, M. C. & Cameron, S. (Eds.). *Self organizing systems.* New York: Pergamon, 1960.

Yovits, M. C., Jacobi, G. T., & Goldstein, G. D. (Eds.). *Self organizing systems 1962.* Washington, DC: Spartan, 1962.

5

K-Lines:
A Theory of Memory*

MARVIN MINSKY

Massachusetts Institute of Technology

Most theories of memory suggest that when you learn or memorize something, a *representation* of that something is constructed, stored and later retrieved. This leads to questions like:

> How is the information represented?
> How is it stored?
> How is it retrieved?
> How is it used?

New situations are never exactly the same as old, so if an old "memory" is to be useful, it must somehow be generalized or abstracted. This leads us also to ask:

> How are the abstractions made?
> When—before or after storage?
> How are they later instantiated?

We try to deal with all these at once, via the thesis that *the function of a memory is to recreate a state of mind*. Hence each memory must embody information that can later serve to reassemble the mechanisms that were active when the memory was formed—thus recreating a "memorable" brain event. *(See Note 1.)* More specifically:

When you "get an idea," or "solve a problem," or have a "memorable experience," you create what we shall call a K-line. *This K-line gets connected to those "mental agencies" that were actively involved in the memorable mental event. When that K-line is later "activated," it reactivates some of those mental agencies, creating a "partial mental state" resembling the original.*

To make this intuitive idea into a substantive theory we have to explain (1) "mental agencies," (2) how K-lines interact with them, (3) "partial mental states," and (4) how all this relates to conventional ideas about meaning and memory.

DISPOSITIONS VS. PROPOSITIONS

In this modern era of "information processing psychology" it may seem quaint to talk of mental states; it is more fashionable to speak of representations, frames, scripts, or semantic networks. But while I find it lucid enough to speak in such terms about memories of things, sentences, or even faces, it is much harder so to deal with feelings, insights, and understandings—and all the attitudes, dispositions, and ways of seeing things that go with them. *(See Note 2.)* We usually put such issues aside, saying that one must first understand simpler things. But what if feelings and viewpoints are the simpler things? If such dispositions are the elements of which the others are composed, then we must deal with them directly. So we shall view memories as entities that predispose the mind to deal with new situations in old, remembered ways—specifically, as entities that reset the states of parts of the nervous system. Then they can cause that nervous system to be "disposed" to behave as though it remembers. This is why I put "dispositions" ahead of "propositions."

The idea proposed here—of a primitive "disposition representing" structure—would probably serve only for a rather infantile dispositional memory; the present theory does not go very far toward supporting the more familiar kinds of cognitive constructs we know as adults. But I would not expect to capture all that at once in one simple theory; I doubt that human memory has the same uniform, invariant character throughout development, and do not want to attribute to infants capacities that develop only later.

MENTAL STATES AND THE SOCIETY OF MIND

One could say little about "mental states" if one imagined the Mind to be a single, unitary thing. Instead, we shall envision the mind (or brain) as composed of many partially autonomous "agents"—as a "Society" of smaller minds. This allows us to interpret "mental state" and "partial mental state" in terms of *subsets of the states of the parts of the mind*. To give this idea substance, we must propose some structure for that Mental Society. In fact, we'll suppose that it works much like any human administrative organization.

On the largest scale are gross "Divisions" that specialize in such areas as sensory processing, language, long-range planning, and so forth.

Each Division is itself a multitude of subspecialists—call them "agents"—that embody smaller elements of an individual's knowledge, skills, and methods. No single one of these little agents need know much by itself, but each recognizes certain configurations of a few associates and responds by altering its state.

In the simplest version of this, each agent has just two states, *active* and *quiet*. A *total mental state* is just a specification of all the agents that are active. A *partial mental state* is a partial such specification: it *specifies the activity-state of just* some *of the agents.*

It is easiest to think about partial states that constrain only agents within a single Division. Thus, a visual partial state could describe some aspect of an imagery process without saying anything about agents outside the visual division. In this paper our main concern will be with yet "smaller" partial states that constrain only some agents within one Division.

This concept of partial state allows us to speak of entertaining *several partial states at once*—to the extent they do not assign different states to the same individual agents. And even if there is such a conflict, the concept may still be meaningful, if that conflict can be settled within the Society. This is important because (we suggest) the local mechanisms for resolving such conflicts could be the precursors of what we know later as *reasoning*—useful ways to combine different fragments of knowledge.

In the next few sections we describe in more detail the K-nodes and K-lines that are proposed as the elements of memory. Activating a K-node will impose a specific partial state upon the Society—by activating the agents connected to its K-line—and this will induce a certain computational disposition. Now, while it is fairly easy to see how such elements could be used in systems that learn to recognize arrangements of sights and sounds, the reader might suppose that it must be much harder so to capture recollections of attitudes, points of view, or feelings. But one must not assume that "concrete" recollections are basically the simplest; that is an illusion reflecting the enormous competence of the adult mental systems we have evolved for communicating about concrete matters. I mention this lest that illusion fool us, as theorists, into trying to solve the hardest problems first.

Concrete concepts are not necessarily the simplest ones. *(See Note 3.)* A novice best remembers "being at" a concert, and something of how it affected him. The amateur remembers more of what it "sounded like." Only the professional remembers much of the music itself, timbres, tones and textures. So, the most concrete recollection may require the most refined expertise. Thus, while our theory might appear to put last things first, I maintain that attitudes do really precede propositions, feelings come before facts. This seems strange only because we cannot remember what we knew in infancy.

MEMORIES AND PARTIAL BRAIN STATES

Old answers never perfectly suit new questions, except in the most formal, logical circumstances. To explain how memories could then be useful, one might consider various theories:

Encode memories in ''abstract'' form.
Search all memory for the ''nearest match.''
Use prototypes with detachable defaults.
Remember ''methods,'' not answers.

Our theory most resembles the latter, in remembering not the stimulus itself but part of the state of mind it caused. When one is faced with a new problem, one may be able to solve it if one is ''reminded'' of some similar problem solved in the past. How does this help? It is not enough just to ''remember the solution'' for, unless the situation is exactly the same, some work will have to be done to adapt it. Better, we suggest, is to get the mind into the (partial) state that solved the old problem; then it might handle the new problem in the ''same way.'' To be more specific, we must sketch more of the architecture in which our Agents are embedded. *(See Note 4.)*

We envision the brain to contain a great lattice of ''agents,'' each one connected to only a few others. We further suppose that an agent's inputs come either from below or from the side, while its outputs go upwards or sideways. Thus information can move only upwards, on the whole. *(See Note 5.)* This is what one might imagine for the lower levels of a visual system: simple feature or

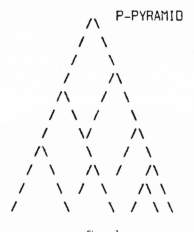

Figure 1.

texture detectors at the bottom, above them edge and region sensing agents, and identifiers of more specific objects or images at higher levels.

Given these connection constraints, if one ''looks down'' from the viewpoint of a given agent P, one will see other agents arranged roughly in a hierarchical Pyramid (see Figure 1). Note that although we shall thus talk about ''pyramids,'' that shape is a mere illusion of the agent's perspective. The network as a whole need not have any particular shape.

CROSS-EXCLUSION AND PERSISTENCE

We mentioned that information can flow laterally, as well as upwards, in a pyramid. Unrestricted lateral connections would permit feedback and reverberatory activity. However, we shall assume that all the cross-connections are essentially inhibitory—which rules out such activity. We assume this because, in our concept of the Society of Mind, agents tend to be grouped in small "cross-exclusion" arrangements; each member of such a group sends inhibiting connections to the others. This makes it hard for more than one agent in each group to be "active" at any time. Any active agent then tends to suppress its associates, which in turn weakens *their* inhibiting effect on itself. This kind of substructure is familiar in physiology.

A network composed of cross-exclusion systems has a kind of built-in "short-term memory." Once such a system is forced into a partial state, even for a moment, that partial state will tend to persist. To reset the network's state one need only activate, transiently, one agent in each cross-exclusion group. Afterwards, the new substates will tend to persist—except for those agents under strong external pressure to change. To an outside observer, these internal persistences will appear as "dispositions"—distinctive styles of behavior. Changing the states of many agents grossly alters behavior, while changing only a few just perturbs the overall disposition a little.

The temporal span of an agent's disposition will depend on its place in the hierarchy. The states of low level agents change frequently, in response to signals ascending from outside or from other P-nets. The state of high level agents are presumably bound to plans and goals of longer durations. In the following theory, it will be the intermediate level agents that are most involved with the memories associated with each particular P-net, because they must help to determine how the agents below them influence those above them. Of course, this notion of "intermediate" probably must be defined in terms of development; its locus will presumably move upwards during cognitive growth. *(See Note 6.)* For example, a lowest level agent in the visual system would always compute the same function of retinal stimulation. But at higher levels, different dispositions induce different "ways of seeing things." Thus, the choice between the three natural perspectives for seeing the Nekker cube is dictated not by ascending sensory information but by decisions in other agencies. Similarly one needs nonsensory information to dispose oneself to regard a certain sound as noise or word—an image as thing or picture.

K-LINES AND LEVEL BANDS

Our theory will propose that around each P-pyramid grows another structure— the "K-pyramid"—that embodies a repertory of such dispositions, each defined by preactivating a different subset of P-agents. The K-pyramid is made of "K-nodes," each of which can excite a collection of P-agents, via its "K-line." To explain the idea, suppose that one part P of your mind has just experienced a mental event E which led to achieving some goal—call it G. Suppose another part of your mind declares this to be "memorable." We postulate that two things happen:

> K-NODE ASSIGNMENT: A new agent, called a *K-node* KE, is created and somehow linked with G.

> K-LINE ATTACHMENT: Every K-node comes with a wire, called its *K-line*, that has potential connections to every Agent in the P-pyramid. The act of "memorizing" causes this K-line to make an "excitatory" attachment to every currently active P-agent.

Consequently, when KE is activated at some later time, this will make P "reenact" that partial state—by arousing those P-agents that were active when E was "memorized." Thus, activation of KE causes the P-net to become "disposed" to behave the way it was working when the original goal G was achieved. What happens if *two* K-nodes are activated? Since we are talking of partial, not total, states it is possible for a single P-pyramid to maintain fragments of *several* dispositions at one time. Of course, if the two dispositions send conflicting signals to an agent there is a problem, which we discuss later.

It might seem impractical to require that every K-line come near to every P-agent. Now we introduce a series of "improvements" that not only alleviate this requirement but also combine to form a powerful mechanism for abstraction and inference.

To begin with, the schema just described would tend to reset the entire P-net. This would amount to making P to virtually "hallucinate" the event EK. *(See Note 7.)* But, on reflection, one sees that it is *not* the purpose of Memory to produce hallucinations. *(See Note 8.)* Rather, *one wants to reenact only enough to "recapture the idea."* Complete hallucination would be harmful; resetting the whole P-net would erase all work recently done—and might even fool one into seeing the present problem as already solved. Instead, memory must induce a state that remains sensitive to the new situation. We conclude that a *memory should induce a state through which we see current reality as an instance of the remembered event*—or, equivalently, see the past as an instance of the present.

THE LEVEL-BAND PRINCIPLE

We propose to accomplish this by connecting KE not to all the P-agents that were active during E, but only to those within an intermediate band of levels. To explain this, I must assume here that KE is somehow associated with some agent PE at a certain level of the P-pyramid. I will return later to discuss this somewhat obscure "P→K" association. But assuming it for the moment, we can formulate two important restrictions:

LOWER BAND-LIMIT: The K-line should not affect agents at levels too far below PE, for this would impose false perceptions and conceal the real details of the present problem. *(See Note 9.)*

UPPER BAND-LIMIT: Nor should that K-line reach up to or above the level of PE itself, for that would make us hallucinate the present problem as already solved, or change it, or impose too strongly the details of the old solution.

These two constraints combine to suggest the first of this paper's two principal ideas:

LEVEL-BAND PRINCIPLE: A K-line should span only a certain band of levels somewhere below PK. This induces a disposition that can (1) exploit higher level agents appropriate to current goals and (2) be sensitive to the current situation as perceived at lower levels.

So, by activating agents only at intermediate levels, the system can *perform a computation analogous to one from the memorable past, but sensitive to present goals and circumstances* (see Figure 2).

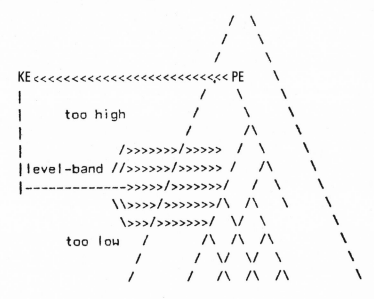

Figure 2.

CONNECTIONS AMONG K-NODES

The second idea: if memories partially recreate previous states, and if those states are in turn based on other memories, this suggests that K-lines should exploit other memories i.e., other K-lines. We can do this via attachments to previously constructed K-nodes. In fact, this idea provides a second way to make the scheme more physically plausible:

K-RECURSION PRINCIPLE: When you solve a problem, it is usually by exploiting memories from the past. The occurrence of a memorable event E is itself usually due in large part to activation of already existing K-lines. So, to ''memorize'' that state, *it will usually suffice to attach the new K-line KE just to active K-nodes*—rather than to all active P-nodes!

Connecting K-lines to K-nodes (rather than P-nodes) allows us to compose new memories mainly from ingredients of earlier memories. This should lead to meaningful cognitive structures—especially when combined with the level-band constraint. So, finally:

We connect KE not to *all* recently active K-nodes, but only to those in a Level Band (of K-nodes) below KE! Note that this creates a ''K-pyramid,'' as discussed below.

Of course, if K-lines were connected *only* to other K-nodes, they would have no ultimate contact with the P-pyramid: the process has to start somewhere! I envision the K-agents to lie anatomically near the P-agents of corresponding levels, making it easy for K-lines to contact *either* P- or K-agents. Perhaps in early stages of growth the connections are primarily to P-agents. Then later, under genetic control, the preferences tend to shift over from P's to K's.

THE CROSSBAR PROBLEM

We digress for a moment into an issue concerning the physical ''hardware.'' Even using both the Recursion and Level-Band principles, each K-node still must have potential junctions with many agents. This problem confronts every brain theory that tries to explain how the mind is capable of any great range of ''associations.'' We shall call it the ''crossbar'' problem. The problem is often ignored in traditional programming because computer memory can be regarded as totally connected in the sense that any register ''address'' can connect to any other in a single step. But the problem returns in systems with multiple processors or more active kinds of memory.

One need not expect to find any general solution to this problem. In the cerebrum the (potential) interconnections constitute almost the entire biomass; the computational hardware itself—the cortical neurons and synapses—is but a thin layer bordering that mass. *The Level-band principle would have a large effect by lowering the dimensionality of the problem by one.* The advantage of using the recursion principle is not so obvious, but it suggests that local, short connections should suffice for most purposes. *(See Note 10.)*

In any case, I would not seek to solve the crossbar problem within the context of K-theory (nor, for that matter, in any clever coding scheme, or chemical diffusion, or holographic phase-detector—although any such invention might make a brain more efficient). Instead, I would seek the answer within the concept of the Society of Mind itself: if the mechanisms of thought can be divided into specialists that intercommunicate only sparsely, then the crossbar problem may need no general solution. For then, most pairs of agents will have no real need to talk to one another; indeed, since they speak (so to speak) different languages, they could not even understand each other. If most communication is local, the crossbar problem scales to more modest proportions.

Still, the reader might complain that any communication limits within the Mind would seem counter-intuitive—cannot one mentally associate *any* two ideas, however different? Perhaps, but it would seem that making unusual connections is unusually difficult and, often, rather "indirect"—be it via words, images, or whatever. The bizarre structures used by mnemonists (and, presumably unknowingly, by each of us) suggest that arbitrary connections require devious pathways.

THE KNOWLEDGE-TREE

It will not have escaped the reader that we have arrived at an elegant and suggestive geometry: The K-nodes grow into a structure whose connections mirror those of the P-pyramid, except that information flows in the other direction. The K-nodes form a K-pyramid, lying closely against the P-pyramid, each with convenient access to the level bands of the other. P-nodes activate units above them, while K-nodes activate units below them. A typical path of computation within the diagram of Figure 3 tends to traverse a counterclockwise spiral. Over time, the locus of this activity could drift either up or down—presumably controlled by other agencies who demand more generality or specificity.

While this "computational architecture" seems very general and versatile, its apparent symmetry is deceptive, because I suppressed some hard questions. I described the connections within K, and of those from K to P. And while I have said little here about the connections within P, that is not a major problem: it is discussed in more detail in Minsky (1977). The real problem concerns the link from P back to K; I said only that ". . . KE is somehow associated with some agent PE at a certain level of the P-pyramid. . . ." We need to provide some relation between P-events and the achievement of Goals represented elsewhere, and the rest of the essay discusses various possible such relations but does not settle upon any particular one; from this point on, the reader can assume that difficulties in understanding are my fault, not his. But I hope I have supplied an adequate enough framework to make plausible these further speculations.

It is tempting to try to find simple ways to restore the symmetry. For example, our K-trees learn to adapt to the P-tree. But the P-tree itself must once have been the learner. Was the P-tree once the K-tree for another P-system? Could they take turns training each other? Alas, nothing so simple will do. We shall argue that nontrivial learning requires at least *three* nets to be involved. For there must be some link from K and P to the rest of the Society, and the P →K connection seems to want that role.

Figure 3.

K-KNOWLEDGE

We started with a naive idea that "memories reenact past states"—without attempting to explain what they "mean." Now we come full circle: since the K-system forms a sort of hierarchical web, one can hardly escape asking what its nodes might mean. It seems natural to try to see it as some sort of abstraction lattice in which *each K-node "represents" some relation among whatever its subordinates represent.*

K-Knowledge Seen as Logical. What kinds of relations? In the simplest case, when partial states do not interact much, a superior simply *superposes* the effects of its subordinates. Concurrent activation of two K-lines at *comparable* levels will dispose P to respond to *either* meaning. Thus, if P were a sensory system, and if detectors for "chair" and "table" are activated, then P will be disposed to react either to a chair or to a table. So K-terms at comparable levels tend to combine "disjunctively."

When the partial states of the subordinates *do* interact, the "logic" of combining K-lines depends upon the "logic" within P. In a version of cross-exclusion that Papert and I favor, the *activation of two or more competitive P-units usually causes their entire cross-exclusion group simply to "drop out" completely,*

96

defaulting to another element at the next higher level. Returning to the previous example, if the dispositions for "chair" and for "table" were in some local conflict (e.g., by requiring both "back" and "no back") the conflicting agencies should disarm each other—leaving the remaining harmonious elements to accept anything in the next higher "furniture" class!

Papert and I see this as a profound heuristic principle: if a single viewpoint produces two conflicting suggestions in a certain situation, it is often better *not* to seek a compromise between them but to find another viewpoint! We introduced this idea as a general principle in Minsky and Papert (1974) after Papert had observed how it might explain how Piagert's Conservation develops in Children.

K-Knowledge Seen as Abstract. Earlier, we spoke only of creating an entirely new K-node for each memorable event. But surely there are more gentle ways to "accumulate" new subordinates to already existing nodes. Suppose that a chimpanzee achieves the too-high banana by using different means at different times—first using a box, then a chair, later a table. One could remember these separately. But, if they were all "accumulated" to one single K-node, this would lead to creation of a more powerful "how to reach higher" node: when reactivated, it would *concurrently* activate P-agents for boxes, chairs, or tables, so that perception of *any* of them will be considered relevant to the "reach higher" goal. In this crude way, such an "accumulating" K-node will acquire the effect of a class abstraction—an extensional definition of "something to stand on."

Indeed, it may do much better than that, in view of our proposed cross-cancellation principle. Suppose, as mentioned above, that conflicts among details cause decisions to be made—by default—by those remaining, nonconflicting, agents. *The effect is that of a more abstract kind of abstraction—the extraction of common, nonconflicting properties!* Thus; combining the concrete "accumulation" of particular instances with the rejection of strongly dissonant properties leads automatically to a rather abstract "unification." *(See Note 11.)*

K-Knowledge as Procedural. This is more speculative: when K-lines interact at different vertical levels, the superposition of several partial states will produce various sorts of logical and "illogical consequences" of them. We already know they can produce simple disjuncts and mutual exclusions. This is probably enough for simple forms of propositional logics. I think that it is possible for such structures also to simulate some kinds of predicate logic. A lower K-line could affect the *instantiation* of a higher level, "more abstract" K-line, just as one can partly instantiate one frame (Minsky, 1975) by attaching other frames to some of its terminals. Thus, a K-line could displace one of a P-agent's "default assignments" by activating instead a specific sensory recognizer. *(See Note 9.)* Other specific kinds of logic could be architecturally embedded in the P-logic. One might even be able to design a "detachment" operation to perform deduction chaining during the overall K-P-K—operation cycle. But I have no detailed proposal about how to do that.

LEARNING AND REINFORCEMENT

Most theories of learning have been based on ideas about "reinforcement" of success. But all these theories postulate a single, centralized reward mechanism. I doubt this could suffice for human learning because the recognition of which events should be considered memorable cannot be a single, uniform process. It requires too much "intelligence." Instead I think that such recognitions must be made, for each division of the mind, by some other agency that has engaged the present one for a purpose.

Hard problems require strategies and tactics that span different time scales. When a goal is achieved, one must "reinforce" not only the most recent events but also the strategies that caused them. At such a moment the traces that remain within the mind's state include all sorts of elements left over from both good and bad decisions. Traditional behavioristic learning theories rely on "recency" to sort these out, but strategy-based activities create "credit assignment" problems too complex for this to work. However, if we segregate different strategic time scales in different G-P-K systems, then they can operate over appropriate time scales. Our everyday activities seem to involve agencies that operate and learn over seconds, minutes, hours and days. Strategies for dealing with ambition and acquisition, loss and grief, may span years. Furthermore, decisions about what and when to "reinforce" cannot be made within the K-P pairs, for those decisions must depend to some extent on the goals of other centers.

We conclude that control over formation of links between K and P must be held by yet a third agency. Based on these intuitions, suppose that a third network, N, has the power to construct new K-nodes for P. Suppose that at some earlier time some goal G (represented in N) is achieved and was connected to a K-node KE that (for example) activates two subnodes K1 and K2. Suppose that at a later time N achieves another instance of G and celebrates this as memorable. If nothing new has happened in P, there is no need to change KE. But if a new element K3→P3 is involved we could add K3 to KE's K-line, making P3 available for achieving G in the future. (See Figure 4).

This raises all the issues about novelty, conflict, adaptation and saturation that any learning theory must face. *(See Note 12.)* What if P3 were a direct competitor of P1 or P2? What if there were a mistake? How do we keep the attachments to KE within bounds? (After all, there is always *something* new.) One can try to invent local solutions to all these problems, but I doubt there is any single answer. Instead, it must be better always to leave link formation under the control of a distinct system that itself can learn, so that the mnemonic strategies in each locale can be made to suit their circumstances. What activates KE? It should be possible for the goal-type G to call upon some variety of P-nets. Selecting P (that is, KE) in particular would presumably depend on use of some "cue" involving P—e.g., by making KE's activation depend on an "and" condition involving G and that P-condition. Through such connections KE be-

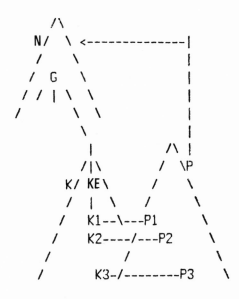

Figure 4.

comes part of the meaning of G—a remembered solution to a problem. This sketchy argument suggests that a minimal learning theory needs at least *three* nets, in which the first controls how the second learns to operate the third. The triplets may not be distinct because the same net might play a P-role in one domain and a G-role in another.

It is commonplace to distinguish between "tacit" knowledge (like how to walk) and "explicit" knowledge (like to solve a quadratic). In a "single-agent" theory, one might wonder how knowledge could possibly be tacit. In a "society of mind" theory, one might wonder how any knowledge could ever become "explicit"—this might require K-nodes to become linked with such cognitive elements as particular senses of particular words. I discuss some such issues in Minsky (1977).

In any case, the "tacit-explicit" distinction is only a simplistic approximation to some richer theory of internal connections. Each subsociety of the mind must still have its own internal epistemology and phenomenology, with most details private, not only from those central processes, but from one another. In my view, self-awareness is a complex, but carefully constructed illusion: we rightly place high value on the work of those mental agencies that appear able to reflect on the behavior of other agencies—especially our linguistic and ego-structure mechanisms. Some form of self-awareness is surely essential to highly intelligent thought, because thinkers must adapt their strategies to the available mental resources. On the other hand, I doubt that any part of a mind can ever see very deeply into other parts; it can only use models it constructs of them.

Any theory of intelligence must eventually explain the agencies that make models of others: each part of the mind sees only a little of what happens in some others, and that little is swiftly refined, reformulated and "represented." We like to believe that these fragments have meanings in themselves—apart from the great webs of structure from which they emerge—and indeed this illusion is valuable to us *qua* thinkers—but not to us as psychologists—because it leads us to think that expressible knowledge is the first thing to study. According to the present theory, this is topsy-turvy; most knowledge stays more or less where it was formed, and does its work there. Only in the exception, not the rule, can one really speak of what one knows. To explain the meanings of memories will need many more little theories beyond this one; we can understand the relations among our mental agencies if—and only if—we can model enough of some of them inside the others. But this is no different from understanding anything else— except perhaps harder.

ACKNOWLEDGMENTS

I gratefully acknowledge valuable discussions about K-lines with D. Hillis, G. J. Sussman, W. Richards, Jon Doyle, R. J. Solomonoff, R. Berwick, and especially S. Papert.

REFERENCES

Clarke, A.C., *The city and the stars*. New York: Signet, 1957.

Doyle, J., *A truth maintenance system*. MIT Artificial Intelligence Memo. No. 521, 1979.

Hebb, D. O., *Organization of behavior*. New York: Wiley, 1949.

Marr, D., A theory of cerebellar cortex. *Journal of Physiology*, 1969, *202*, 437–470.

Marr, D., A theory for cerebral neocortex. *Proceedings of the Royal Society of London*, 1970, *176B*, 161–234.

Minsky, M., A framework for representing knowledge. In P. Winston (Ed.), *The psychology of computer vision*. New York: McGraw-Hill, 1975.

Minsky, M., Plain talk about neurodevelopmental epistemology. Proceedings of the Fifth International Joint Conference on Artificial Intelligence, Boston, Mass., 1977. [Condensed version in P. Winston and R. Brown (Eds.), *Artificial intelligence*, Vol. 1, Boston: MIT Press, 1979.]

Minsky, M. & Papert, S. *Artificial intelligence*, Condon Lectures, University of Oregon, Eugene, Oregon, 1974.

Mooers, C. E., Datocoding and developments in information retrieval. *ASLIB Proceedings*, 1956, *8*, 3–22.

Mountcastle, V. In F. Schmitt (Ed.), *The mindful brain*, Boston: MIT Press, 1978.

Willshaw, P. J., Buneman, O. P. & Longuet-Higgins, H. C., Nonholographic associative memory. *Nature*, 1969, *222*, 960–962.

Winston, P., Learning structural descriptions from examples. In P. Winston (Ed.), *The psychology of computer vision*. New York: McGraw Hill, 1975.

NOTES

Note 1:Background. The references to the "Society of Mind" relate to a theory I have been evolving, jointly with S. Papert, in which we try to explain thought in terms of many weakly interacting (and often conflicting) specialists. It is described briefly in Minsky (1977), which the present paper complements in several areas. The C-lines of that paper correspond roughly to the K→P connections here. The discussion in Minsky (1977) of *cognitive cases* and of *differences* supplement the discussion here of goals, but there is not enough detail, even in both papers, to specify exactly what happens in P-nets. We hope to clarify this in a forthcoming book.

Note 2: Dispositions. I use "disposition" to mean "a momentary range of possible behaviors;" technically it is the shorter term component of the state. In a computer program, a disposition might depend upon which items are currently active in a data base, e.g., as in Doyle's (1979) flagging of items that are "in" and "out" in regard to making decisions.

The term "representation" always should involve three agents—*A* represents *B* as *C*. In a mind theory, *A* might be part of the mind or part of the theorist himself; most discussions are muddled about this. In the present paper, "K-nodes" impose dispositions on P-nets hence, *for us as theorists*, K-nodes can represent dispositions. But what they represent *for the mind that contains them* is another matter we address only in passing at the end of the paper.

Note 3: Modularity. Most people would assume that understanding memories of feelings should be harder than understanding memories of facts. But I think the latter appear simpler only in the adult perspective of "modular" knowledge, based on a lifetime of constructing our orderly, commonsense epistemological hierarchies. A fragment of incremental knowledge—e.g., that ducks have webbed feet—seems easy to "represent," once we have only to link together a few already established structures. But this apparent, surface smoothness should not be mistaken for underlying simplicity, for it conceals the deeper ways in which each event's meanings become involved in the total "web" of our dispositions. I think it no accident that in popular culture, feelings are considered inexplicably complex, while thoughts are simple. But, in the culture of psychiatry, of professional concern with real mental activity, it is feelings that are analyzed (more or less successfully) while thoughts are found to be too intricate to understand in any useful detail.

Note 4: Brains. Not enough is known about the nervous system to justify proposing specific details. In our references to brains our intention is to suggest that it might be useful to consider architectural hypotheses compatible with the general ideas of the society of mind approach.

Note 5: Unidirectionality. It is technically very difficult to theorize about systems that allow large degrees of circular behavior. On the other hand, no mind can be based on undirectional networks, because loops and feedback are essential for nontrivial behavior. This, I think, is why so little has happened in the field of "neural net" models, since the works of Hebb (1949) and Marr (1969; 1970). A feature of the present theory is how it introduces the required circularity in a controlled way: it begins with a nearly unidirectional network, avoiding some of those problems. (The lateral cross-exclusion still leaves basically unidirectional behavior.) Then, feedback loops are built up as steps in training the K-net, yielding a strategy that lends itself to circuits that are manageable and debuggable. With the loops introduced a little at a time, one can watch for instability and oscillation, distraction and obsession.

Now consider a speculation: perhaps the difficulty of dealing with too-circular networks is no mere human limitation. Evolution itself probably cannot cope with uncontrolled recursive behaviors. If the present theory were correct, this suggests an evolutionary pressure behind its development: even the individual nervous system must evolve its circularities by controlled interconnection of unidirectional flows.

Finally, we note that K-logic must be more complex than as described here, because K-node activation should not propagate to subordinates all the way down. That would vitiate the level-band idea. This suggests that perhaps the activity band of a K-P pair should be controlled, not locally, but by some other agency that uses a low spatial resolution signal to enhance the activity in a selected level band. Such an agency could control the ascent or descent of the K-P computation—e.g., to instruct K-P to "try a more general method" or to "pay more attention to the input" or, perhaps, to "try another like that." Such an agency would provide a locus for high-level heuristic knowledge about how to use the knowledge within K-P, and would be useful for implementing plans, looking ahead, and backing up.

   Note 6: Global Architecture. An entire brain would contain many different P-structures associated with different functions: sensory, motor, affective, motivational, and whatever, interconnected according to genetic constraints. The present theory might apply only to the common properties of neocortex; the brain contains many other kinds of structures. Incidentally, the idea of "middle level" agent is not precisely defined. In my image of mental development, the definition of this intermediate region of agents will tend to move upwards during cognitive growth.

   Note 7: Excitation. We do not need to add "negative" K-line connections to agents that were inactive when E occurred; many of them will be automatically suppressed by cross-exclusion via AK. Others may persist, so that the partial hallucination may include additional elements. According to Mountcastle (1978), all lines entering the cortex from other centers are excitatory.

   Note 8: Accuracy. Only a naive theory of memory would require first-time perfect recollection. Many agents active during E will be "inessential" to new situations, so we need not demand exact replication. (Indeed, the theory will need a way to undo serious errors.) In the early days of neural modeling one found some workers who welcomed "sampling noise" as a desirable source of "variety". I consider that view obsolete now, when the problem is instead to find control structures to *restrict* excessive variation.

   Note 9: Fringes and Frames. In this sense, a K-node acts like a "frame," as described in Minsky (1975). When a K-node activates agents in the level-band below it, these correspond to the essential, obligatory terminals of the frame. If K-lines have "weaker" connections at their lower fringes, we should obtain much of the effect of the loosely bound "default assignments" of the frame theory, for then the weakly activated agents will be less persistent in cross-exclusion competition. What about the upper fringe? This might relate to the complementary concept of a "frame-system", emphasized in Minsky (1975): A failure of a P-net to do anything useful could cause control to pass, by default, to a competitive goal or plan (via the weak cross-exclusion), or to move upwards to a slightly higher-level goal type. It would be interesting if all this could emerge simply from making weaker connections at the fringes of the level-band.

   I recognize that my arguments concerning upper fringes are weaker than those for lower fringes. My intuition that a level-band not include those agents that activate it embodies the idea of controlled circularity, but it is responsible also for the murkiness of my explanation of how the "P→K" connections relate P-structures to goals and actions. In fact, P-K was defined, in the first place, to give the reader a mental reference point for describing the level structures, but the P→K connection itself, involving at least another network, is only a functional concept. Incidentally, in regard to *motor* behavior, some of the image probably must be inverted because action is somewhat dual to perception, with flow from intent to detail rather than from detail to recognition.

   Note 10: Crossbar Problem. I conjecture that the popularly conceived need for holistic mechanisms may be ameliorated if we envision the mind as employing a few thousand P-nets, each with a few thousand Agents. This would factor the problem into two smaller crossbar problems, each involving only thousands of lines, not millions. In fact, we argue in Minsky (1977) that one need not suppose all P-nets can or need to communicate with each other.

   While, in this view, there might well be enough white matter for the connections among P-nets, there do exist communication-hardware schemes more physically efficient than point-to-point wiring—e.g., the schemes of Mooers (1956) or Willshaw et al. (1969). To implement one of these within a K-net, one might use a 100-line bundle of descending conductors. To simulate a K-line, attach the K-node to excite a small, fixed, but randomly assigned, subset of these. Then, connection to another K-node needs a conjunctive recognizer for that subset. Ten-line subsets of a 100-line bundle would suffice for very large K-pyramids, and the recognizer might be a rather elementary perceptron.

Note 11: Winston Learning. Because Winston (1975) describes the most interesting constructive theory of abstraction, I will try to relate it to the present theory. "Emphasis links" are easily identified with K-lines to members of cross-exclusion groups, but "prevention pointers," which must enable specific P-agents to disable higher level class-accepting agents, are a problem that perhaps must be handled within P-rather than within the K-line system. Perhaps more basic to Winston's scheme is the detection and analysis of Differences; this suggests that K-line attachment should be sensitive to P-agents whose activation status has recently changed.

Generally, in this essay, I have suppressed any discussion of sequential activity. Of course, a K-node could be made to activate a sequence of other K-nodes. But I considered such speculations to be obvious, and that they might obscure the simplicity of the principal ideas.

Winston's scheme emphasizes differences in "near miss" situations. In a real situation, however, there must be a way to protect the agents from dissolution by responding too actively to "far misses." Perhaps a broader form of cross-exclusion could separate the different senses of a concept into families. Then, when a serious conflict results from a "far miss," this would disable the confused P-net so that a different version of the concept can be formed in another P-net.

Note 12: Saturation. In the present theory, one only adds connections and never removes them. This might lead to trouble. Does a person have a way to "edit" or prune his cognitive networks? I presume that the present theory will have to be modified to allow for this. Perhaps the Winston theory could be amended so that only imperative pointers long survive. Perhaps the cross-exclusion mechanism is adequate to refer low-level confusion to higher level agents. Perhaps, when an area becomes muddled and unreliable, we replace it by another—perhaps using a special revision mechanism. Perhaps in this sense we are all like the immortal people in Arthur Clarke's novel (1957), who from time to time erase their least welcome recollections.

6
Language and Memory*

ROGER C. SCHANK

Yale University

PREFACE

As an undergraduate, I naturally developed a simultaneous interest in the problem of cognition and its computer simulation. I also had a strong interest in language. Attempting to combine these three interests led me to the conclusion that there existed no academic discipline that could comfortably accommodate my interests. Linguists were not seriously interested in cognition. Psychologists were, but did not take seriously the idea of a computer program as the embodiment of a theory. Computer Science was still nascent and in many ways resistant to the "mushiness" of Artificial Intelligence (AI). Where AI did exist, concern with people as opposed to machines was frequently lacking.

In the last few years the situation in all three fields has begun to change. In AI, cognitive concerns have not only been accepted but are considered to be of prime importance. Many linguists have abandoned their overriding concern with syntax for a more balanced view of language phenomena. Psychologists are learning how to build computer models themselves and have begun to run experiments to test hypotheses taken directly from work in AI.

What we are seeing is the beginning of Cognitive Science.

*I would like to thank the following people for their help both in the writing of and the information of ideas in this paper: Wendy Lehnert, Christopher Riesbeck, Robert Abelson, Michael Lebowitz, Janet Kolodner, Mark Burstein, Lawrence Birnbaum, and Margot Flowers. I would also like to thank Donald Norman for his help in editing a previous version of this paper. This work was supported in part by the Advanced Research Projects Agency of the Department of Defense, monitored by the Office of Naval Research under contract N00014-75-C-1111.

INTRODUCTION

In this paper I will attempt to outline some of the issues and basic philosophy that have guided my work and that of my students in the last ten years. I will end by outlining some of the problems that I am currently working on in the area of the modelling of memory.

My initial research focused on the representation of meaning as it would be used for the generation of natural language sentences. I believed (and still do believe) that because people could easily translate from one language to another and, in a sense, think in neither, there must be available to the mind an interlingual, i.e., language-free, representation of meaning. I was very interested in the problem of mechanical translation of language and hoped that any representation I developed would be useful for solving that problem. Since I was looking for this interlingual representation based upon the assumption that people actually thought with such a thing, I developed an intense interest in making any representation I came up with as psychologically correct as possible. Unfortunately, psychologists were at this point very concerned with phenomena that could shed light on the validity of transformational grammars (e.g., Fodor et al., 1966; Mehler, 1963). This work did not provide much in the way of evidence one way or the other for the things I was interested in, so, since I was not trained to do experiments myself, I had only my intuitions to rely on for psychological evidence.

I began to think about the problem of representing meaning; but, since my guiding interest at the time was mechanical translation, I was particularly interested in the computational properties of any representation that I came up with. I was especially concerned with the question of how a meaning representation could be of use in the generation of natural language sentences and in the parsing of natural language sentences.

The first representation that I developed looked a lot like English words with arrows connecting them. The arrows were taken from dependency theory, which had been written about by Hays (1964) and used quite a bit by Klein (1965) and, to some extent, Lamb (1964). My contribution, as I saw it at that time, was to make the representation more conceptual.

The main claim that Conceptual Dependency made at that time (Schank, 1969) had nothing to do with the primitives with which the work has been primarily associated in recent times. Conceptual Dependency theory claimed that there was a predetermined set of possible relationships that made up an interlingual meaning structure. These relationships (or conceptual rules as I termed them) could be used either to predict conceptual items that were implicit in a sentence or, coupled with syntactic rules, to inform a parser what was missing from a meaning and where it might be found in a sentence (Schank & Tesler,

1969). In generation, these rules could be used as the basis for generating meanings from which sentences could be formed. This changed generation to a process that was more realistic than one beginning with $S = NP + VP$ (Schank, 1968).

The key issue from my point of view, then—and my philosophy has not changed on this—was the creation of expectations about what slots needed to be filled in a conceptualization and the embodiment of those expectations to guide both parsing and generation. If information about the properties of a coherent meaning structure is available to parsers and generators, there seems no reason not to use it. Folk wisdom decided that I ''didn't believe in syntax'' because I pointed out the necessity of using meaning information to drive the parser. But, the only way to write such a parser is to use meaning-driven rules which have their basis in syntactic information about the input sentence. This is what we tried to do (Schank et al., 1973). The basic idea of slot filling and top down expectations drives our work today (Carbonell, 1979; DeJong, 1979; Gershman 1979; Riesbeck & Schank, 1976; Wilensky, 1978). The notion of scripts (Schank & Abelson, 1977), and to some extent frames (Minsky, 1975), uses this same basic philosophy.

As we began to work on building programs that mapped English into and out of Conceptual Dependency, we ran into a problem with ambiguous sentences whose resolution depended on world knowledge considerations. Prior to this time parsers were purely syntactic, so no good solution had been found for this problem.

As an example of the kind of issue I was concerned about at that time, consider the following sentences:

I hit Fred on the nose.
I hit Fred in the park.

In order to parse these sentences correctly it was necessary to know where a person can be located. Here, ''correctly'' depended on what had to be represented in CD. There was a locative relationship for entire conceptualizations and a ''part of'' relationship for objects, and either could be expressed in English with a locative prepositional phrase. To solve this problem I used the conceptual semantics I had invented for generation. [These were simple world knowledge rules that were tied to each CD conceptual rule (Schank, 1968). Thus the conceptual rule that actors can act would be modified by lists of what could do what according to semantic categories, such as ''animals can eat,'' ''planes can fly,'' and so on.] The rules that mapped from syntactic relationships to conceptual ones checked for acceptability according to the conceptual semantics each time a mapping was attempted.

Gradually, it became clear that the final parse of most sentences into Conceptual Dependency wound up adding information that was not in the original sentence explicitly. This took our work out of the domain of linguistics, since we had gone beyond language phenomena. This work was Cognitive Science, but since that field didn't then exist, a good home became a nontrivial problem.

CONCEPTUAL REPRESENTATIONS

In 1970 we started to make our representations more conceptual (Schank et al., 1970) than they had been. Until this point our supposedly language-free representations had a great deal of language in them. Our representation seemed to require us to put in a great deal more than was in the surface or deep structure representation of the sentence in order to make conceptual sense. There did not seem to be any way to avoid this introduction of elements that were not present in the utterance initially if we were to represent the meaning of what had been said. Examining our representations, we began the search for some regularities in the representation that would give us a more canonical form. What we had until that point was so free form that we could create anything at any time. This did not seem very sensible. In particular, there was a problem of determining which sense of the various multiple-sense verbs we had at any given time. We could not just continue writing ''have'' with subscripts to differentiate ''have a soda'' from ''have ten dollars'' from ''have cancer.'' There had to be some underlying basic forms. Was ''understand1'' equal to ''see3''? Which sense was more basic? And, more important, how many senses of a word would there turn out to be and what would their intersections be? In the case of partial overlap of senses, there was a definite problem with the subscript method.

As a side issue at this time, we attempted to clean up the mess in which we had left our representation of prepositions. We had been using an arrow to mean any prepositional relationship, in the faith that higher level processes that used our representations would figure out the true relationship that held between an action and its associated objects. We tried to think about what kinds of prepositional relationships there were.

We had already dealt adequately for our purposes with locations and ''part of'' relationships (Schank, 1969). Aside from these two classes of prepositions we found that there were only three kinds of prepositional relationships: instrumental, directional, and recipient. These relationships described the way an action could relate to an object in an event regardless of what preposition was being used. Since we were describing relationships and not prepositions, we realized that English could be considered to have a kind of null preposition denoting objective relationships. However, this objective relationship was not any less of a relationship between action and object than the others. We knew that Fillmore (1968) had said similar things about syntactic relationships in

English, so we christened our relationships "conceptual cases." The differences between the two systems were a lot greater than their names suggested and in retrospect this was probably a poor choice of names. [See Schank (1972) for a discussion of those differences.]

This new system of cases had immediate ramifications throughout our entire representation system. For example, we had previously represented "I want money" as:

```
I <==>want
      ↑              to
 money <==>go   < _ I
```

However, adding a recipient to this representation caused us to come up with the following representation:

```
I <==>want
     ↑            O          R I--->I
Someone <=>   ??   <--money<--I
                             I---<someone
```

that is, we knew that we had a Recipient here and it had to be "I." Similarly there had to be an Object because what else could "money" be? It did not seem like an actor. The actor was unknown, but we knew he was the same person as the donor of the recipient case. Of course, the above diagram had a glaring hole. What was the action? Still this representation seemed to make a lot more sense than the first one where money was an actor doing the action "go."

What was needed at this point was a name for our unknown action, and since it obviously involved a kind of transfer of the money, we called it "trans."

"Trans" helped us with other problems as well. It solved the partial overlap problem in the meaning of words such as "give," "take," "buy," and "sell." Furthermore, it eliminated the need for elaborate meaning transfer rules of the kind Katz (1967) had been proposing for mapping words like "buy" into "sell." We began to wonder what other actions like "trans" were around.

We began at this point to look more closely at the concept of an action. We attempted to classify the verbs we had been using according to the cases they took and the properties of their objects. This left us with S(tate)-ACTS, P(hysical)-ACTs, E(motional)-ACTs, and so on (Schank et al., 1970). Using this classification for verbs, we could now predict the missing cases that were implicit and that thus had to be inferred. We continued to look for effective groupings that would facilitate inference. Thus, although we did not actually set out to discover primitives, the considerations that we had in representation issues forced us to come up with some workable classification of actions that fit within our framework.

Inference was not yet a major issue in this regard, but other problems forced us to focus on it. For example, consider the sentence "I fear bears" and our proposed representation of it at that time:

```
I<=>fear
    ↑
bears<=>harm<--I
```

In the same paper where we were wrestling with the issue of representation
of actions (Schank et al., 1970), we also introduced an idea we called "associative storage of concepts." In order to adequately represent sentences of the above
type, it was necessary to have available a conceptualization that could serve as
the object of the verb "fear." (At this point we viewed such a verb as a kind of
stative ACT. We later realized such states were not ACTs but states of objects.)
Obviously this conceptualization had to have in it both "bears" and "I" as part
of the object of "fear." Here again we were faced with the question of what was
the ACT? The answer we chose was an ACT called "harm." As we were not
particularly interested in primitives, this should not seem strange. The focus of
our interest was: how were we going to find the concept "harm" to add to our
representation?

We tried using "associative storage of concepts." What we meant by this
was that there had to be some connection between fear and bears that would
allow us to infer "harm" as the missing ACT. Quillian (1966) had used the idea
of a linked network of concepts that could be searched from two paths in order to
find their shortest intersection. This idea had been used for disambiguation, but it
now seemed that it could be extended for use here as well.

However, that seemed like a lot of work for so little. When we looked at
other examples of the phenomenon we were trying to account for, an easier
solution presented itself. For example, the sentence "I like books" clearly
needed something about "I read books" inside the conceptualization that represented its meaning. It was obvious that this could be done simply by listing
"books" in the dictionary as a "READ object." If we had an empty slot
requiring an ACT, and an object of "book," we would simply infer "read."
This depended on treating "like" as a state and not an ACT, of course.

This did not solve the problem when the object was not the source of the
inference, however. A functional object like a "book" could well be listed as a
"READ object," but what were we to do when "bears" or "Nixon" was the
object of a stative ACT? Since these objects were not functional in the same way,
it seemed that the missing ACT would have to be supplied as a part of the
meaning of the word "fear." Here again we had, without quite intending to,
decomposed the meaning of a word (fear) into more basic elements (fear plus
expected harm). The reason for this was again attributable to the requirements we
had placed on CD with respect to what slots there were in a conceptualization and
how they were to be filled. So, we were left at this point with a representation
like:

I fear Nixon
I<=>fear
↑
Nixon<=>do
⁀///⁀
something <=>harm<——I

Thus at this point we were now freely adding to our representation concepts that were not present in the English sentence in the first place and, perhaps more importantly, concepts that were only probably part of the meaning. These were the first explicit inferences that we had.

INTENTIONS, BELIEFS, AND MEMORY

We began to focus on the problem of inferencing intentions (Schank, 1971). We got into this problem because of a peculiar use of language that we happened to come across, which we realized was crucial for a reasonable understanding system to handle. The example was:

Q: Do you want a piece of chocolate?
A: I just had an ice cream cone.

Clearly, it is necessary to understand the answer given here as meaning "no." In attempting to figure out how to do this, we realized that it was necessary to fill out the structure of the conceptualizations underlying both sentences so that a match could be made from the answer to the question. To do this required inferences that were different from the "fill in the ACT" ones we had been working on. Thus we needed a structure like:

want → trans → eat → satisfied

To get this structure we had to postulate that when a "trans" was present, the object of the "trans" might enable an actor to perform the usual functional ACT done to this object. Furthermore we had to examine the result of this action, because whatever state it caused was the key for the pattern match. That is, a paraphrase of this question might be: "Do you want me to 'trans' you an object which is edible so you can eat it so that it will make you feel some feeling (full, happy, etc.)?" The answer would then be: "I already have that feeling because I just did an action that resulted in that feeling." To do all this required a new set of resultative and enabling inferences, and caused us to begin to focus on the question of what kinds of inferences there were and where they came from.

One of the first issues, however, was the potential use of such inferences. Since we were primarily concerned with parsing at this stage, we focused initially on the issue of what expectations existed in processing that came from places other than the CD or syntactic expectations themselves.

We looked at an example of a conversation where a person, in a fit of anger at his wife, asks his friend for a knife and, when he is refused it, says:

I think I ought to . . .

The question we asked was: What different kinds of things do you expect at this point? We isolated the following (Schank, 1971):

1. sentential   a verb is coming
2. conceptual   an entire conceptualization is coming
3. contextual   "ought to have fish" is excluded by the fighting context—
                     something violent is expected
4. conversational   inference about the reason the person is talking—why talk
                     about your future violence unless you want someone to stop it?
5. memory   what kind of person is John?
                     should we take his anger seriously?
6. cultural   what happens in situations of this sort?
                     memory structure inferences are used

These questions started us looking seriously at what else was going on in understanding besides parsing. Clearly we needed a memory full of facts about the world to do any sensible understanding. At this point our focus began to change. The issues of representation and parsing still existed of course, but memory, belief and inference were obviously at least as crucial.

Hemphill (1975) began to work on identifying how parsing was influenced by beliefs implicitly referred to in a text. I concentrated my efforts on representation; in particular, it was necessary, in order to handle the above example, to postulate a set of beliefs that could account for our expectations about an actor's behavior. To understand that John was not likely to want to sit down now and be friendly in the above example, we needed to know that when you are angry you do not like to be with the people you are angry with. This was represented as:

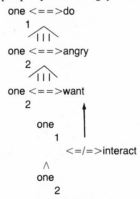

Beliefs of this sort were useful for predicting the future actions of an actor. Adding beliefs to the representation changed the idea of inference from that of simply additional information that would help in the parsing of a sentence. It suggested instead that we had to concentrate on problems having to do with the representation of information in memory and with the overall integration of incoming data with a given memory model. It thus became clear that natural language processing was a bit of a misnomer for our enterprise. What we were doing was not essentially different from what Colby (1967) or Abelson and Carroll (1965) were doing. That is, we had to deal with the problem of belief systems in general. But added to that was the problem of representation of meaning, knowledge, and memory.

The integration of all these problems caused us to deal with sentences whose meaning was a product of the combination of all these issues. For example, "He acts like Harry" means different things if Harry is a cat, a child, or an aged man. What is the correct representation for the meaning of such a sentence? Clearly it cannot be determined in any way apart from the memory structures its meaning relies on. Similarly, the sentence "He is dog-like in his devotion" means nothing if there is no belief available in memory about the devotion (or lack of it) of dogs.

We thus began to work on issues of memory and belief. But, in order to do this, we needed an adequate language for encoding beliefs and memory in general.

We returned to attempting to make the CD representations that we were using more rigorous so that we could better establish what was within the domain of a system like CD and what was outside of it. To do this, we considered the nature of the ACTs we had been using. At that point we had been using "trans" and a hodgepodge of others that suited us. To remedy this situation we looked at the mental verbs which we had, to this point, virtually ignored.

The significance of the primitive ACTs for us was that we could now be sure that we had a given agreed-upon representation for most of the sentences we were dealing with. This made our system usable by the large group of students who were beginning to concern themselves with programming systems that could communicate with each other. Further, we now knew what was in the bounds of the theory and what was not. We knew that to do the kind of work we were interested in, a canonical form was necessary. We were not as concerned with the ultimate correctness of that system as we were with its usability. No other canonical form existed, and transformational deep structure representations and predicate calculus, which were the major well-known alternatives, neither adequately represented meaning nor were in any sense canonical. The most important part of the primitives of CD for us was that they facilitated our getting on to the more interesting problems at hand. They did this because they gave us a language in which to describe those problems.

ORGANIZING INFERENCES

Eventually we began to realize that the most important problem in natural language processing was inference. The single most important fact about the primitive ACTs was that they helped to organize the inference problem (Schank,

1973). No primitive ACT meant anything in the system at all, other than the conceptualizations that might come to exist as inferences from it. Primitive ACTs served to organize the inference process, thus giving us a starting point from which to attack the problem.

We began to concern ourselves therefore with two principle kinds of inference: results from ACTs and enablements for ACTs. Then, having exhausted the inferences derivable from the ACTs themselves, we began to attempt to categorize the kinds of inferences that needed to be made in general. In Schank and Rieger (1974) we delimited 12 kinds of inference. Using these ideas, Rieger, Riesbeck, Goldman, and I began to design a computer implementation of these ideas in 1972 which resulted in the MARGIE system (Schank et al., 1973). During the implementation of these ideas our views on parsing, generation, and inference were altered by the task of attempting to specify precise algorithms for these processes. Rieger created a new classification of inferences based on his experiences with MARGIE (Rieger, 1975).

CAUSALITY

At this point we began to take seriously the problem of codifying the kinds of causal relations that there were. This work was crucial to the inference problem since we had come to believe that the major inferences were (forward) consequences and (backward) reasons. Thus the primary task of the inference process was to fill in causal chains. We identified four kinds of causal links: RESULT, REASON, INITIATE, and ENABLE. RESULT and ENABLE were the forward and backward causal rules for physical ACTs, and REASON and INITIATE were the forward and backward links for mental ACTs. We also added the rule that ACTs could only result in states and only states could enable ACTs. This had the consequence of making our causal chains, and thus our CD representations, both very precise and very cumbersome. The precision was of course important for any canonical form, but the cumbersomeness was obviously a problem that needed to be dealt with.

One of the advantages of all the detail necessary to connect all possible causal relations, aside from those already mentioned is that it provided a facility for tying together sentences in a text. Thus, a paragraph will frequently consist of a series of conceptualizations that can be related by their implicit causal connections.

THE REPRESENTATION OF TEXT

We began, therefore, to work on the problem of representing text. This was, after all, the major issue all along. We were not particularly interested in isolated sentences out of context. Dealing only with isolated sentences was probably the

root of many of the problems involved with the theories proposed by transfor-
mationalists and computational linguists. People do not understand sentences in a
null context. Why then did our theories try to deal with sentences out of context?
The answer was obviously that this was thought to be a simplification that would
facilitate research. But the problem was really significantly changed by this
supposed simplification. Certainly parsing sentences in context is a more reasonable problem with respect to word sense disambiguation than is parsing out of
context.

    We had never dealt with texts of more than one sentence before because we
just did not know how to represent them. Now, with the idea of causal chains, we
could tie together texts in terms of their causal relations. Such causal chaining,
when applied to real texts (Schank, 1975), helped to explain certain memory
results (particularly those of Bartlett, 1932). Now we had a theory that said that a
crucial piece of information had many causal connections and an irrelevant piece
of information had no causal consequences.

    The work on causal connectedness gave us a theory that was helpful in
explaining problems of forgetting and remembering, and also helped tie together
text. However, it could not explain how to tie together texts whose parts were not
relatable by chains of results and enablements; something else was needed for
those situations.

    The something else was obvious once we thought about it. The answer was
scripts. That is, scripts are really just prepackaged sequences of causal chains.
Some causal chains are used so often that we do not spell out enough of their
details for an understander to make the connections directly. Scripts are a kind of
key to connecting events together that do not connect by their superficial features
but rather by the remembrance of their having been connected before. The
prototypical script we chose to examine described what goes on in a restaurant.
In a story involving the setting of a restaurant, we cannot infer the causal
connection to either ordering or paying from hearing simply that someone has
entered a restaurant. However, speakers assume that you know this connection
and they do not bother to mention it. There is a causal chain there, but inferring it
bit by bit is impossible, which makes scripts necessary.

HIGHER LEVEL KNOWLEDGE STRUCTURES

We set about testing our assumptions about how scripts would facilitate the
processing of connected text by building SAM (Script Applier Mechanism, described in Cullingford, 1978). While we worked on SAM we began to wonder
about where scripts came from. In thinking about this we came up with the idea
that plans gave rise to scripts and that goals gave rise to plans (Schank &
Abelson, 1975). Meehan (1976) began to develop a story generator that served as
a vehicle for developing our ideas about plans and goals. Wilensky (1978)
developed a program to understand stories by tracking goals and plans. All this

work is adequately described in Schank and Abelson (1977), so we will not deal with it here.

OUR PRESENT VIEW

The last four years have found us developing the system of plans, goals, themes, and scripts for use in understanding systems. This work produced many working systems (Carbonell, 1979; Cullingford, 1978; DeJong, 1979; Wilensky, 1978) and has greatly broadened our ideas about inference. We now believe the following:

There are a great many possible levels of description. Each of these levels is characterized by its own system of primitives and conceptual relationships. [For example, we have recently introduced a set of ''basic social acts'' (Schank & Carbonell, 1979) to account for actions that have societal consequences] inferences occur at each of these levels. Thus, for every set of primitives there exists a set of inferences that applies to it. Some of these levels have been described in Schank and Abelson (1977) and will not be dealt with in any detail here. We currently make use of the following kinds of inferences.

Micro-CD

All events in a story can be connected at a level where each event is connected to the events that follow from it, and to the states which enable it. This produces a very detailed causal chain made up of the events and states that were actually mentioned in the text as well as those that had to be inferred in order to complete the chain. The causal chain made by the low level expression of facts is one part of understanding. Thus, in order to read a magazine, you must: ATRANS it; OPEN it; ATTEND to it; and MTRANS from it. When any one of these events is discerned, the others must be inferred.

Macro-CD

Another type of causal chain exists at the macro-CD level. There, events connect to other states and events in the same way as they did at the micro-CD level, but the level of description is different. Thus, going to Boston enables eating in a Boston restaurant at the macro-CD level; but, at the micro-CD level, the locations would have to be further specified, such that going to Boston results in being in Boston which enables beginning to look for and go to a restaurant. This latter level of description can regress in infinite detail where, for example, walking is enabled by putting one foot in front of the other. The level of detail of inferences is extremely important and is dependent on the purposes the understander has in mind.

In the magazine situation mentioned above, Micro-CD is concerned with opening the magazine, holding it, turning the pages, etc. Each of those ACTs also uses causal chains but at a much more detailed level. Macro-CD simply involves having a magazine, which enables reading it. Neither one of these levels of description is more correct than the other.

For causal chaining, then, the needed inference types are:

> What Enables
> What Results
> What are Reasons
> What Initiates

These apply at both the macro level and the micro level.

Filling in Missing Information

For every object and person we hear about we are always tracking where they are, the state they are in, what they know and believe, and how they feel. All these inferences are possibly appropriate at any given time. Thus, other kinds of inference types that are necessary are:

> Locational specifications
> Object specifications
> Emotional specifications
> Belief specifications

Scripts

Inferring the presence of scripts and the unstated parts of scripts is an important part of the understanding process. The following kinds of inference are significant:

> Filling in missing causal chains in a script
> Inferring what script is being used
> Inferring what unstated script was used instrumentally

Thus, when we hear that "John robbed the liquor store," it is appropriate to ask how he got there, how he got in, where he got his weapon, and so on. Such inquiries are a part of the inference process, since it is only by knowing what we do not know that we can seek to infer it.

One of the main problems with regard to inferences about scripts is the question of why a script is being pursued. This leads to the problem of inferring plans.

Plans

For any given event, it is often important to know the motivations and intentions of the actors in that event. This means knowing the plans being pursued by an actor. Thus it is necessary to make the following kinds of inferences:

Inferring the plan being used
Why was a particular plan chosen?
Inferring facts about an actor given
  his choice of plans
Inferring other plans an actor is likely
  to pursue to get his goal
Predictive inferences about future plans
What goal is he operating under?

This last inference leads to another class of information that spawns new inferences.

Goals

Detecting the presence of a goal causes the following goal-based inferences to be made:

Why was this goal chosen?
What might it be in conflict with?
Can it be subsumed?
Given this goal, what other goals can we infer?
Under what circumstances will it be abandoned?

Actually these inference types represent only the tip of the numerous kinds of goal-based inferences that have been isolated by Wilensky (1978) and Carbonell (1978).

Since goals are dominated by higher level structures which we call themes, detecting what theme is present and making the appropriate inferences is also necessary.

Themes

The theme-based inferences include finding out:

What kinds of goals is an actor likely to pursue?
What themes are likely to coexist with the given one?
Are there any conflicts in themes?
How might theme conflicts that are detected be resolved?
Where did a given theme come from?

HOW INFERENCES LOOK TO US NOW

Our current work has led us to believe there are, in general, six kinds of inferences. These inference types apply at all the levels of analysis we have worked on so far (i.e., scripts, goals, plans, themes, and some others):

1. *Specification:* Given a piece of an event, what else can be specified about the rest of the pieces?

2. *Motivation:* Why did an event happen? Why this event and not another? What did the actor believe he was doing?
3. *Enablement:* What was necessary for the event to occur?
4. *Results:* What are the results or effects of this event?
5. *Structure:* What higher level structure does this fit into?
6. *Other Events:* What other events are known to occur with this event? What could not have happened if this event happened?

Scripts, plans, and so on fit in as events in the above description. Thus we can ask for *Specification, Motivation, Enablement, Results, Structure* and *Other Events* for a script, a plan, a goal, a theme, or probably any other higher level structure we are likely to invent.

Inference, then, is the fitting of new information into a context that explains it and predicts other facts that follow from it. Since these explanations can occur at many levels, inference is a very complex problem and one we expect to continue working on in an attempt to find out how people understand and how computers could understand.

THE CURRENT SITUATION

Our work started out as a linguistic theory, albeit one with a computer-based bias. Some linguists have explicitly rejected it as a possible linguistic theory (see, for example, Dresher & Hornstein, 1976). In one sense they are right. The phenomena we have become interested in over the years are not particularly phenomena of language per se; rather they are phenomena having to do with the processing of language in general and the issue of the representation of knowledge in particular.

At the same time that *our* work was going on, the field of Artificial Intelligence had been evolving too. When I first arrived at the Stanford AI lab, the major issues in AI were theorem proving, game playing, and vision. Natural language was not considered to be a serious part of AI until Winograd (1972) presented the AI community with SHRDLU. This work contributed substantially to the evolution of AI. The major concern of AI would now seem to be the issue of the representation of knowledge, which of course makes the work in natural language processing quite central.

In the future I expect that many of the relevant fields will begin to become less separate. AI must come to terms with the fact that it is concerned with many issues that are also of interest to philosophers. I hope that the cooperation here will be of more use than was the head-butting that has gone on between AI people and linguists. (Recently this too has changed, however, as the more liberal forces in linguistics have become both stronger and more interested in AI.) Also, the interaction between psychologists and AI people hopefully will continue to flourish. The works of Bower, Black, and Turner (1979) and Smith, Adams, and

Schorr (1978) have already served to bolster the relationship between our group
and cognitive psychology.

We now turn to where we are today. The mood in psychology has changed
considerably since our early work. Psychologists have made various attempts to
test experimentally some of the ideas that we have developed. As Cognitive
Science develops, researchers whose original interests were in AI will have to
take account of experimental results in their programs if they believe they are
developing cognitive models. Of course, not all experiments necessarily reveal
God's truth, but some undoubtedly will produce results that should cause Cognitive Scientists with computational orientation to alter their theories and thus their
programs.

Our work on scripts has caused many people to use such notions for both
programs and experiments. One piece of work in psychology that relates to
scripts is that of Bower, Black, and Turner (1979). In addition to showing that
script-like considerations are relevant in story understanding, one of the most
valuable things to come out of that work was a problem it presented to us.
Recognition confusions were found by Bower et al. to occur between stories
about visits to the dentist and visits to the doctor. In no intuitive sense can this
result be called surprising, since most people have experienced such confusions.
But what accounts for it? Should we posit a ''visit to a health care professional''
script to explain it? Such a script is beyond our initial conception of what a script
was, because it was not specific enough. We had always believed that scripts
were rooted in actual experiences rather than in abstractions and generalizations
from experiences.

The right question to ask at this point is: What phenomena are scripts
supposed to explain? Previously we had used scripts, plans, etc., as data structures in terms of which we could make the right inferences to create connected
causal chains. But we also always believed that scripts were more than just useful
data structures. Scripts ought to tell us something about memory as well as
processing. In Schank and Abelson (1977) we claimed that final memory representations for stories involving scripts would use the packaged scripts as the basis
for those representations. For example, we would remember the RESTAURANT
script (denoted $RESTAURANT) only and could ''recall'' INGEST by recogniz-
ing that INGESTING was a normal occurrence in $RESTAURANT. This is
easily accomplished by saving the particular values of variables assigned to each
script in a story. Under this view we remember only the salient new information
and do not pay attention to the old stereotyped information. $RESTAURANT
(lobster, John, Lundy's) should be enough to regenerate a rather dull story.

Our problem here, however, is not the final form of the story, but the initial
form and level of the information that we use in understanding the story in the
first place. If we used $DENTIST to interpret a relevant story, why should the
remembrance of the story get confused with one that used $DOCTOR? If we
used $HEALTHCAREVISIT, are we saying that there is no possibility of confus-

ing a dentist story with a visit to an account's office? If we use $OFFICEVISIT, what kind of entity is that? Do we really have information stored at that level to help us understand stories? If we do, then understanding such a story becomes much more complex than we had initially imagined. We cannot get away with simply applying scripts. Rather we will have to consult many levels of information at once.

Why would we store new inputs about dentists in terms of a structure which might confuse it with a visit to an accountants? It seems unreasonable on the surface unless we simply do not have a dentist script available at all. Is it possible that there is no dentist script?

Why haven't we run headlong into this problem before? The answer is, I think, that whereas psychologists worry about recognition confusions in due course, as a part of their natural interest in memory, people working in AI never really concern themselves with memory at all. We have not been in the habit of actually remembering very much at all in our programs, so the issue has not really come up. Once the issue has been raised, however, it seems obvious that what we posit as a processing structure is likely to be a memory structure as well, and this has profound implications for what we do.

LEVELS OF MEMORY

The problem that we must deal with is the question of the kinds of knowledge available to an understander. Every theory of processing must also be a theory of memory. To put this another way, if psychologists show that recognition confusions occur between two entities in memory, this would have to be taken as evidence against a theory that said those two entities existed and were proceeded entirely separately.

Thus, in order to address the question of what kinds of processing structures people have, we should investigate the kinds of things people are capable of remembering (and confusing). We have to become a special kind of psychologist—one who has available to him computer and thought experiments, in addition to more standard methods.

To begin our discussion about memory, it seems clear that there are many types of memory. The first we shall discuss is Event Memory.

Event Memory (EM)

One thing that people remember is a particular experience, often in some detail. So, we postulate a level of memory that contains specific remembrances of particular situations—*Event Memory*. Examples of Event Memory include all the details of "going to Dr. Smith's dental office last Tuesday and getting your tooth pulled" and "forgetting your dental appointment and having them call you up and charge you for it.'' Events are remembered as they happened, but not for long. After a while, the less salient aspects of an event fade away (e.g., where you got the phone call or why you forgot your appointment). What is left are Generalized Events plus the unusual or interesting parts of the original event from Event Memory.

Generalized Event Memory (GEM)

A *Generalized Event* is a collocation of events whose common features have been abstracted. This is where general information about situations that have been experienced numerous times is held. Particular experiences are initially a part of Event Memory. However, when such particular experiences refer to a common generalized event, that generalized event is brought in to help in the processing of the new input. Once the connection between an event and the generalized event that it references is established, the event itself is liable to gradually fade away leaving only the pointer to the generalized event and the salient features of the event not dominated by the generalized event.

Situational Memory (SM)

Memory for generalized events relies in a similar way upon what we shall call *Situational Memory*. Situational Memory contains information about specific situations in general. Thus while information about dentists resides in GEM, Situational Memory contains more general information. "Going to a health professional's office" or "getting a health problem taken care of" rely on knowledge about such instances in general. SM contains the kind of knowledge we have about waiting rooms and other things that doctors and dentists share.

In the understanding process, information found in Situational Memory is used to provide the overall context for a situation. When we go to a dentist's office and something happens there (e.g., you are overcharged), the specifics of the dental part of the experience are unimportant in the same way that what telephone you were using is unimportant in the event given as an example for Event Memory above. Situational Memory serves as a repository for relevant contextual knowledge as well as the final storage place for the relevant parts of new events in memory; thus it contains relevant contexts and the rules and standard experiences associated with a given situation in general.

Intentional Memory (IM)

The next level of memory experience is *Intentional Memory*. Experiences are encoded in Intentional Memory in terms of the generalizations relevant behind the information encoded in Situational Memory. Information encoded in Intentional Memory would include that relevant to "getting any problem taken care of by a societal organization." What resides here are the rules for getting people to do things for you and other plan-like information. But the decomposition can go on as before. Thus, specific events would lose the particulars that were best encoded at other levels on their way up to the Intentional level.

People often cannot recall the full details of a situation they are trying to remember. Often they can recall just their goals and the resolution of those goals. The specifics of the situation are often more elusive to recall. This suggests that events can be decomposed into the pieces having to do with their intentional basis and these intentions can then serve as the organizational focus where the relevant parts of such experiences can be found.

THE PLACE FOR SCRIPTS IN THE ORGANIZATION OF MEMORY

Where do scripts fit into this partitioning of memory? In particular, what is the dentist script and where can it be found in memory? The answer is that there is no dentist script in memory at all, at least not in the form of a list of events of the kind we have previously postulated. A more reasonable organization of memory would allow for the following kinds of information:

EM   Particular dental visits are stored in event memory (EM). These visits decay over time and thus are not likely to last in EM for a very long time. Rather, what will remain are particularly unusual, important, painful, or otherwise notable visits or parts of visits. These particulars are stored at the EM level.

GEM   At the level of General Event Memory (GEM), we find the information we have learned about dental visits in general that is applicable only to dental visits. Thus, "sitting in the waiting room" is not stored at the GEM level. The reason it is not stored at that level is clear; the lack of economy of storage would be fearsome. We know a great deal about office waiting rooms that has little to do with whether or not they were part of a dentist's office. In addition, any abstraction and generalization mechanism that we posit is likely to be so powerful that it would not be likely to stop operating at any given level. Thus if commonalities between DENTIST and DOCTOR are brought to its attention, it would *naturally* produce this result.

What is particular to a dentist's office is, perhaps, the X-ray machine, or the dental chair, or the kind of light that is present, and so on. These items are not scriptal in nature. Rather, they are just pieces of information about dental offices that are stored as part of what we know about them. For example, one might expect to find a giant toothbrush in a dentist's office. Such information is stored at the GEM level. However, it is also available from the EM level in terms of those particular experiences that can be remembered at that level of detail. (Such memories fade fast, however.) That is, to answer questions about dental offices, there is nothing to prevent us from consulting our knowledge of dental offices in general (GEM) or of particular prior experiences (EM) to the extent that they still can be found.

So where is the dentist script? So far it has not surfaced. The next two levels complete the framework for allowing *dynamic creation of the pieces of the dental script that are applicable in a given situation for use on demand*. The dentist script itself does not actually exist in memory in one precompiled chunk. Rather, it, or more likely its needed subparts, can be constructed as needed. The economy of such a scheme is very important. Moreover, the memory use and probable psychological sensibility of such a solution is highly significant. Now we will consider how that might work.

SM   In Situational Memory (SM) resides information about a situation in general. Here is where we find the kind of knowledge that would include facts such as "nurses wear white uniforms," "doctors frequently have many rooms so that they can work on lots of patients at once," "there are history charts that must be selected and updated by women in white outfits who might not actually be nurses," etc. We also find information about situations in general. This includes information such as the flow of events in an office, for example. Thus, the bare bones of the dentist script and, most importantly, many other scripts are found in SM. Here we have information such as: "If you need help you can go to the office of a professional who gives that help. You may have to wait for that help for a while in a waiting room. You may report your problem to an underling of the professional's. You will get a bill for services, etc."

IM   Intentional Memory contains more goal-based memories. Trips, romances, improving one's health, and other general contexts whose immediate goals are known are IM structures. Intentional Memories organize inputs according to their reason for existence. As a consequence of this, memory confusions at the IM level involve different situations whose intentions are the same.

According to this view of the information in memory, then, scripts do not exist as extant memory structures. Script-like structures (corresponding to what we have called scenes or even parts of scenes) are constructed from higher-level general structures *as needed* by consulting rules about the particular situation from the three other levels.

The words "as needed" are very important. Why bring an entire script in while processing if it will not be used? Since scripts are being constructed rather than being pulled in whole from memory, only the parts that there is reason to believe will be used (based upon the input text) need to be brought in.

As for retrieval and storage of the incoming information, new stories are available at the EM level for only a very short time. In the course of processing an initial input, pointers are created that preclude the necessity of storing all the details. These pointers are not to the dentist script, but to the relevant subscenes that are to be found at the various memory levels. Thus, something that happens in the waiting room is stored with a pointer to the waiting room scene. However, and this is the main point, the waiting room scene came from knowledge about waiting rooms that was only picked up for the occasion from the highest level (IM). Thus, it was not connected to any dentist script initially, and whatever has happened in the waiting room, unless it was of particular interest, will be stored at the IM level, virtually disassociated from the dentist sequence. Under this scheme, recognition confusions will occur among various waiting room scenes with regard to the question of the original overall situation of which they were a part. The only time when it will be clearly remembered which waiting room scene belongs to which story will be when the continuity is provided between scenes by the story itself. For example, if something special happens in the waiting room scene that affects later scenes, the connection would be a causal link and such connections should be more easily remembered.

MEMORY FOR DENTIST INFORMATION

To see how what we have outlined would work, it is perhaps useful to look at a diagram of the structure of memory for a story (shown at the EM level) involving a dentist:

IM   HEALTHPROBLEM
             FIND PROFESSIONAL + MAKE CONTRACT
             + PROFOFFICEVISIT

SM   GO TO OFFICE + WAITING ROOM + ENTER INNER OFFICE
             + HELP + LEAVE + BILLSENT

GEM   Dentist visits include:
             getting teeth cleaned—dentist puts
                funny tooth paste on teeth
                turns on machine
                etc.
             getting teeth drilled
                D does x-ray
                D gives shot of novocain
                D drills
                etc.
             also: Dentists fill the health care professional role in
                   HEALTHCAREVISIT

EM   The time I went to the dentist last week:
             I drove to the dentist.
             I read Newsweek. There were holes in all the pictures.
             I entered.
             He cleaned my teeth.
             He poked me in the eye with his drill.
             I yelled at him.
             He didn't charge me.

The events in EM are remembered in terms of the highest level memory structures that were activated.

After some time, decay sets in and allows the magazine reading to be stored as part of the WAITING ROOM scene of PROFOFFVISIT. It thus gets disassociated from the rest of the event. Similarly, the "eye poking" gets stored under HELP and is thus disconnected from the magazine experience. But, since HELP is filled by specific Dentist information from GEM, it is remembered as part of a Dentist experience whereas the magazine experience can get completely confused with any other situation in which one might read a magazine.

The main point is that memory breaks down its new information into appropriately interesting pieces and stores those pieces in the context to which they are relevant, i.e., the context which originally recognized them and explained them.

MEMORY ORGANIZATION PACKETS (MOPs)

What we have been addressing here is the overall question of how information is organized in memory. The old issue of semantic memory versus episodic memory and the newer issue of what kinds of memory structures are available are the key elements with respect to memory organization. To summarize so far: we are saying that scripts are not data structures that are available in one piece in some part of memory. Rather, script application is a reconstructive process. We build pieces of scripts as we need them from our store of knowledge to help us interpret what we hear. Thus the next key question is: What is the organization of the knowledge store? This is another way of asking the question: What kinds of knowledge do we have and how is that knowledge represented and used in the understanding process?

There are thus two relevant questions to ask of memory: First, how does any given experience get stored so that it will provide a capability for understanding new experiences in terms of it? And second, why do recognition confusions occur at all?

Situational level memory structures help us understand the experiences we have. They do this by generating parts of scripts. But, in addition, they tend to enable recognition confusions in two ways: First, since new events are understood by using these structures to interpret them, a connection is established between the new event as entered in EM and the memory structure that was used to interpret that event. This connection is established by means of two different kinds of pointers. The first, a *processing pointer,* connects the memory structure with the new event in order to help in the processing of that event. The second, a *memory pointer,* is established because the memory structure is itself affected by the new event. We call memory structures at the SM level Memory Organization Packets or MOPs. MOPs both organize episodic memories and help to process new inputs; that is, they are the means by which an appropriate episode in memory can be accessed for aid in processing a new input. At the basis of a MOP at the SM level is an abstraction of a mass of input events that have been mushed together in memory. A MOP is a collocation of all the events that have come to be stored under it. Thus, memory pointers must be established from a relevant MOP to the detailed event which that MOP is helping to process at the EM level.

Of these two pointers, only the memory pointer needs to last very long. When the processing is finished, the processing pointer is easily forgotten since it can always be regenerated as needed. The memory pointer stays but decays over time. Details that are insignificant in the EM event are forgotten. Significant or interesting details are remembered by virtue of there being more than one memory pointer available; that is, if more than one Situational or Intentional structure has been accessed, then more than one pointer has been established. The number of the possibly relevant structures at these levels may be high since a new event may call many kinds of structures in to help interpret it during processing. For every structure that is called in during processing, a memory pointer is established. The combination of what these pointers point to is what remains of the event at the EM level of memory.

Thus, since each new piece of information is stored in terms of the high level structure that was needed to interpret it, two kinds of confusions occur. Connections between items in the same episode that are interpreted by different high-level structures will tend to break down. A waiting room scene will tend to disconnect from the dentist script of which it was a part because it was interpreted by a different MOP (one having to do with office visits perhaps) than other parts of the story.

The second kind of confusion will occur within a script. When a high level structure is deemed relevant, all inputs are interpreted in terms of the norm. This causes small details not normally part of a script to get lost and normalized. Normalization does not occur for very interesting or weird deviations from a script. The reason for this has to do with the answer to the first question above.

REMINDING

Sometimes during the processing of new inputs an interesting phenomenon occurs: You are reminded of a previous experience that is somehow similar to the new input currently being processed. Such reminding experiences are not random. Rather they are dependent upon the very nature of the understanding and memory processes we have outlined.

The answer to the question of why one experience reminds you of another is of primary importance to any theory of human understanding and memory. If people are reminded of things during the natural course of a conversation, or while reading, or when seeing something, then this tells us something of great importance about the understanding process. It tells us that a particular memory piece—that is, a specific memory—has been excited or "seen" during the natural course of processing the new input. We can then ask two important questions:

1. Why did processing naturally pass through this piece of memory? That is, what is there about the processing of new information that requires a particular related piece of information to be noticed?

2. How did such a mechanism as reminding develop? That is, what is the purpose of reminding? Why is this phenomenon available consciously when so many other processing phenomena are not?

We can begin to attempt to answer these questions by considering the kinds of reminding experiences that people have. For example, there is a restaurant in Boston where you pay first, then eat, called Legal Seafood. Going to another such restaurant, and saying, "This restaurant reminds me of Legal Seafood," would of course be quite natural. According to our view of memory, the restaurant script is merely a first approximation of where search should begin for the most appropriate memory structure to be used in processing a new input. Thus, initial access of the restaurant script merely serves to begin our search for the high-level structure that will be used to understand this new experience. Accessing the restaurant script just means finding a relevant entry point to memory. We have, rather than a discrete set of such high-level structures, a potentially infinite set. There is not one restaurant script but thousands. The various refinements on restaurants all serve as nodes in memory that help to reconstruct a needed high level structure. By saying to ourselves, "Gee, you pay first here," we have caused our minds to traverse a particular path within the information organized by restaurants in order to complete our search for the highest level structure (i.e., the structure that explains the most information). At the end of that path is Legal Seafood, so reminding occurs.

More important than reminding, however, is that all the predictions from that previous experience are now available to help interpret the new input. Such predictions function no differently if the new input calls up a once-seen prior relevant experience or a multitude of experiences expressed in terms of high-level generalizations such as "the restaurant script."

The logical consequence of all this is that there is a potentially infinite set of such structures and that most people's sets would be extremely large and idiosyncratic. For example, an expert at chess would be able to recognize "famous games" or positions that have been seen before. Such recognition depends on the use of a high-level structure in the first place of the kind we have been discussing that would have been part of the understanding process. That is, during understanding, we are constantly seeking the highest level of analysis we can get. This works for understanding chess as well as for anything else. Former chess understandings are stored at particular subparts of the appropriate knowledge structures.

UNDERSTANDING

We can now reevaluate what it means to understand. When we enter Burger King, having before been to McDonald's but never having been to Burger King, we are confronted with a new situation which we must attempt to "understand."

We can say that a person has understood such an experience (i.e., he understands Burger King in the sense of being able to operate in it) when he says, "Oh, I see, Burger King is just like McDonald's."

To put this another way, we might expect that at some point during his Burger King trip he might be "reminded" of McDonald's. The point I want to make is that understanding means being reminded of the closest prior experienced phenomenon and being able to use the expectations generated by that reminding. When we are reminded of some event or experience in the course of undergoing a different experience, this reminding behavior is not random. We are reminded of this experience because the structures we are using to process this new experience are the same structures we are using to organize memory. Thus, we cannot help but pass through the old memories while processing a new input. There are an extremely large number of such high level memory structures. Finding the right one of these, (that is, the one that is most relevant to the experience at hand) is what we mean by understanding.

Is it any wonder that we are reminded of similar events? Since memory and processing structures are the same, sitting right at the very spot needed will be the experience most like the current one.

But all experiences are not identical to all others. A key issue then is the creation of new structures. This is done in terms of the old ones. To return to our fast food example, when Burger King reminds you of McDonald's, what you are doing goes as follows: "Ah yes, Burger King is just like McDonald's except the waitresses wear red and yellow and you can have it your way." A new discrimination on the net that contains McDonald's is then made, creating a node in which Burger King is a high-level structure that shares most, but not all, of its properties with the old McDonald's node. The differences are significant in that they themselves may form the basis of reminding experiences.

In this view, then, understanding is finding the closest higher-level structure available to explain an input and creating a new memory node for that input that is IN TERMS OF the old node's closely related higher-level structure. Understanding is a process that has its basis in memory, particularly memory for closely related experiences accessible through reminding and expressible through analogy.

MEMORY DISCRIMINATIONS

Now the question is: How do we go about finding what is stored in memory? If there are "have it your way" discriminations, in what way could they be used? The answer clearly depends on effective initial categorization of the input.

Memory is highly idiosyncratic. One person's organization is not another's. How people categorize experiences initially is how they remember them later. If Burger King is seen as an instance of McDonald's, it will be stored in terms of whatever discriminations the understander noticed as relevant at that time. However, it is possible for a person to make multiple discriminations as well as multiple categorizations. Thus, a person can see Burger King as "something tasteless that kids love," a "place where red and yellow uniforms are worn," and a "place where you can have it your way." Each of these is used as a path by which Burger King can be accessed. A fight with one's child in a Burger King might be stored solely as an instance of a child fight, or as a fight in a restaurant, or as a fight in a Burger King. If the latter categorization were used, fights with a child in McDonald's might not be noticed. Thus, an intelligent understander stores his experiences as high up and as generally as possible so as to be able to learn from them, i.e., so as to make them available for use as often as possible or in as many situations as possible.

One question often asked of these ideas is: "Why, when you enter a restaurant, are you not reminded of all restaurants, or even reminded of that particular restaurant?" I believe the answer to both questions is that you most certainly are. When you enter Naples (a Yale hangout) you are reminded of Naples. You then use that reminding as the source of predictions about what will happen next; that is, you use the most particular script available to help you process what you are experiencing. When Naples reminds you of Naples, you do not experience the same sensation of reminding for an obvious reason. The more appropriate a reminding experience is, the less it seems like reminding. But reminding is simply the bringing to mind of highly relevant memories to help in the processing of new inputs. To say or to feel upon entering a new restaurant that "this place reminds me of a restaurant" is rather absurd, but remind you it does. If this were not the case, how would you know that it was a restaurant? Thus, reminding is not just a rather interesting phenomenon that I have been seeking to explain. Reminding, in a very serious sense, is the most significant memory phenomenon that there is to explain.

WHAT MEMORY LOOKS LIKE INSIDE

We are now ready to take a look at a specific proposal for handling memory (and handling scripts in particular) in order to account for the issues we have been discussing. For old times' sake, we will again use restaurants. The difference between what we have said in the past and our new view has to do with how restaurant experiences are organized in memory. Consider two restaurant experiences that are virtually identical except for what was ordered. The chance for confusion in memory here is enormous. Which waitress (if there were two different ones in the same restaurant) served which food might be confused, for example. Such confusions are not accounted for by our original conception of scripts where each story, including information about the waitress and the food eaten, is uniquely stored with its own copy of the script.

SCRIPT EMBELLISHMENT

Scripts are formed for actual use by building them up from scenes. However, in building up a script we are also allowing for the possibility of memory experiences being allowed to generalize and be stored at the high-level structure that best explains them. This causes the script that was temporarily built up for processing purposes only to be broken down again, thus causing memory confusions and a certain lack of connectivity between the scenes of a story as it is stored in memory.

Recall that our purpose is to integrate the structures of processing with those of memory. We desire to have episodes stored in such a way that each one of them can serve as a kind of script itself; that is, we want predictions to be available from *all* prior experiences, not just from those we have labelled officially as "scripts" or "script pieces." After all, people make predictions about what will happen next from past experiences. Are scripts the only kind of past experience that aids processing by making predictions and filling in causal chain inferences? Obviously this cannot be. A person who has experienced something only once will expect his second time around to conform to the initial experience and will be "surprised" in some sense every time the second experience does not conform to the first.

This is how scripts get put together in the first place: first one experience, then another on top of it, strengthening those areas of agreement and beginning to solidify a script. But obviously there are times when "new" experiences for which there is one or no prior experience can occur in the middle of an old, well-understood experience. Thus, when you go to Legal Seafood, you modify your restaurant script so as to indicate that the PAYING scene has been placed immediately after the ORDERING scene in memory. What I want to propose is that what is happening here is *not* the creation of a new part or "track" in a script. I see very little evidence for tracks at all. Rather, the entire memory experience is being stored under this PAYING interruption or abnormality following the ORDERING scene.

Two kinds of reminding exercises are accounted for by this. First, any other script readjustment occurring after ORDERING might remind one of Legal Seafood. Second, a new placement of the PAYING scene in the restaurant script might be expected to remind one of Legal Seafood. This reminding would occur as a result of having categorized Legal Seafood as weird with respect to PAYING. This gets placed as a part of what we know about PAYING. So, when PAYING is placed in a new spot, the Legal Seafood experience is brought in because it is hanging off a "PAYING reassignment" discrimination.

Now what does this reminding buy you? The reminding actually causes the whole rest of the reminded experience to be brought into memory at this point just as would happen with any new experience not accounted for by a well-

trodden script. This experience is now used, just as any script is used, to predict
what will happen next.

Thus, deep down inside the guts of a script, we find all the pointers to
every specific memory experience we have had that has been organized in terms
of that script and that has not been obliterated by multiple identical experiences.
Thus script application is embellished by going down paths which the script itself
organizes, that contain all prior deviant (that is, not completely standard) experiences. These experiences are functionally identical to scripts and thus are an
integral part of the application process. This can occur within any script-piece at
all.

As an example of all this, consider Figure 1, a picture of a possible set of
memory experiences tied to, or organized by, the restaurant script.

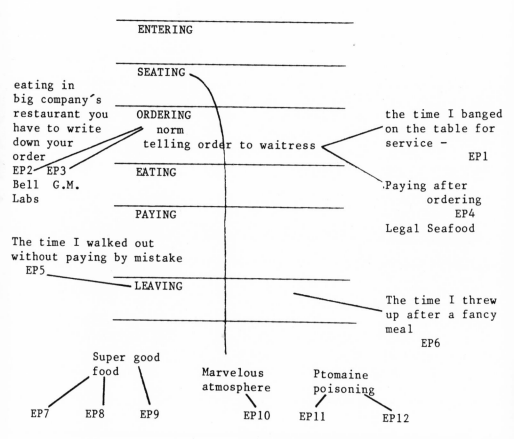

Figure 1.

From this diagram we can see that the ultimate purpose of scripts is as organizers of information in memory. The restaurant script that we have used in the past is no more than the standard default path, or basic organizing principle, that serves as the backbone for all remembered restaurant experiences that have been stored as restaurant experiences. Thus, we are saying that every deviation from the standard script is stored as a modification of the particular scene in which the deviation occurred.

So, one experience in Legal Seafood causes a deviation (these were previously referred to as being on the ''weird list'' in Schank & Abelson, 1977) in the ordering scene. This deviation serves as both the beginning of a reminding experience and the start of the script application process. As we have been saying, storage and processing must be taken care of by the same mechanism in order to get natural reminding to take place. In addition, the scheme that I am proposing allows for the use of all prior experiences in the interpretation of new experiences rather than a reliance on only standard normalized experiences (i.e., what we have previously called scripts).

If the new experience does have a counterpart, i.e., if similar deviations have been met before, *at some point* these experiences are collected together to form a scriptal subscene whose predictions are disembodied from actual episodes like the higher-level script itself. When enough of these are encountered, a new subscene is created that will *not* cause one to be reminded of the particular experiences that caused the creation of this subscene. As this subscene is created, all pointers to the relevant episodes that helped to create that subscene are erased, although other pointers not a part of this subscene but pointing to the same episode would still exist.

Memory collects similar experiences from which to make predictions; these are of general utility above some threshold of a number of prior experiences. Below that threshold, remindings of prior experiences serve as the source of relevant experiences. Thus uniqueness of experience, or, more accurately, unique classifications of experience, serve as a rich source of understandings about new experiences.

In the process of script embellishment via deviant paths we access entire episodes, many of which may have next to nothing to do with the story currently being processed. It is important to be able to separate the relevant from the irrelevant. On the other hand, it is hard not to be reminded of the parts of that experience that are connected to the scene that you have been reminded of. This is one aspect of *intelligence* that comes into play here. The discrimination of those experiences that are relevant for prediction and those that are irrelevant is one of the most formidable tasks facing an understander. *Such discriminations must be done at processing time since one cannot know beforehand where relevant similarities might lie for future inputs.* Thus, a very important part of understanding is the analysis of what is happening to you now with respect to the issue of how relevant newly encountered events might be for predictive purposes to handle future inputs. The collocation of arguments and "paying right after ordering" is not a useful category for experience-based prediction. Clearly we are not born knowing such things. What form such knowledge takes and how we go about acquiring it is, it seems to me, one of the very big issues for the future.

HIGH-LEVEL MEMORY STRUCTURES

The key point in the issue of what is and what is not a script has to do with where we expect information to be found in memory. From the point of view of processing it makes sense to talk about having a restaurant script available. We have shown that such scripts will facilitate the processing of stories; but just because an entity facilitates processing, it does not necessarily follow that that entity exists as a chunk that has been prestored in memory. It is quite plausible that such entities are constructed on demand from information that is stored directly in memory. The key question before us, then, is whether scripts and other high level structures have only a processing role, or whether they are also memory pieces, useful for storage of information that has previously been processed using those high level structures. That is, are high level structures solely processing devices or are they also memory devices?

If the chunks we have been calling scripts are not solely processing devices, the demands on them change. Just as we would not expect that a sensibly organized memory would have the fact that George Washington was the first President stored in fifteen different places, we would not expect that "you eat when you are hungry," or "you order after reading a menu," or "if you don't pay your dentist bill you can be sued" to be stored in fifteen different places either.

Once the requirement that you have to find *one* and *only one* place to store general information comes into play, the question of where that information is stored becomes extremely important. To decide that question, notions such as scripts must be tightened up considerably so that general information shared by any two scripts is held outside them in some other memory store. To do this requires ascertaining what it might mean for two scripts to share the same information, and finding out when such sharing is "realized" by memory and when it is not.

The Creation of MOPs

When a child discovers that its personal restaurant script is also shared by other people, he or she can resort to a new method of storage of restaurant information: a standardized restaurant script with certain personal markings that store idiosyncratic points in view; that is, the child can begin to organize experiences in terms that separate out what is unique and what is shared by the culture. For example, adults know that getting in a car is not part of the restaurant script, but this may be a very salient feature of the child's personal restaurant script. It is very important for the child to separate the car experience from the restaurant experience. The child must learn to reorganize memory according to cultural norms.

This reorganization of stored information can continue indefinitely. New experiences are constantly being reorganized on the basis of similar experiences and cultural norms. The abstraction and generalization process for experientially acquired knowledge is thus a fundamental part of adult understanding. When you go to the dentist for the first time, everything in that experience is stored as one chunk. Repeated experiences with the same dentist, other dentists, and vicarious experiences of others serve to reorganize the original information in terms of what is peculiar to your dentist, yourself in dental offices, dentists in general, and so on. This reorganization process never stops. When similarities between doctors and dentists are seen, a further reorganization can be made in terms of health care professionals. When doctors' and lawyers' similarities are extracted, yet another organization storage point emerges. The key to understanding is the continual creation of *Memory Organization Packets* (MOPs), which record the essential parts of the similarities in experience of different episodes.

The purpose of a MOP is to provide expectations that enable the prediction of future events on the basis of previously encountered, structurally similar events. These predictions can be at any level of generality or specificity. Thus, such predictions can come from nearly identical or quite different contexts or domains, since a context or domain can be described at many different levels of generality. The creation of a suitable MOP provides a class of predictions organized around the common theme of that MOP. The more MOPs that are available for processing a given input, the more prediditions will be available to help in understanding that input. The ability of MOPs to make useful predictions in situations for which there is no direct experience but for which there are relevant analogous experiences is crucial to our ability to understand.

Seen this way, a MOP is a kind of high-level script. The restaurant script is itself a kind of MOP, but it is also related to many different and more general MOPs. There is a MOP about social situations, a MOP about requesting service from people whose profession is that service, and a MOP about business contracts—to name three that are relevant to restaurants.

Viewed as a whole, then, memory is a morass of MOP strands, each connected at the base to the relevant abstractions and generalizations that are the base of the MOP. At the end of each strand are particular experiences (i.e., individual episodes) or groups of experiences (i.e., scripts).

Using MOPs

Consider the information relevant in a visit to a doctor's office. At least five MOPs are relevant to the construction of the processing structures necessary for understanding a doctor's office visit. They are: PROFOFFVISIT; CONTRACT; FIND SERVICE PROFESSIONAL; USE SERVICE; and FIX PROBLEM.

As we will see, these five MOPs overlap quite a bit. There is nothing wrong with that; indeed it should be expected that any memory theory would propose overlapping structures since they are the source of both memory confusions and the making of useful generalizations across domains.

When a script is available it can be used without really looking at a MOP. However, because storage of information needs to be economical, we would not expect what is best stored in a MOP to be found in a script as well. Thus, the doctor script would not have the doctor suing the patient for nonpayment of the bill directly in it. Neither would the bill itself be in the domain of the doctor script. Each of those is best stored as part of a MOP for a CONTRACT, with strands pointing to the doctor script. A doctor visit is perhaps not best viewed as a contract, but it is one nonetheless, and the CONTRACT MOP must help to construct what we can sloppily call the DOCTOR "script" that might actually be useful in processing.

It is important to mention that $DOCTOR is connected to the CONTRACT MOP by a strand of the MOP, but that $DOCTOR does not contain that strand, i.e., it does not contain information about payment other than the presence of that MOP strand. Thus, $DOCTOR is smaller than is obvious at first glance, since we have essentially taken the paying scene out of the script. The actual DOCTOR script that exists in memory contains only the doctor-specific parts of the doctor experience.

Thus, waiting room information is not part of $DOCTOR; waiting rooms are part of PROFOFFICEVISITS, which are also MOPs. But PROFOFFICEVISITS are different from CONTRACTs, which are different from HUNGER and PROFSERVICE. Each of these are MOPs, but they represent different kinds of MOPs. PROFOFFICEVISIT has a strong structure that it imposes on any situation to which it is applied. This structure is in essence a kind of search procedure that helps one sort through the strands in a MOP.

MOPs are memory organization packets. Thus PROFOFFICEVISIT will grab up particular experiences and store them. An experience in a waiting room of an office will get disembodied from the rest of the visit. What happens in the waiting room will be stored with the PROFOFFVISIT MOP, but the actual consultation with the doctor or lawyer will be stored with a different MOP.

WAITINGROOM is a content strand of the PROFOFFVISIT MOP. That is, it has a great deal of information attached to it, such as what a waiting room looks like, what is in it, what happens there, and so on. The HELP strand, on the other hand, is entirely empty. It is a kind of place holder, the only content of which is what is connected temporarily to it on either side. This is where $DOCTOR or $DENTIST comes in. Under this view, scripts are very particular structures about a situation that can fill in an empty strand in a MOP. Actually, these scripts are strands of different MOPs. Thus, just as WAITINGROOM is a contentful strand of the PROFOFFVISIT MOP, so DENTIST is a contentful strand of the HEALTHCARE MOP.

There are also a great many other relevant structures. Some are relevant because MOPs can themselves be strands of other MOPs. There is a *twining* mechanism that can cause strands from many MOPs to fill the same empty strands in another MOP. In the end, then, what we are doing is constructing a DOCTOR superscript (shown at the bottom line of Figure 2). This superscript is constructed for use as needed by taking the strands of relevant MOPs and ordering them by time and enablement conditions. Often multiple strands account for one scene in a superscript. Below, the DELIVER strand of CONTRACT as well as the HELP strand of HEALTHCARE and the SERVICE strand of PRO-FOFFVISIT all relate to $DOCTOR. That is, they each explain to some extent the role that the doctor is playing.

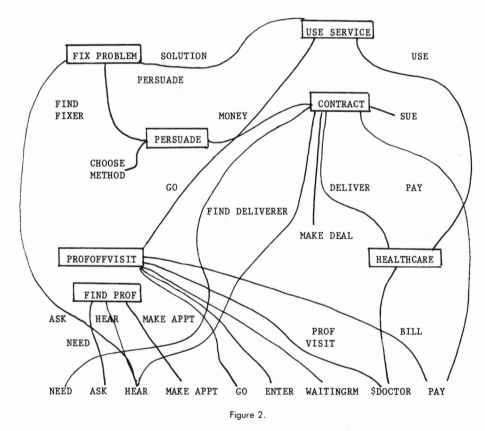

Figure 2.

Taking a look at Figure 2 for the construction of the doctor superscript, we see that a MOP has one clear characteristic: It organizes a class of information by the creation of sequences of slots that can be filled by various structures. In essence, the true differentiation of the kinds of MOPs that exist depends on the types of entities that can fill the slots in the MOP.

Processing Using MOPs

Memory Organization Packets serve as the basis of memory and of processing. In order to understand an input it is necessary to find in memory the structure or particular episode most like the new input. Reminding is one way of telling that such things are happening.

Processing an input means finding a relevant memory piece. When such a piece is found, expectations are created that some from all the pieces to which the initial memory piece is connected. Thus, when we receive an input, we look for a relevant MOP. Upon finding this MOP, we create expectations at every level to which that MOP is naturally connected. Expectations from scripts that have been activated create demands for certain conceptualizations. Expectations are simultaneously generated from the relevant script that filled the slots of the MOPs.

To illustrate how some of this works, consider a story beginning "My drain pipe was overflowing." Now for our purposes the point is not whether this is the first line of the story or not; rather, it is important that this simply be an input to a cognitive system. The fact that you might hear such a thing in everyday conversation is important also. The questions we need to address are:

1. What comes to mind upon hearing such a sentence?
2. What structures are being activated in memory that cause such things to come to mind?
3. What state is the mind in after having received this input?

At Yale in recent years and among researchers in general who are concerned with scripts or schemata, it has seemed plausible to answer these questions with something called the "plumber script." Such a script implies that any body of knowledge can be a script. Clearly a body of knowledge about plumbing can be assembled from the various corners of memory in which it resides in order to create such an entity as a plumber script. One issue is whether such an entity preexists in memory or is constructed, and, if the latter is true, then the real issue is "constructed from what pieces by what method?" A second issue is where are our episodic memories to be found that will help us respond to what we have heard? It seems unlikely that every experience we have had with plumbers is organized by $PLUMBER. Clearly a great many memory structures are likely to be active.

Thus far we have taken the position that to have precompiled chunks of memory such as a plumber script is unrealistic, particularly when we consider facts of memory such as recognition confusions, memory searches, and forgetting based upon the breaking up of an experience into chunks. A great deal of information can be retrieved about plumbers (e.g., what a plumber is likely to wear, the estimated size of the bill, etc.) that is in no sense a part of the script, so it seems safe to say that some reconstruction is going on, or at least that various pieces of memory are being searched when an input is being processed. In our discussion we will assume that there is no plumber script in anything but the simplest of all forms, and that the main problem in responding to an input such as the one above is the accessing of the memory structures relevant to the creation of the plumber superscript.

What kind of high level structures might be relevant to "My drain pipe is overflowing"? Clearly at least the following information is relevant: Drains must be understood to be part of sinks in houses, thus determining the general location of the item in question. Such information is part of the meaning of "drain." It is unlikely that there would be a "drain MOP" available with that information in it. The existence of such a MOP implies that memories about drains are organized together in one place. This seems unlikely; however, there is nothing immutable about what can be a MOP. Different individuals with different levels of expertise are likely to have different needs in memory organization.

"Drain" points to information about bathrooms and kitchens, etc. Such information is stored in what Minsky (1975) refers to as a "room frame." These frames contain primarily visual information rather than episodic information (although again the latter is possible). The visual information attached to the room frame here is helpful for understanding future inputs such as: "To fix it I sat on the toilet," or "The overflow ruined $20 worth of cleanser stored underneath." Such statements would be quite impossible to understand without these active and ready frames. But such frames are not MOPs, they are just, upon occasion, used by MOPs.

One way they are used by MOPs here is that, since these rooms are parts of houses, the combination of the implicit house and the possessive "my" causes information about HOMEOWNERSHIP to be activated. HOMEOWNERSHIP has information in it derived from preservation goals (P-GOALS; see Schank & Abelson, 1977) and, among other things, points to the FIX-PROBLEM MOP.

Of course people have drains in places they rent as well. This possibility is activated in the absence of knowledge to the contrary by activating D-AGENCY (Schank & Abelson, 1977). D-AGENCY points to knowledge about AGENCY relationships (which is what "landlords" are) so that HOMEOWNERSHIP can still be used although it would be mediated by D-AGENCY.

Until we see "overflowing" we do not really know what is being told to us. But, after we have seen it, a great many structures must become active. First, the conceptualization that is to be constructed here contains empty CD slots for what object is being PROPEL-ed (which comes from "overflow") and to where. The OBJECT defaults to "water" by consulting the "normal contents" part of the conceptual dictionary item for "drain." The "TO" slot is filled by consulting the relevant frames, in this case the candidates being "in house," "on floor," or "on carpet."

The activation of FIXPROBLEM causes an attempt at the creation of a solution. FIXPROBLEM has as its strands FINDFIXER, PERSUADE, and SOLUTION. Each of these, it turns out, is a possible topic of conversation where the first input is our above sentence. Thus we might hear:

1. I know a good plumber.

2. My, that's going to cost a lot of money.
3. Have you tried Drain–Fixing Drano?

The fact that all these are quite possible as responses here is an important indication that all these structures are active in the mind of the understander of these sentences. To test further the validity of the active high-level structures in this way, consider other possible responses based on the other ones given above:

1. That sink of yours has been rotten for ages.
2. I told you not to get such an old house.
3. Boy, isn't it a pain to own a house?

Each of these is perfectly plausible as a response. We attribute this to the fact that some high-level memory structure would have to have been activated by the input. What other kinds of statements might be acceptable here? Some candidates are:

4. Oh, isn't that awful.
5. Did you have to stay home from work?
6. Water can be awfully damaging.
7. Do you know how to fix it?
8. Would you like to borrow my Stilson wrench?
9. And with your mother coming to visit, too!
10. This has certainly been a bad month for you, hasn't it?

Assuming that these too are all legitimate, what structures do they come from?

The ultimate questions here are what kinds of MOPs are there and how many of them are likely to be active at any given time? It seems plausible that the following high-level structures are likely to be active during the processing of our input sentence:

JOB; FAMILY RELATIONS
HOMEOWNERSHIP

FIX PROBLEM; PERSUADE
USE SERVICE

PROF HOME VISIT
FAMILY VISIT TO HOME
FIND PROFESSIONAL
MAKE CONTRACT

$PLUMBER

Are all these structures MOPs? Returning to our definition of a MOP, we can see that some of them clearly are and some of them fall into a rather grey area. Recall that a MOP is an organizer of information that can be used to create a superscript. Recall further that MOPs serve to organize terminal scenes that have within them a backbone of a sequence of events that are episodes from memory organized in terms of that backbone. These terminal scenes are either script-like (in which case they contain deviations from the normal flow of the script encoded as actual memories) or else they are locative in nature (in which case they contain actual episodes that are organized in a nonevent-based manner, possibly visually). Thus, a MOP is an organizer of terminal scenes or actual memory episodes. By this analysis, PROF HOME VISIT, FAMILY VISIT TO HOME, FIND PROFESSIONAL, and MAKE CONTRACT are all MOPs. They each organize terminal scenes such as PAY, PHONING FOR AN APPOINTMENT, FAMILY DINNER and so on. As we have said these terminal scenes are whether actual memories are to be found.

FIX PROBLEM, PERSUADE, and USE SERVICE are meta-MOPs; that is, they do not have memories in them directly. Rather, they are structures that serve to organize MOPs.

This leaves us with JOB, FAMILY RELATIONS, and HOMEOWNERSHIP as active knowledge structures that do not fit in with our previously established definition of MOPs and the structures that both organize and are organized by MOPs. What then are these structures and how do they differ from MOPs?

The first thing to notice about these labels is that we have a great deal of information about them in our memories. In fact, we have so much information and it is of such great importance to us (i.e., it concerns our high-level goals) that to begin to think that we can break such structures down into MOPs that organize terminal scenes is absurd. There is, for example, a JOB MOP that contains scenes about applying for jobs, getting paid, terminating employment, and so on. But there is a great deal more information about one's job or knowledge of jobs in general that could not be neatly contained in the JOB MOP. The point here is that such information is at a higher level than that of MOPs. We cannot begin to talk about that information here, since it is extremely complex, but later on we shall have a bit more to say about the role of the structures that are at a higher level than MOPs.

The MOPs that we have specified and the other high-level structures that we have not specified relate for this story as shown in Figure 3.

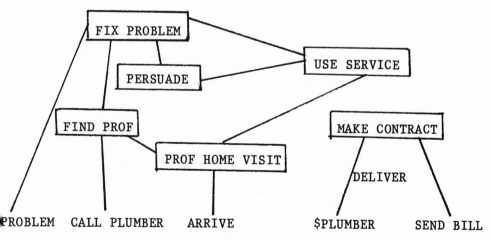

Figure 3.

All of the MOPs mentioned here are capable of making useful predictions about what is going on in this situation. The big questions, then, are exactly when such predictions are made, how they are called into play in processing, and where they come from.

MOPs REVIEWED

A MOP is a packet of knowledge that can be called into play for initial processing and memory storage. Thus, a MOP is a bundle of memories organized around a particular subject that can be brought in to aid in the processing of new inputs. All the subjects that we have considered so far have been events. Thus, MOPs are used insofar as we have described them for understanding and storing event-based information. The criteria we have been using for determining what can be a MOP has depended on the following questions:

1. Why is the information contained in that MOP contained there and not anywhere else?
2. How can we search that MOP?
3. What is the output (i.e., what is at the end of the strands) of that MOP?
4. How is that MOP known to be relevant and subsequently accessed?
5. What kind of processing help (i.e., what predictions are made) is available from having accessed that MOP?

First Conclusion

There are several technical conclusions we can make from what we have said here. In the next section I shall make some more general conclusions.

First, we are now in a position to see what a script really is. Scripts are a particular kind of MOP which we might call subMOPs. They are subject to temporal precedence search, produce Conceptual Dependencies, and contain memories—so they are obviously MOPs. But they are very particular. MOPs tend to organize information in general about an area and thus at one level of suborganization are methods of filling the various strands of the MOP. Scripts are standardized memory chunks that are particular methods of filling one or more strands in a MOP.

A second technical issue revolves around the kind of thing that is going on with respect to high-level structures in memory. We can see that there are basically three overall kinds of memory events: those that are classified uniquely, those that are mushed into a MOP for retrieval through that MOP, and those that have recurred so frequently that a MOP would be useless for aid in retrieval of these events.

Events that are uniquely classified can be retrieved by a variety of aids. For example, sometimes a particular word can have an episode attached to it in memory if that word is strongly identified with only one event. Such attachments can be made off of particular concepts as well. Such concepts are not MOPs, but they can and do have unique memories stored as a part of them.

At the other extreme, we have events that occur so frequently that they cannot be recalled at all. These would originally be grouped as MOPs, but a tremendous number of events can overwhelm a MOP and thus make that MOP effectively useless as a memory organizer. For example, "toothbrushing experiences" are likely to have been grouped as a MOP at one time, but eventually that MOP gets to be useless for retrieval.

A MOP, then, is in between these two extremes. A MOP must organize information in such a way as to provide useful processing structures (i.e., predictions) off the backbone or temporal precedences of the MOP and still have pointers to unique episodes that have been classified in terms of that MOP. As those unique episodes begin to get mushed with other episodes, they cease to be unique and become MOPs themselves. As those new MOPs begin to grow they develop pointers to unique episodes that they organize. But, if they grow too big, they lose their power as memory aids and become merely subMOPs, or scripts with no memory capabilities (what we had previously referred to as Instrumental Scripts in Schank & Abelson, 1977).

Second Conclusion

This paper has taken us through a number of issues in the area of the representation of language and memory. There seem to be two points worth mentioning— one theoretical and one methodological.

The theory I have been trying to build here is an attempt to account for the facts of memory to the extent that they are available. In order to do natural language understanding effectively (whether by humans or machine) it is necessary to have as part of the working apparatus of such a system as episodic memory. Scripts and other higher-level knowledge structures are not simply static data structures in such a memory. Rather, they are active processors as well as the organizers of memory. Processing and storage devices must be the same in order to account for the phenomenon of reminding. In order to account for the fact that reminding and recognition confusions in memory both can be disembodied from large notions of a script to much smaller pieces, it was necessary to restructure our notion of a script to be much more particular. Full blown scripts of the kind SAM used would have to be reconstructed by memory. This reconstruction implies a subsequent decomposition. Thus, we can expect pieces of stories or experiences to be stored in different parts of memory, commonly breaking the link between them. The advantage of this setup is to more effectively understand the world around us. This more effective understanding manifests itself in better predictions about what will happen in particular, well-constructed experiences that have been built up over time. But these predictions are only as good as the initial categorizations of the world that we make. Thus, an effective categorization of new experience is the major problem for an understander as well as the major research problem facing those of us who work on understanding.

The negative effect of this breaking up of experience in order to make more effective predictions about the world is imperfect memory. People have imperfect memories because they are looking to make generalizations about experience that will serve as a source of useful predictions in understanding. That imperfect memory is a by-product of predictive understanding capabilities is a very important point for those of us working in computer modelling. I do not believe that there is any other alternative available to us in building intelligent machines other than modelling people. People's supposed imperfections are there for a reason. It may be possible that in the distant future we will build machines that improve upon what people can do; but machines will have to equal people first, *and I mean equal very very literally.*

This brings me to my methodological point. It is absolutely crucial that AI researchers and psychologists, as well as cognitively oriented linguists, begin to work together on the issues facing us. To pretend that we are interested in different things is folly—we are all working on the nature of the mind. The fact that we bring different tools to bear on this subject is terrific. So much the better for getting potentially different results and thus learning from each other. The field of Cognitive Science can have its computer modellers, its experimentalists, its field workers, and so on. When we stop arguing (and reporting on) methodology and begin to listen to what we have to say to each other, Cognitive Science will really begin to exist.

REFERENCES

Abelson, R. P., & Carroll, J. Computer simulation of individual belief systems. *American Behavioral Science*, 1965, *8*,

Bartlett, R. *Remembering: A study in experimental and social psychology*. London: Cambridge University Press, 1932.

Bower, G. H., Black, J. B., & Turner, T. J. Scripts in text comprehension and memory. *Cognitive Psychology*, 1979, *1*, 177–220.

Carbonell, J. G. *Subjective understanding: Computer models of belief systems*. Ph.D. Thesis, Yale University, Computer Science Dept., Research Report 150, 1979.

Colby, K. M. Computer simulation of change in personal belief systems. *Behavioral Science*, 1967, *3*, 248–258.

Cullingford, R. E. *Script application: Computer understanding of newspaper stories*. Ph.D. Thesis, Yale University, Computer Science Dept., Research Report 116, 1978.

DeJong, G. F. *Skimming stories in real time: An experiment in integrated understanding*. Ph.D. Thesis, Yale University, Computer Science Dept., Research Report 158, 1979.

Dresher, B. E., & Hornstein, N. On some supposed contribution of artificial intelligence to the scientific study of language. *Cognition*, 1976, *4*, 321–398.

Fillmore, C. The case for case. In E. Bach & R. Harms (Eds.), *Universals in linguistic theory*. New York: Holt, Rinehart and Winston, 1968.

Fodor, J. A., Jenkins, J. J., & Saporta, S. Some tests of implications from transformation grammar. Unpublished study cited in R. Brown & R. J. Hernstein, *Psychology*. Boston: Little, Brown and Co., 1966.

Gershman, A. V. *Knowledge-based parsing*. Ph.D. Thesis, Yale University, Computer Science Dept., Research Report 156, 1979.

Hays, D. G. Dependency theory: A formalism and some observations. *Language*, 1964, *40*, 511–525.

Hemphill, L. G. A conceptual approach to automated language understanding and belief structures. Stanford University, Computer Science Dept., AI Memo AIM-273, 1975.

Katz, J. Recent issues in semantic theory. *Foundations of Language*, 1967, *3*.

Klein, S. Control of style with a generative grammar. *Language*, 1965, *41*.

Lamb, S. M. On alternation, transformation, realization, and stratification. *Monograph Series on Languages and Linguistics*, 1964, *17*, 105–122.

Meehan, J. *The metanovel: writing stories by computer*. Ph.D. Thesis, Yale University, Computer Science Dept., Research Report 74, 1976.

Mehler, J. Some effects of grammatical transformations on the recall of English sentences. *Journal of Verbal Learning and Verbal Behavior*, 1963, *2*, 346–351.

Minsky, M. A framework for representing knowledge. In P. H. Winston (Ed.), *The psychology of computer vision*. New York: McGraw-Hill, 1975.

Quillian, R. *Semantic memory*. Cambridge, Mass.: Bolt, Beranek and Newman, 1966.

Rieger, C. Conceptual memory. In R. C. Schank (Ed.), *Conceptual information processing*. Amsterdam: North Holland, 1975.

Riesbeck, C. K. & Schank, R. C. Comprehension by computer: Expectation-based analysis of sentences in context. Yale University, Computer Science Dept., Research Report 78, 1976. Also in W. J. M. Levelt and G. B. Flores d'Arcais (Eds.), *Studies in the Perception of Language*. Chichester, England: John Wiley & Sons, Ltd., 1979.

Schank, R. C. A notion of linguistic concept. Stanford University, Computer Science Dept., A.I. Memo 75, 1968.

Schank, R. C. Outline of a conceptual semantics for computer generation of coherent discourse. *Mathematical Biosciences*, 1969, *5*, 93–119.

Schank, R. C. Finding the conceptual content and intention in an utterance in natural language conversation. *Proceedings of the Second International Joint Conference on Artificial Intelligence*. London, England, 1971.

Schank, R. C. Conceptual dependency: A theory of natural language understanding. *Cognitive Psychology*, 1972, *3*, 552–631.

Schank, R. C. Identification of conceptualizations underlying natural language. In R. C. Schank & K. Colby (Eds.), *Computer Models of Thought and Language*. San Francisco: W. H. Freeman, 1973.

Schank, R. C. *Conceptual Information Processing*. Amsterdam: North Holland, 1975.

Schank, R. C., & Abelson, R. P. Scripts, plans, and knowledge. *Proceedings of the Fourth International Joint Conference on Artificial Intelligence*. Tbilisi, USSR, 1975.

Schank, R. C., & Abelson, R. P. *Scripts, plans, goals, and understanding*. Hillsdale, N.J.: Lawrence Erlbaum, 1977.

Schank, R. C., & Carbonell, J. G. Re: The Gettysberg Address: Representing social and political acts. In N. Findler (Ed.), *Associative networks: Representation and use of knowledge by computers*. New York: Academic Press, 1979. Also Yale University, Computer Science Dept., Research Report 127, 1978.

Schank, R. C., & Rieger, C. Inference and the computer understanding of natural language. *Artificial Intelligence*, 1974, *5*, 373–412.

Schank, R. C., & Tesler, L. A conceptual parser for natural language. *Proceedings of the International Joint Conference on Artificial Intelligence*. Washington, D.C., 1969.

Schank, R. C., Goldman, N., Rieger, C., & Riesbeck, C. MARGIE: Memory, analysis, response generation and inference in English. *Proceedings of the Third International Joint Conference on Artificial Intelligence*. Stanford, California, 1973.

Schank, R. C., Lebowitz, M., & Birnbaum, L. Integrated partial parsing. Yale University, Computer Science Dept., Research Report 143, 1978.

Schank, R. C., Tesler, L., & Weber, S. SPINOZA: Conceptual case-based natural language analysis. Stanford University, Computer Science Dept., A.I. Memo AIM-109, 1970.

Smith, E. E., Adams, N., & Schorr, D. Fact retrieval and the paradox of interference. *Cognitive Psychology*, 1978, *10*, 438–464.

Wilensky, R. *Understanding goal-based stories*. Ph.D. Thesis. Yale University, Computer Science Dept., Research Report 140, 1978.

Winograd, T. *Understanding natural language*. New York: Academic Press, 1972.

7

Mental Models
in Cognitive Science

P. N. Johnson-Laird

University of Sussex

INTRODUCTION

If cognitive science does not exist then it is necessary to invent it. That slogan
accommodates any reasonable attitude about the subject. One attitude—an op-
timistic one—is that cognitive science already exists and is alive and flourishing
in academe: we have all in our different ways been doing it for years. The
gentleman in Molière's play rejoiced to discover that he had been speaking prose
for forty years without realizing it: perhaps we are merely celebrating a similar
discovery. And, if we just keep going on in the same way, then we are bound to
unravel the workings of the mind. Another attitude—my own—is more pessimis-
tic: experimental psychology is *not* going to succeed unaided in elucidating
human mentality; artificial intelligence is *not* going to succeed unaided in modelling the mind; nor is any other discipline—linguistics, anthropology, neuroscience, philosophy—going to have any greater success. If we are ever to understand cognition, then we need a new science dedicated to that aim and based only
in part on its contributing disciplines. Yet pessimism should not be confused with
cynicism. We should reject the view that cognitive science is merely a clever ruse
dreamed up to gain research funds—that it is nothing more than six disciplines in
search of a grant-giving agency.

Cognitive science does not quite exist: its precursors do, but it lacks a clear
identity. Perhaps the major function of this conference should be to concentrate
our minds on what that identity might be. At present, there appear to be two
distinct ideas wrapped up in it: one topic-oriented, and the other methodological.

The topic-oriented idea is that workers from several disciplines have con-
verged upon a number of central problems and explanatory concepts. George

Miller and I became aware of this convergence when we were caught in the toils of *Language and Perception*. It soon became clear to us that psychology was ill-equipped to provide a semantic theory for natural language, but that other disciplines were tackling some of the problems in a useful way. We, in turn, became embroiled with these different disciplines in an effort to create a psychological plausible lexical semantics. Very much the same process must have occurred, I imagine, in the LNR project (Norman, Rumelhart, *et al*, 1975), in the development of FRAN and HAM (Anderson & Bower, 1973) and in a number of other recent research projects.

Perhaps the most striking example of a concept that has been worked over in radically different fields is that of the *prototype*. Wittgenstein (1953) was the first (at least in modern times) to use the notion. He was reacting to the Fregean doctrine that predicates can be analyzed in terms of sets of necessary and sufficient conditions. Subsequently, Hilary Putnam (1970, 1975) took up the idea, amplified it, and came to the startling conclusion that if meanings are what determine the reference of terms then meanings are not in the mind.[1] Meanwhile, psychologists and anthropologists had been busy establishing the mental reality of prototypical information (see e.g. Berlin & Kay, 1969; Rosch, 1973); workers in artificial intelligence had devized programs for representing prototypes and for exploiting them in visual perception (Falk, 1972; Marr & Nishihara, 1976); and even certain linguists had taken up the idea (see Fillmore, 1975; Lakoff, 1977).

There are other cases where a particular problem or concept has been a focus for work in a number of different disciplines. The study of parsers has been pursued by mathematical linguists, psychologists, and computer scientists; rhythm has been investigated by linguists interested in prosody, psychologists interested in the mental structuring of events, and artificial intelligencers interested in music; decision making has been analyzed by logicians, statisticians, economists and psychologists. Doubtless, we all have our favorite examples, and there must be many more that show an increasing overlap in the research carried out in different academic departments. Unfortunately, cognitive science is unlikely to achieve very much if it is simply involves people with diverse intellectual backgrounds who happen to work on the same problems. "Well," the optimists will say, "there needs to be a *collaboration* between these different individuals." At this point, the question of methodology arises, for the nature of the collaboration calls for more than the interchange of results.

Part of the underlying motivation for Cognitive Science is a dissatisfaction with the orthodox methods of studying cognition, and an impetus to change the fashion in which we think about the mind and investigate its operations. It is tempting to demonstrate the shortcomings of experimental psychology and artificial intelligence, but there are already plenty of such arguments in the literature. The purpose of this paper is certainly to contribute to the process of change, but it is more appropriate on this occasion, and more important in general, to show that

---

[1]For an attempt to repudiate this thesis, see Johnson-Laird (1979).

we can learn from both experiments and intelligent software. Philosophers distinguish between a correspondence theory of truth and a coherence theory. An assertion is true according to the first theory if it corresponds to some state of affairs in the world; and it is true according to the second theory if it coheres with a set of assertions constituting a general body of knowledge. Psychologists want their theories to correspond to the facts; artificial intelligencers want their theories to be coherent; both groups have adopted the methods best suited to their aims. Cognitive science, however, needs theories that both cohere and correspond to the facts. Hence a rapprochement is required. I will have something more to say on this point later, but in case these observations strike you as ancient truths, my first task is to explore some of the major problems confronting cognitive science.

I will consider (1) the form of mental representations and the questions of whether images differ from sets of propositions, (2) the mental processes that underlie ordinary reasoning and the question of what rules of inference they embody, and (3) the representation of the meanings of words and the question of whether they depend on a decompositional dictionary or a set of meaning postulates. These three questions have stimulated much research, but we still do not know the answers. Moreover, although the questions have been independently pursued, they are intimately related to one another. Their answers all implicate the notion of a *mental model*.

The idea that an organism may make use of an internal model of the world is not new. Even before the advent of digital computers, Kenneth Craik (1943) wrote:

> If the organism carries a "small-scale model" of external reality and of its possible actions within its head, it is able to try out various alternatives, conclude which is the best of them, react to future situations before they arise, utilize the knowledge of past events in dealing with the present and the future, and in every way to react in a much fuller, safer, and more competent manner to the emergencies which face it.

The power of such a model is illustrated in a simple robot, designed by my colleague, Christopher Longuet-Higgins, which moves freely around the surface of a table, and which, whenever it reaches an edge, rings an alarm bell to summon its human keeper. It possesses neither pressure sensors for detecting edges, nor any sort of electronics. How then does it respond to the edge of the table? The answer turns—literally—on a model. As the robot travels around the table, two small wheels, driven by its main wheels, move a piece of sandpaper around on its baseplate. The position of the small wheels on the paper corresponds exactly to the robot's position on the table. The edge of the paper has a double thickness so that whenever one of the smaller wheels is deflected by it, a simple circuit is closed to ring the alarm. Few cognitive scientists are likely to doubt the power of internal models. What is more problematical is the way in which they are mentally represented and the use to which they are put in cognition.

INFERENCE AND MENTAL MODELS

Aristotle at least by his own account was the first to write on the processes of inference, and he remains in at least one respect in advance of many modern psychologists. Of course, as every schoolgirl knows, there has been an enormous growth in formal logic, particularly since 1879—the year in which both modern logic and experimental psychology began. But logic is not psychology. Aristotle's contribution was to formulate a set of principles governing the syllogism. Syllogisms are extremely simple, consisting of two premises and a conclusion, as this example from Lewis Carroll illustrates:

All prudent men shun hyaenas
All bankers are prudent men
All bankers shun hyaenas

Despite their logical simplicity, however, they have some interesting psychological properties. One such property can be illustrated by the following example. Suppose you are told that in a room full of various people:

Some of the parents are drivers
All of the drivers are scientists

and then asked to state what follows from these two premises. You may care to commit a conclusion to paper before reading on.

We have found in a number of experiments, and many informal observations, that the overwhelming majority of subjects are able to make a valid inference from these premises, but they show a very striking bias. They almost always draw a conclusion of the form:

Some of the parents are scientists

rather than its equally valid converse:

Some of the scientists are parents

This phenomenon, which I have dubbed the "figural effect," does not depend on the fact that the subject of the first premise is "Some of the parents," because it is also observed if the order of the premises is reversed. The results of one study that corroborated the figural effect are summarized in Table 1. The reader will observe that where a syllogism has the form $\frac{AB}{BC}$, as in the example above, 51.2% of the subjects drew a conclusion of the " . . . A . . . C," and only 6.2% drew a conclusion of the converse form. The effect is much less pronounced for syllogisms with symmetric figures:

$$\frac{AB}{CB} \text{ and } \frac{BA}{BC}$$

TABLE 1
The "Figural Effect" Observed in Syllogistic Inference
(from Johnson-Laird & Steedman, 1978)
The Percentages of A-C and C-A Conclusions as a Function of the Figure of the Premises

Form of Conclusion	Figure of Premises			
	A-B B-C	B-A C-B	A-B C-B	B-A B-C
A-C	51.2	4.7	21.2	31.9
C-A	6.2	48.1	20.6	17.8

Note: The table includes both valid and invalid conclusions: the effect is equally strong for both of them. The balance of the percentages corresponds almost entirely to responses of the form, "No valid conclusion can be drawn."

Although the figural effect is virtually unknown among psychologists, it was evident to Aristotle. He argued that a syllogism of the form:

All A are B
All B are C

$\therefore \lambda$ All A are C

was a "perfect" one, because the transitivity of the connection between the terms was immediately obvious. The validity of the argument, he claimed, is self-evident and requires no further support. Indeed, part of his doctrine of the syllogism is to show how arguments in other figures may be "reduced" to the perfect figure (see Kneale & Kneale, 1962, p. 67 et seq.). Unfortunately for psychology, this doctrine was largely supplanted by the rules of the syllogism developed by the medieval Scholastic logicians. Unlike Aristotle, they proposed a set of figures that did not contain the perfect one:

B - A	A - B	B - A	A - B
C - B	C - B	B - C	B - C
C - A	C - A	C - A	C - A

and psychologists have invariably followed this formulation with the result that for fifty years of experimentation they neglected half of the possible syllogisms[2] and failed to detect the potent effect of figure.

[2]Each statement in a syllogism has four possible forms, and hence there are $4^3 = 64$ possible "moods". Psychologists typically go on to claim: "Since each of two terms in each of two premises may appear either first or second, there are 2^2, or 4 possible figures. The variables of mood and figure combine to yield a total of 64×4, or 256 different syllogisms." This number is wrong. There are twice that number of syllogisms. Logicians ignored the order of the premises and made an arbitrary decision to cast their figures so that the subject of the conclusion, 'C' in the examples in the text, occurs in the second premise. Logic is not affected if the subject occurs in the first premise, but plainly the self-evidence of an argument may be affected.

The development of formal logic has not helped psychologists to elucidate the mental processes that underlie inference. There is of course a temptation to treat logic as model of "competence"—as a set of principles that human beings have somehow internalized but depart from occasionally as a result of "performance" limitations. This view is implicit in Boole's (1854) essay on the Laws of Thought, and in our time Piaget and his collaborators have rendered it wholly explicit. The trouble is there are many different logics—there is an infinite number of different modal logics; and any given logic can be formulated in many different ways. If formal logic is to be treated as a model of competence, we need to know which logic or logics human beings have internalized, and the nature of their mental formulation.

The orthodox formulation of a logical calculus consists of specifying (1) the syntactic rules governing well-formed formulae, (2) a set of axioms, and (3) a set of rules of inference that govern deductions from the axioms or from statements derived from them. Since ordinary human beings are little concerned in proving logical theorems, and more concerned with passing logically from one contingent assertion to another, the mental representation of logic should primarily consist of internalized rules of inference: axioms play little part in the logical business of daily life. But what rules of inference do we possess? We have no introspective access to them. It is unclear how we could have come to acquire them or pass them on to the next generation, especially since many everyday inferences appear, at least superficially, to be invalid. It is difficult to imagine that logic is innate—that merely passes the puzzle over to the geneticists—though perhaps an extreme Rationalist might opt for this alternative. The problem about the origin and transmission of rules of inference is so perplexing that I shall argue that there is something mistaken about any conception of reasoning that leads one to pose it.

Theories of syllogistic inference. Although psychologists have studied reasoning experimentally for over seventy years (see e.g. Storring, 1908, for an early study), only in the last five years have they got as far as venturing any hypotheses about the mental processes that underlie syllogistic inference. By far the most typical activity has been the investigation of the hypothesis that the "atmosphere" created by the premise predisposes an individual to accept certain conclusions rather than others. Although the original formulation of the hypothesis was complicated, (see Sells, 1936; Woodworth & Sells, 1935), its essence can be captured in two principles formulated by Begg and Denny (1969):

1. Whenever at least one premise is negative, the most frequently accepted conclusion will be negative; otherwise, it will be affirmative.
2. Whenever at least one premise is particular (i.e. contains the quantifier *some*), the most frequently accepted conclusion will be particular; otherwise it will be universal (i.e. contains either *all* or *none*).

These principles characterize the nature of a putative bias, but they say nothing about the mental processes that underlie it. Moreover, they closely resemble two of the traditional laws of the syllogism formulated by the Scholastic Logicians (see Cohen & Nagel, 1934). This resemblance makes the atmosphere predictions difficult to test because they often correspond to valid conclusions, and it is accordingly necessary to examine the invalid inferences that people make. Unfortunately, there is little consensus in the literature: some experimenters claim to have confirmed the atmosphere effect (e.g. Begg & Denny, 1969) others claim to have disconfirmed it (e.g. Ceraso & Provitera, 1971; Mazzocco, Legrenzi & Roncato, 1974). One datum that is difficult to reconcile with the effect is that certain premises from which a valid conclusion can be drawn tend to be judged not to imply any conclusion. Here is an example:

Some of the beekeepers are artists
None of the chemists are beekeepers

When such premises were presented in one experiment, 12 out of 20 subjects declared that there was no valid conclusion that could be drawn from them (see Johnson-Laird & Steedman, 1978). In fact, there is a valid conclusion:

Some of the artists are not chemists.

and, moreover, it is entirely congruent with the atmosphere effect: particular because the first premise is particular, and negative because the second premise is negative. Only 2 out of the 20 subjects drew this conclusion. Such findings require at the very least some modification of the atmosphere hypothesis.

It is obviously more important to give an account of the mental processes that underlie syllogistic inference than to attempt to explain the putative effects of "atmosphere." In fact, three major theories have been developed in the last few years.

1. Erickson (1974, 1978) argues that the premises of a syllogism are mentally represented in a form that corresponds to Euler circles. He postulates that only a single representation is used for each premise and so, for example, he assumes that a premise of the form *All A are B* is represented by two co-incident circles on 75% of occasions, and by one circle, A, within another, B, on 25% of occasions. An inference is made by combining the separate representations of the two premises, though Erickson does not specify any effective procedure for making such a combination. It is generally possible to combine such representations in more than one way. In one version of his theory, Erickson supposes that subjects consider all the different possible combinations; in another version, he supposes that they consider only one selected at random from the set of possible combinations. Unfortunately, this latter procedure will always yield a conclusion, and the theory is accordingly unable to predict responses of the form, "There is no valid conclusion." Moreover, if only a single combination is constructed, then there will be occasions where an overlap between sets ought to lead to a conclusion of the form, "Some A are C", and other occasions where it ought to lead to a conclusion of the form, "Some A are *not* C." Erickson accordingly invokes the atmosphere effect to account for the fact that subjects tend to make the appropriate response. A major difficulty with both versions of

the theory is that Euler circles are symmetrical: if they correspond to a conclusion, *Some A are C*, then they equally correspond to the conclusion *Some C are A*. The theory is accordingly totally unable to account for the figural effect.

2. An alternative theory is based on the idea that subjects illicitly convert both *All A are B* to *All B are A*, and *Some A are not B* to *Some B are not A* (Chapman & Chapman, 1959). This notion has been elevated into an information-processing model by Revlis (1975a,b). In its most recent formulation (Revlin & Leirer, 1978), the theory assumes that, during the process of encoding the premises, the reasoner converts each premise unless the result is an assertion that is obviously factually false. The reasoner then applies entirely logical processes to the resulting representations in order to derive a conclusion (though the theory does not specify the nature of these processes). It follows that the premises:

> All A are B
>
> Some B are C

should be converted during their encoding to yield:

> All B are A
>
> Some C are B

which logically imply the conclusion:

> Some C are A

though this conclusion, of course, fails to follow from the original premises. Unfortunately, the theory leads naturally to a prediction exactly contrary to the figural effect: if subjects automatically convert premises, then there is no reason to suppose that they will be biased towards a conclusion of one form rather than another.

3. Robert Sternberg and his colleagues have recently proposed a model that attempts to remedy some of the difficulties of manipulating Euler circle representations (Guyote & Sternberg, 1978; Sternberg & Turner, 1978). This theory assumes that subjects represent premises in a logically correct way. Hence, a premise of the form *All A are B* requires two separate representations: one corresponding to the inclusion of set A within B, and one corresponding to an equivalence in the extension of the two sets. The first of these representations has a form corresponding to:

$$a_1 \rightarrow B \quad b_1 \rightarrow A$$
$$a_2 \rightarrow B \quad b_2 \rightarrow -A$$

where the lower case letters denote disjoint, exhaustive partitions of the corresponding sets denoted by capital letters, and the arrow denotes class inclusion. Thus the left-hand side of the representation states that each of the two partitions of set A, a_1 *and* a_2, is included in set B, and the right-hand side of the representation states that one of the partitions of set B, b_1, is included in set A and the other of the partitions of set B, b2, is included in not−A, the complement of A; in other words, set A is a proper subset of B. The choice of the number of partitions is arbitrary. Although the representation of premises is logically correct, according to the theory their combinations can give rise to errors. In particular, Sternberg and his colleagues assume that a subject never makes more than four combined representations; the particular four depend on an ordering postulated by the theory. The final state of an inference requires the subject to find a verbal description that is consistent with the set of combined representations. If there is no such label, then the premises are indeterminate. If there are two such labels, the theory assumes that subjects are biased both by the atmosphere effect and by a preference for descriptions that are consistent with the smallest number of alternatives. The theory also proposes that subjects are prone to become confused if the set of final representations appears not to be consistent with any verbal description. Although the representations postulated by this theory are very much easier to manipulate than Euler circles, they share with them precisely the same difficulty of being unable to account for the figural effect. Any representation that leads to the conclusion *Some A are C* will lead equally to the conclusion *Some C are A*.

Criteria for Evaluating Theories of Syllogistic Inference

An adequate theory of syllogistic inference should satisfy the following points.

First, the theory should account for the systematic mistakes, and the habitual biases, including the figural effect, that are observed in experiments, and also for the fact that many valid inferences are drawn.

Second, the theory should be readily extendable so that it applies to all sorts of quantified assertions. It should accommodate sentences that contain more than one quantifier, e.g. "Every man loves a woman who loves him." It should also accommodate sentences that contain such quantifiers as *most, many, several*, and *few*.

Third, the theory should provide an account of how children acquire the ability to make deductive inferences.

Fourth, the theory should be at least compatible with the development of formal logic, that is to say, it should allow that human beings are capable of rational thought, and that they have been able to formulate principles that govern valid inference.

All three of the theories described above fare poorly on these criteria, and it is therefore worth considering a different approach based on the notion of a mental model (Johnson-Laird, 1975).

Syllogistic Inference as the Manipulation of Mental Models

One way in which you could interpret a pair of premises such as:

> All of the singers are professors
> All of the poets are professors

would be by actually gathering together a number of individuals—actors, say—in a room, and then assigning them the roles of singer, professor, and poet, in a way that satisfies the premises. Logical principles can determine whether a given conclusion is valid, but they cannot even in principle specify what particular conclusion to draw from some premises on a given occasion, because there are always infinitely many valid conclusions that could be drawn. Most of them are trivial, of course, such as a disjunction of the premises.[3] Hence, in order to derive a specific conclusion from the premises, you need some extra-logical principle to guide you. Let us suppose that you work according to the heuristic procedure of always trying to establish as many identities as possible between the different roles that you assign. This heuristic is designed to cut down on the number of actors that you have to employ by maximizing the number of connections that are formed between the different roles. It keeps matters simple. Thus, you get together, say, six actors. The first premise asserts that all of the singers are professors, and so you arbitrarily assign three actors to play the part of singers, and, in accordance with the premise, you specify that each of them is also a professor. Of course there may be professors in the room who are not singers, and so you arbitrarily assign that role to the remaining three actors, but since the premise does not establish that they definitely exist, these individuals represent only a possibility. You have accordingly interpreted the first premise by establishing the following scenario:

```
singer = professor
singer = professor
singer = professor
        (professor)
        (professor)
        (professor)
```

where the parentheses indicate that the relevant individuals may, or may not, exist. You interpret the second premise, *all of the poets are professors*, in a similar way, using your heuristic principle in order to establish as many identities as possible:

```
singer = professor = poet
singer = professor = poet
singer = professor = poet
        (professor)
        (professor)
        (professor)
```

At this point, you might conclude (invalidly) as did a certain proportion of the subjects in our experiment (Johnson-Laird & Steedman, 1978) that *all of the singers are poets*, or conversely that *all of the poets are singers* since the form of the premises is not such as to give rise to the figural effect. However, if you are

[3]The inability of logic alone to provide the formulation for a theory of inference has been overlooked in nearly every psychological theory of reasoning—most notably in the Piagetian school (cf. Inhelder & Piaget, 1958, 1964), but also in other theories (e.g. Martin, in press).

prudent, you might refrain from drawing a conclusion until you have checked its logical validity. You must establish whether the identities between the various roles are irrefutable: you must attempt to destroy them without doing violence to the meaning of the premises. You should discover that you can break at least one of the identities without violating the premises:

```
singer = professor = poet
singer = professor = poet
singer = professor
         professor = poet
         (professor)
         (professor)
```

At this point, you may be tempted—again like some subjects—to conclude (invalidly) that *some of the singers are poets*, or conversely that *some of the poets are singers*. However, if you are really prudent, you may try to extend your destructive manoeuvre to all the identities. This step leads to the following re-assignment of roles, in which all the original identities are destroyed:

```
singer = professor
singer = professor
singer = professor
         professor = poet
         professor = poet
         professor = poet
```

Since you have been able to arrange matters so that none of the singers are poets, and hitherto you had arranged them so that all of the singers are poets, now at last you should appreciate—as some subjects do—that you cannot draw any valid inference about the relations between the singers and the poets.

The present theory of quantified inferences assumes that you can carry out the whole of the above procedure as a "thought experiment." You construct a mental model of the relevant individuals, you form identities between them according to the heuristic, and, if you are logically prudent, you attempt to test your mental model to destruction.

An Evaluation of the Mental Model Theory of Inference

How does the present theory measure up to the criteria on our shopping list? First, it provides an account of both the figural effect and the systematic errors that tend to occur in syllogistic reasoning. The representation of identities such as: $a = b$, depends on a list-structure in which there is an asymmetry in ease of search: given a it is relatively easy to establish its identity with b, but given b it is relatively hard to establish its identity with a. Premises that give rise to the figural effect yield a uniform direction of search, whereas the others do not. Likewise, the theory obviously predicts that those premises for which the heuristic yields a valid conclusion should be easier to cope with than those premises for which a valid conclusion emerges only after submitting the model to a logical test. This prediction was readily confirmed: 80.4% of responses to the first sort of premises were correct whereas only 46.5% of responses to the second sort of premises were correct, and this pattern of results was obtained from each of the subjects who was tested (see Johnson-Laird & Steedman, 1978, for a detailed account).

Second, mental models can obviously be generated so as to represent all sorts of quantified assertions. They accommodate multiply-quantified assertions such as "Every man loves a woman who loves him," which cannot be represented by Euler circles. They can even represent sentences that are claimed to demand "branching" quantifiers that go beyond the resources of the ordinary predicate calculus, such as "Some relative of each villager and some relative of each townsman hate each other," (see Hintikka, 1974.) They can accommodate such quantifiers as *most*, *many*, *several* and *few*. They enable distinctions to be drawn between *each* and *every*, and *any* and *all*, as Janet Fodor (1979) has independently shown in a theory with a striking resemblance to the present account. Models also allow a clear distinction to be drawn between class-inclusion and class-membership. The assertion:

John is a Scotsman

concerns class-membership and can be represented as:

John = Scotsman
      Scotsman
      Scotsman
        .
        .
        .
        .

The assertion:

Scotsmen are numerous

also concerns class-membership and can be represented as:

Scotsman
Scotsman = numerous
Scotsman   numerous
   .   numerous
   .   .
          .
          .

In other words, the set of Scotsmen is identical to one of the members of the set of sets of numerous entities. The combination of the two premises

John is a Scotsman
Scotsmen are numerous

leads to a representation from which one can *not* conclude:[4]

John is numerous

Third, the theory of mental models does illuminate the way in which children learn to make inferences and the problematical question of the nature of the rules of inference that they internalize. The theory contains no rules of inference. Its logical component consists solely in a procedure for testing mental models: the aim is to establish the falsity of a putative conclusion by destroying the model from which it derives, but the manipulations that attempt to carry out this process of destruction are constrained in that they must never yield a model that is inconsistent with the premises. The reader will recall that a rule of inference specifies in an essentially "syntactic" way a set of premises and a conclusion that can be derived from them. No such rules are invoked by the theory. This claim may be confusing, so let me elaborate it.

In addition to the formal or syntactic stipulation of rules of inference that enable certain formulae to be derived, a logician can give a semantic characterisation of a logical calculus. He can do so by providing a *model-structure* for it, which consists of a model—a set of entities that provide the referents for the terms in the calculus, an interpretation function that specifies the referents (in the model) for the terms and predicates of the language, and a set of rules governing the way in which the interpretations of complex expressions are built up from the interpretations of their simpler constituents. Any well-formed sentence in the calculus will have a determinate truth value with respect to the model-structure, whose function is precisely to provide such interpretations. A rule of inference should accordingly yield only *valid* conclusions, that is, if it is applied to premises that are true with respect to the model structure, then it should yield only conclusions that are also true with respect to the model structure. Logicians are seldom interested in a particular model structure: the principle of validity must hold over any and every model that can be formulated for the calculus. There is an interesting relation between the model structures of formal logic and the mental models postulated in the present theory. The psychological theory posits a process of inference that involves, not the mobilization of quasi-syntactic rules of inference, but the direct manipulation of a model of the assertions in the premises. The notion is not wholly foreign to formal logic: the theory of *natural deduction* is based essentially on the same principle (see Beth, 1971). It is perhaps for this reason that the formal aspects of natural deduction have had some popularity amongst psychologists (see Johnson-Laird, 1975; Osherson,

---

[4]Unfortunately, such inferences are sanctioned by the theory proposed by Guyote and Sternberg (1978). They remark: ". . . the choice of the number of partitions [in their representation] is arbitrary, and of course, the most accurate representation of a set would have as many partitions as there are members of the set". However, a partition is a subset of the set whereas a member is not a subset. Guyote and Sternberg represent "X is a B", where "X" denotes an individual, as X→B, that is, in exactly the same way as they represent the subset relation. The arrow stands for class-inclusion.

1975; Braine, 1978) and artificial intelligencers (see Bledsoe, Boger & Henne-man, 1972; Reiter, 1973).

The reader may be tempted to suppose nevertheless that somewhere in the theory of mental models for syllogistic inference there lurks some machinery equivalent to a set of rules of inference. The temptation must be resisted. A computer program that I have devised works according to the theory and uses no rules of inference. Its power resides in the procedures for constructing and manipulating models—a power which in turn demands at the very least the recursive power of list-processing operations.

Fourth, and finally, although the theory contains no rules of inference it is entirely compatible with the development of formal logic. Another computer program devised by Mark Steedman showed that simplifying the operation of the psychological principles embodied in the theory by natural computational "short cuts" led to the recovery of all the traditional laws of the syllogism. For exam-ple, with affirmative premises, it transpires that whenever one identity can be broken, then, as in the example above, all of them can be broken. Steedman implemented an extremely simple version of this principle: the relevant proce-dure looked for a middle item that was not linked by an identity to any end items, and whenever such an item was found the program indicated that no valid conclusion could be drawn about the relations between the end items. This procedure sacrifices psychological plausibility for the sake of simplicity: it cuts out a whole series of processes that are likely to occur when logically naive individuals reason, and that are modelled in the first program. However, the abstraction that Steedman's program embodies corresponds directly to the tradi-tional law that the middle term must be distributed at least once in a valid syllogism (see Cohen & Nagel, 1934, p. 79). A logician's conscious reflection on the invariant properties of his own deductions could well have played an analogous role in the development of logic. Aristotle's own procedure for dem-onstrating that a pair of premises does not yield a conclusion bears a striking resemblance to a consciously applied method of manipulating models (see Kneale & Kneale, 1962, p. 75). He compares two different instances of a syllogism of the same form. The syllogism

> Every man is an animal
> No stone is a man
> ———————————
> ∴.No stone is an animal

might be thought to be valid, but he compares it with:

> Every man is an animal
> No horse is a man
> ———————————
> ∴.No horse is an animal

Aristotle's technique is accordingly to show by such examples that premises of the form:

Every B is A
No   C is B

are consistent with

Every   C is A (e.g. Every horse is an animal)
No   C is A (e.g. No stone is an animal)
Some   C is A
Some   C is not A.

The method is wholly semantic and, in effect, externalizes the method of destroying putative conclusions by manipulating models.

The theory of mental models is compatible with the origins of logic. It allows that human beings are capable of rational thought; that they may fall into error if they fail to carry out a comprehensive destructive test of the models that they create, and that their discovery of this tendency to err may have led, in part by reflection on the invariant properties of deduction, to the formulation of logical laws.

MEANING AND MENTAL MODELS

There is a controversy about the proper form of a psychologically adequate semantic theory that can be resolved by following through the implications of the theory of mental models. Psychologists have generally agreed that a major burden for the meaning of words is to account for the relation between such assertions as "Polly is a parrot" and "Polly is a bird"—if the first assertion is true, then plainly so is the second. What they disagree about is the nature of the semantic machinery needed to explain such relations.

One school of thought, whose recent ancestry can be traced back to the work of Katz and Fodor (1963)—though it has a much longer history reaching back into antiquity—holds that the meaning of a word such as "parrot" is represented in the mental lexicon as a set of semantic elements that includes, amongst others, those corresponding to "bird." The relation between the two sentences is accordingly captured by the decomposition of the entries in the mental lexicon. A wide variety of psychological theories of meaning are committed to some sort of decomposition into semantic primitives (Clark & Clark, 1977; Collins & Quillian, 1972; Miller & Johnson-Laird, 1976; Norman & Rumelhart, 1975; Schank, 1975; Smith, Shoben & Rips, 1974).

An alternative view is that there are neither semantic primitives nor decompositional lexical entries (Fodor, 1976; Fodor, 1977; Fodor, Fodor, & Garrett, 1975; Kintsch, 1974; Lyons, 1977). Entailments that depend upon the meanings of words are, according to these theorists, captured by meaning postulates (see Carnap, 1956). Meaning postulates stipulate the semantic relations between words, e.g. *for any x, if x is a parrot then x is a bird.* Such rules are introduced into a model-theoretic semantics of a language in order to render some models inadmissible, namely, those for which the meaning postulates are not true. Latterly, the idea has been cut loose from formal semantics and imported into psychological theory. Kintsch (1974) and Fodor et al (1975) assume that sentences in a natural language are translated into 'propositional representations' in a corresponding mental language, and that meaning postulates couched in the mental vocabulary are used to make inferences from these propositional representations.

Two Problems for Meaning Postulates

Although there have been attempts to resolve the controversy about meaning experimentally, the results so far are equivocal. Some findings appear to count against decomposition (Kintsch, 1974; Fodor et al, 1975); other findings appear to count against meaning postulates (Clark & Clark, 1977; Johnson-Laird, Gibbs & de Mowbray, 1978). But, as yet, there are no results sufficiently decisive to resolve the issue. Indeed, there has been a tendency to accept the view of Katz and Nagel (1974) that there is no fundamental distinction between the two sorts of theory. There are, in fact, several arguments that could be made to establish a difference in their psychological plausibility. I shall present two: the first concerns simple inferences based on premises in ordinary language, and the second the relation between language and the world.

Consider the following simple inference:

> The pencil is in the box
> The box is in the envelope
> ―――――――――――――――――――――
> ∴.The pencil is in the envelope

Obviously, it is valid since no one in practice would doubt the truth of the conclusion given the truth of the premises. Meaning postulates provide an initially plausible basis for such an inference. The premises are translated into a propositional representation, which according to Kintsch (1974) might take the following sort of form:

(IN, PENCIL, BOX)
(IN, BOX, ENVELOPE)

and then the meaning postulate that captures the transitivity of "in":

For any x, y, z, (If (IN, x, y) & (IN, y,z)) then (IN, x, z)
is applied to yield the conclusion:

(IN, PENCIL, ENVELOPE)

And this propositional representation can, if necessary, be translated back into natural language.

Although the details of the various processes of translation have not been formulated explicitly by any theorist, they are not problematical as far as the present argument is concerned. It covers any processes that lead parsimoniously to propositional representations and to the application of meaning postulates to them. There is nothing privileged about meaning postulates here, they may be replaced by any rules of inference that apply to such propositional representations.

The heart of the argument depends on the following sort of inference:

> Luke is on Mark's right
> Mark is on Matthew's right
> ―――――――――――――――――
> ∴ Luke is on Matthew's right

It is not immediately clear whether this inference is valid. If the three individuals are sitting in a straight line on one side of a table, then the relation referred to by "on x's right" is transitive, and the inference is valid. But if they are sitting at equal intervals round a small circular table, then the relation referred to by "on x's right" is not transitive, and the inference is invalid.

A natural way to try to accommodate this phenomenon within the framework of a propositional theory is to propose two different meanings for "on the right" and its cognates, one to which a meaning postulate expressing transitivity applies, and one to which a meaning postulate expressing intransitivity applies. However, if a number of people are seated round a *large* circular table, then the previous inference could be valid, but one might have doubts about the following one:

> John is on Luke's right
> Luke is on Mark's right
> Mark is on Matthew's right
> ―――――――――――――――――
> ∴ John is on Matthew's right

As more and more individuals are added round the table, there will inevitably come a point where transitivity breaks down. (As a matter of fact, there is likely to be a region of uncertainty, but this possibility merely exacerbates the problems of a meaning postulate theory.) In general, the particular relation referred to by "on the right" may be intransitive or the extent of its transitivity may vary over any number of items from three to an arbitrarily large number. Each of these extents would require its own separate meaning postulate with the number of premises in its antecedent directly correlated with the number of items over which transitivity holds—two premises for transitivity over three items, three premises for transitivity over four items, and so on *ad infinitum*. Because there is no limit to the number of items at which transitivity ceases to hold, there is no limit to the number of separate meaning postulates that are required to cope with the semantics of this single term. This conclusion is psychologically unacceptable on the reasonable criterion, decisive in other contexts (Miller & Chomsky, 1963), that human beings do not have an unlimited capacity for storing information, or the ability to learn an infinite number of rules.

It should be emphasized that these difficulties are not peculiar to ''right'' and ''left.'' English vocabulary is plagued by the same sorts of problem, and it is hard to find any simple spatial terms that have an unequivocal meaning. Inferences based on such terms as ''at,'' ''between,'' ''near,'' ''next to,'' ''on,'' and ''in'' can all reflect the uncertainties of transitivity.

A proponent of meaning postulates might argue that once the transitivity of ''on the right'' ranges over some large number of items, say, 100, then it can be taken to have an unlimited extent. This *ad hoc* proposal has at least the virtue of limiting the required meaning postulates to a finite number. Yet, it does not solve the problem: no matter how large the radius of a circle and how densely the individuals are packed around it, it *is* a circle and transitivity must break down. Moreover, this proposal highlights another difficulty: how is the appropriate meaning postulate recovered by someone attempting to make an inference? It is clear that any feasible answer to this question will depend on some mechanism for determining the nature of the situation referred to explicitly or implicitly by the premises. In the case of our examples, it will depend on information about the table and the seating arrangements, which in turn will be used to select the appropriate meaning postulate.

Once the need to deal with reference situations is admitted, the second argument against the meaning postulate account can be made. The theory contains an obvious, though deliberate, gap which is again best illustrated by a simple example. Given the following arrangement of letters:

B   A

any competent speaker of English knows that it is true to say of them, ''A is on the right of B'' and false to say of them, ''A is on the left of B''. This distinction reflects the difference in meaning between ''right'' and ''left''; yet, there is no way to capture it using meaning postulates. One can, of course, establish that there is a difference in meaning between the two terms, e.g. *for any x and y, x is on the right of y if and only if y is on the left of x*, and *for any x and y, if x is on the right of y then x is not on the left of y*. These postulates establish that a difference exists, but they do not specify its nature. For that, it is necessary to make explicit what it is that underlies our knowledge that A is indeed on the right of B in the example above.

Procedures for Manipulating Mental Models

The idea lying behind the psychological exploitation of meaning postulates, and indeed most decompositional theories of meaning too, is that it is feasible to specify the semantic relations between words without considering how they relate to the world: intensions can be profitably pursued independently from extensions. The principle seems plausible for meaning postulates in their original context of formal semantics, where the real world is replaced by a model structure in which the extensions of terms are assigned directly. But the precedent is misleading for natural language where, as we shall see, the only way to account for the proper relations between words, and for inferences based upon them, is by giving a specification of their meanings that includes their relations to the world. What is missing in the meaning postulate account is a *definition* of how "right" and "left" relate to the world. The reason for this omission is obvious: the relations are so basic that there is no way to define them in ordinary English. It is for this reason that a complete theory of meaning must rely upon some sort of decomposition into more primitive notions.

Is it possible to save a propositional theory by sacrificing meaning postulates? The answer depends, of course, on what processes are used to make inferences in their stead. Any system that relies on rules that manipulate propositions will have to introduce some machinery to handle transitive relations, and hence it will be in imminent danger of falling into precisely the same difficulties. The only escape route will be a method for handling the facts of transitivity without relying on rules, postulates, or productions, for transitivity itself. Once again, we need to get rid of rules of inference. This prescription may seem to be impossible to fulfill; fortunately, there is at least one way in which it can be met.

The semantics of spatial terms and the uncertainties of their transitivity can be accommodated within a sort of decompositional theory that has come to be known as "procedural semantics" (see Davies & Isard, 1972; Johnson-Laird, 1977; Miller & Johnson-Laird, 1976; Woods, 1967, 1979). The theory can be illustrated by considering a computer program (written in POP-10) that I have devised in order to investigate spatial inference. The purpose of the program is to evaluate premises about the spatial relations between objects. It works by building up a two-dimensional spatial model that satisfies the premises given to it, and indicates whether a premise is implied by, or is inconsistent with, what it has already been told. It accordingly contains a number of *general procedures* for constructing, recursively manipulating, and interrogating sets of models. One procedure constructs a new model for any premise that refers only to entities that have not been mentioned previously. Another procedure, given the location in the model of one item mentioned in a premise, puts another item into the same model at a place that satisfies the premise. Another general procedure is used to verify whether the relation specified to hold between two items, say A and B, obtains within a model. It works by locating B and then by looking along a line from B in order to determine whether or not A is somewhere on that line. If A is found to lie on the line then the premise is true, otherwise it is false. The verification procedure contains two parameters, DX and DY, whose values specify the direction of the line: they give the respective increments on the x and y axes of the model that define the locations to be examined. This use of parameters to specify directions is common to all the general procedures used by the program, including those for inserting new items into a model. This uniformity makes it possible to define the meanings of relational terms as procedures that work in a way that is utterly remote from meaning postulates and conventional decompositional theories.

The meaning of "on the right of" consists of a single procedure: FUNCT(% 0, 1 %). This takes whatever general procedure is about to be executed, and which has been assigned as the value of the variable, FUNCT, and "freezes in" the value of 0 to its DY parameter and the value of 1 to its DX parameter. The decorated parentheses are a standard device in POP-10 for freezing in the values of parameters, with the effect of converting a general procedure into a new more specific procedure that takes fewer arguments—one less for each argument that has had its value frozen in. The effect of FUNCT(% 0, 1%) on the verification procedure is accordingly to produce a procedure that scans a specified sequence of locations lying in a particular orientation. Since DY = 0, they have the same y-coordinate as the object B; and since DX = 1, they are spelt out by successive increments of 1 on the X-coordinate. In other words, if you imagine the spatial array laid out on a table in front of you, the procedure examines a sequence of locations lying progressively further to the right of B: it looks to see whether A is on the right of B. The same process of freezing in the values of parameters is used to convert the program's other general procedures into specific ones that depend on the relation specified in a premise.

The program's lexical entries define how words relate to its model of the world; but they stipulate nothing about transitivity or intransitivity. However, in the program's simple rectilinear world, a relation such as "on the right of" has the emergent property of transitivity, that is to say, whenever A is on the right of B and B is on the right of C, then as a matter of fact A will be on the right of C, whether the program is building, manipulating, or interpreting a model. The program can accordingly make transitive inferences even though it contains no rules, postulates, or productions, for transitivity itself. This facility depends crucially on its use of spatial models and procedural definitions that relate directly to them. The definitions decompose meanings into the primitive components of specific coordinate values that are only interpretable with respect to the spatial models. The meaning of a word is accordingly not a procedure that can do anything by itself; it is a procedure that applies to other procedures. If the locus of the entities in a reference situation is circular rather than rectilinear, then exactly the same lexical procedures will give rise to transitivity locally, but sooner or later it will fail as the entities depart further and further from the required sequence of locations passing through the initial object in the series.

The program is intended neither as an exercise in artificial intelligence nor as a computer simulation of spatial inference. It is far too simple to be psychologically realistic—for example, human beings do not just consider single lines, and whether objects lie on or off them, in determining spatial relations. Its purpose is merely to establish the feasibility of a theory of semantics based on the assumption that the meanings of words are decompositional procedures that relate to mental models of the world, and, in particular, on the use of lexical procedures that interact with the general procedures for constructing manipulating and evaluating mental models. There is a twofold advantage of this approach over any theory based on meaning postulates. First, the procedural theory gives an account of the extensions of expressions, which meaning postulates are neither intended nor able to do. Second, the vagaries of transitivity, which the meaning postulate theory is presumably intended to handle, emerge in a wholly natural way from the operation of procedures on mental models.

IMAGES, PROPOSITIONS, AND MENTAL MODELS

The concept of a mental model, which has been used throughout this paper, has yet to be analyzed in any detail. Undoubtedly, it resembles some of the current conceptions of an image. However, there is little agreement about the properties of images other than that they give rise to an obvious subjective experience, whereas this characteristic is wholly irrelevant to mental models, which need not possess any immediately "pictorial" attributes. In order to specify their positive characteristics, however, I need to resolve the controversy about images and propositional representations.

Images versus Propositional Representations

Many human beings claim to be able to form and to manipulate mental images in the absence of corresponding visual stimuli. The phenomenon has been studied empirically for a century, dating from Galton's questionnaire on his correspondents' ability to imagine their breakfast tables (Galton, 1928, originally published in 1880). More recent studies have examined a variety of aspects of images, including their use as mnemonics (Bower, 1972; Paivio, 1971), their mental rotation and transformation (Cooper, 1975; Shepard, 1975), their suppression by other tasks (Brooks, 1967, 1968; Byrne, 1974), and their use in retrieving information about objects (Hayes, 1973; Holyoak, 1977; Kosslyn, 1975, 1976; Moyer, 1973; Paivio, 1975). No one seriously doubts the existence of the psychological phenomena of imagery. What is problematical, however, is the explanation of the phenomena and the ultimate nature of images as mental representations. It seems unlikely that they are simple pictures in the head, because this conjecture leads to a number of undesirable consequences including the need for an homunculus to perceive the pictures, and thus to the danger of an infinite regress (Dennett, 1969). There remain two schools of thought.

On the one hand, there are those who argue that an image is distinct from a mere representation of propositions (Bugelski, 1970; Kosslyn & Pomerantz, 1977; Paivio, 1971, 1977; Shepard, 1975, 1978; Sloman, 1971). These authors attribute a variety of properties to images. The consensus, in so far as one can be detected, embodies the following points:

1. The mental processes underlying an image are similar to those underlying the perception of an object or a picture.
2. An image is a coherent and integrated representation in which each element of a represented object occurs only once with all its relations to other elements readily accessible.
3. An image is amenable to apparently continuous mental transformations, such as rotations or expansions, in which intermediate states correspond to intermediate states (or views) of an actual object undergoing the corresponding physical transformation. Hence, a small change in the image corresponds to a small change in the object (or its appearance).
4. Images represent objects. They are *analogical* in that the structural relations between their parts correspond to those between the parts of the objects represented. There may indeed be an isomorphism between an image and its object, though this claim makes sense only with respect to an object viewed as decomposed into parts with particular relations between them.

On the other hand, there are theorists who argue that the subjective experience of an image is epiphenomenal and that its underlying representation is propositional in form (Anderson & Bower, 1973; Baylor, 1971; Kieras, 1978; Morgan, 1973; Palmer, 1975; Pylyshyn, 1973). The main properties of such a representation, again in so far as there is a consensus, are as follows:

1. The mental processes underlying a propositional representation are similar to those underlying the perception of an object or picture.
2. The same element or part of an object may be referred to by many of the different propositions that constitute the description of the object. However, when propositions are represented in the form of a semantic network, then the representation is coherent and integrated, and each element of the represented object occurs only once with all its relations to other elements readily accessible.
3. A propositional representation is discrete and digital rather than continuous. However, it can represent continuous processes by small successive increments of the relevant variable(s), such as the angle of an object's major axis to a frame of reference. Hence, a small change in the representation can correspond to a small change in the object (or its appearance).
4. Propositions are true or false of objects. Their representations are *abstract* in that they do not resemble either words or pictures, though they may be needed to provide an

interlingua[5] between them (Chase & Clark, 1972). Their structure is not analogous to the structure of the objects that they represent.

The critics of imagery often allow that an image can be constructed from its propositional description, but such an image does not introduce any new information, it merely makes the stored description more accessible and easier to manipulate. Gelernter's (1963) program for proving geometric theorems, and Funt's 1977) program for making inferences about the stability of arrangements of blocks, are both considerably enhanced by the use of procedures that operate on diagrammatic representations. However, Pylyshyn (1973) argues that picturelike representations are not necessary for such purposes: the same function can be served by propositional descriptions. This view has been pushed still further by Palmer (1975):

> The arguments in favor of analogical representations tend to emphasize the relative ease with which certain operations can be performed on them compared to the difficulty in performing the same operations on propositional representations. These arguments, however, generally overlook the fact that propositions can encode quantitative as well as qualitative information. In addition, it is not often recognized that propositions are capable of encoding an analog image.

Palmer then goes on to establish both a way in which a shape such as a triangle can be encoded propositionally and a method for rotating such representations once they have been decomposed into their propositional constituents.

Evidently, the two sorts of representation share a number of properties: they differ mainly on the fourth of the characteristics listed above—the function served by the representation. Otherwise, their apparent similarity and the view that they are readily transformed into one another has indeed led some commentators to conclude that the controversy is neither fundamental (Norman & Rumelhart, 1975) nor resolvable (Anderson, 1976, 1978). In particular, Anderson (1978) argues that "any claim for a particular representation is impossible to evaluate unless one specifies the processes that will operate on this representation." He shows that a theory based on images can be mimicked by one based on propositions provided that certain conditions are satisfied.

Anderson's Theorem on "Mimicry"

Anderson's argument is intended to establish that given a theory which embodies assumptions about mental representations and processes, it is possible, in principle, to construct other theories with different sorts of representations that

---

[5]There is danger of an infinite regress here. If an interlingua is needed to mediate between words and pictures, then perhaps a language is needed to mediate between words and the interlingua, or between the interlingua and pictures, and so on and on (see Anderson, 1978).

nevertheless behave in an equivalent manner. Suppose, for instance, that one wishes to show that with suitable mental operations, a propositional theory can mimic an imaginal theory. The trick is to embed the whole of the imaginal theory within the operations carried out on the propositional representations. The imaginal theory assumes, say, that a stimulus is encoded as an image, which can be mentally rotated in order to determine whether it coincides with another stimulus. The propositional theory assumes only that a stimulus is encoded as a set of propositions. The following operations can accordingly be postulated as part of the propositional theory:

1. Apply the inverse of the propositional encoding to the set of propositions in order to recover the original "stimulus" (i.e. its sensory image).
2. Apply the imaginal encoding to this stimulus in order to obtain the corresponding image.
3. Rotate the image.
4. Apply the inverse of the imaginal encoding to the rotated image in order to obtain the corresponding stimulus.
5. Apply the propositional encoding to the stimulus in order to obtain the set of propositions corresponding to the rotated image.

The decision about whether these propositions match the second stimulus can again, if necessary, relay on the imaginal theory:

6. Apply the inverse of the propositional encoding in order to obtain the stimulus corresponding to the rotated image.
   (This stimulus is, of course, identical to the one obtained in step 4.)
7. Apply the imaginal encoding to the stimulus to obtain the corresponding image.
   (This image is identical to the one obtained from step 3.)
8. Compare the image to the one obtained from the second stimulus, and make the appropriate response.

Although this chain of operations can be postulated, its feasibility depends on a crucial condition: it must be possible to apply the inverse of the propositional encoding to obtain the original stimulus, or, more plausibly, a sensory representation isomorphic to the original stimulus. However, since perception is likely to involve a many-one mapping, the inverse may fail to yield the original "stimulus." It is for this reason that Anderson imposes the condition that there must be a one-to-one mapping between the respective representations of the two theories. Granted this condition, the inverse of the propositional encoding can yield any of the "stimuli" that could have given rise to the relevant set of propositions, and it will not matter which stimulus is selected, because they will all be equivalent for the imaginal theory, too.

That a propositional theory can mimic an imaginal theory by importing the whole apparatus of images is plainly a trivial result. What is of interest is the possibility of a more direct method of mimicry that does not depend upon embedding one theory within another. Unfortunately, there is no guarantee that a direct method can always be found for two alternative representational theories.

Anderson makes only the modest claim: " . . . it seems we can usually construct [the required operation] more simply than its formally guaranteed specification." Moreover, if one theory encodes stimuli into classes that do not correspond one-to-one with the encodings of the other theory, then the whole system of mapping breaks down.

Considerable care needs to be exercised in drawing conclusions on the basis of Anderson's demonstration. He himself (Anderson, 1976, p. 74) makes the following claim:

> Any behavior that can be computed from inspecting semantic primitives can be computed with the aid of "meaning postulates" that interpret more complex semantic units. This follows from the theorem . . . that any representation can mimic the behavior of any other, provided they impose the same equivalence class on their inputs.

The first assertion has, of course, proved to be false: meaning postulates cannot handle the reference of expressions or the uncertainties of transitivity, but lexical entries based on procedural primitives can accommodate them. It follows that the two sorts of theory do not impose the same equivalence classes on their inputs. And this conclusion is clinched by considering sentences of the form: "A is in front of B, which is behind C." The sentence is unambiguous[6] and should accordingly receive a single propositional representation, but it is referentially indeterminate—the relation between A and C is unspecified—and can accordingly be represented by a number of different mental models. Once one has constructed a particular model, it is impossible to recover the original premises on which it is based. This distinction drives a wedge between sets of propositions and mental models that is not easily removed.

It might be supposed that the propositional representation could mimic the model representation, and yield two alternatives: one in which A is in front of C, and one in which C is in front of A. But, before such alternatives could be specified, it would be necessary to detect the indeterminacy in the first place. In general, a scheme for detection would have to be able to infer that the relation between certain items in a propositional representation was indeterminate. Unfortunately, this requirement leads straight back to the problems of transitivity: whether the relation between certain items is determinate or indeterminate may depend entirely on whether a transitive inference is valid or invalid. Since no finite system of rules based on a propositional representation can handle this problem, it follows that no such system can detect indeterminacies, or *a fortiori* set up alternative representations when they occur. Hence, a theory of propositional representation does not yield the same equivalence class of repre-

---

[6]Expressions such as "in front of," in fact, have two distinct spatial senses, a deictic sense that depends on the speaker's point of view, e.g. "Stand in front of the rock," and another sense that depends on the intrinsic parts of certain sorts of object, e.g. "The river was in front of the house" (see Fillmore, 1971; Miller & Johnson-Laird, 1976, Sec. 6.1.3). This complication is not relevant to the present argument and I have otherwise ignored it.

sentations as the class yielded by the theory of mental models. The wedge remains securely in place: there is a difference between the theory of mental models and the theory of propositional representations. The way is now clear to attempt to draw some lines of demarcation and to provide some evidence in support of them.

The Characteristics of Propositional Representations

The nature of a propositional representation obviously depends on what a proposition is. One view, which has much to commend it, is a generalization of the commonplace notion that to understand a proposition is to know what the world would have to be like for it to be true. If one considers all the different ways in which the world might be, as well as the way it actually is, that is, the set of all "possible worlds," then a proposition is, in principle, either true or else false of each member of the set. Hence, a proposition can be treated as a function from the set of possible worlds onto the set of truth values.[7] A logician might, in turn, treat this function as a set of ordered pairs, each comprising a possible world and a truth value (of the proposition in that world), but this conception is highly abstract since the set of possible worlds is plainly infinite. A mental *representation* of a proposition, however, can be thought of as a function which takes a state of affairs (perceived, remembered, or imaginal) as an argument, and whose body is capable of returning a truth value. The fact that a propositional representation is a function, however, does not imply that it is automatically evaluated every time the proposition is brought to mind. It does not even imply that the function could be evaluated. Many propositions may be only partial functions, yielding no truth values for certain states of affairs; many propositions may be functions for which there is no effective computational procedure. Yet, at least some propositional representations must sometimes be evaluated and return a truth value. Otherwise, propositional representations and truth itself would be idle wheels in our minds. A view common to many proponents of a "procedural semantics" is accordingly that grasping a proposition is analogous to compiling a function,

---

[7]We might also wish to include possible times and other aspects of the context in the domain of the function (see Lewis, 1972). An alternative way of handling pragmatics has been proposed by Kaplan (1977). He points out that it is necessary to distinguish the context of an utterance from the circumstances of its evaluation. For example, the sentence, "I am speaking now" is true in any context in which it is uttered, but it is not thereby logically true—the speaker does not necessarily have to be speaking. There are circumstances of evaluation—possible worlds and times—in which the sentence is false. The machinery for distinguishing context and circumstances of evaluation was originally provided by Hans Kamp (1971) in his analysis of that tricky word, "now." It depends on a system of double indexing in which a set of possible worlds (and a set of times) is used twice, once for context and once for circumstances of evaluation. Since a proposition is a function from possible worlds to a truth value, the *propositional concept* expressed by a specific utterance is a function from pairs of possible worlds to a truth value, that is to say, it is a function from possible worlds representing contexts to an intension, which in turn is a function from possible worlds representing circumstances of evaluation to a truth value (see also Stalnaker, 1978).

whereas verifying it is analogous to evaluating a function. This idea can be generalized to allow other mental operations based on propositions, and to allow functional representations for questions and commands (cf. Davies & Isard, 1972; Miller & Johnson-Laird, 1976; Woods, 1967, 1979).

If a proposition is a function, then its representation is the representation of a function. The way to represent a function is to express it in a language, and, as Fodor et al., (1975, & Fodor, 1976) have argued, it is useful to think of a propositional representation as an expression in a mental language. Although we may never delineate the details of the mental language, we do know that it must have both a syntax and a semantics. It must be capable, for example, of representing conjunction, and its mental syntax could take a variety of forms, e.g. "$(\alpha K\beta)$," "$K(\alpha,\beta)$," or "$(\alpha,\beta)K$," where the Greek letters range over representations of propositions, and "K" stands for some mental token representing conjunction. Whatever form the syntax takes, it must be associated with the appropriate semantics: the function representing a conjunction will return the truth value if and only if each of the functions representing the conjoined propositions returns the value true[8]. A crucial point about the mental representation of propositions, however, is that the choice of their syntactic structure, though perhaps innately determined, is not governed by any logical or analogical considerations. It is essentially free in the same way that the discursive structure of any language is free. That is to say, although nature may have decided that conjunction is represented by a structure of the form, "$K(\alpha,\beta,$" she might just as well have settled for "$(\alpha K\beta)$." It will make no difference provided that the structure receives the appropriate semantic interpretation.

The same principle of *arbitrary syntactic structure* applies to simple propositions, and in particular to the way in which their predicates and arguments are syntactically arranged. This freedom of choice is actually exercised by the designers of programming languages: they determine the syntax of the language and how it relates to its semantics; they may even elect, perhaps unwisely, to lay down the syntactic rules independently of the semantic interpretation (Hamish Dewar, personal communication)—a strategy that Chomsky (1957) also adopted in his initial studies of natural language, but which has been emphatically repudiated by students of formal semantics (e.g. Montague, 1974).

The propositional description of a complicated state of affairs may consist of a large number of propositions. The question arises as to the nature of the structural relations between them. In fact, one paradigm case of a propositional representation is simply an unordered set of expressions in some symbolic language such as the predicate calculus. Uniform theorem provers will evaluate inferences made in such a formalism, relying on procedures that will search the

---

[8]I have assumed here a simple truth-functional account of conjunction. Natural language is more complicated: conjunction may require a more complex connective that is not truth–functional (cf. "and then"), or conversational principles that impose a further layer of interpretation on what is fundamentally a truth–functional connective.

set for any particular atomic proposition, looking within complex propositions to check whether it is a constituent of them (Robinson, 1965, 1979). However, advocates of propositional theories have often relied on some sort of semantic network (see Anderson, 1976, 1978; Anderson & Bower, 1973; Baylor, 1971; Kintsch, 1974; Moran, 1973; Norman & Rumelhart, 1975; Palmer, 1975). In a network, propositions about the same entity are gathered together and attached to the single node for that entity. Plainly this use of structure is not essential, it simply facilitates the processes that encode or retrieve information.

The Characteristics of Mental Models

Mental models and propositional representations can be distinguished on a number of criteria. They differ pre-eminently in their function: a propositional representation is a description. A description is true or false, ultimately with respect to the world. But human beings do *not* apprehend the world directly; they possess only internal representations of it. Hence, a propositional representation is true or false with respect to a mental model of the world. In principle, this functional difference between models and propositions could be the only distinction between them: there need be nothing to distinguish them in form or content. Model-theoretic semantics often uses the device of allowing a set of sentences to be a model of itself, because various neat proofs can thereby be established. Likewise, Hintikka (1963) has formulated a semantic theory of modal logic in which the model consists of a set of sentences. PLANNER, too, uses a set of assertions in its data-base (Hewitt, 1972). However, in the case of mental models, there is reason to suppose that their form is distinct from that of propositional representations. A model *represents* a state of affairs and accordingly its structure is not arbitrary like that of a propositional representation, but plays a direct representational or analogical role. Its structure mirrors the relevant aspects of the corresponding state of affairs in the world.

Mental models of quantified assertions introduce only a minimal analogical role for structure: the use of elements to stand for individuals in a one-to-one fashion, and links to stand for identities between them. But, they possess one other feature characteristic of models as opposed to propositional representations. They represent a set of entities by introducing an arbitrary number of elements that denote exemplary members of the set. Propositional representations of the sort proposed by Fodor et al., (1975) do not contain arbitrary features, whereas models based on verbal descriptions ordinarily do so. A model representing the assertion, "Two boys kissed one girl," might contain two elements standing for the boys, and one element standing for the girl; and the links between them might have a simple propositional label standing for the relation, "kiss." There might be nothing arbitrary about this representation, yet I should still be tempted to describe it as a (hybrid) model. It has a strong analogical feature: two elements to represent two boys, one element to represent one girl. The point to be emphasized is that the inferential heuristic of maximizing the number of identities can only apply if there are entities to be identified: it demands the use of models, because it cannot operate on a propositional representation of the sort, following Kintsch (1974, p. 18) consisting of a formula: (KISS, BOY, GIRL) & (NUMBER, BOY, TWO) & (NUMBER, GIRL, ONE).

Images, like models, have the property of arbitrariness, which has often drawn comment from philosophers. You cannot form an image of *a triangle in general*, but only of a specific triangle. Hence, if you reason on the basis of a model or image, you must take pains to ensure that your conclusion goes beyond the specific instance you considered. Hume (1896, vol I) made the point, somewhat optimistically, in this way:

> For this is one of the most extraordinary circumstances in the present affair, that after the mind has produced an individual idea, upon which we reason, the attendant custom, revived by the general or abstract term, readily suggests any other individual, if by chance we form any reasoning that agrees not with it. Thus, should we mention the word triangle, and form the idea of a particular equilateral one to correspond to it, and should we afterwards assert, *that the three angles of a triangle are equal to each other*, the other individuals of a scalenum and isosceles, which we overlooked at first, immediately crowd in upon us, and make us perceive the falsehood of this proposition . . .

The heuristic advantage of a model is balanced by the need for procedures that test the conclusions that can be derived from it—a point that is borne out by the way in which the models for quantified assertions and spatial relations have to be manipulated in order to ensure validity.

Of course models can have a richer analogical structure than those required for quantifiers. They may be two- or three-dimensional; they may be dynamic; they may take on an even higher number of dimensions in the case of certain gifted individuals. One advantage of their dimensional structure is that they can be scanned in any direction, regular or irregular, since the dimensional variables controlling the search can be determined from moment to moment by any mentally computable function. In the case of a propositional representation, as Simon (1972) points out, direct scanning can be performed only in those directions that have been encoded in the representation. Simon also draws attention to the fact that people who know perfectly well how to play tic-tac-toe (noughts and crosses) are unable to transfer their tactical skill to number scrabble, a game which is isomorphic to tic-tac-toe. He comments:

> The number scrabble evidence is particularly convincing, not merely in pointing to semantic processing, but in showing how translation to an encoding that uses isomorphs of visual linear arrays to provide the (implicit) information as to the winning combinations causes a striking change in performance. Just as the collinearity of positions can be determined on an external tic-tac-toe array by visual scanning, so collinearity can be detected on an array in the "mind's eye" by an apparently isomorphic process of internal scanning.

This process of scanning is precisely what is modelled by the spatial inference program described above.

Models and propositions are interesting to compare on the criterion of economy. If a series of assertions are highly indeterminate, and no profound inferences have to be drawn from them, it may be more economical to remember the propositions that were asserted rather than to interpret them in the form of a model: a single propositional representation will suffice, whereas many alternative models will be needed to represent the discourse accurately. Miller (1979) makes exactly this point, and suggests that discourse may accordingly be encoded in both sorts of representation. There is certainly a limit to the extent that human beings can manipulate models in order to ensure validity, and even certain syllogisms appear to be taxing for this reason.

The theory of mental models assumes that they can be constructed on the basis of either verbal or perceptual information, though only in the former case will their construction necessitate the introduction of arbitrary assumptions. It follows that images correspond to those components of models that are directly perceptible in the equivalent real-world objects. Conversely, models may underlie thought processes without necessarily emerging into consciousness in the form of images. Models are also likely to underlie the perception of objects by providing prototypical information about them (see Roberts, 1965; Marr & Nishihara, 1976) in a form that can be directly used in the interpretation of what Marr (1976) has referred to as 'the primal sketch,' the output of lower level visual processes.

LEVELS OF DESCRIPTION

Is it really true that images and models are not necessarily equivalent to sets of propositions? That was the conclusion of the previous section, but doubtless it will be resisted by propositional theorists. There is one way in which they can sustain their objection, but only at the cost of trivializing the whole controversy. It depends on a source of much confusion in theoretical discussions, the level at which a particular theory is described. The issues can be illustrated by considering the problem of how to characterize the computer program that embodies the theory of spatial inference.

One approach is that since the program must ultimately be translated into the machine language of a computer before it can be run, we should concern ourselves with what the machine language instructions cause to happen in the machine—the shifting of bits from one location in store to another, and so on. But this approach is misguided: the details of a specific implementation should not concern us. We should not worry about the particular computer and its machine code, since the program could be executed on some very different machines, and we do not want to make a separate characterization for all these different sorts of computer. An alternative approach is provided by Scott and Strachey (1971), the pioneers of formal semantics for computing languages:

Compilers of high-level languages are generally constructed to give the complete translation of the programs into machine language. As machines merely juggle bit patterns, the concepts of the original language may be lost or at least obscured during this passage. The purpose of mathematical semantics is to give a correct and meaningful correspondence between programs and mathematical entities in a way that is entirely independent of an implementation.

There is a very important lesson for psychologist here: their subject can be pursued independently from neurophysiology (the study of the machine and the machine code) and other disciplines that reductionists often suppose underlie psychology. The argument also provides a useful antidote to the excessive scepticism that can be induced by theorems demonstrating how one sort of representational theory can be mimicked by another. In order to try to substantiate this claim, and to clear up the confusion over levels of description, let us continue the characterization of the spatial inference program.

The Reconstruction of a Theory at a Lower Level of Description

"It works by building up a two-dimensional array that satisfies the premises given to it." This description of the program is informal, but at a high level, the level of "psychological" discourse. You may wonder how exactly an array is represented by the programming language. It is, in fact, a data structure of one or more dimensions in which the elements can be accessed and updated by giving appropriate coordinates. (An array can also be represented by a function in POP-10, which permits it to be specified by a rule rather than an explicit table.) A programmer needs to know no more: one can write procedures for manipulating arrays simply by thinking of them as n-dimensional spaces where each location is specified by an n-tuple of integers. A student of the "psychology" of computers, however, may be curious about the invisible machinery that makes such an array possible. Its representation in the computer does not involve an actual physical array of locations in core store. That is quite unnecessary. Indeed, the physical embodiment of an array is irrelevant. What matters is that it should *function* as an array, that is, it has a set of addresses that are functionally equivalent to an array, its elements can be accessed as in an array, and its contents displayed or printed out in the form of an array. A psychological description should accordingly be a functional one.

Consider a program for spatial inference in which an assertion such as, "A is on the right of B" is represented by the following formulae: AT(A, 1, 6), AT(B, 1, 2) and the general procedure for verification works by looking for sequences of ordered pairs of integers as parts of such formulae. In order to verify the above assertion, it starts with B and its associated pair (1, 2), and then looks for formulae corresponding to the sequence: (1, 3), (1, 4), (1, 5) . . . up to some arbitrary number. If the program finds A associated with a pair of integers in the series (which of course it will do in this example), then the assertion is true; otherwise, it is false. The series is defined by the procedure representing "on the right of," which freezes in the appropriate values for the incremental parameters of the verification process.

It should be clear that the whole of the original theory of spatial inference can be reconstructed in this way, even to the extent of coping with the problems of transitivity. Indeed, many adherents of propositional theories may wish to claim that a propositional theory of spatial inference has here been constructed that counters all the earlier criticisms. They would be wrong; but wrong in a way that is most instructive. The construction of the new propositional theory of spatial inference is in reality simply a reconstruction of the original theory *at a lower level of description*. The whole of the propositional apparatus, the ordered pairs of integers, the definition of "on the right of" in terms of incremental values of parameters, is parasitic upon the unacknowledged presence of a spatial array. Perhaps it is easiest to grasp this point by asking oneself how such a system could have been set up in the first place, how it could have been learned, and where the definition of "on the right of" could have come from. The program *functions* as though it uses an array, and one seen from a particular viewpoint, too.

Any Psychological Theory Can Be Based (Vacuously) on Propositional Representations

In general, a model is only a model at a certain level of description: that level at which it functions as one. A listing of the original spatial inference program in machine code is a level of description that obscures the program's use of models. The new "propositional" theory is similarly a redescription of the old theory at a level that obscures its reliance on models; it is a description that could well pass as a slightly more detailed account of how to set up and manipulate arrays in a certain programming language.

There is, of course, nothing inconsistent about calling such a representation a propositional theory. Indeed, the controversy can be resolved in a still more direct way to support the view that any plausible theory of any psychological phenomenon is propositional. If you accept Church's thesis that any "effective procedure" can be computed by a Turing machine, then it follows that the psychological theory, granted the reasonable criterion that it is intended to characterize an effective procedure, can also be computed by a Turing machine. This device, however, can be completely described by a set of propositions— linear strings of symbols from a defined alphabet—that characterize the rules governing its change of state and behaviour as a function of its current state and input (see e.g. Minsky, 1967, p. 106 *et seq*). The only form of representation required by a Turing machine is a tape divided into cells in which there is either a symbol, "1", or a blank: everything that can be computed at all can be computed on the basis of this preeminently propositional representation by a device that can be specified propositionally in exactly the same code. To characterize a theory as propositional is accordingly to say nothing of any empirical consequence.

How to Give the Notion of a "Propositional Representation" an Empirical Content

If the term "propositional representation" is to have empirical content, then it must be constrained in some way. Hence, the view espoused earlier in this paper is that a propositional representation is based on symbols that correspond in a one-to-one fashion with the lexical items of natural language—a view proposed for other reasons by Kintsch (1964) and Fodor et al., (1975). It is unclear whether those who advocate propositional representations for images intend to make a trivial point of the sort that can be established directly by a reduction to machine code or by the parallel conceptual reduction to a Turing machine. What is noteworthy, however, is that they have freely introduced propositions expressing polar coordinates, vectors, and other spatial notions. Such concepts can obviously be expressed in scientific language, but there is no corresponding terminology for them in the ordinary language of simple shapes that they are being used to analyze. Hence, by the criterion introduced to ensure that "propositional representation" has an empirical content, what a theorist proposes in such cases is, not a propositional theory, but a reconstruction of a theory of mental models at a lower level of description.

The purpose of introducing lists, strips, arrays, and a whole variety of data structures and facilities into high-level programming languages is to enable the programmer to forget about the detailed implementation of something that can be functionally specified. Plainly these representations do not increase the computational power of the language or necessarily improve the actual running of the programs. What they do facilitate is the programmer's task of developing and testing programs. On the plausible supposition that the mind possesses the capability of devizing programs for itself (see Miller, Galanter & Pribram, 1960), precisely the same advantage is obtained from high level procedures for manipulating both models and propositional representations. My next task, having shown how they can be usefully distinguished in principle, is to examine some evidence that distinguishes them in practice.

EXPERIMENTS ON MENTAL MODELS AND PROPOSITIONAL REPRESENTATIONS

Ordinary discourse is often indeterminate. If you were to come across the following passage in a story, then you would probably form only a rather vague idea of the actual spatial layout:

> I opened the door and went in. The room was at the corner of the building and on my right there was a long window overlooking the bay. A plain but tasteful table ran the

length of the room and there were chairs on either side. A large colour television set
stood flickering on one side of the table beneath the window, and on the other side
there was a small safe, its door ajar. At the head of the table facing the door, Willis sat
deep in thought, or so it seemed. The room was very quiet. And Willis was very quiet,
frozen in a posture of unnatural stillness.

A few details would stand out—the open safe, the TV, and the corpselike
appearance of the man—but you would be unlikely to have gone beyond the
description to have figured out whether the safe was on the right hand side or the
left hand side of the room from where the narrator viewed it. Yet, if you read the
passage again with the aim of determining the answer to this question, then you
can form a very much more complete mental picture of the room. There accordingly appear to be different levels of representation, and the hypothesis that I
wish to advance is that they differ in kind. The result of a superficial understanding is a propositional representation: a fairly immediate translation of the discourse into a mental language. A more profound understanding leads to the
construction of a mental model which is based on the propositional representation, but which can rely on general knowledge and other relevant representations
in order to go beyond what is explicitly asserted.

We have carried out a number of experiments in order to investigate this
hypothesis. In one experiment (see Ehrlich, Mani & Johnson-Laird, 1979) the
subjects listened to three sentences about the spatial relations between four common objects, e.g.:

> The knife is in front of the spoon
> The spoon is on the left of the glass
> The glass is behind the dish

and then attempted to make a drawing of the corresponding layout using the
names of the objects. We assumed that in order to carry out this task the subjects
would construct a mental model of the layout as they heard each premise. Hence,
we predicted that the task would be straightforward if the premises came in an
order (like those in the example above) that permitted a model to be built up
continuously, but that the task would be very much harder if the premises were
arranged in a discontinuous order:

> The glass is behind the dish
> The knife is in front of the spoon
> The spoon is on the left of the glass

in which the first two assertions refer to no item in common. In this case a subject
must either construct two models and then combine them in the light of the third
premise or else simply represent the premises in a propositional form until the
time comes to make the drawing. The results reliably confirmed the prediction:
69% of the drawings based on continuous premises were correct, whereas only
42% of the drawings based on discontinuous premises were correct. It might be
argued that the subjects only ever use a propositional representation of the premises and that it is easier to form such a representation from continuous premises

than discontinuous premises. One suggestive piece of evidence to the contrary is the relative ease of a third sort of ordering of the premises:

> The spoon is on the left of the glass
> The glass is behind the dish
> The knife is in front of the spoon

in which the third assertion has nothing in common with the second. This ordering was not significantly harder than the continuous premises, yielding 60% of correct drawings. The point to be noted is that although the second and third premises are discontinuous, they always contain at least one item that would already have been represented in a mental model.

A further experiment corroborated the existence of two modes of representation. The subjects again listened to three assertions about the spatial relations between some common objects. They described either a determinate layout (as in the previous examples) or else an indeterminate one, e.g.

> The knife is in front of the spoon
> The spoon is on the left of the glass
> The fork is on the right of the spoon

where the relation between the glass and the fork is undetermined. The subjects' task was rather different in this experiment. After each set of premises, they were shown a diagram of a layout and they had to decide whether or not it satisfied the description in the premises. I assumed that the subjects would be inhibited from forming a model of the indeterminate premises since they might easily form the ''wrong'' one, i.e. one that failed to correspond with the picture, though it was consistent with the premises. Hence, I predicted that they would use a propositional representation and would accordingly be better able to remember the premises. At the end of the experiment, the subjects received an unexpected recognition test of their memory for each set of premises. Each test involved the original premises, a paraphrase of them that had the same meaning, and two sets that differed in meaning from the originals. The major result was that my prediction was completely false: determinate premises were reliably better recalled than indeterminate premises. Not one of the twenty subjects that Kannan Mani tested went against this trend. However, there was an interesting incidental finding. If a subject remembers the meaning of the original premises, then he will pick out the originals and the paraphrases of them before he picks out the other two confusion items. In this case, it is possible to work out the likelihood that he can remember the original premises *verbatim*, picking them out prior to the paraphrases. This probability was 63% for the indeterminate problems, which was significantly better than chance; it was 57% for the determinate premises, which was not significantly better than chance.

A natural explanation for these results rests on the assumption that mental models are constructed from propositional representations. It follows, of course, that a greater amount of processing is required to construct a mental model than to construct a propositional representation. We have found independently that other things being equal the greater the amount of processing the better an item will be remembered: the phenomenon applies both to individual words (Johnson-Laird, Gibbs & de Mowbray, 1978) and to sentences (Johnson-Laird & Bethell-Fox, 1978). It follows that in general mental models should be better remembered than propositional representations—as indeed the experiment established. However, a propositional representation is directly obtained from discourse: if it is recalled, then there should be a good chance that the original sentences on which it is based should be recalled *verbatim;* whereas a mental model, through relatively easy to recall, contains no direct information about the sentences on which it is based: even if it is recalled, there is no guarantee that they will be recalled *verbatim*.

Work in other laboratories provides similar support for two modes of representation for discourse. Scribner and Orasanu (1979), for example, examined their subjects memory for syllogistic premises, comparing trials on which a subject had answered a question about them that required an inference to be made with trials where the question did not require an inference to be made. They found that adults and older children tended to remember the premises more accurately when they had made an inference from them—a finding that corroborates the hypothesis that inferences depend on the construction and testing of mental models.

CONCLUSIONS

Language can be used to talk about real, imaginary, and hypothetical states of affairs: domains for which logicians and philosophers have often advocated a "possible worlds" semantics. However, a psychologically plausible account of such discourse cannot be based on an infinite set of possible worlds, but, as I have suggested elsewhere, should be founded on the mental ability to construct representations of alternative states of affairs to those that actually obtain (see Johnson-Laird, 1978). The same mode of representation can be used to represent beliefs about others' beliefs, and in general propositional attitudes about others' propositional attitudes (see Johnson-Laird, 1979). A crucial characteristic of discourse, whether conversation or text, is reference and referential continuity. The referents of expressions depend in part on context, and, as Alan Granham and I have recently argued, following in the steps of Karttunen (1976), Stenning (1978), and others, the real context of an utterance consists of the mental models of the current conversation that the speaker and the listener maintain. These models represent the relevant individuals, events, and relations. They also represent what is known about the other participants' state of mind. Hence, a speaker chooses his words partly on the basis of his model of the listener's discourse model; and a listener interprets these remarks partly on the basis of his model of the speaker's discourse model. A number of referential phenomena depend critically on the characteristics of mental models, as we were at pains to demonstrate (Johnson-Laird & Garnham, 1979). For example, what really controls the use of a definite description is, not uniqueness in the world, but uniqueness in a model. Hence, when a speaker remarks:

The man who lives next door drives to work

then the definite description should not be taken to imply that there is only one man living next door to the speaker. It designates the only neighbor who is relevant in the context.

Likewise, the most important characteristic underlying the coherence of texts is continuity of reference—a feature that was explicitly manipulated in the experiments on spatial inference. A simple illustration of this point is to consider the following text (after Rumelhart, 1976):

> Margie was holding tightly to the string of her beautiful new balloon. Suddenly, a gust of wind caught it and carried it into a tree. It hit a branch and burst. Margie cried and cried.

As Rumelhart points out, if the sentences are put into random order, their cohesion is destroyed:

> It hit a branch and burst. Suddenly a gust of wind caught it and carried it into a tree. Margie cried and cried.Margie was holding tightly to the string of her beautiful new balloon.

Obviously, the causal sequence of events is disrupted. Yet, if the original noun-phrases are replaced by ones that reestablish continuity of reference, the cohesion of the randomized text is greatly enhanced:

> Margie's beautiful new balloon hit a branch and burst. Suddenly, a gust of wind caught it and carried it into a tree. Margie cried and cried. She was holding tightly to the string of the balloon.

Moreover, if continuity of reference is destroyed by replacing the original noun-phrases with new ones, even in the original order the passage ceases to be cohesive:

> Margie was holding tightly to the string of her beautiful new balloon. Suddenly, a gust of wind caught a newspaper and carried it into a tree. A cup hit a wall and broke. John cried and cried.

There are of course other aspects of coherence, but none is likely to be so preeminent as referential continuity: if a text never refers to the same entity more than once, it rapidly acquires the characteristics of a telephone directory rather than a passage of prose.

Mental models evidently play a part in a variety of phenomena other than those that I have considered in detail in this paper. They appear to have a unifying role to play in Cognitive Science. To return to the three questions with which I began, first, there are indeed distinctions to be drawn between propositional representations and mental models:

1. A propositional representation is a description of a state of affairs, which may be true or false. It is evaluated with respect to a model representing that state of affairs.
2. The initial, and sometimes perhaps only, stage in comprehension consists in creating a propositional representation: a linear string of symbols in a mental language that has an arbitrary (and as yet unknown) syntactic structure and a lexicon that closely corresponds to that of natural language. This representation can be used to construct a mental model, which represents information analogically: its structure is a crucial part of the representation. Models can also be set up directly from perception.
3. A propositional representation encodes determinate and indeterminate information in a uniform way, and makes no use of arbitrary assumptions. A mental model of the state of affairs described in a proposition may embody a number of arbitrary assumptions since language is inherently vague. Indeterminate information is encoded either by utilizing a set of alternative models, or else by incorporating a propositional representation in a 'hybrid' way. The two sorts of representation do not necessarily yield the same equivalence classes, and hence there is no guarantee that a theory embodying one can be made to mimic the other.
4. A model represented in a dimensional space can be directly constructed, manipulated, or scanned, in any way that can be controlled by dimensional variables. A propositional representation lacks this flexibility and can be directly scanned only in those directions that have been laid down between the elements of the representation.

Second, there are likewise distinctions to be drawn between a decompositional semantics and a set of meaning postulates:

1. Insofar as language relates to the world, it does so through the action of the mind, and in particular through its innate ability to construct models of reality. The extension of such words as *right* and *left* is specified by decompositional procedures that operate on the general procedures for constructing and evaluating mental models. Meaning postulates are not intended to perform this function and contain no machinery for doing the job.
2. The logical properties of a term need not be specified within a procedural definition, rather they are emergent properties of that definition. Only in this way can such phenomena as the vagaries of transitivity be explained: they are not an intrinsic part of the meaning of the term, but properties that emerge in the construction of mental models. Meaning postulates, however, as rules that explicitly specify the logical properties of terms, and the logical relations between them.

Third, it is possible to account for the psychological principles underlying deductive reasoning:

1. The capacity to draw inferences rests fundamentally on the ability to construct and to manipulate mental models. The major inferential heuristic for quantified assertion can only be stated for a domain of individuals: it can be summarized in a principle of economy aimed to keep models simple by identifying individuals playing different roles. Inferential ability also depends on submitting putative conclusions to logical test by attempting to destroy the model on which they are based while maintaining its faithfulness to the premises.
2. Insofar as human beings have internal rules of inference that operate on propositional representations, they derive them from invariant outcomes in the manipulation of models e.g. whenever *a is greater than b* and *b is greater than c* then the resulting model is always such that *a is greater than c*.

3. The origins of formal logic as an intellectual discipline are likely to be found in the awareness of potential error as a result of failing to carry out the test procedures exhaustively, and in a self-conscious attempt to externalize such test procedures. Once a set of valid inferences has been determined in this way, an attempt can be made to formalize rules that characterize the set.

These conclusions have been based partly on the results of experiments and partly from ideas derived from developing computer programs. The reader will recall that at the outset I stressed the need for theories in cognitive science that are both coherent and correspond to the facts. The time has come to consider the arguments that favour the use of experiments, programs, and their methodological combination.

A Methodological Moral

There are many reasons for carrying out psychological experiments, and by no means all of them need concern the elucidation of mental phenomena. You may be primarily concerned with the practical application of your findings, as, for example, in the design of a more legible typeface, in the development of better procedures for teaching foreign languages, or in tests of the reliability of police identity parades. Such studies can be useful without directly revealing anything about mental processes. But even those investigations that have that as their primary aim can differ strikingly in how they achieve it. Experiments in cognitive psychology typically address specific hypotheses or sets of alternative hypotheses, and are designed to allow you to come to a decision about them. However, a view that is common amongst devotees of artificial intelligence is that psychological experiments are a waste of time because the theoretical alternatives are not sufficiently articulated to need to worry about experimental tests between them. The business of providing such theories can be pursued within AI on the basis of general knowledge and common observation. After a number of years of arguing with Max Clowes and other vigorous champions of AI, I confess to considerable sympathy with this view. One sort of experiment, however, still seems eminently worthwhile: it is that relatively rare variety that yields a significant pattern of results such as the figural effect, or the greater memorability of determinate descriptions, that is totally unexpected to you. Although experiments may be useful in corroborating your hypotheses, or in showing that they survive potentially falsifying tests, their major value is in causing a significant change in the way in which you think about a problem. An experiment should astonish you. Unfortunately, there are no methodological principles that can guarantee you success; but if you obtain a surprising result, then it may lead to an insight that could have been acquired in no other way.

Computer programming is too useful to cognitive science to be left solely in the hands of the artificial intelligenzia. There is a well established list of advantages that programs bring to a theorist: they concentrate the mind marvelously; they transform mysticism into information processing, forcing the theorist to make intuitions explicit and to translate vague terminology into concrete proposals; they provide a secure test of the consistency of a theory and thereby allow complicated interactive components to be safely assembled; they are "working models" whose behavior can be directly compared with human performance. Yet, many research workers look on the idea of developing their theories in the form of computer programs with considerable suspicion. The reason for the suspicion is complex. In part it derives from the fact that any large-scale program intended to model cognition inevitably incorporates components that lack psychological plausibility. To take an example from a masterly program, Winograd's (1972) procedure for recovering the referents of pronouns is manifestly implausible.[9] Certain aspects of any such program must be at best principled and deliberate simplifications or at worst *ad hoc* patches intended merely to enable the program to work. The remedy, which I have struggled to express on a number of occasions (see e.g. Johnson-Laird, 1977), is *not* to abandon computer programs, but to make a clear distinction between a program and the theory that it is intended to model. For a cognitive scientist, the single most important virtue of programming should come not from a finished program itself, or what it does, but rather from the business of developing it. Indeed, the aim should be neither to simulate human behavior—often a species of dissimulation—nor to exercise artificial intelligence, but to force the theorist to think again. As Jackson Pollock remarked in a different context: the end product does not matter so much as the process of making it. The development of small-scale programs that explore part of a general theory can be a genuinely dialetical process leading to new ideas both about the theory and even about how to test it experimentally. Students of human reasoning would long ago have discovered that it is unnecessary to postulate a mental schema for transitivity, or other internalized rules of inference, if only they had attempted to devise some simple inferential programs.

Cognitive science does not exist: it is necessary to invent it. A crucial part of its invention may prove to be a methodological synthesis of experimental psychology and artificial intelligence. On the one hand, the experimenter's concept of truth exerts a dangerous pull in the direction of empirical pedantry, where the only things that count are facts, no matter how limited their purview. On the other hand, the programmer's concept of truth exerts a dangerous pull in the direction of systematic delusion, where all that counts is internal consistency, no matter how remote it is from reality. One way ahead is to develop general and comprehensive theories of the mind, couched in the theoretical vernacular of the discipline; to make explicit models of at least parts of them in the form of computer programs; and to combine this process with a regime of experimental investigation. This route may lead us to a discipline that is a general science of the mind.

[9]Til Wykes (1979), however, has found that very young children do interpret pronouns in a "syntactic" manner closely resembling the principles embodied in Winogard's programs.

ACKNOWLEDGMENT

This research was supported by a grant from the Social Science Research Council (G.B.) Many individuals have helped wittingly and unwittingly in the preparation of this paper. I am particularly indebted to Bruno Bara, Anne Cutler, Kate Ehrlich, Alan Garnham, Gerald Gazdar, Dave Haw, Steve Isard, Ewan Klein, Christopher Longuet-Higgins, George Miller, Don Norman, Stan Peters, Stuart Sutherland, Patrizia Tabossi, and Eric Wanner for many useful ideas and criticisms.

REFERENCES

Anderson, J. R. *Language, memory and thought.* Hillsdale, N.J.: Lawrence Erlbaum Associates, 1976.

Anderson, J. R. Arguments concerning representations for mental imagery. *Psychological Review,* 1978, *85,* 249–277.

Anderson, J. R. & Bower, G. H. *Human associative memory.* New York: V. H. Winston & Sons, 1973.

Baylor, G. W. Programs and protocol analysis on a mental imagery task. *First International Joint Conference on Artificial Intelligence,* 1971.

Begg, I. & Denny, J. P. Empirical reconciliation of atmosphere and conversion interpretations of syllogistic reasoning errors. *Journal of Experimental Psychology,* 1969, *81,* 351–354.

Berlin, B. & Kay, P. *Basic colour terms: Their universality and evolution.* Berkeley and Los Angeles: University of California Press, 1969.

Beth, E. W. *Aspects of modern logic.* Dordrecht, Holland: Reidel, 1971.

Bledsoe, W. W., Boger, R. S. & Henneman, W. H. Computer proofs of limit theorems. *Artificial Intelligence,* 1972, *3,* 27–60.

Boole, G. *An investigation of the laws of thought.* London: Macmillan, 1854.

Bower, G. H. Mental imagery and associative learning. In L. Gregg (Ed.) *Cognition in learning and memory.* New York: Wiley, 1972.

Braine, M. D. S. On the relation between the natural logic of reasoning and standard logic. *Psychological Review,* 1978, *85,* 1–21.

Brooks, L. The suppression of visualization by reading. *Quarterly Journal of Experimental Psychology,* 1967, *19,* 280–299.

Brooks, L. Spatial and verbal components of the act of recall. *Canadian Journal of Psychology,* 1968, *22,* 349–368.

Bugelski, B. R. Word and things and images. *American Psychologist,* 1970, *25,* 1002–1012.

Byrne, B. Item concreteness vs. spatial organization. *Memory and cognition,* 1974, *2,* 53–59.

Carnap, R. *Meaning and necessity: A study in semantics and modal logic.* Second edition. Chicago: University of Chicago Press, 1956.

Ceraso, J. & Provitera, A. Sources of error in syllogistic reasoning. *Cognitive Psychology,* 1971, *2,* 400–410.

Chapman, I. J. & Chapman, J. P. Atmosphere effect re-examined. *Journal of Experimental Psychology,* 1959, *58,* 220–226.

Chase, W. G. & Clark, H. H. Mental operations in the comparison of sentences and pictures. In L. W. Gregg (Ed.) *Cognition in learning and memory.* New York: Wiley, 1972.

Chomsky, N. *Syntactic structures.* The Hague: Mouton, 1957.

Clark, H. H. & Clark, E. V. *Psychology and language: An introduction to psycholinguistics.* New York: Harcourt Brace Jovanovich, 1977.

Cohen, M. R. & Nagel, E. *An introduction to logic and scientific method.* London: Routledge & Kegan Paul, 1934.

Collins, A. M. & Quillian, M. R. Experiments on semantic memory and language comprehension. In L. W. Gregg (Ed.) *Cognition in learning and memory.* New York: Wiley, 1972.

Cooper, L. A. Mental rotation of random two-dimensional shapes. *Cognitive Psychology,* 1975, *7,* 20–43.

Craik, K. *The nature of explanation.* Cambridge: Cambridge University Press, 1943.

Davies, D. J. M. & Isard, S. D. Utterances as programs. In D. Michie (Ed.) *Machine intelligence 7.* Edinburgh: Edinburgh University Press, 1972.

Dennett, D. C. *Content and consciousness.* New York: Humanities Press, 1969.

Ehrlich, K., Mani, K. & Johnson-Laird, P. N. Mental models of spatial relations. Mimeo, Centre for Research on Perception and Cognition, Laboratory of Experimental Psychology, University of Sussex, 1979.

Erickson, J. R. A set analysis theory of behavior in formal syllogistic reasoning tasks. In R. Solso (Ed.) *Theories in cognitive psychology: The Loyola symposium.* Potomac, MD: Lawrence Erlbaum Associates, 1974.

Erickson, J. R. Research on syllogistic reasoning. In R. Revlin & R. E. Mayer (Eds.) *Human reasoning.* Washington, DC: V. H. Winston & Sons, 1978.

Falk, G. Interpretation of imperfect line data as a 3-dimensional scene. *Artificial Intelligence,* 1972, *3*, 101–144.

Fillmore, C. J. Toward a theory of deixis. Paper delivered to the Pacific conference on contrastive linguistics and language universals. University of Hawaii, 1971.

Fillmore, C. J. An alternative to checklist theories of meaning. *Proceedings of the First Annual Meeting of the Berkeley Linguistics Society,* 1975, 123–131.

Fodor, J. A. *The language of thought.* Hassocks, Sussex: Harvester Press, 1976.

Fodor, J. D. *Semantics: Theories of meaning in generative grammar.* Hassocks, Sussex: Harvester Press, 1977.

Fodor, J. D. The mental representation of quantifiers. Paper presented to the Symposium on Formal Semantics and Natural Language, University of Texas at Austin, 1979.

Fodor, J. D., Fodor, J. A. & Garrett, M. F. The psychological unreality of semantic representations. *Linguistic Inquiry,* 1975, *4*, 515–531.

Funt, B. V. WHISPER: A problem-solving system utilizing diagrams. *Fifth International Joint Conference on Artificial Intelligence,* 1977, 459–464.

Galton, F. *Inquiries into human faculty and its development.* London: Dent, 1928 (originally published 1880).

Gelernter, H. Realization of a geometry-theorem proving machine. In E. A. Feigenbaum & J. Feldman (Eds.) *Computers and thought.* New York: McGraw-Hill, 1963.

Guyote, M. J. & Sternberg, R. J. A transitive-chain theory of syllogistic inference. Technical Report No. 5, Department of Psychology, Yale University, 1978.

Hayes, J. R. On the function of visual imagery in elementary mathematics. In W. G. Chase (Ed.) *Visual information processing.* New York: Academic Press, 1973.

Hewitt, C. Description and theoretical analysis of PLANNER. MIT AI Laboratory Report MIT-AI-258, 1972.

Hintikka, J. The modes of modality. *Acta Philosophica Fennica,* 1963, *16*, 65–82.

Hintikka, J. Quantifiers vs. Quantification theory. *Linguistic Inquiry,* 1974, *5*, 153–177.

Holyoak, K. J. The form of analog size information in memory. *Cognitive Psychology,* 1977, *9*, 31–51.

Hume, D. *A treatise of human nature.* Vol I. Edited by L. A. Selby-Bigge. Oxford: Clarendon, 1896.

Inhelder, B. & Piaget, J. *The growth of logical thinking from childhood to adolescence: An essay on the construction of formal operational structure.* London: Routledge & Kegan Paul, 1958.

Inhelder, B. & Piaget, J. *The early growth of logic in the child: Classification and seriation.* London: Routledge & Kegan Paul, 1964.

Johnson-Laird, P. N. Models of deduction. In R. J. Falmagne (Ed.) *Reasoning: representation and process in children and adults.* Hillsdale, N.J.: Lawrence Erlbaum Associates, 1975.

Johnson-Laird, P. N. Procedural semantics. *Cognition,* 1977, *5*, 189–214.

Johnson-Laird, P. N. The meaning of modality. *Cognitive Science,* 1978, *2*, 17–26.

Johnson-Laird, P. N. Formal semantics and the psychology of meaning. Paper presented at the Symposium on Formal Semantics and Natural Language, University of Texas at Austin, 1979.

Johnson-Laird, P. N. & Bethell-Fox, C. E. Memory for questions and amount of processing. *Memory and Cognition*, 1978, *6*, 496–501.

Johnson-Laird, P. N. & Garnham, A. Descriptions and discourse models. *Linguistics and Philosophy*, in press.

Johnson-Laird, P. N. & Steedman, M. J. The psychology of syllogisms. *Cognitive Psychology*, 1978, *10*, 64–99.

Johnson-Laird, P. N. Gibbs, G. & de Mowbray, J. Meaning, amount of processing, and memory for words. *Memory and Cognition*, 1978, *6*, 372–375.

Kamp, H. Formal properties of "Now." *Theoria*, 1971, *37*, 227–273.

Kaplan, D. Demonstratives: an essay on the semantics, logic, metaphysics and epistemology of demonstratives and other indexicals. Paper presented at the meeting of the Pacific division of the American Philosophical Association, March, 1977.

Karttunen, L. Discourse referents. In J. D. McCawley (Ed.) *Syntax and semantics Vol. 7: Notes from the linguistic underground*. New York: Academic Press, 1976.

Katz, J. J. & Fodor, J. A. The structure of a semantic theory. *Language*, 1963, *39*, 170–210.

Katz, J. J. & Nagel, R. Meaning postulates and semantic theory. *Foundations of Language*, 1974, *2*, 311–340.

Kieras, D. Beyond pictures and words: Alternative information-processing models for imagery effects in verbal memory. *Psychological Bulletin*, 1978, *85*, 532–554.

Kintsch, W. *The representation of meaning in memory*. Hillsdale, N.J.: Lawrence Erlbaum Associates, 1974.

Kneale, W. & Kneale, M. *The development of logic*. Oxford: Clarendon, 1962.

Kosslyn, S. M. Information representation in visual images. *Cognitive Psychology*, 1975, *7*, 341–370.

Kosslyn, S. M. Can imagery be distinguished from other forms of internal representation? Evidence from studies of information retrieval time. *Memory and Cognition*, 1976, *4*, 291–297.

Kosslyn, S. M. & Pomerantz, J. R. Imagery, propositions and the form of internal representations. *Cognitive Psychology*, 1977, *9*, 52–76.

Lakoff, G. Linguistic Gestalts. *13th Regional Meeting, Chicago Linguistic Society*, 1977.

Lewis, D. General semantics. In D. Davidson & G. Harman (Eds.) *Semantics of natural language*. Dordrecht, Holland: Reidel, 1972.

Lyons, J. *Semantics*. Vols. 1 and 2. Cambridge: Cambridge University Press, 1977.

Marr, D. Early porcessing of visual information. *Philosophical Transactions of the Royal Society of London*, Series B, 1976, *275*, 483–519.

Marr, D. & Nishihara, H. K. Representation and recognition of the spatial organization of three-dimensional shapes. MIT AI Laboratory Memorandum, 337, 1976.

Martin, E. The psychological unreality of quantificational semantics. In W. Savage (Ed.) *Minnesota studies in philosophy of science*, Vol. 9. Minnesota, in press.

Mazzocco, A., Legrenzi, P. & Roncato, S. Syllogistic inference: The failure of the atmosphere effect and the conversion hypothesis. *Italian Journal of Psychology*, 1974, *2*, 157–172.

Miller, G. Images and models, similes and metaphors. In A. Ortony (Ed.) *Metaphor and thought*. Cambridge: Cambridge University Press, 1979.

Miller, G. A. & Chomsky, N. Finitary models of language users. In R. D. Luce, R. R. Bush, & E. Galanter (Eds.) *Handbook of mathematical psychology*, Vol. II. New York: Wiley, 1963.

Miller, G. A., Galanter, E. & Pribram, K. *Plans and the structure of behavior*. New York: Holt Rinehart & Winston, 1960.

Miller, G. A. & Johnson-Laird, P. N. *Language and perception*. Cambridge, Mass: Harvard University Press; Cambridge, Cambridge University Press, 1976.

Minsky, M. *Computation: Finite and infinite machines*. Englewood Cliffs, N.J.: Prentice-Hall, 1967.

Montague, R. *Formal philosophy*. Edited by R. H. Thomason. New Haven: Yale University Press, 1974.

Moran, T. P. The symbolic nature of visual imagery. *Third International Joint Conference on Artificial Intelligence*, 1973, 472–477.

Moyer, R. S. Comparing objects in memory: Evidence suggesting an internal psychophysics. *Perception and Psychophysics*, 1973, *13*, 180–184.

Norman, D. A., & Rumelhart, D. E., Memory and knowledge. In D. A. Norman, D. E. Rumelhart & the LNR Research Group, *Explorations in cognition*. San Francisco: Freeman, 1975.

Osherson, D. Logic and models of logical thinking. In R. J. Falmagne (Ed.) *Reasoning: Representation and process in children and adults*. Hillsdale, N.J.: Lawrence Erlbaum Associates, 1975.

Paivio, A. *Imagery and verbal processes*. New York: Holt, Rinehart & Winston, 1971.

Paivio, A. Perceptual comparisons through the mind's eye. *Memory and Cognition*, 1975, *3*, 635–647.

Paivio, A. Images, propositions and knowledge. In J. M. Nicholas (Ed.) *Images, perception and knowledge*. Dordrecht, Holland: Reidel, 1977.

Palmer, S. E. Visual perception and world knowledge: Notes on a model of sensory-cognitive interaction. In D. A. Norman, D. E. Rumelhart & the LNR Research Group, *Explorations in cognition*. San Francisco: Freeman, 1975.

Putnam, H. Is semantics possible? In H. Putnam (Ed.) *Mind, language and reality: Philosophical papers*, Vol. 2. Cambridge: Cambridge University Press, 1975. (Originally published 1970.)

Putnam, H. The meaning of 'meaning'. In H. Putnam (Ed.) *Mind, language and reality: Philosophical papers*, Vol. 2, Cambridge; Cambridge University Press, 1975.

Pylyshyn, Z. W. What the mind's eye tells the mind's brain: A critique of mental imagery. *Psychological Bulletin*, 1973, *80*, 1–24.

Reiter, R. A semantically guided deductive system for automatic theorem-proving. In *Third International Joint Conference on Artificial Intelligence*, 1973.

Revlin, R. & Leirer, V. O. The effect of personal biases on syllogistic reasoning: Rational decisions from personalized representations. In R. Revlin & R. E. Mayer (Eds.) *Human reasoning*. Washington, DC: V. H. Winston & Sons, 1978.

Revlis, R. Two models of syllogistic reasoning: Feature selection and conversion. *Journal of Verbal Learning and Verbal Behavior*, 1975(a), *14*, 180–195.

Revlis, R. Syllogistic reasoning: Logical decisions from a complex data base. In R. J. Falmagne (Ed.) *Reasoning: Representation and process in children and adults*. Hillsdale, N.J.: Lawrence Erlbaum Associates, 1975(b).

Roberts, L. G. Machine perception of three-dimensional solids. In I. J. T. Tippett et al., (Eds.) *Optical and electro-optical information processing*. Cambridge, Mass: MIT Press, 1965.

Robinson, J. A. A machine-oriented logic based on the resolution principle. *Journal of Association for Computing Machinery*, 1965, *12*, 23–41.

Robinson, J. A. *Logic, form and function: Mechanization of deductive reasoning*. Edinburgh: Edinburgh University Press, 1979.

Rosch, E. Natural categories. *Cognitive Psychology*, 1973, *4*, 328–350.

Rumelhart, D. E. Notes on a schema for stories. In D. G. Bobrow & A. Collins (Eds.) *Representation and understanding: Studies in cognitive science*. New York: Academic Press, 1975.

Schank, R. C. *Conceptual information processing*. Amsterdam: North-Holland, 1975.

Scott, D. & Strachey, C. Toward a mathematical semantics for computer languages. *Proceedings of the Symposium on Computers and Automata*. Polytechnic Institute of Brooklyn, April, 1971.

Sells, S. B. The atmosphere effect: An experimental study of reasoning. *Archives of Psychology*, 1936, *29*, 3–72.

Scribner, S. & Orasanu, J. Syllogistic recall. Mimeo. Rockefeller University, 1979.

Shepard, R. N. Form, formation and transformation of internal representations. In R. Solso (Ed.) *Information processing and cognition: The Loyola symposium*. Hillsdale, N.J.: Lawrence Erlbaum Associates, 1975.

Shepard, R. N. The mental image. *American Psychologist*, 1978, *33*, 125–137.

Simon, H. A. What is visual imagery? An information processing interpretation. In L. W. Gregg (Ed.) *Cognition in learning and memory*. New York: Wiley, 1972.

Sloman, A. Interactions between philosophy and artificial intelligence: The role of intuition and non-logical reasoning in intelligence. *Artificial Intelligence*, 1971, *2*, 209–225.

Smith, E. E., Shoben, E. J. & Rips, L. J. Structure and process in semantic memory: A featural model for semantic decisions. *Psychological Review*, 1974, *81*, 214–241.

Stalnaker, R. C. Assertion. In P. Cole (Ed.) *Syntax and semantics*. Vol. 9: *Pragmatics*. New York: Academic Press.

Stenning, K. Anaphora as an approach to pragmatics. In M. Halle, J. Bresnan, & G. A. Miller (Eds.) *Linguistic theory and psychological reality*. Cambridge, Mass.: M.I.T. Press.

Sternberg, R. J. & Turner, M. E. Components of syllogistic reasoning. Technical Report No. 6. Department of Psychology, Yale University, 1978.

Störring, G. Experimentelle Untersuchungen über einfache Schlussprozesse. *Archiv ges. Psychologie*, 1908, *11*, 1–127.

Winograd, T. *Understanding natural language*. New York; Academic Press.

Wittgenstein, L. *Philosophical investigations*. Oxford: Blackwell, 1953.

Woods, W. A. Semantics for a question-answering system. Mathematical linguistics and automatic translation report, NSF-19, Harvard computational Laboratory, 1967.

Woods, W. A. Procedural semantics. Paper presented at the Symposium on Formal Semantics and Natural Language, University of Texas at Austin, 1979.

Woodworth, R. S. & Sells, S. B. An atmosphere effect in formal syllogistic reasoning. *Journal of Experimental Psychology*, 1935, *18*, 451–460.

Wykes, T. D.Phil. dissertation. Laboratory of Experimental Psychology, University of Sussex, 1979.

8
The Metaphorical Structure
of the Human Conceptual System

GEORGE LAKOFF

University of California, Berkeley

MARK JOHNSON

Southern Illinois University

I. METAPHORICAL CONCEPTS

If anything is central to Cognitive Science, it is the nature of the human conceptual system. We have found that that system is fundamentally metaphorical in character. That is, it contains metaphorical as well as nonmetaphorical concepts, and the metaphorical structure is extremely rich and complex. *Nonmetaphorical concepts* are those that emerge directly from our experience and are defined in their own terms. These include at least (1) *spatial orientations* (e.g., UP–DOWN, IN–OUT, NEAR–FAR, FRONT–BACK), (2) *ontological concepts* arising in physical experience (e.g., ENTITY, SUBSTANCE, CONTAINER, PERSON), and (3) *structured experiences and activities* (e.g., EATING, MOVING, TRANSFERRING OBJECTS FROM PLACE TO PLACE, etc.). *Metaphorical concepts* are those which are understood and structured not merely on their own terms, but rather in terms of other concepts. This involves conceptualizing *one kind* of object or experience in terms of *a different kind* of object or experience.

Paralleling the kinds of nonmetaphorical concepts, there are roughly three types of metaphorical concepts, which are realized by a vast number of linguistic expressions:

(1) Orientational Metaphors

These structure concepts linearly, orienting them with respect to nonmetaphorical linear orientations.

More Is Up

The number of books printed each year keeps going up. You made a high number of mistakes. My income rose last year. The amount of artistic activity in this state has gone down in the past year. His humber of errors is incredibly low. His income fell last year.

Control Is Up

I have control over her. I am on top of the situation. He's in a superior position. He's at the height of his power. He's in the high command. His power rose. He's in a dominating position. He ranks above me in strength. He is under my control. He fell from power. His power is on the decline.

Good Is Up

Things are looking up. We hit a peak last year, but it's been going downhill ever since. Things are at an all-time low. The quality of life is high these days.

Rational Is Up

The discussion fell to the emotional level, but I raised it back up to the rational plane. We put our feelings aside and had a high-level intellectual discussion of the matter. He couldn't rise above his emotions.

(2) Ontological Metaphors

These involve the projection of entity or substance status on something that does not have that status inherently.

Ideas Are Entities and Words Are Containers

It's hard to get that idea across to him. Your reasons came through to me. It's difficult to put my ideas into words. When you have a good idea, try to capture it immediately in words. Try to pack more thought into fewer words. His words carry little meaning. Your words seem hollow. The ideas are buried in terribly dense paragraphs.

The Mind Is a Container

I can't get the tune out of my mind. He's empty-headed. His brain is packed with interesting ideas. Do I have to pound these statistics into your head? I need to clear my head.

The Mind Is a Machine

We're still trying to grind out the solution to this equation. My mind just isn't operating today. Boy, the wheels are turning now! I'm a little rusty today. We've been working on this problem all day and now we're running out of steam.

The Mind Is a Brittle Object

She's very fragile. You have to handle him with care since his wife's death. He broke under cross-examination. The experience shattered him. I'm going to pieces. His mind snapped.

Vitality Is a Substance

He overflows with energy. She's brimming with vim and vigor. Toward the end of the day I just run out of energy. There's no life in him anymore since his accident. Her vitality shows up in everything she does.

(3) Structural Metaphors

These involve the structuring of one kind of experience or activity in terms of another kind of experience or activity.

Understanding Is Seeing

I see what you're saying. It looks different from my point of view. What is your outlook on that? Now I've got the whole picture. Let me point something out to you. That's an insightful idea.

Life Is a Gambling Game

I'll take my chances. The odds are against us. I've got an ace up my sleeve. It's a toss-up. If you play your cards right, you can do it. He's a real loser. Where is he when the chips are down?

II. METAPHORS HAVE ENTAILMENTS

Since metaphorical concepts are defined in terms of nonmetaphorical concepts, they show entailment relations parallel to those for the corresponding nonmetaphorical concepts. For example, MONEY is a LIMITED RESOURCE, and LIMITED RESOURCES ARE VALUABLE COMMODITIES. Paralleling these, we have the metaphorical concept TIME IS MONEY, which entails that TIME IS A LIMITED RESOURCE and TIME IS A VALUABLE COMMODITY.

Time Is Money

How do you spend your time these days? That flat tire cost me an hour. I've invested a lot of time in her. You need to budget your time. You don't use your time profitably.

Time Is a Limited Resource

I don't have the time to give you. You're running out of time. Put aside some time for ping pong. Do you have much time left? I lost a lot of time when I got sick.

Time Is a Valuable Commodity

This gadget will save you hours. My time is precious right now. You're wasting my time. Is that worth your while? Thank you for your time.

III. METAPHORICAL DEFINITIONS: PARTIAL, INCONSISTENT, AND OVERLAPPING

Most of our concepts are abstract—concepts like TIME, EMOTIONS, COM-MUNICATION, THE MIND, IDEAS, INSTITUTIONS, INTERPERSONAL RELATIONSHIPS. In general, abstract concepts are defined metaphorically in terms of concepts that are more concrete and more clearly structured on their own terms—concepts like SPACE, MOTION, FOOD, OBJECTS, etc. However, no single, concrete, nonmetaphorical concept is ever structured in exactly the right way to completely and precisely define any single abstract concept. As a result, abstract concepts are typically defined metaphorically in terms of more than one concrete concept. Each metaphor defines only certain aspects of an abstract concept. Thus, we understand abstract concepts in terms of many metaphorical definitions, each of which captures part of the concept. For example, the concept of an IDEA is defined by a rich and complex cluster of metaphors.

(1) Ideas Are Organisms (with Respect to Life and Death)

Ideas Are People

He conceived a brilliant theory of molecular motion. The University of Chicago was the birthplace of the nuclear age. This concept is the brainchild of one of our finest young executives. Edward Teller is the father of the hydrogen bomb. Cognitive psychology is still in its infancy.

Ideas Are Plants

His ideas have finally come to fruition. That idea died on the vine. That's a budding theory. It will take years to come to full flower. He views chemistry as a mere offshoot of physics. The seeds of his great ideas were planted in his youth. She has a fertile imagination.

Ideas Are Products

We're really turning (churning, cranking, grinding) out new ideas. We've generated a lot of ideas this week. He produces ideas at an astounding rate. His intellectual productivity has decreased in recent years. We need to take the rough edges off that idea, hone it down, smooth it out. It's a rough idea; it needs to be refined.

Ideas Are Commodities

It's important how you package your ideas. He won't buy that. That idea just won't sell. There is always a market for good ideas. That's a worthless idea. He's been a source of valuable ideas. Your ideas don't have a chance in the intellectual marketplace.

Ideas Are Resources

He ran out of ideas. Don't waste your thoughts on small projects. Let's pool our ideas. He's a resourceful man. We've used up all our ideas. That's a useless idea. That idea will go a long way.

Ideas Are Money

Let me put in my two cents. He's rich in ideas. That book is a treasure-trove of ideas. He has a wealth of ideas.

Ideas Are Cutting Instruments

That's an incisive idea. That cuts right to the heart of the matter. That was a cutting remark. He's sharp. He has a razor wit. He has a keen mind. She cut his argument to ribbons.

Ideas Are Food

What he said left a bad taste in my mouth. There are too many facts in the paper for me to digest them all. I just can't swallow that claim. Let me stew over that for a while. Now there's a theory you can really sink your teeth into. That's food for thought. He's a voracious reader. He devoured the book. Let's let that idea simmer on the back burner for a while. This is the meaty part of the paper.

Ideas Are Fashions

That idea went out of style years ago. I hear sociobiology is in these days. Marxism is currently fashionable in Western Europe. That idea is old hat! That's an outdated idea. What are the new trends in English criticism? He keeps up to date by reading *The New York Review of Books*. Berkeley is a center of avante-garde thought. Semiotics has become quite chic. That old hypothesis is really behind the times.

Each of these defines some aspect of the concept of an IDEA. However, these metaphors taken together do not provide a *consistent* definition for the concept of an IDEA. Some metaphors have parts that are inconsistent with parts of other metaphors. Thus, IDEAS ARE CUTTING INSTRUMENTS is inconsistent with IDEAS ARE PEOPLE, since PEOPLE are not used for cutting and CUTTING INSTRUMENTS are made, not born. IDEAS ARE FASHIONS is not fully consistent with IDEAS ARE FOOD, since we do not eat and digest fashions. Moreover, IDEAS ARE MONEY is inconsistent with IDEAS ARE PLANTS, since, as we all know, money doesn't grow on trees.

In some cases the inconsistencies between metaphors are cases where properties and functions are inconsistent (e.g., people aren't used for cutting). But in other cases the inconsistency is even more radical. These are cases where the metaphors have conflicting ontologies. Each metaphor imposes an entity-structure of a certain kind on the concept IDEA. The IDEAS ARE PEOPLE metaphor brings along the associated entities PARENTS and (possibly) PRO-GENY. PLANTS have SEEDS as associated entities, and FOOD has associated cooking implements. But these ontologies are not consistent with each other. Thus, the IDEAS ARE PRODUCTS metaphor has neither SEEDS nor PAR-ENTS, and the IDEAS ARE MONEY metaphor has no associated cooking implements.

But even though parts of the various metaphors for IDEAS are inconsistent with other parts, the metaphors do have partial overlaps in many respects. In other words, there are some aspects of the concept IDEA which have correlates in more than one metaphor. Thus PACKAGING in the IDEAS ARE PROD-UCTS metaphor corresponds to FASHIONS. PARENTS in the IDEAS ARE PEOPLE metaphor corresponds to PRODUCERS in the IDEAS ARE PROD-UCTS metaphor. Both PRODUCTS and FOOD can be consumed. Both PLANTS and PEOPLE develop and die.

In summary, abstract concepts are not defined by necessary and sufficient conditions. Instead they are defined by clusters of metaphors. Each metaphor gives a partial definition. These partial definitions overlap in certain ways, but in general they are inconsistent, and typically have inconsistent ontologies. Elsewhere we have given an elaborate theoretical and empirical account of metaphorical definition (Lakoff & Johnson, 1980), but here we would only like to stress that the usual concept of definition in terms of necessary and sufficient conditions will not do.

It is extremely important to note that abstract concepts are defined in terms of a system of related metaphors *in the conceptual system*. The definitions are given for general concepts, not individual words. No lexicon for individual words and phrases will be adequate for definitions of this kind. Such definitions must be made in terms of metaphors *on the conceptual level*, and not in terms of words on the linguistic level (for discussion, see Lakoff & Johnson, 1980).

The fact that abstract concepts are defined by clusters of partially overlapping metaphors has another important consequence. Each metaphor highlights certain aspects of the concept and implicitly hides others. The IDEAS ARE PEOPLE metaphor focuses on COMING INTO EXISTENCE, DEVELOPMENT, and GOING OUT OF EXISTENCE. In doing so, it downplays or hides what the IDEAS ARE COMMODITIES metaphor stresses—namely that ideas have a commercial value, can be bought and sold, etc. It follows from this that no single metaphor even *comes close* to being definitive. In general, each metaphor hides more than it highlights. It takes many different and inconsistent metaphorical perspectives to comprehend each abstract concept.

IV. THE GROUNDING OF METAPHORICAL CONCEPTS IN EXPERIENCE

Metaphorical concepts of all types arise naturally from physical and cultural experience. The orientational metaphor MORE IS UP, for example, appears to be based on the observed correlation between increasing a substance or adding objects to a pile and seeing the level of the substance or pile rise. Such metaphors are good candidates for universal concepts, since they have such a strong physical basis. Most metaphorical concepts, however, are clearly dependent on culturally relative activities and experiences. One would not expect to encounter the same metaphors for ideas or the mind across widely divergent cultures, nor would the same metaphor (say, IDEAS ARE FASHIONS) have the same meaning across cultures (since FASHIONS might be differently understood).

V. METAPHORICAL CONCEPTS AS EXPERIENTIAL GESTALTS

(1) The Nature of Experiential Gestalts

One of the most principal claims of Lakoff and Johnson (1980) is that metaphorical concepts are based on complex experiential gestalts. In order to see what it means for a metaphor of the form A IS B to be based on a complex gestalt, we need to see what it means for the constituent concepts A and B to be grounded on gestalts. An *experiental gestalt* is a multidimensional structured whole arising naturally within experience. We hypothesize that such gestalts can be represented formally in terms of semantic networks. Our proposal is a generalization of the concepts of scripts (Schank & Abelson, 1977), frames (Fillmore, 1975; Minsky, 1975), and schemas (Norman & Rumelhart, 1975), all of which involve theories of the organizational structure of types of experience. To date we have identified basic aspects or dimensions of structure for both ACTIVITY and OBJECT gestalts. As an example of a gestalt for ACTIVITY consider the simple activity of polite conversation, which has at least the following natural dimensions of structure:

Gestalt Structure for Conversation

1. Participants: Here they are PEOPLE who take the role of SPEAKERS.
2. Parts: These are natural kinds of activity, namely, TALKING, consisting of TURNS at talking.
3. Stages: Conversations typically have a set of INITIAL (or enabling) CONDITIONS and pass through various stages, such as BEGINNING, CENTRAL PART, and END.
4. Linear sequence: Participants' turns at speaking are ordered in a linear sequence, with alternating turns at speaking.
5. Causation: The finish of one turn at talking typically results in the beginning of another.
6. Purpose: There are a number of possible purposes which any given conversation might serve.

These six dimensions of structure (and others) can be used to characterize the structure of activities. What distinguished one activity from another is primarily a matter of the particular content or determination that each dimension receives. This can be seen by considering the more complex activity of war. Here we have the same six dimensions of structure.

Gestalt Structure for War

1. Participants: People or groups of people playing the role of ADVERSARIES.
2. Parts:
   a. The two POSITIONS
   b. PLANNING STRATEGY
   c. ATTACK
   d. DEFENSE
   e. RETREAT
   f. MANEUVERING
   g. COUNTERATTACK
   h. STALEMATE

   i. TRUCE
   j. SURRENDER/VICTORY
3. Stages:
   a. INITIAL CONDITIONS: PARTICIPANTS have different POSITIONS. ONE or BOTH wants the other to surrender, etc.
   b. BEGINNING: one ADVERSARY ATTACKS
   c. MIDDLE: combinations of DEFENSE, MANEUVERING, RETREAT, etc.
   d. END: TRUCE or STALEMATE or SURRENDER/VICTORY
   e. FINAL STATE: PEACE, VICTOR HAS DOMINANCE
4. Linear Sequence:
   RETREAT after ATTACK
   DEFENSE after ATTACK
   COUNTERATTACK after ATTACK, etc.
5. Causation: ATTACK results in DEFENSE or COUNTERATTACK or RETREAT, etc.
6. Purpose: VICTORY

The two examples just given illustrate the way in which certain recurring natural dimensions of structure for ACTIVITIES are the basis for our concepts of those activities. In addition, our experience of OBJECTS involves another set of structuring dimensions, e.g., PERCEPTUAL (how the object appears to us), MOTOR ACTIVITY (what we do in manipulating the object), FUNCTIONAL (how it operates), and PURPOSIVE (the uses to which it may be put).

VI. METAPHORICAL CONCEPTS AS COMPLEX GESTALTS

One of the central tenets of the Lakoff–Johnson (1980) study is that metaphorical concepts are based on complex experiential gestalts, in the following way: In the metaphor A IS B, some of the dimensions of structure for B are imposed upon the gestalt for A, forming a complex gestalt. This can be illustrated by considering the gestalts for CONVERSATION and WAR as they are related in the ARGUMENT IS WAR metaphor. Understanding a conversation as being an argument involves being able to superimpose the multidimensional structure of part of the concept of WAR upon the corresponding structural dimensions of CONVERSATION. In the ARGUMENT IS WAR metaphor, the gestalt for CONVERSATION is structured further by means of correspondences with selected elements of the gestalt for WAR. Thus one activity, talking, is understood in terms of another, physical fighting. This way of conceptualizing arguments in terms of war is reflected in our use of war terminology to speak about *corresponding parts* of arguments, and it is the superimposition of the gestalts that defines the correspondence. Thus we speak of winning or losing an argument, gaining or losing ground, being on the defensive, even shooting down our opponent. Structuring our experience in terms of such multidimensional gestalts is what makes our experience coherent.

VII. COMPLEXITY OF THE EXPERIENTIAL
BASIS FOR METAPHOR

A metaphor can serve as a vehicle for understanding a concept *only by virtue of its experiential basis*. Describing metaphors as isolated cases, using the A IS B formula, misses the fact that no metaphor can be comprehended, or even adequately represented, independently of its experiential basis. For example, MORE IS UP has a very different *kind* of experiential basis than HAPPY IS UP or CONTROL IS UP. As we say, the experiential basis for MORE IS UP has to do with seeing the level rise when we add more of a substance. The experiential basis for CONTROL IS UP has to do with physical dominance, where the winner in a fight typically winds up above the loser and where parents, who are much larger, control infants. Though the concept UP is the same in these metaphors, verticality enters into our experience in many different ways, which gives rise to many different UP–DOWN orientations.

To emphasize the inseparability of metaphors from their experiential bases it is necessary to build the experiential bases into the representations themselves. Thus, instead of writing MORE IS UP and CONTROL IS UP, we might have:

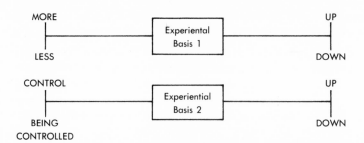

Such a representation would emphasize that the two parts of each metaphor are linked only via an experiential basis and that it is only by means of this basis that the metaphor can serve the purpose of understanding.

The role of the experiential basis is important in understanding the workings of metaphors that do not fit together because they have very different kinds of experiential bases. For instance, some of the metaphors that give concepts an UP–DOWN orientation seem not to fit together coherently if one ignores their experiential bases. Consider the case of UNKNOWN IS UP/KNOWN IS DOWN (e.g., That's up in the air. The matter is settled) as opposed to HAPPY IS UP (e.g., I'm feeling up today. My spirits rose). One would not expect that UNKNOWN would have the same orientation as HAPPY. This apparent inconsistency disappears when we recall that these two metaphors have very different experiential bases and that the orientations are given only via these experiential bases. HAPPY IS UP is based on the typical correlation between being in a happy mental state and having an erect rather than drooping posture. KNOWN IS DOWN/UNKNOWN IS UP is based on the fact that if something is fixed on the ground, one can locate it, see how to reach it, and perhaps get hold of it, whereas if something is floating or flying through the air, it is harder to fix your gaze on it, locate it, and figure out how to reach it. It is not that there are two different kinds of UP, nor are these orientations inconsistent. Rather they just have two different bases in our experience. Thus, it is of the utmost importance to have a detailed account of the nature of experiential bases for metaphors.

In summary, we have suggested that metaphors are grounded in experience and that metaphorical concepts are understood only in relation to their experiential bases. And as we have said, a metaphor of the form A IS B is a shorthand for a partial mapping of the structure of concept B onto concept A. But a mere mapping of B onto A does *not* include the experiential basis for the metaphor A IS B. Thus such mappings are inadequate for representing how we understand the metaphor; all they do is show how the metaphor is structured. What we need in addition is something showing how concepts A and B are linked in our experience. We would like to propose, though we have not even begun to work out the details, that the experiential basis for a metaphor of the form A IS B would be an experiential gestalt that shows explicitly how A and B are related.

VIII. EXPERIENTIAL GESTALTS AND REPRESENTATIONS OF THEM

We would now like to take up the problem of representations for experiential gestalts. In order to do this, we must make the following distinctions.

1. A particular experience or occurrence in the world.
2. A particular experiential gestalt: (a) a structure within a person's experience that identifies that experience as being of a certain kind; or (b) a structure in terms of which a person understands some external occurrence and that identifies that occurrence as being of a certain kind.
3. A concept (or generalized experiential gestalt): A mental structure that characterizes a category of personal experiences or occurrences in the external world. Concepts emerge both from constant direct interaction with our environment and from knowledge we gain as members of our culture. Concepts have certain natural dimensions of structure, each of which is based on some aspect of our personal or cultural experience.
4. A representation of a concept (or generalized experiential gestalt): A mathematical object which is a model of a concept (or generalized experiential gestalt). That is, a representation of a concept is a mathematical model of the structure of a category of personal experiences or a model of a structure in terms of which we understand external occurrences.

The progression from (1) to (4) involves more and more abstraction from lived experiences. The structuring of particular experiences is a product of our genetic endowment plus a lifetime of constant interaction as a part of our environment. A particular experiential gestalt picks out the structure in terms of which we understand a particular experience and function (whether consciously or automatically) within that experience. But it is important to distinguish the *structure* of the experience from the experience itself, which is infinitely richer. To focus on the structure of the experience is to downplay the infinite richness beyond the structure.

The structuring of a particular experience involves the application of general concepts that have a basis both in our direct experience and in the understanding we achieve as members of a culture. For example, an individual's concept of LOVE depends both on his or her own experiences plus the metaphorical concepts for LOVE provided by the culture. There are three points to be made here. The first is that our concepts do not only emerge from direct experience but are also structured by dominant cultural metaphors. Second, concepts (whether they are culturally learned or acquired through direct experience) have the form of experiential gestalts, which have natural dimensions of structure; that is, culturally learned concepts have the same dimensions of structure as naturally emergent concepts. Third, concepts serve the purpose of understanding only in relation to the experiences that have given rise to them and that they have previously structured. Thus understanding is a matter of an individual's experiential history as well as his cultural heritage. *Consequently, the conceptual structure of an experience must be distinguished from an understanding of that experience by a person with a history and heritage.* What the conceptual structure of a person's experience hides is that history and that heritage.

The most important distinction we wish to make is the one between a concept (or experiential gestalt) and a representation of it. Concepts exist within the experience of people. They are structures through which we categorize personal experiences and external occurrences. Representations of concepts are mathematical objects which we, as cognitive scientists, construct as models for concepts. Such representations are not themselves the concepts, or experiential gestalts, that exist within our experience. It is one of the principal goals of Cognitive Science to work out an adequate theory of representations for human concepts. This is both an empirical and a mathematical endeavor. At present no adequate theory exists.

However, even if relatively adequate models for human conceptual structure were to be worked out, they would still not provide an account of human understanding and meaning to people, which we take as included in the domain of Cognitive Science. The reason is this: At best, structural representations can represent salient and categorized aspects of an experience but never the full richness of the lived experience itself. Structural or model-theoretic representations of meaning are meaningful *to us* only because we are able to link them to our lived experiences. We therefore disagree with those in artificial intelligence who have suggested, or might suggest, that computers can in principle understand things in the same way humans do. We would suggest that they cannot, since they do not have the experiences that make human understanding possible. Likewise, model-theoretical accounts of "meaning" can never give an account of meaningfulness to a person, since they too ignore the link to lived experience.

This does not mean, however, that one cannot learn a great deal about the structural and inferential aspects of human understanding through the study of artificial intellegence and model theory. Such endeavors have supplied important tools for the study of how the human conceptual system is structured—tools that we have been making use of. But what weighs on our minds is what is hidden when Cognitive Science is defined solely in terms of the use of available formal tools for investigating the structural and inferential aspects of cognition. What is hidden is an indefinitely large amount about human understanding.

IX. THE METAPHORS OF COGNITIVE SCIENCE

Metaphorical concepts are necessary for understanding most of what goes on in our world. A Scientific Theory attempts to provide an understanding of some class of phenomena through the consistent elaboration of some set of metaphorical concepts. When the basic metaphors of a scientific theory are extensions of basic metaphors in our everyday conceptual system, then we feel that such a theory is "intuitive" or "natural."

Much of modern cognitive psychology uses extensions of metaphors for the mind and ideas that are in our ordinary conceptual system: THE MIND IS A CONTAINER, IDEAS ARE OBJECTS, LINGUISTIC EXPRESSIONS ARE CONTAINERS, and THE MIND IS A MACHINE. Computer models for the mind are the result of taking metaphors like these seriously and trying to elaborate them in some consistent way. THE MIND IS A COMPUTER metaphor gives rise to the associated metaphor of MENTAL PROCESSES. When the MENTAL PROCESS metaphor is taken seriously, it becomes reasonable to ask whether certain processing occurs serially or in parallel—since those are the only alternatives in this metaphor. Like any metaphor, the MENTAL PROCESS metaphor will highlight certain aspects of mental activity and hide others. Thus it is not surprising that psychologists have been able to find phenomena that will fit this metaphor—phenomena that can be classified as instances of serial or parallel processing. Similarly, it is common to devise theories of memory which are extensions of the metaphors THE MIND IS A CONTAINER and IDEAS ARE OBJECTS. Memory can then be viewed as a warehouse or other storage space with memories stored in various "locations." Within this metaphor, it makes sense to ask whether memories are stored close to one another or not, how we get access to them, and how well they are preserved. Again assuming the IDEAS

ARE OBJECTS metaphor and adding the LINGUISTIC EXPRESSIONS ARE CONTAINERS metaphor, we get metaphorical concepts like encoding (PUT-TING IDEAS INTO WORDS) and decoding (TAKING IDEAS OUT OF WORDS). We can then ask how much time the packaging and unpackaging takes.

We are not suggesting that there is anything wrong with using such metaphors. In fact, metaphorical concepts are essential to scientific thought—without them we could understand very little beyond our direct physical experience. It is the genius of a good scientist that he can come up with a consistent set of natural metaphors that, when elaborated, fit a wide range of phenomena. It is important to recognize the indispensibility of metaphors for science; but it is equally important to understand that the metaphors of a science, like any other metaphors, typically hide indefinitely many aspects of reality.

The way ordinary people deal implicitly with the limitations of any one metaphor is by having many metaphors for comprehending different aspects of the same concept. As we saw, people in our culture have many different metaphors for IDEAS and the MIND, some of which are elaborate in one or another branch of Psychology and some of which are not. These clusters of metaphors serve the purpose of understanding better than any *single* metaphor could—even though they are partial and very often inconsistent with each other. Scientists, however, have tended to insist on complete and consistent theories. While consistency is generally desirable, there are times when it does not best serve the purpose of understanding. In particular, the insistence on maintaining a consistent extension of one metaphor may blind us to aspects of reality that are ignored or hidden by that metaphor. We would like to suggest that there are times when scientific understanding may best be served by permitting alternative metaphors even at the expense of completeness and consistency. If Cognitive Science is to be concerned with human understanding in its full richness, and not merely with those phenomena that fit the MIND IS A MACHINE metaphor, then it may have to sacrifice metaphorical consistency in the service of fuller understanding. The moral: Cognitive Science needs to be aware of its metaphors, to be concerned with what they hide, and to be open to alternative metaphors—even if they are inconsistent with the current favorites.

REFERENCES

Fillmore, C. J. An alternative to checklist theories of meaning. In *Proceedings of the First Annual Meeting of the Berkeley Linguistics Society*. Berkeley Linguistics Society, 1975.

Lakoff, G., & Johnson, M. *Metaphors we live by*. Chicago: University of Chicago Press, 1980.

Minsky, M. A framework for representing knowledge. In P. Winston (Ed.), *The psychology of computer vision*. New York: McGraw-Hill, 1975.

Norman, D. A., & Rumelhart, D. E. *Explorations in cognition*. San Francisco: W. H. Freeman, 1975.

Schank, R. C., & Abelson, R. P. *Scripts, plans, goals, and understanding*. Hillsdale, NJ: Erlbaum, 1977.

9

The Intentionality
of Intention and Action*

JOHN R. SEARLE

University of California, Berkeley

I

What exactly are the relationships between the intention I had at the time of the
last election to vote for Jones and the action that I performed when I did vote for
Jones? And what exactly are the relations between these and the desire I had at
the time of the last election to vote for Jones, or the belief that I had at that time
that I would vote for Jones? It is quite commonly said that actions are caused by
beliefs and desires, but if that is so, then what role do intentions play? On the
face of it, actions would appear to be caused by intentions, and an argument for
this view would be that intentions enable us to justify counterfactuals in a way
that is typical of causal phenomena: e.g. if I hadn't intended to vote for Jones at
the last election, I wouldn't have voted for him. But if we say that intentions
cause actions, then what happens to beliefs and desires? Can they still be causes
too? And if so, how does their causal role relate to that of intentions? What is an
action anyhow? I think that the problems of the relation of action and intention is
one of the messiest tangles of puzzles in contemporary philosophy and the aim of
this paper is to unravel at least part of the tangle.

Since my method of achieving that aim will be to locate the relation of
intention and action within a general theory of Intentionality, I need to begin with
a brief account of Intentional states.[1] Intentional states are *directed at* or *about*

---

*I am indebted to Julian Boyd, Hubert Dreyfus, Dagmar Searle, Bruce Vermazen and Steve
White for comments on earlier drafts of this paper.

[1]The account which follows is a very brief summary of the theory of Intentionality advanced
in Searle (1971 & 1979). In order to distinguish the technical sense of "Intentionality" from the
ordinary English intend, intention, etc., I will capitalize the technical occurrences.

objects and states of affairs in the world—states such as beliefs, hopes, fears, desires and intentions. All Intentional states consist of a representative content in a psychological mode. Thus, for example, I can hope that you will leave the room, fear that you will leave the room or believe that you will leave the room, and in each case we have the same representative content, expressed by "that you will leave the room" in a different psychological mode—hope, fear, or belief. The form of such Intentional states we can therefore symbolize as $S(r)$, where the "S" is a variable for psychological mode and "r" for representative content.[2] Furthermore, such Intentional states as these can be said to be *satisfied* or *not satisfied* depending on whether the representative content actually matches or represents anything in reality. Thus if I believe that you will leave the room and you do indeed leave the room, my belief is said to be *true*, and if I fear that you will leave the room and you do leave the room, my fear is not said to be true but to have been *realized*. If I hope that you will leave the room and you do leave the room, my hope is said to have been *fulfilled*. "True" and "false" are used to assess success in representing states of affairs in the *mind-to-world* direction, of fit, and terms like "fulfilled" and "realized" are used to assess success in representing states of affairs in the *world-to-mind* direction of fit. Beliefs have the mind-to-world direction of fit, desires and intentions have the world-to-mind direction of fit. Intuitively the idea of direction of fit is that if the fit doesn't come off, one side or the other is amiss. If my belief is false, my belief is at fault, not the world (hence mind-to-world direction of fit); if my desires are unfulfilled it is the world that disappoints me (hence world-to-mind direction of fit). Not every Intentional state has a direction of fit. If, for example, I am sorry that you left the room, my sorrow has no direction of fit, though it does contain the belief that you left the room and the wish that you had not left the room, and that belief and wish have directions of fit. Indeed if the belief is not satisfied (i.e. true) then my sorrow is misplaced or inappropriate. The state of affairs that makes the Intentional state with a direction of fit satisfied I call its *conditions of satisfaction*. Where the conditions of satisfaction contain actual things (objects, events, etc.) I call these the *Intentional objects* of the Intentional states. But if we are to allow ourselves to speak in the jargon of "Intentional objects," it is important to emphasize that they have no special ontological status; they are just the objects which Intentional states happen to be about. Thus, for example, if I believe that Carter is a Democrat, the conditions of satisfaction of my belief are that Carter is

---

[2]In what follows I will frequently use this form to represent Intentional states. Thus, e.g., the desire reported by "I want to go to the movies" will be represented as

I want (I go to the movies)

and the content of the desire simply by

(I go to the movies).

a Democrat and the Intentional object is Carter, but if I believe that the King of France is bald, my belief has no Intentional object. We might summarize this brief account by saying that the key to understanding Intentionality is representation, and the key to understanding representation is conditions of satisfaction. All Intentional states with a direction of fit represent their conditions of satisfaction (there will be some refinements on these views later).[3]

Now at first sight the relation between intention and action seems to fit nicely into this general account of Intentionality. As we will see later, we are inclined to say: just as my belief is satisfied iff the state of affairs represented by the content of the belief actually obtains, and desire is satisfied iff the state of affairs represented by the content of the desire comes to pass, so my intention is satisfied iff the *action* represented by the content of the intention is actually performed. If I believe that I will vote for Jones, my belief will be *true* iff I vote for Jones, if I desire to vote for Jones my desire will be *fulfilled* iff I vote for Jones, and if I intend to vote for Jones my intention will be *carried out* iff I vote for Jones. Besides these "semantic" parallels, there are also syntactical parallels in the sentences reporting intentional states. Leaving out problems of tense, the deep structure of the three sentences reporting my belief, desire, and intention respectively are:

I believe + I vote for Jones.
I want + I vote for Jones.
I intend + I vote for Jones.

We ought to be impressed by the apparent tightness of fit between the syntax and semantics: each sentence represents an Intentional state; each state represents its conditions of satisfaction and these conditions are represented by the sentence "I vote for Jones", which is exactly the embedded sentence in the sentences representing the Intentional states. The latter two sentences, but not the first, permit an equi NP deletion of the repeated "I" and the insertion of the infinitive in the surface structure, thus:

I want to vote for Jones.
I intend to vote for Jones.

Furthermore, the way in which intention and action fit into this general account of Intentionality enables us to give a simple (but provisional) statement of the relations between intentions and intentional actions: an intentional action is simply the realization of the conditions of satisfaction of an intention. On this view

[3]Also, for purposes of this exposition, I am confining my discussion to the so-called propositional attitudes and ignoring those Intentional states such as love and hate that don't normally have whole propositions as representative contents.

anything that can be the satisfaction of an intention can be an intentional action. Thus, for example, spilling one's beer is not normally the condition of satisfaction of an intention, because people don't normally spill their beer intentionally; but such a thing can be an intentional action, for it can be the condition of satisfaction of an intention.

As it stands this account won't quite work, because it seems to admit too much. For example, if I intend to weigh 160 pounds by Christmas and I succeed, it won't do to say I performed the intentional action of weighing 160 pounds by Christmas nor will it do to say that weighing 160 pounds by Christmas can be an intentional action. What one wants to say rather is that if I fulfilled my intention to weigh 160 pounds by Christmas, I must have performed certain *actions by means of which* I came to weigh 160 pounds; and that needs to be further explained. Furthermore, the account says nothing about general intentions. But worse yet, this account seems to have very little explanatory power: what we want to know is, what is an intention? What is an action? And what is the character of the relation between them that is described by saying that one is the condition of satisfaction of the other? Still, I believe this provisional account is on the right track and I will come back to it later.

One advantage of it, by the way, is that it ties in with our intuition that there is a close connection between intentional actions and what one can tell people to do. Since when one gives orders, one orders people to perform intentional actions, one can only order people to do things that they can do intentionally, and indeed it does not make any clear sense to say "I order you to perform *A* unintentionally."

II

So far we seem to be moving quite smoothly in our efforts to assimilate action and intention to a theory of Intentionality. However, now our troubles begin. There are some interesting asymmetries between the relation of intention to action on the one hand and the relation between the other Intentional states and their conditions of satisfaction on the other. A theory of intention and action ought to be able to explain them.

To begin with, it ought to strike us as odd that we have a special name such a "action" and "act" for the conditions of satisfaction of intentions at all. We have, for example, no special names for the conditions of satisfaction of beliefs and desires. Furthermore, the connection between what is named and the Intentional state which it satisfies is much more intimate in the case of intentions than in such other states as beliefs and desires. We saw that my belief will be satisfied iff the state of affairs I believe to obtain really does obtain, and my desire will be satisfied iff the state of affairs I desire to obtain does obtain, and, similarly, my intention to do an action will be satisfied iff the action I intend to perform actually is performed. But notice that whereas there are lots of states of affairs which are not believed to obtain or desired to obtain, there are no actions without intentions. Even where there is an unintentional action such as Oedipus's marrying his mother, that is only because there is an identical event which is an action he performed intentionally, namely marrying Jocasta. There are many states of affairs without corresponding beliefs and many states of affairs without corresponding desires but there are in general no actions without corresponding intentions.[4] Why should there be this asymmetry?

Furthermore, even though an event represented in the content of my intention occurs, it isn't necessarily the satisfaction of my intentions. As many philosophers have remarked, it has to come about "in the right way," and this again has no analogue for beliefs and desires. Thus, if I believe it's raining and it is raining, my belief is true no matter how it got to be raining. And if my desire is to be rich and I become rich, that desire is satisfied no matter how I got rich.

But a variation on an example of Chisholm (1966, p. 37) will show that this condition does not hold for actions. Suppose Bill intends to kill his uncle, then it might come about that he kills his uncle and yet the conditions of satisfaction of his intention do not obtain. They may not obtain even in some cases where his intention to kill his uncle actually caused him to kill his uncle. Suppose he is out driving thinking about how he is going to kill his uncle, and suppose his intention to kill his uncle makes him so nervous and excited that he accidentally runs over and kills a pedestrian who happens to be his uncle. Now in this case it is true to say that he killed his uncle and true to say that his intention to kill his uncle was (part of) the cause of his killing his uncle, but not true to say that he carried out his intention to kill his uncle or that his intention was satisfied because he didn't kill his uncle *intentionally*.

III

In this section I want to develop an account of the relations between intention and action that will both show how the relations fit into the general theory of Intentionality sketched in Section I and yet account for the paradoxical features of the relation of action and intention discussed in Section II. For the sake of simplicity I will start with very simple actions such as raising one's arm. Later I will

---

[4]On my account such things as snoring, sneezing, sleeping, and many reflex movements are not actions. Whether or not I am right about ordinary usage is less important than whether I can give an account of intention and action that shows such cases to be fundamentally different from those that I count as actions.

consider more complex cases. In this article I will say nothing about purely mental actions, though I think the account can be extended to them as well.

We need first to distinguish those intentions that are formed prior to actions and those that are not. The cases we have considered so far are cases where the agent has the intention to perform the action prior to the performance of the action itself, where, for example, he knows what he is going to do because he already has an intention to do that thing. But not all intentions are like that: suppose you ask me, "When you suddenly hit that man, did you first form the intention to hit him?" My answer might be, "No, I just hit him". But even in such a case I hit him intentionally and my action was done with the intention of hitting him. I want to say about such a case that the intention was *in the action* but that there was no *prior intention*. The characteristic linguistic form of expression of a prior intention is "I will do A" or "I am going to do A". The characteristic form of expression of an intention in action is "I am doing A". We say of a prior intention that the agent acts on his intention, or that he carries out his intention, or that he tries to carry it out. But in general we can't say such things of intentions in action, because the intention in action just is the Intentional content of the action; the action and the intention are inseparable in ways that I will shortly try to explain.

There are at least two ways to make the distinction between an intention in action and a prior intention clearer. The first, as our previous example suggests, is to note that many of the actions one performs, one performs quite spontaneously, without forming, consciously or unconsciously, any prior intention to do those things. For example, suppose I am sitting in a chair reflecting on a philosophical problem and I suddenly get up and start pacing about the room. My getting up and pacing about are clearly intentional actions, but in order to do them I do not need to form an intention to do them prior to doing them. I don't in any sense have to have a plan to get up and pace about. Like many of the things one does, I just do these actions; I just act. A second way to see the same distinction is to note that even in cases where I have a prior intention to do some action there will normally be a whole lot of subsidiary actions which are not represented in the prior intention but which are nonetheless performed intentionally. For example, suppose I have a prior intention to drive to my office. As I am carrying out this prior intention I might perform a series of subsidiary actions for which I need not have formed a prior intention: opening the door, starting the engine, depressing the clutch, etc. When I formed my intention to drive to the office I might not have given these subsidiary acts a thought. Yet such actions are intentional. For such cases I have an intention, but no prior intentions.

All intentional actions have intentions in action but not all intentional actions have prior intentions. I can do something intentionally without having formed a prior intention to do it, and I can have a prior intention to do something and yet not act on that intention. Still, in cases where the agent is acting on his prior intention there must be a close connection between the prior intention and the intention in action, and we will also have to explain this connection.

Prior intentions are selfreferential in the sense that the representative content of the intention refers to the intention of which it is a part. This thesis can be illustrated with the following example. Suppose I intend to raise my arm. The content of my intention can't be that my arm goes up, for my arm can go up without me raising my arm. Nor can it be simply that my intention causes my arm to go up, for we saw in our discussion of the uncle example that a prior intention can cause a state of affairs represented by the intention without that state of affairs being the action that would satisfy the intention. Nor, oddly enough, can it be

(that I perform the action of raising my arm)

because I might perform the action of raising my arm in ways that had nothing to do with this prior intention. I might forget all about this intention and later raise my arm for some other independent reason. The representative content of my intention must be

(that I perform the action of raising my arm
by way of carrying out *this intention*).

Now this formulation raises lots of questions we will need to answer later: what is meant by "action", what is meant by "carrying out," and what is the exact role of the selfreference?

In the meantime, this selfreferential character of intentions will seem less mysterious if we compare it with a similar phenomenon in the realm of speech acts (and incidentally it is always a good idea when you get stuck in the theory of Intentionality to go back to speech acts, because the phenomena of speech acts are so much more accessible). Suppose I order you to leave the room. And suppose you respond by saying "I am going to leave the room, but not because you ordered me to, I was just about to leave the room anyhow. But I would not have left the room because you ordered me to." If you then leave the room, have you *obeyed my order*? Well, you certainly didn't *disobey* the order, but there is a sense in which you did not obey it either, because the order did not function as a reason for what you did. We would not, for example, on the basis of a series of such cases describe you as an "obedient" person. But what this illustrates is that the content of my order is not simply that you leave the room, but that you leave the room by way of obeying *this order*; that is, the logical form of the order is not simply

I order you (that you leave the room)

but rather it is selfreferential in the form

I order you (that you leave the room by way of obeying this order).[5]

In order to examine intentions in action I need to say a little more about different forms of Intentionality. I said before that such Intentional states as beliefs, fears, desires, etc. are representations of their conditions of satisfaction; but not all forms of Intentionality really sit comfortably with this account, and one form which does not is perception. Suppose I am seated in front of a table and I see the table. In so doing I will have a visual experience of the table. But now the visual experience is not identical with the table, for I don't see the visual experience. I *see* the table, and I *have* the visual experience when I see the table. "But," someone might say in the style of classical epistemology, "suppose that the experience is an hallucination and there is nothing there. What do you see then?" And the answer is: when I have the visual experience but there is no table there, I *see* nothing. I have the visual experience and thus it seems to me as if I were seeing the table, but I do not in fact see anything. But now notice, and this is the crucial point, *the visual experience has Intentionality*, and the argument for this is that even when I am having an hallucination, I know what the hallucination is an hallucination of: that is, I know what must be the case in order that this experience not be an hallucination, and to say that is just to say that in having the visual experience I know its conditions of satisfaction. The conditions of satisfaction are that there should be a table there, and additionally that it should have such and such properties and should cause my visual experience. Part of the difference between the Intentionality of a state like belief and the Intentionality of visual experience is that the visual experience is not a *representation* of the object, but one might say, a *presentation* of the object. When I see an object I directly perceive it and do not represent it to myself.

So, the truth conditions of a sentence of the form "*x* saw a table" involve two components (besides *x*), a visual experience and a table; but the two are not independent, for the visual experience is a presentation *of* the table. And that is another way of saying that the Intentionality of the visual experience is such that its conditions of satisfaction require that there be a table there and that the table play a certain sort of causal role in the production of the visual experience. Subtract the fact that there is a table there from the event of seeing the table and what is left is a visual experience, but the visual experience is not a neutral "sense datum," it has Intentionality, and its Intentionality is presentational rather than representational. Just to have a clear distinction in terminology I will use "visual perception" as the name of the complex event that involves both the Intentional component and its conditions of satisfaction, and I will use "visual experience" as the name of the Intentional component.

[5]The selfreference does not lead to an infinite regress. When I order you to do *A*, I am indeed creating a reason for your doing *A* such that the order will be obeyed iff you do *A* for that reason, i.e. because I ordered you to do it; but I do not in addition create a reason for it to be a reason, nor do I give a second-level order to you to obey my first-level order.

Now let us apply all this to Wittgenstein's (1953) question: If I raise my arm, what is left over if I subtract the fact that my arm went up? The question seems to me exactly analogous to the question: If I see the table what is left over if I subtract the table? And in each case the answer is that a certain form of presentational Intentionality is left over, but the direction of fit and the direction of causation is different in the two cases. When I raise my arm I have a certain experience, and like my visual experience of the table, this arm-raising experience has a certain form of Intentionality, it has conditions of satisfaction. For if I have this experience and my arm doesn't go up, the Intentional content of the experience is not satisfied. Furthermore, even if my arm goes up, but goes up without this experience, I didn't raise my arm, it just went up. That is, just as the case of seeing the table involves two related components, an Intentional component (the visual experience) and the Intentional "object" or conditions of satisfaction of that component (the table), so the act of raising my arm involves two components, an Intentional component (the experience of acting) and the Intentional "object" or conditions of satisfaction of that component (the movement of my arm). As far as Intentionality is concerned the differences between the visual experience and the experience of acting are in the direction of fit and in the direction of causation: the visual experience stands to the table in the mind-to-world direction of fit. If the table isn't there, we say that I was mistaken, or was having an hallucination, or some such. And the direction of causation is from the object to the visual experience. If the Intentional component is satisfied it must be caused by the object. But in the case of the experience of acting, the Intentional component has the world-to-mind direction of fit. If I have this experience but the event doesn't occur we say such things as that I *failed* to raise my arm, or that I *tried* to raise my arm but did not succeed. And the direction of causation is from the experience of acting to the event. Where the Intentional content is satisfied, that is, where I actually succeed in raising my arm, the experience of acting causes the arm to go up. If it didn't cause the arm to go up, but something else did, I didn't raise my arm; it just went up for some other reason. And just as the visual experience is not a representation of its conditions of satisfaction but a presentation of those conditions, so I want to say, the experience of acting is a presentation of its conditions of satisfaction. On this account, action, like perception, is a causal and Intentional transaction between mind and the world.

Now, just as we don't have a name for that which gives us the Intentional content of our visual perception but have to invent a term of art, "the visual experience," so there is no term for that which gives us the Intentional content of our intentional action, but have to invent a term of art, "the experience of acting." But the term would mislead if it gave the impression that I thought that such things were passive experiences or sensations that simply afflict one, or that they were like what some philosophers have called volitions or acts of willing or anything of that sort. They are not acts at all, for we no more *perform* our experience of acting than we *see* our visual experiences. Nor am I claiming that there is any special feeling that belongs to all intentional actions. There are (at least) two ways to come to understand what I am driving at. Suppose you were in a situation where you couldn't perceive your arm, and suppose someone gave you the order to raise your arm and you carried out that order. Now if in such a case we subtract the fact that your arm goes up, what we have left over is what I am calling the experience of acting. What is left over will normally involve certain feelings and bodily sensations, but for our purposes the phenomenal properties of these sensations and feelings are not what matters, rather what matters are the logical properties of the experience, and the logical properties are that the experience in question has certain conditions of satisfaction and those conditions of satisfaction are internal to the experience in the sense that it couldn't be that experience if it didn't have those conditions of satisfaction and there is no way to have that experience without knowing that it has those conditions of satisfaction.

And this last point leads to the second way to try to clarify this notion. It is generally the case, as several philosophers[6] have remarked, that at any point in a man's waking life he is doing something; there is an answer to the question, what is he doing now? But also, and we ought to allow ourselves to be struck by this fact, at any point in a man's conscious life *he knows what he is doing*. A man knows without observation the answer to the question, what are you doing now? He may of course make all sorts of mistakes and blunders: he may think he is stirring pancake batter when in fact he is grinding peanuts, but even in such a case he knows what he is trying to do. Now the knowledge of what one is doing in this sense, in the sense in which such knowledge does not guarantee that one knows that one is succeeding, and does not depend on any observations that one makes of oneself, characteristically derives from one's awareness[7] of the conditions of satisfaction of the experience of acting. And, again, the parallel with perception holds. Just as at any point in a man's conscious life he knows the answer to the question, ''What are you doing now?'' so he knows the answer to the question, ''What do you see now?'' In both cases the knowledge in question is simply an awareness of the conditions of satisfaction of a certain sort of presentation.

Anyone who is still in doubt about the existence of the sort of phenomena I am describing as the experience of acting would do well to ponder the distinction

[6]See, for example, Hampshire, 1959.

[7]Again my use of phrases like ''knowledge of the conditions of satisfaction'' or ''awareness of the conditions of satisfaction'' will be misleading if we do not prevent two sorts of misunderstanding at the outset. First, I do not mean that we are always thinking about or conscious of the conditions of satisfaction. If you say to me ''What exactly are you doing now?'' I may say ''I am passing the green Chevrolet on the right.'' But that needn't imply that I was thinking about or conscious of passing the green Chevrolet before you ask me the question. Secondly, knowledge or awareness of the conditions of satisfaction are not second-order Intentional states. If they were, we would get an infinite regress.

between intentional actions and the sorts of cases described by Dr. W. Penfield (1975):

> When I have caused a conscious patient to move his hand by applying an electrode to the motor context of one hemisphere I have often asked him about it. Invariably his response was: "I didn't do that. You did." When I caused him to vocalize, he said, "I didn't make that sound. You pulled it out of me." (p. 76)

There is clearly a difference between the case where the patient moves his hand in an intentional action and the case where the patient's hand moves as a result of Penfield's electrical stimulation of his brain. But since the physical movements in the two cases are identical, what exactly is the difference? And how does the patient know in one case that he is moving his hand and in the other that he is not doing anything ("I didn't do that. You did"). And as an answer to these questions I am suggesting that first there is an obvious phenomenal difference between the case where one moves one's hand and the case where one observes it move independently of one's intentions—the two cases just feel different to the patient—and secondly that this phenomenal difference carries with it a logical difference in the sense that the experience of moving one's hand has certain conditions of satisfaction. Such concepts as "trying," "succeeding," and "failing" apply to it in ways that they do not apply to the experiences the patient has when he simply observes his hand moving. Now this experience with its phenomenal and logical properties I am calling the experience of acting. And I am not claiming that there is a characteristic experience common to every intentional action, but rather that for every intentional action there is the experience of performing that action, and that experience has an Intentional content.

The parallel between the Intentionality of visual perception and the Intentionality of Intentional action can be made explicit as in Table 1.

TABLE 1

	Visual perception	Intentional action
Intentional component	visual experience	experience of acting
Conditions of satisfaction of the Intentional component	that there be objects, states of affairs, etc. and that these have certain features and certain causal relations to the visual experience	that there be certain bodily movements, states, etc., of the agent, and that these have certain causal relations to the experience of acting
Direction of fit	mind-to-world	world-to-mind
Direction of causation	world-to-mind (i.e. the object causes the experience)	mind-to-world (i.e. the experience causes the movements, etc.)
Corresponding features of the world	objects and states of affairs	movements, and states involving the agent

So far I have tried to establish three claims; first, that there is a distinction between prior intentions and intentions in action; secondly, that prior intentions are selfreferential; and thirdly, that the action, for example, of raising one's arm, contains two components—the experience of acting, which has a form of Intentionality that is both presentational and causal, and the event of one's arm going up. Next I want to put these conclusions into a general account of the relations of prior intentions, intentions in action, and actions.

The Intentional content of the intention in action and the experience of acting are identical. Indeed as far as Intentionality is concerned the experience of acting just is the intention in action. The only difference between them is that the experience may have certain phenomenal properties that are not essential to the intention. In exactly the same way the visual experience has the same Intentionality as its presentational content but the experience has certain phenomenal properties that are not essential to that Intentionality (as the Weiskrantz (1977) experiments indicate).[8]

Our problem now is to lay bare the relations between the following four elements: the prior intention, the intention in action (the experience of acting), the bodily movement, and the action. The method is to take a simple example and make fully explicit the Intentional contents of the two intentions. Now why is that the method? Because our aim is to explain the relations between intentions and actions; and since an action is, in some sense at least, the condition of satisfaction of the intention to perform it, any attempt to clarify these relations must make completely explicit how the Intentional content of the intentions represents (or presents) the action (or the movement) as their conditions of satisfaction. And this method differs somewhat from the standard methods of the philosophy of action because we don't stand way back away from the action and see which *descriptions* we can make of it, we have to get right up close to it and see what these descriptions are actually describing. The other method incidentally produces such true but superficial results as that an action "can be intentional under one description, but not intentional under another"—one might as well say that a fire engine can be red under one description but not red under another. What one wants to know is: What facts exactly are these various descriptions describing? What fact about the action makes it "intentional under one description" and what fact about it makes it "not intentional under another?"

Suppose I recently had a prior intention to raise my arm and suppose, acting on that intention, I now raise my arm. How does it work? The representative content of the prior intention can be expressed as follows:

(I perform the action of raising my arm
by way of carrying out this intention.)

[8]Briefly, Weiskrantz's (1977) studies concern patients who have brain lesions that produce "blind sight:" they are able to report events that occur in their visual fields but they report no visual experience of these events. They thus have the Intentionality of the visual experience without the accompanying phenomenal properties.

TABLE 2

A comparison of the forms of Intentionality involved in seeing a flower and remembering seeing a flower on the one hand, and (prior) intending to raise one's arm and raising one's arm on the other.

	Visual perception	Memory	Intentional action	Prior intention
How reported	I see the flower	I remember seeing the flower	I am raising my arm	I intend to raise my arm
Nature of the Intentional component	visual experience	memory	intention in action (=experience of acting)	prior intention
Presentation or representation	presentation	representation	presentation	representation
Conditions of satisfaction of the Intentional component	That there be a flower and the flower causes *this visual experience*	that there be an event of seeing the flower consisting of two components, the *flower* and the *visual experience* and the event causes *this memory*	that there be an event of my arm raising and *this intention in action* causes that event	that there be an *action* of raising my arm, consisting of two components, the event of the arm raising and the intention in action, and *this prior intention* causes the action
Direction of fit	mind-to-world	mind-to-world	world-to-mind	world-to-mind
Direction of causation	world-to-mind	world-to-mind	mind-to-world	mind-to-world
Nature of the self-reference of the Intentional component	as part of the conditions of satisfaction of the visual experience, it must be caused by the rest of its own conditions of satisfaction (i.e., by its own Intentional object)	as part of the conditions of satisfaction of the memory, it must be caused by the rest of its own conditions of satisfaction (i.e., by its own Intentional object)	as part of the conditions of satisfaction of the intention in action it must cause the rest of its own conditions of satisfaction (i.e., its own Intentional object)	as part of the conditions of satisfaction of the prior intention, it must cause the rest of its own condition and satisfaction (i.e., its own Intentional object)
Corresponding objects & events in the world (Intentional objects)	flower	flower / event of seeing the flower	movement of the arm	movement of the arm / action of raising the arm

The prior intention thus makes reference to the whole action as a unit, not just the movement, and it is selfreferential. But the action as we have seen contains two components, the experience of acting and the movement; where the Intentional content of the experience of acting and the intention in action are identical. The next step then is to specify the Intentional content of the intention in action and show the relation of its Intentional content to that of the prior intention. The presentational content of the intention in action is:

(My arm goes up as a result of this intention in action.)

Now at first sight the contents of the prior intention and the intention in action look quite different, because the prior intention represents the whole action in its conditions of satisfaction, but the intention in action presents, but does not *re*present, the physical movement and not the whole action as its conditions of satisfaction. In the former case the whole action is the "Intentional object" in the latter case the movement is the "Intentional object." The intention in action is selfreferential in the sense that its Intentional content determines that it is satisfied only if the event that is its Intentional object is caused by it. Another difference is that in any real life situation the intention in action will be much more determinate than the prior intention, it will include not only that my arm goes up but that it goes up in a certain way and at a certain speed, etc.[9]

Well, if the content of the prior intention and the Intention in action are so different, how do they ever—so to speak—get together? In fact the relationship is quite simple, as we can see by unpacking the content of the prior intention and making explicit the nature of the selfreference of the prior intention. Since the whole action is represented as a unit by the prior intention and since the action consists of two components, the experience of acting and the physical movement, in order to make the content of the prior intention fully explicit, we can represent each component separately. Furthermore, the nature of the selfreference of the prior intention is (like the selfreference of the intention in action)

---

[9]The relative indeterminacy of prior intentions is most obvious in the case of complex actions. In our earlier examples of carrying out my intention to drive to my office, there will be a large number of subsidiary acts that are not represented by the prior intention but are presented by the intentions in action: I intentionally start the engine, shift gears, pass slow-moving vans, stop at red lights, swerve to avoid cyclists, change lanes—and so on with dozens of subsidiary acts that are performed intentionally but need not have been represented by my prior intention. This difference has also been a source of confusion in philosophy. Several philosophers have remarked that not everything I do intentionally is something I have an intention to do. For example, the particular movements of my hand when I brush my teeth are done intentionally, even though I had no intention to do them. But this view is a mistake that derives from a failure to see the difference between prior intentions and intentions in action. I may have had no prior intention to make just these hand movements but I had an intention in action to make them.

causal.[10] The prior intention causes the intention in action which causes the movement. By transitivity of causation we can say that the prior intention causes both the intention in action and the movement, and since this combination is simply the action, we can say that the prior intention causes the action. The way to see this is to see that if we break the causal connection between the prior intention and the intention in action we no longer have an action which is a case of carrying out that intention, even though the action may have been performed intentionally. Suppose I intend to raise my arm in thirty seconds, and suppose I forget all about that intention in such a way that it plays no role, conscious or unconscious, in my subsequent behavior. Suppose in thirty seconds I raise my arm "just for the hell of it." In such a case I had a prior intention to raise my arm and I did raise my arm but since the prior intention played no causal role in my raising my arm I didn't carry out that intention. This also enables us to see what was wrong in the Chisholm-style counterexample I presented earlier. Bill had the prior intention to kill his uncle and his intention caused him to kill his uncle but his prior intention didn't cause an intention in action that presented the killing of his uncle as Intentional content, it just presented his driving his car or some such. (More about this later.) Since, as we have seen, the form of selfreference of the prior intention is causal and since the representation of the action can be split into two components, the Intentional content of the prior intention can now be expressed as follows:

(I have an intention in action which is a presentation of my arm going up, which causes my arm to go up, and which is caused by this prior intention).

And thus the prior intention causes the intention in action. By transitivity of causation, the prior intention represents and causes the entire action, but the intention in action presents and causes the bodily movement.

I think these points can be made clearer by pursuing our analogy with perception a bit farther. Roughly speaking, the prior intention to raise my arm is to the action of raising my arm as the memory of seeing the flower is to seeing the flower; or, rather, the formal relations between the memory, the visual experience of the flower, and the flower are the mirror images of the formal relations between the prior intention, the intention in action, and the bodily movement. The seeing consists of two components, the visual experience and the flower, where the flower causes the visual experience and the visual experience has the flower as Intentional object. The visual experience is *of* the flower, and it is selfreferential in the sense that unless the flower causes this experience the conditions of satisfaction do not obtain; i.e. I do not actually see the flower. The

---

[10]It is perhaps worth emphasizing that this view does not imply determinism. When one acts on one's desires or carries out one's prior intention, the desire and intention function causally, but it is not necessarily the case that one could not have done otherwise, that one simply could not help oneself.

memory of seeing the flower represents both the visual experience and the flower, and is selfreferential in the sense that unless the memory was caused by the visual experience which in turn was caused by the flower, I didn't really remember seeing the flower. Now similarly the action consists of two components, the experience of acting and the movement as Intentional object. The experience of acting is *of* the movement of my arm, and it is selfreferential in the sense that unless the movement is caused by this experience the conditions of satisfaction do not obtain; i.e. I do not actually raise my arm. The prior intention to raise my arm represents both the experience of acting and the movement, and is selfreferential in the sense that unless this intention causes the experience of acting which in turn causes the movement, I don't really carry out my prior intention. These relations can be made explicit by expanding our earlier table into Table 2.

A few things about Table 2 are worth special mention. First, neither the memory nor the prior intention is essential to the visual perception or the intentional action respectively. I can see a lot of things that I have no memory of seeing and I can perform a lot of intentional actions without any prior intention to perform those actions. Secondly, the asymmetry of the direction of fit and the direction of causation is too neat to be accidental. Put crudely the intuitive explanation is this: when I try to make the world be the way I want it to be, I succeed if the world comes to be the way I want it to *be* (world-to-mind direction of fit), but only because I *make* it be that way (mind-to-world direction of causation). Analogously, if I see the world the way it really *is* (mind-to-world direction of fit), it is only because the way the world is *makes* me see it that way (world-to-mind direction of causation). Thirdly, for the sake of simplicity I have left out of Table 2 the fact that the conditions of satisfaction of the Intentional components will contain various details about what the flower looks like and how the raising of the arm is performed. I have not tried to include everything. Fourthly, the formal structure of the table is not meant to suggest that perception and action function independently of each other. For most complex actions, such as driving a car or eating a meal, I have to be able to perceive what I am doing in order to do it; and similarly there is an intentional element in most complex perceptions, as when I am looking at a painting or feeling the texture of a rug. Fifthly, because of the transitivity of causation, I have allowed myself to oscillate between saying the memory of seeing the flower is caused by the event of seeing the flower and the memory of seeing the flower is caused by the visual experience which is in turn caused by the flower. Similarly I oscillate between saying the prior intention causes the action and the prior intention causes the intention in action which causes the movement. Since in each case the complex event contains a component which is both Intentional and causal, and since in each case the Intentional component stands in certain causal relations to another Intentional state which represents the whole complex event, it doesn't seem to me to matter which of the two ways of speaking we adopt.

Before showing how this account solves the problems of Section II, I want to tie up a few loose ends.

If intentions really cause actions in the way described, then why is it that we can't normally explain an action by stating its intention? If I am asked, "Why did he raise his arm?" it sounds odd to say: "Because he intended to raise his arm." The reason it sounds odd is because by identifying the action as "raising his arm" we have already identified it in terms of the intention in action. We already reveal an implicit knowledge that the cause of the arm going up was the Intentional component in the action of raising it. But notice it doesn't sound at all odd to specify the intention in action as the cause of *the movement*: why did his arm go up? He raised it. Nor does it sound odd to give some *further* intention as the cause of the action. Why did he raise his arm? He was voting / waving goodbye / reaching for the book / exercising / trying to touch the ceiling. This is what people are driving at when they say that we can often explain an action by redescribing it. But if we redescribe it truly there must be some facts we are redescribing which were left out of our first description, and these facts are that the action has an Intentional component which was left out of the first description and which causes the other component, e.g. his prior intention to vote by raising his arm causes his intention in action of raising his arm which causes his arm to go up. Remember, on this account all actions consist of an Intentional component and a "physical" (or other sort of) Intentional object component. We can always explain this non-Intentional component by the Intentional component, and the Intentional component can be as complex as you like. Why is that man wriggling around like that? He's sharpening an axe. But to say he's sharpening an axe is to say his action has at least two components, an axe-sharpening intention in action and the series of movements caused by that intention. But we can't answer the question, "Why is he sharpening an axe?" by identifying that intention, because we have already identified the axe-sharpening intention when we asked the question. But we can say, e.g., he's preparing to chop down a tree.

What do people mean when they say that an action can be "intentional under one description but not intentional under another?" The action consists of two components, an Intentional component and its Intentional object, the intention in action is the Intentional component and it presents the Intentional object as its conditions of satisfaction. But the complex event which constitutes the action will also have all sorts of other features not presented as a part of the Intentional content of the intention in action. Oedipus intended to marry Jocasta but when he married Jocasta he was marrying his mother. "Marrying his mother" was not part of the Intentional content of the intention in action, but it happened anyhow. The action was intentional under the description "marrying Jacosta," it was not intentional under the description "marrying his mother." But all that means is that the total action had elements which were parts of the conditions of satisfaction of the intention in action and other elements which were not. It is misleading to state these facts about actions in terms of descriptions of actions because it suggests that what matters is not the action but the way we describe the action, whereas, according to my account, what matters are the facts that the descriptions describe.

This distinction will be clearer if we consider intentional actions performed by animals, and it is no more puzzling, incidentally, to ascribe intentional actions to animals than it is to ascribe visual perceptions to them. Suppose my dog is running around the garden chasing a ball; he is performing the intentional action of chasing the ball and the unintentional action of tearing up the Lobelias, but this has nothing to do with anybody's descriptions. The dog certainly can't describe himself, and the facts would remain the same whether or not any human being ever did or could describe them. The sense in which one and the same event or sequence of events can be both an intentional action and an unintentional action has no intrinsic connection with linguistic representation but rather with Intentional presentation. Some aspects of the event may be conditions of satisfaction of the Intentional content, some other aspects may not; and under the first set of aspects the action is intentional, under the second set, not; even though there need be nothing linguistic about the way an Intentional content presents its conditions of satisfaction.

A question I don't know the answer to is, how do we distinguish between those features of the complex event which are unintentional actions and those features which are so far from the intention that they are not actions at all? When Oedipus married his mother he moved a lot of molecules, caused some neurophysiological stuff in his brain, and altered his spatial relationship to the North Pole. These are all things he did unintentionally and none of them are actions of his. Yet I feel inclined to say that marrying his mother, though it was something he did unintentionally, was still an action, an unintentional action. Perhaps the reason for this difference in our (my) intuitions is that the description "marrying his mother" is closer to the content "marrying Jocasta" than is "moving a lot of molecules." I think that there must be a principle in operation here, but I do not know what it is.

We have so far been talking mostly about very simple cases such as raising one's arm and I will now very briefly sketch how this account could be extended to account for complex intentions and the relations between complex intentions, the accordion effect (see Feinberg, 1970, p. 134) and basic actions (see Danto, 1968, pp. 43–58).

Consider Gavrilo Princip and his murder of the Archduke in Sarajevo. Of Princip we say that he:

    pulled the trigger
    fired the gun
    shot the Archduke
    killed the Archduke
    struck a blow against Austria
    avenged Serbia

Furthermore, for each member of this list we can say that it is the action by means of which the next member is achieved. Thus he fired the gun by means of pulling the trigger, he shot the Archduke by means of firing the gun, etc. Now to the extent that each of these descriptions expresses the content of an intention in action we can say that under each description the action is intentional. Furthermore, the representation of the by-means-of relation forms a part of the content of the complex intention. Thus he intended to strike a blow against Austria by means of killing the Archduke, which action he intended to perform by means of shooting the Archduke, which he intended to perform by means of firing the gun, etc. Starting in the middle we can extend the accordion up or down by earlier or later members of the sequence of intentions. But notice that we can't go on indefinitely. As far as the causal story is concerned there are lots of things that happened up above the top, down below the bottom, and off to the side which are not part of the accordion. Thus we could add to the list as follows:

He produced neuron firings in his brain
   contracted certain muscles in his arm and hand

---

   pulled the trigger
   fired the gun
   shot the Archduke   moved a lot of air molecules
   killed the Archduke
   struck a blow against Austria
   avenged Serbia

---

   ruined Lord Grey's summer season
   convinced the Emperor Franz Josef that God was punishing the family
   angered Wilhelm II
   started the first World War

But none of these things above, below or to the side are Intentional actions of Princip, and I am inclined to say none of them are actions of his at all. They are just unintended things that happened as a result of his actions. As far as *intentional* action is concerned the boundaries of the accordion are the boundaries of the complex intention; and indeed we have the accordion effect for Intentional actions because we have complex intentions that represent the "by means of" relation, both of causal and of other sorts. But the complex intention does not quite set the boundaries of the *action*, because of the possibility of unintentional actions; and, as I said earlier, I don't know how to distinguish those unintended results, consequences, upshots, and effects of our intentional actions which are not actions, not even unintentional actions, from those which are unintentional actions.

If we are going to have any use for the concept of a basic action at all, we might say that the top member of any such accordion is a basic action, and we might indeed define a basic action as follows: A is a basic action for an agent S iff S can do A and S can intend to do A without intending to do any other action by means of which he intends to do *A*. (For this formulation I am indebted to the work of Charles Taylor, though I don't know if he would accept it.) Notice that this definition would make an action basic only relative to an agent and his skills; what is basic for one agent might not be basic for another. But that may be a useful way to describe the facts: for a good skier making a left turn can be a basic action. He just intends to do it and he does it. For a beginner to make a left turn he must put the weight on the downhill ski while edging it into the slope, stem the uphill ski, then shift the weight from left to right ski, etc., all of which are reports of the content of his intentions in action. For two agents the physical movements might be indistinguishable even though one was performing a—for him—basic action and the other was performing the same action by means of performing a basic action. Furthermore, this definition would have the consequence that for any one agent there may be no sharp dividing line between his basic and nonbasic actions. But, again, that may be the right way to describe the facts.

IV

In this section I will try to show how the account of the relations of intention and action that I have presented will explain the paradoxical asymmetries of Section II.

First, the reason there is a more intimate connection between actions and intentions than there is between, say, beliefs and states of affairs is that actions contain intentions in action as one of their components. An action is a composite entity of which one component is an intention in action. If the composite entity also contains elements which constitute the conditions of satisfaction of the Intentional component in the way described earlier, the agent succeeded in the performance of an intentional action. If not, he only tried but failed. Thus to take our overworked example: the action of my raising my arm consists of two components, the intention in action and the movement of the arm. Take away the first and you don't have an action—only a movement—take away the second and you don't have success, but only a failed effort.

The sense in which we can say that an intentional action is caused by an intention or simply is the condition of satisfaction of an intention can now be made more precise. The condition of satisfaction of a prior intention really is an action, but not all actions are performed as the result of prior intentions. There can be actions without corresponding prior intentions, e.g. when I just haul off and hit somebody without any prior intention to hit him. But there can't be any actions, not even unintentional actions without intentions in action. Actions thus necessarily contain intentions in action, but are not necessarily caused by prior intentions. But the Intentional content of the intention in action is not that it should cause the action, but rather than it should cause the movement (or state) of the agent which is its condition of satisfaction, and the two together, intention in action and movement constitute the action. So it wasn't quite right to say that an intentional action just is the condition of satisfaction of an intention; it was wrong for two reasons: actions don't require prior intentions and though they do require intentions in action, the condition of satisfaction of the intention in action is just the movement or state of the agent, not the action. What it is correct to say, I believe, is that an action is any composite event or state that contains the occurrence of an intention in action. If that intention in action causes its conditions of satisfaction the event or state is a successfully performed intentional action; if not, it is unsuccessful. An unintentional action is an intentional action which has aspects which were not intended in it, i.e. were not presented as conditions of satisfaction of the intention in action. However, lots of things I do unintentionally, e.g. sneezing, are not actions at all, for though they are things I cause, they contain no intentions in action.

We now have a very simple explanation of the Chisholm-style counterexamples to the view that actions which are caused by intentions are intentional actions. In the uncle example the prior intention caused the killing of the uncle, but the killing of the uncle was unintentional. Why? In our analysis we saw there are three stages: the prior intention, the intention in action, and the physical event. The prior intention causes the event by way of causing the intention in action, which causes and presents the event as its conditions of satisfaction. But in the uncle example this middle stage was left out. We did not have the death of the uncle as the condition of satisfaction of any intention in action, and that is why he was killed unintentionally.

There are several such puzzling examples in the philosophical literature on this subject, and I believe the approach I am advocating will account for all those I have seen, because they all rest on a failure to understand intentions in action. Consider the following from Davidson (1973), which he says illustrates the sources of his

> despair of spelling out . . . the way in which attitudes must cause action if they are to rationalize the action . . . A climber might want to rid himself of the weight and danger of holding another man on a rope, and he might know that by loosening his hold on the rope he could rid himself of the weight and danger. This belief and want might so unnerve him as to cause him to loosen his hold, and yet it might be the case that he never *chose* to loosen his hold, nor did he do it intentionally. (pp. 153–154) [Emphasis in the original]

I believe the way to dispel the despair is to recognize the role of the intention in action and to make fully explicit the Intentional contents of the relevant Intentional states. The reason the climber's loosening of his hold is unintentional in the case as described is that he has no intention in action of loosening his hold. There is no moment at which he could say "I am now loosening my hold" as a way of articulating the content of his intention in action i.e. as a way of making explicit the conditions of satisfaction of his intention, even though he might say just that as a way of describing what was happening to him. Even if on the basis of his belief and desire he formed a secondary desire to loosen his hold and this desire caused him to loosen his hold, it is still not an intentional action if he does not have an intention in action to loosen his hold. In an intentional action, on the other hand, the standard way the sequence of Intentional states would work is as follows:

> I want (I rid myself of weight and danger)
> I believe (the best way to rid myself of weight
> and danger is to loosen my hold).

And by practical reason this leads to a secondary desire:

> I want (I loosen my hold).

And this leads, either with or without a prior intention, to an intention in action: the climber says to himself "Now!" And the content of his intention in action is:

> I am now loosening my hold.

That is:

> This intention in action causes my hand
> to loosen its hold on the rope.

The whole structure is both Intentional and causal; the sequence of Intentional states causes the bodily movement. There are various problems about how practical reason works, but I must say I do not see any deep mystery here, much less cause for despair in analyzing how Intentionality explains intentional actions.

Another (equally homicidal) example derives from Dan Bennett (see Davidson, 1973, pp. 152–153). A man may try to kill someone by shooting at him. Suppose he misses him, but the shot stampedes a heard of wild pigs which tramples the intended victim to death. In this case the man's intention in action presents the death of the victim as part of the conditions of satisfaction and the victim dies as a result, but all the same we are reluctant to say that it was an intentional killing. And the reason is obvious. The intention in action had a whole lot of other details about how the killing was to be accomplished as parts of its conditions of satisfaction, and these conditions were not satisfied. Some people have thought that the problem in all these cases has to do with the oddity of the causal sequences, but the causal sequence only matters if it is part of the Intentional content of the intention in action. To see this we can vary the above example as follows: the killer's assistant, knowing about the pigs in advance, tells the killer, "Shoot your gun in that direction and you will kill him." The killer does as instructed with the death of the victim as the result; and in this case the killing is intentional, even though the events are as causally bizarre as in Bennett's original example.

Could we get similar counterexamples where something gets between the intention in action and the event so that, though we could say the intention in action caused the physical event, the action was not intentional? The only plausible cases I can think of are cases where some other intention in action intervenes to bring about the event. Thus, suppose that unknown to me my arm is rigged up so that whenever I try to raise it, somebody else causes it to go up, then the action is his, not mine, even though I had the intention in action of raising my arm and in some sense that intention caused my arm to go up. (The reader will recognize this as essentially the Occasionalist solution to the mind–body problem. God does all of our actions for us.)

But this class of potential counterexamples is eliminated in these simple cases by construing relation of the intention in action to its conditions of satisfaction as precluding intervention by other agents or other Intentional states. And that this is the right way to contrue intentions in action is at least indicated by the fact that for such simple cases as raising my arm, when my intentions in action make explicit reference to the intentions of other agents, the actions then become the actions of those agents. Thus suppose I know how my arm is rigged up and I want it to go up. My intention in action then is *getting the other agent to raise it*, not *raising it*. *My* action is getting him to raise it, *his* action is raising it.

But as long as there is no intervening Intentionality it doesn't matter how weird the physical apparatus might be. Even if unknown to me my arm is rigged up to a whole lot of electrical wires that go through Moscow and return via San Diego and when I try to raise my arm it activates this whole apparatus so that my arm goes up, all the same, I raise my arm. For some complex acts one can perform the act by getting others to perform it. We say 'Louis XIV built Versailles' but the actual construction was not done by him.

However, this account is still incomplete because there is a class of possible counterexamples I have not yet discussed, cases where the prior intention causes something else which causes the intention in action. Suppose, for example, Bill's intention to kill his uncle causes him to have a stomach ache and his stomach ache makes him so angry that he forgets all about his original intention but in his rage he kills the first man he sees whom he recognizes as his uncle. I believe that such possible counterexamples can also be eliminated, but to do so requires an analysis of Intentional causation that goes beyond the scope of this article.

A final word about desires and beliefs. Nothing in this account is inconsistent with the view that actions are caused by desires, for desires may lead to the formation of prior intentions, often through deliberation, or they may directly cause intentions in action, e.g. I am thirsty so I take a drink of water. But it is at least misleading to say that actions are caused by both desires and beliefs, for beliefs have the wrong direction of fit and they lack the logical connection between cause and effect necessary for the Intentional causation of actions. When beliefs function in the causal account of actions it is characteristically as part of the cause of secondary desires. Thus suppose I want to go to Paris and I believe the only way I can go to Paris is by first buying a plane ticket. Now the way this conjunction of belief and desire functions as the cause of my buying a plane ticket is by first causing a secondary desire to buy a plane ticket, through "practical reason." And the way to see this is to note that if I don't have any desire to buy the plane ticket I won't perform the intentional action of buying it, regardless of my beliefs. In the direct way that desires cause actions, beliefs don't cause actions, though in conjunction with primary desires they do cause secondary desires. Nor will it do to say that when my desire causes me to raise my arm it is only because I also have the belief that *this* is raising my arm, for the fact that *this* satisfies the desire must already be determined by the desire, since the desire represents its conditions of satisfaction.

REFERENCES

Chisholm, R. M. Freedom and action. In K. Lehrer (Ed.) *Freedom and determinism*. New York: Random House, 1966.
Danto, A. Basic actions. In A. R. White (Ed.) *The philosophy of action*. London: Oxford University Press, 1968.
Davidson, D. Freedom to act. In T. Honderich (Ed.) *Essays on freedom of action*. London: Routledge & Kegan Paul, 1973.
Feinberg, J. *Doing and deserving*. Princeton, N.J.: Princeton University Press, 1970.
Hampshire, S. *Thought and action*. London: Chatto & Windus, 1959.
Penfield, W. *The mystery of mind*. Princeton, N.J.: Princeton University Press, 1975.
Searle, J. R. Intentionality and the use of language. In A. Margalit (Ed.) *Meaning and use*. Dordrecht, Holland: Reidel, 1971.
Searle, J. R. What is an intentional state? *Mind,* 1978, *88*, 74–92.
Weiskrantz, L. Trying to bridge some neurological gaps between monkey and man. *British Journal of Psychology*, 1977, *68*, 431–445.
Wittgenstein, L. *Philosophical investigations*. New York: Macmillan, 1953.

10
What Does It Mean
to Understand Language?

TERRY WINOGRAD

Stanford University

INTRODUCTION

In its earliest drafts, this paper was a structured argument, presenting a comprehensive view of cognitive science, criticizing prevailing approaches to the study of language and thought and advocating a new way of looking at things. Although I strongly believed in the approach it outlined, somehow it didn't have the convincingness on paper that it had in my own reflection. After some discouraging attempts at reorganization and rewriting, I realized that there was a mismatch between the nature of what I wanted to say and the form in which I was trying to communicate.

The understanding on which it was based does not have the form of a carefully structured framework into which all of cognitive science can be placed. It is more an orientation—a way of approaching the phenomena—that has grown out of many different experiences and influences and that bears the marks of its history. I found myself wanting to describe a path rather than justify its destination, finding that in the flow, the ideas came across more clearly. Since this collection was envisioned as a panorama of contrasting individual views, I have taken the liberty of making this chapter explicitly personal and describing the evolution of my own understanding.

My interests have centered around natural language. I have been engaged in the design of computer programs that in some sense could be said to "understand language," and this has led to looking at many aspects of the problems, including theories of meaning, representation formalisms, and the design and construction of complex computer systems. There has been a continuous evolution in my understanding of just what it means to say that a person or computer "understands," and this story[1] can be read as recounting that evolution. It is

---

[1] This is a "story" because like all histories it is made up. In an attempt to make sense of the chaos of past events one imposes more of a sense of orderliness than they deserve. Things didn't actually happen exactly in this order, and the events contain inconsistencies, throwbacks, and other misfortunes that would make it much harder to tell.

231

long, because it is still too early to look back and say "What I was *really* getting at for all those years was the one basic idea that . . ." I am too close and too involved in its continuation to see beyond the twists and turns. The last sections of the paper describe a viewpoint that differs in significant ways from most current approaches, and that offers new possibilities for a deeper understanding of language and a grasp on some previously intractable or unrecognized problems. I hope that it will give some sense of where the path is headed.

2. UP THROUGH SHRDLU

The Background

In the mid 1960s, natural language research with computers proceeded in the wake of widespread disillusionment caused by the failure of the highly touted and heavily funded machine translation projects. There was a feeling that researchers had failed to make good on their early confident claims, and that computers might not be able to deal with the complexities of human language at all. In AI research laboratories there were attempts to develop a new approach, going beyond the syntactic word-shuffling that dominated machine translation and other approaches based on key word search or statistical analysis. It was clear that for effective machine processing of language—whether for translation, question answering, or sophisticated information retrieval—an analysis of the syntactic structures and identification of the lexical items was not sufficient. Programs had to deal somehow with what the words and sentences meant.

There were a number of programs in this new vein described in the early collections of AI papers.[2] Each program worked in some very limited domain (baseball scores, family trees, algebra word problems, etc.) within which it was possible to set up a formal representational structure corresponding to the underlying meaning of sentences. This structure could be used in a systematic reasoning process as part of the overall language comprehension system. The model of language understanding that was implicit in those programs and in many AI programs since then is illustrated in Figure 1.

This model rests on some basic assumptions about language and representation:

1. Sentences in a natural language correspond to facts about the world.
2. It is possible to create a formal representation system such that
   (a) For any relevant fact about the world there is a corresponding structure in the representation system;

---

[2]Green et al. and Lindsay in Feigenbaum and Feldman (1963); Black, Bobrow, Qullian, and Raphael in Minsky (1967).

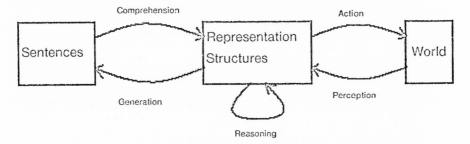

Figure 1. Basic AI model of language understanding.

(b) There is a systematic way of correlating sentences in natural language with the structure in the representation system that correspond to the same facts about the world; and

(c) Systematic formal operations can be specified that operate on the representation structures to do "reasoning." Given structures corresponding to facts about the world, these operations will generate structures corresponding to other facts, without introducing falsehoods.

This somewhat simplistic formulation needs some elaboration to be comprehensive. It is clear, for example, that a question or command does not "correspond to facts" in the same manner as a statement, and that it is unlikely that any actual reasoning system will be error-free. We will discuss some of these elaborations later, but for a first understanding, they do not play a major role.

The critical element in this model that distinguishes it from the pre-AI programs for language is the explicit manipulation of a formal representation. Operations carried out on the representation structures are justified not by facts about language, but by the correspondence between the representation and the world being described. This is the sense in which such programs were said to "understand" the words and sentences they dealt with where the earlier machine translation programs had "manipulated them without understanding."

This general model was not a new idea. It corresponds quite closely to the model of language and meaning developed by philosophers of language like Frege, drawing on ideas back to Aristotle and beyond. There has been a good deal of flag waving at times about the ways in which the "artificial intelligence paradigm" is new and superior to the older philosophical ideas. In large degree (some exceptions are discussed later) this has been a rather empty claim. As Fodor (1978) has pointed out, to the extent they are clearly defined, AI models are generally equivalent to older philosophical ones. A formal logical system can play the role of a representation system as described in the figure, without being explicit about the nature of the processing activity by which reasoning is done.

In fact, AI programs dealing with language do not really fit the model of Figure 1, since they have no modes of perception or action in a real world.

Although they converse about families, baseball or whatever, their interaction is based only on the sentences they interpret and generate. A more accurate model for the programs (as opposed to the human language comprehension they attempt to model) would show that all connection to the world is mediated through the programmer who builds the representation. The reason that "dog" refers to dog (as opposed to referring to eggplant parmesan or being a "meaningless symbol") lies in the intention of the person who put it in the program, who in turn has knowledge of dogs and of the way that the symbols he or she writes will be used by the interpreter. This difference is important in dealing with questions of "background" discussed later.

SHRDLU

SHRDLU (Winograd, 1972) was a computer program for natural language conversation that I developed at MIT between 1968 and 1970.[3] The program carried on a dialog (via teletype) with a person concerning the activity of a simulated "robot" arm in a tabletop world of toy objects. It could answer questions, carry out commands, and incorporate new facts about its world. It displayed the simulated world on a CRT screen, showing the activities it carried out as it moved the objects around.

SHRDLU had a large impact, both inside and outside the field, and ten years later it is still one of the most frequently mentioned AI programs, especially in introductory texts and in the popular media. There are several reasons why so many people (including critics of AI, such as Lighthill (1973)) found the program appealing. One major factor was its comprehensiveness. In writing the program I attempted to deal seriously with all of the aspects of language comprehension illustrated in the model. Earlier programs had focussed on one or another aspect, ignoring or shortcutting others. Programs that analyzed complex syntax did not attempt reasoning. Programs that could do logical deduction used simple patterns for analyzing natural language inputs. SHRDLU combined a sophisticated syntax analysis with a fairly general deductive system, operating in a "world" with visible analogs of perception and action. It provided a framework in which to study the interactions between different aspects of language and emphasized the relevance of nonlinguistic knowledge to the understanding process.

Another factor was its relatively natural use of language. The fact that person and machine were engaged in a visible activity in a (pseudo-)physical world gave the dialog a kind of vitality that was absent in the question-answer or problem-solution interactions of earlier systems. Further naturalness came from the substantial body of programs dealing with linguistic phenomena of conversation and context, such as pronouns ("it," "that," "then," etc.), substitute

---

[3]Winograd (1971) was the original dissertation. Winograd (1972) is a rewritten version that owes much to the editing and encouragement of Walter Reitman. Winograd (1973) is a shortened account, which also appears in various reworkings in several later publications.

nouns ("a green *one*"), and ellipsis (e.g., answering the one-word question "Why?"). Dialog can be carried on without these devices, but it is stilted. SHRDLU incorporated mechanisms to deal with these phenomena in enough cases (both in comprehension and generation) to make the sample dialogs feel different from the stereotype of mechanical computer conversations.

In the technical dimension, it incorporated a number of ideas. Among them were:

1. Use of a reasoning formalism (MicroPlanner) based on the "procedural embedding of knowledge." Specific facts about the world were encoded directly as procedures that operate on the representation structures, instead of as structures to be used by a more general deductive process. The idea of "procedural embedding of knowledge" grew out of early AI work and had been promoted by Hewitt (1971). SHRDLU was the first implementation and use of his Planner language. The difference between "procedural" and "declarative" knowledge has subsequently been the source of much debate (and confusion) in AI.[4] Although procedural embedding in its simplistic form has many disadvantages, more sophisticated versions appear in most current representation systems.

2. An emphasis on how language triggers action. The meaning of a sentence was represented not as a fact about the world, but as a command for the program to do something. A question was a command to generate an answer, and even a statement like "I own the biggest red pyramid" was represented as a program for adding information to a data base. This view that meaning is based on "imperative" rather than "declarative" force is related to some of the speech act theories discussed below.

3. A representation of lexical meaning (the meaning of individual words and idioms) based on procedures that operate in the building of representation structures. This contrasted with earlier approaches in which the lexical items simply provided (through a dictionary lookup) chunks to be incorporated into the representation structures by a general "semantic analysis" program. This was one of the things that made it possible to deal with conversational phenomena such as pronominalization. Some equivalent device is present in most current natural language programs, and there is a formal analog in the generality of function application in Montague Grammar formalizations of word meaning.

4. An explicit representation of the cognitive context. In order to decide what a phrase like "the red block" refers to, it is not sufficient to consider facts about the world being described. There may be several red blocks, one of which is more in focus than the others because of having been mentioned or acted on recently. In order to translate this phrase into the appropriate representation structure, reasoning must be done using representation structures corresponding to facts about the text preceding the phrase, and structures corresponding to facts about which objects are "in focus."

The attempt to deal with conversational phenomena called for an extension to the model of language understanding, as illustrated in Figure 2. It includes additional structures (as part of the overall representation in the language understander) labelled "model of the text" and "model of the speaker/hearer." The label

---

[4]See Winograd, (1975) for discussion.

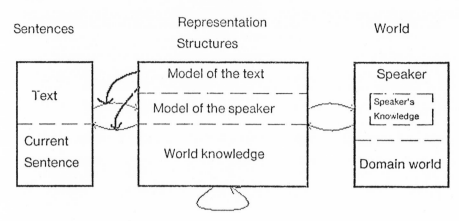

Figure 2. Extended AI model of language understanding.

"model of the speaker" was chosen to reflect the particular approach taken to the problem. It is assumed that inferences about which objects are in focus (and other related properties) can be made on the basis of facts about the knowledge and current internal state (presumably corresponding to representation structures) of the other participant in the conversation. The question "could I use this phrase to refer to object X?" is treated as equivalent to "if I used this phrase would the hearer be able to identify it as naming object X?" On the other side, "what does he mean by this phrase?" is treated as "what object in his mind would he be most likely to choose the phrase for?"

In addition to reasoning about the domain world (the world of toy blocks), the system reasons about the structure of the conversation and about the hypothesized internal structure and state of the other participant. In SHRDLU, this aspect of reasoning was not done using the same representation formalism as for the domain world, but in an *ad hoc* style within the programs. Nevertheless, in essence it was no different from any other reasoning process carried out on representation structures.[5]

3. SEEING SOME SHORTCOMINGS

SHRDLU demonstrated that for a carefully constrained dialog in a limited domain it was possible to deal with meaning in a fairly comprehensive way, and to achieve apparently natural communication. However, there were some obvious problems with the approach, summarized here and discussed below:

[5]For a more elaborate version of this model, along with many examples of conversational phenomena not handled by SHRDLU or any other existing computer system, see Winograd (1977a). Winograd (in preparation) presents an overview of syntactic and semantic structures within a viewpoint drawn from this model.

1. The explicit representation of speaker/hearer internal structure was *ad hoc,* and there was no principled way to evaluate extensions.
2. The notion of word definition by program, even though it opened up possibilities beyond more traditional logical forms of definition, was still inadequate.
3. It took rather strained reasoning to maintain that the meaning of every utterance could be structured as a command to carry out some procedure.
4. The representation and reasoning operations seemed inadequate for dealing with common-sense knowledge and thought reflected in language.

The Internal Structure

In building a simpler system as illustrated in Figure 1, the programmer is creating a model of the language comprehension process. In creating the representation structures corresponding to facts about the domain, he or she is guided by an idea of what is true in the domain world—in representing facts about blocks, one can draw on common-sense knowledge about physical objects. On the other hand, in trying to create structures constituting the model of the speaker/hearer as in Figure 2, there is no such practical guide. In essence, this model is a psychological theory, purporting to describe structures that exist in the mind. This model is then used in a reasoning process, as part of a program whose overall structure itself can be thought of as a hypothesis about the psychological structure of a language understander.

Experimental psychology provides some suggestive concepts, but little else of direct use. A language comprehension system depends on models of memory, attention, and inference, all dealing with meaningful material, not the well-controlled stimuli of the typical laboratory experiment. Research in cognitive psychology has focussed on tasks that do not clearly generalize to these more complex activities. In fact, much current psychological research on how people deal with meaningful material has been guided by AI concepts rather than the other way around.

The problem is hard to delimit, since it touches on broad issues of understanding. In SHRDLU, for example, the program for determining the referent of a definite noun phrase such as "the block" made use of a list of previously mentioned objects. The most recently mentioned thing fitting the description was assumed to be the referent. Although this approach covers a large number of cases, and there are extensions in the same spirit which cover even more, there is a more general phenomenon that must be dealt with. Winograd (1974a) discusses the text "Tommy had just been given a new set of blocks. He was opening the box when he saw Jimmy coming in."

> There is no mention of what is in the box—no clue as to what box it is at all. But a person reading the text makes the immediate assumption that it is the box which contains the set of blocks. We can do this because we know that new items often come in boxes, and that opening the box is a usual thing to do. Most important, we assume that we are receiving a connected message. There is no reason why the box has to be

connected with the blocks, but if it weren't, it couldn't be mentioned without further
introduction. (Winograd, 1974a)

Important differences in meaning can hinge on subtle aspects of the
speaker/hearer model. For example, in the first sentence below, it is appropriate
to assume that the refrigerator has only one door, while in the second it can be
concluded that it has more than one. On the other hand, we cannot conclude from
the third sentence that the house has only one door.

When our new refrigerator arrived, the door was broken.
When our new refrigerator arrived, a door was broken.
When we got home from our vacation, we discovered that the door had been broken open.

The problem, then, is to model the ways in which these connections are made. In
general this has led to an introspective/pragmatic approach. Things get added to
the representation of the speaker/hearer because the programmer feels they will
be relevant. They are kept because with them the system is perceived as performing better in some way than it does without them. There have been some interesting ideas for what should be included in the model of the speaker/hearer, and
how some of it might be organized[6] but the overall feeling is of undirected and
untested speculation, rather than of persuasive evidence or of convergence towards a model that would give a satisfactory account of a broad range of language phenomena.

Word Definition

The difficulty of formulating appropriate word definitions was apparent even
in the simple vocabulary of the blocks world and becomes more serious as
the domain expands. In SHRDLU, for example, the word "big" was translated
into a representation structure corresponding to "having X,Y, and Z coordinates
summing to more than 600 units (in the dimensions used for display on the
screen)." This was clearly an *ad hoc* stopgap, which avoided dealing with the
fact that the meaning of words like "big" is always relative to an expected set.
The statement "They were expecting a big crowd" could refer to twenty or
twenty thousand, depending on the context. By having word definitions as programs, it was theoretically possible to take an arbitrary number of contextual
factors into account, and this constituted a major departure from more standard
"compositional" semantics in which the meaning of any unit can depend only on
the independent meanings of its parts. However, the mere possibility did not
provide a guide for just what it meant to consider context, and what kind of
formal structures were needed.

On looking more closely, it became apparent that this problem was not a
special issue for comparative adjectives like "big," but was a fundamental part

---

[6]See for example Schank and Abelson (1975), Hobbs (1978). and Grosz (1980).

of the meaning of most words. Linguists have pointed out that a natural language categorization cannot be equated with a finite set of logical predicates to be applied to the situation.[7] The applicability of a word depends on an understanding of the purposes of speaker and hearer. Winograd (1976) discusses the meaning of "bachelor." In classical discussions of semantics, "bachelor" has been used as an example of a word with a clear paraphrase in more elementary terms—"unmarried adult human male."[8] But if someone refers to a person as a "bachelor" in normal conversation, much more is meant. It is inaccurate if used in describing the Pope or a member of a monogamous homosexual couple, and might well be used in describing an independent career woman.

The issue is not that the definition of bachelor is complex and involves more terms than usually accounted for. There is no coherent checklist of any length such that objects meeting all of its conditions will consistently be called "bachelors" and those failing one or more of them will not. The question "Is X a bachelor?" cannot be answered without asking "Why do you want to know?". Of course, it is possible to create artificial strict definitions, but these do not account for the normal use of language. When we move to a larger vocabulary, the problem becomes even more obvious. Each of the nouns in the sentence "The administration's dishonesty provoked a crisis of confidence in government" raises a significant problem of definition, and it is clear that purpose and context play a major role in determining what will be called a "crisis," "dishonesty," or even in deciding just what constitutes an "administration."

The problem of considering the contextual background in the meaning of words is not solved simply by moving from a "declarative" form of definition to a "procedural" one, as in SHRDLU. The activity of a program in any bounded amount of time can be described in purely logical terms, and a logical formula can be written which can be proved true in exactly those cases where the program would return the answer "yes" and false when it would say "no."

Meaning as Command

SHRDLU was based on a formalism in which the meaning of a sentence was represented as a command to carry out some action. A question is a command to generate a sentence satisfying a set of constraints, and a statement is a command to add a formula to the data base. This shift of viewpoint from meaning-as-statement to meaning-as-command provided some interesting ways of talking about sentences, but in its naive form it is clearly unworkable.

The good part of the idea was the view of an utterance as triggering some kind of activity in the hearer. The bad part of the idea was the analogy with

[7]See, for example, Fillmore (1975) and Labov (1973).
[8]This is, of course, only one of its definitions. Others, as pointed out by Katz and Fodor (1964), relate to fur seals and chivalry.

computer programming languages, in which there is a direct correspondence between the linguistic form and the sequence of activities to be carried out. In the case of natural language, much more is going on. Both speaker and hearer are engaged in ongoing processes of trying to make sense of their conversation and the world they inhabit. The interpretation of utterances is only one of many activities, and interacts with perception, reasoning, memory, and all the other aspects of cognition mentioned by Norman (this volume). When I utter a sentence, I have no way of anticipating in any detail the processing it will invoke in the hearer. It clearly includes much more than simply obeying or storing away a fact. The following simple examples illustrate some of what goes on.

1. Tom has never failed a student in Linguistics 265.
2. I'm sorry I missed the meeting yesterday. My car had a flat tire.
3. There's an animal over there in the bushes.

Sentence 1 is true in many circumstances, including the one in which Tom has never taught Linguistics 265. However, in ordinary conversation, the hearer makes the additional implication that Tom has taught the course, and is justified in accusing the speaker of bad faith if the implication is not warranted. Similarly in sentence 2, the hearer assumes that there is a coherence to the events being described. If the second sentence were "There are fifteen million people in Mexico City" the hearer would be puzzled, and if the flat tire had nothing to do with missing the meeting (even though it actually did happen), the speaker is practicing deception.

Sentence 3 is a more subtle case. If the hearer looks over and sees a dog in the bushes, and finds out that the speaker knew it was a dog, he or she will feel that the statement was inappropriate, and might say "If you knew it was a dog, why didn't you say so?". On the other hand, the statement "There's a dog over there in the bushes" is perfectly appropriate even if both speaker and hearer know that it is a beagle,[9] and sentence 3 would be fine for a dog if it were a response to something like "There are no animals anywhere around here."

The common element in all of these is that the "meaning" for a hearer is the result of a complex process of trying to understand what the speaker is saying and why. In effect, every statement is the answer to a question, which may be implicit in the context. Its meaning depends as much on the question as on the form of the answer. There is an important germ of truth in saying that the meaning of a sentence "is" the process it invokes, but this view is not compatible with a formal compositional semantics of the kind that has generally interested linguists and philosophers. What is needed is an understanding of meaning-as-triggering, which deals with the interaction between the utterance and the full range of cognitive processes going on in the language user.

---

[9]These phenomena are related to the properties of human categorization systems studied by Rosch (1975).

[10]See the discussion in Fodor (1978).

Natural Reasoning

In looking at any significant sample of natural language, it becomes quickly apparent that only a small fraction of human "reasoning" fits the mold of deductive logic. One is often presented with a fragmentary description of some object or situation, and on the basis of knowledge about what is "typical" jumps to a number of conclusions that are not justifiable as logical deductions, and may at times be false. Most AI systems have been based (either explicitly or unwittingly) on a notion of deduction that does not account for this style of reasoning. In the "opening the box" example quoted above, it was assumed that "the box" was the one in which the blocks arrived even though this is not rigorously deducible from the text, or even from knowledge of the world. This kind of inference is a predominant aspect of reasoning and one which calls for formal systems having very different properties from deductive logic.[11]

4. KRL: TOWARD A NEW FORMALISM

My recognition of these problems with the approach underlying SHRDLU came at the time (1972–73) I participated in a series of discussions in the Artificial Intelligence Lab at MIT about the problems of natural reasoning. These discussions led among other things to Minksy's (1975) formulation of "frames" and to my own attempts to make these intuitions more precise (1974b, 1975). The next major step toward clarifying them was in the specification and construction of KRL (Knowledge Representation Language), a project done jointly with Daniel Bobrow at Xerox PARC.[12] The project has included two rounds of design and implementation, with a limited amount of testing in small applications. Each implementation has covered only a fraction of the overall intended features of the language, and the discussion below (except where otherwise indicated) deals with the basic concepts, not the current implentations.

The Formalism

Viewed as a language for use in building systems of the kind described in Figures 1 and 2, KRL was intended to have the following properties:

1. *Resource-limited processing as a basis for reasoning.* In any act of interpretation or reasoning, a system (biological or computer) has a finite quantity of processing resources to expend. The nature of these resources will be affected by the details of the processor, its environment, and previous history. The outcome of the process is determined by the interaction between the structure of the task and the allocation of process-

---

[11]Winograd (1980) and several other papers in the same issue of *Artificial Intelligence* deal with problems of "nonmonotonic logic" related to this problem.

[12]See Bobrow and Winograd (1977).

ing. The ability to deal with partial or imprecise information comes from the ability to do a finite amount of processing, then jump to a conclusion on the basis of what has happened so far.

2. *Separation of logical form from memory form.* In order to build a theory of resource use in processing, it is necessary to consider the details of how memory processes operate. Two pieces of information may be logically equivalent but differ in how easily they can be accessed or stored. Most representation systems have either ignored memory properties (as in most theories of formal logic), or assumed that they followed from the logical properties of the information. In KRL, stored knowledge has separable dimensions of logical content and memory "chunking." The memory structure depends not just on the logical content, but also potentially the particular history of the way it was entered into the structures.

3. *The integration of meta-knowledge.* In order to use information about the knowledge structures in a systematic way, the system needs a capacity of partial self-description. Formal structures can be used to represent objects in an "outside world" such as blocks, other structures of the same form can be used to represent those structures in turn, and so on indefinitely. This makes it possible to formulate algorithms for resource-limited processing in the same language that is used for other representation.

4. *An overall control structure based on matching.* The basic organization of KRL provides a framework for an extended "matching" process in which the choice of what to do at each point is driven by an attempt to match stored "prototypes" against the current inputs. This matching can involve complex deductions.

The development of KRL led to deeper thinking about the nature of representation formalisms and the reasoning operations done with them. Looking from one point of view, a KRL system can be thought of as a purely logical formal system—it operates with precise rules on well-defined structures as does any computer program. At the same time, there is another view from which the system can be seen as carrying out a kind of informal reasoning—one that comes to conclusions based on partial evidence, makes assumptions about what is to be expected in typical cases, and leaves open the possibility of mistake and contradiction. A KRL system (or any system using resource-limited reasoning) can draw some conclusion, then reverse it on the basis of further reasoning.

The key to this paradox lies in the system's use of formal rules that make reference to the structure of the system of itself. In coming to a conclusion about some world being represented (such as a world of toy blocks,) a KRL system can come to conclusions on the basis not only of statements about the world, but also on the basis of the form of its structures (for example, concluding something is false because it is normally false, and its truth in this case does not emerge in some bounded amount of reasoning). There is a fundamental philosophical and mathematical difference between truth-based systems of logic, and process-based systems like KRL.[13] One of the major theoretical directions of the KRL effort is to make this difference clear and understand its consequences.

[13]These issues are discussed at length in Winograd (1980).

Reasoning and Language

KRL was designed to make possible a different formal basis for the definition of words in natural language. In a standard deductive system, the definition of a word is a formula specifying a set of necessary and sufficient conditions for its applicability. Some terms are designated as *primitive,* and the rest are defined in terms of them. Although nonprimitive terms can appear in definitions, there can ultimately be no *circular definitions*—every nonprimitive term can be expanded through its definition (and the definitions of the terms appearing in it, recursively) to a formula containing only connectives and primitives. In deciding whether a word applies to an object, this expansion is carried out and the primitive terms are checked against the case at hand. If (and only if) they all check out, the word applies.

Formalisms like KRL provide another way of looking at this.[14] A word is associated with a "prototype" in the representation formalism. This prototype (like a definition) includes a description of the object in other terms. However, unlike a definition, this further description is not taken to be sufficient or necessary for determining the applicability of the prototype. It can include things that are typical (but not always the case) or that are relevant only in some contexts. In deciding whether a word applies to an object, the reasoning system compares these further descriptions to what is known about the object. It does so in a resource-dependent way, possibly looking at only some of the description, and choosing which to do on the basis of context. After a limited amount of processing, it makes a decision (as to whether the word applies) on the basis of what has been examined so far.

A process of this type has the potential to treat word meanings in the open-ended way discussed for the "bachelor" example above. Although there is a "checklist" of further descriptions, the process of checking is context dependent and limited. It is possible to imagine strategies for deciding which items on the list to examine, depending on the current purposes and background. The KRL framework does not specify how this is to be done in detail, but through the combination of resource-limited reasoning and meta-description it provides tools that can be used.

Similarly, these tools can be applied to the other problems raised in the critique of SHRDLU above. The whole concept of resource-limited reasoning grew out of an analysis of the kinds of "natural reasoning" that cannot be done with a straightforward deductive system. The idea of "self-description" was partly an attempt to provide an explicit way of allowing the system to have a model of itself and, by reflection, of a hypothesized dialog partner. The matching framework provides a way to treat inputs to the system as elements of an overall

---

[14]The problem of word definition, and the notions of "prototype" and "primitive" are discussed at length in Winograd (1976, 1978) and Bobrow and Winograd (1979).

pattern being matched, rather than as items to be stored or commands to be carried out.

With all of these KRL provided only a framework. It was designed to facilitate exploration of these problems, not to embody solutions to them. In that sense it is a kind of "calculus" of natural reasoning, just as the predicate calculus provides a formal basis for systems of deduction and the differential calculus serves as language for describing physical systems. Having this calculus is not the same as having a solution to the specific problems, or a theory of language understanding; but it is a potentially valuable tool. The experience in using it so far is difficult to evaluate. No substantial project has been done that uses its capabilities to really address the kinds of problems that motivated its creation. In trying to use it more fully, technical difficulties (including everything from slow execution speed to user interfaces) are intertwined with conceptual difficulties (which are hard to isolate clearly). As discussed below, there are deep questions of just what could be expected if KRL were to "succeed," but in any event it is clear that it cannot realistically be evaluated in its current implementations.

5. THE HERMENEUTIC CONNECTION

At the same time that KRL was being developed I took part in a series of informal discussions in Berkeley about the nature of language and cognition. These discussions included philosophers, linguists, and computer scientists and ranged from the narrowest technical details to the broadest philosophical concerns. They raised questions about what it was that KRL (and all other computer representations) were claimed to achieve. Among the works discussed were those of Maturana (1977) on the biological foundations of cognition, and the literature on hermeneutics.[15] This paper is not the place for a detailed exposition of these ideas,[16] but there were some elements of both that were applicable to the problem of building programs that interacted in natural language. The following paragraphs attempt to lay them out in outline, but for a more thorough understanding, it is necessary to go to the original sources.

The Nervous System as a Closed, Plastic, Structure-determined System

Maturana proposes an understanding of the nervous system that is not built around the usual notions of input, output, memory, perception, etc. He adopts instead an orientation toward it as a system of components whose activities

---

[15]Gadamer (1976) was an important source, and Palmer (1969) is an excellent overall introduction.

[16]Flores and Winograd (in preparation) does so at some length.

trigger further activity within the system. The system is "structure determined" in that its activity at any moment is fully determined by the structure (or state) at that moment. It is "plastic" in that its structure can be changed by the activity, so that its structure at any moment is a product of the entire previous history of activity and changing structure. It is "closed," in the sense that the system can do only that which is determined by its own structure and activity—its action cannot be understood as a reflection of an external world it perceives.

At first reading, for most people this approach seems bizarre, apparently denying the obvious fact that we see, hear, and generally perceive a world outside of our own nervous system. It is not a denial, but a change of stance. Instead of looking at vision as a mapping of external reality onto mental structures, we can look at it biologically as a change to the structure of the nervous system, in particular to the chemical and electrical properties of various cells in the retina. The subjective introspection is that we "see something," but from a neurophysiological standpoint, there is a structure-determined causal network in which "perturbations" to the structure of the system lead to patterns of activity that are different from those that would have happened with different perturbations. The focus is shifted away from the structure of the phenomena that led to the perturbations toward the structure of changes in the ongoing activity of the system as it is perturbed.

This view meshed well with the "triggering" view of language understanding described above. An utterance is neither a description of something in the world, nor a command specifying what the hearer is to carry out. It is a "perturbation" to an active ongoing cognitive system that is trying to make sense of things. The central questions to be asked of an utterance are those dealing with the changes in activity that it triggers, not with its correspondence to a world it describes.

The Hermeneutic Circle

Hermeneutics is the study of interpretation. It began as a discipline with the problem of interpreting sacred texts, but has come to encompass not only the interpretation of language, but also the larger understanding of how we interpret the world in which we live. One of the fundamental insights of hermeneutics is the importance of *pre-understanding*. In any situation where we are interpreting language, we begin with a system of understanding that provides a basis within which to generate an interpretation. This pre-understanding in turn arises and evolves through the acts of interpretation. This circle, in which understanding is necessary for interpretation, which in turn creates understanding, is called the *hermeneutic circle*.

> But there is a contradiction here. How can a text be understood, when the condition for its understanding is already to have understood what it is about? The answer is that somehow, by a dialectical process, a partial understanding is used to understand still further, like using pieces of a puzzle to figure out what is missing . . . A certain

pre-understanding of the subject is necessary or no communication will happen, yet
that understanding must be altered in the act of understanding. (Palmer, 1969)

The parallel with the issues of reasoning with frame representations should
be obvious. The set of stored schemas in a system is its "pre-understanding."
The use of these schemas affects the interpretation of what is said:

In comprehension, the set of stored schemas is actively used in a process of "pattern
recognition." The hearer assumes that the discourse is made up of instances of known
discourse and reasoning patterns. . . . Some feature of an utterance, together with the
current context, can trigger a hypothesis that an instance of some particular schema is
being conveyed. This hypothesis is tested by attempting to fit other parts of the
utterance in as pieces of the hypothesized schema. As a result the way in which the
input is analyzed can be controlled (or biased) by the fact that it is being processed as
part of looking for an instance of a specific hypothesized schema. (Winograd, 1977a)

Although little has been said within AI and cognitive science about how
new schemas are generated, it is clear that it must be the result of a history of
previous interactions, each of which is mediated through other schemas in a
hermeneutic circle.[17] In emphasizing the relationship between an act of interpretation and the history of previous interpretations by the system, hermeneutics
raises some of the same questions as Maturana's approach to plastic, structure-
determined systems.

6. FOUNDERING ON THE OPPOSITE SHOALS

My course to this point was a gradual steering away from the logical-deductive
model and its view of language understanding based on objective truth. Starting
with the essentially conventional semantic underpinnings of SHRDLU, I had
become more and more concerned with the properties of language and thought
that could not easily be embodied in traditional logical systems. Maturana and
Gadamer provided some philosophical wind for the rudimentary KRL sails, and
this new direction seemed ripe for exploration. Structure-dependent resource-
limited reasoning offered a way of formalizing natural kinds of inference, and
its dependence on the specific past history of the language understander opened
up room for systematically dealing with the "nonlogical" phenomena of language.

In many ways, this direction is still open for development and there are
many areas to be explored. But early *en route* I was exposed to some troubling
questions about the rocks we faced on the other shore. Two basic issues stood
out: the problem of subjective relativism and the problem of representation. In
this section, we will lay out these problems without proposing solutions. The
directions described in later sections were guided in part by an attempt to solve
them.

---

[17]The development of schemas is of growing concern in AI, as indicated by Minsky (this
volume) and Schank (this volume.)

Subjective Relativism

The first issue can be described in simplistic terms as a dispute about two different starting points for understanding language:

> *Objectivity:* an utterance has meaning by virtue of corresponding to a state of affairs. We approach the study of language by analyzing how the structures of utterances correspond systematically to the states of affairs they describe.

> *Subjectivity:* an utterance has meaning by virtue of triggering processes within a hearer whose cognitive structure depends on prior history and current processing activity. We approach the study of language by analyzing the nature of those cognitive structures and activities.

The examples given above suggest that a subject-dependent view must be taken even in such seemingly objective issues as the appropriate use of "John is a bachelor." If we are seriously interested in understanding the regularities in the use of real language in real situations we will be misled by persisting with idealizations of objective truth. As Lakoff (this volume) points out, ordinary language leans more to metaphor than to mathematics.

But there is a problem with unbridled relativism. If the "meaning" of an utterance can only be described in terms of its effects on a particular understander with a particular history, how do we talk about inter-subjective meaning at all? Since no two people have identical histories, and since any aspect of cognitive structure can potentially have an effect on the processing triggered by a particular utterance, there is a different meaning for every hearer. There is no objective "right meaning"—only a meaning for a particular person at a particular moment in a particular situation. Carried to an extreme, if you interpret my use of the word "dog" as referring to eggplant parmesan, what allows me to argue that you are wrong? We want to understand meaning in a way that makes sense of the fact that you and I may not have identical (or even mutually consistent) understandings of "democracy" or "system," but we cannot ignore the common sense intuition that there are broad areas of obvious agreement.

The most obvious fix is to take some kind of behaviorist or operationalist criterion. There is a long history in discussions of AI of using these criteria in arguing about whether a program can be said to "think" or "understand." The Turing test (Turing, 1950) is the most often cited form of an operational criterion, and many defenses of AI naively take for granted that it is the only sensible (scientific) way to deal with the philosophical issues. Even though no two individuals have the same internal structure, we can talk about equivalent classes of behavior and say that a person "understands" something if he behaves in the appropriate ways upon hearing it. But this is only sweeping the problem under a different rug. In trying to define what constitutes the class of "appropriate behavior on hearing the word 'dog' " we are stuck with a problem no easier than that of defining the meaning of "dog." If we posit some objective standards by which the behavior can be tested, we are making the same kinds of assumptions as in setting objective definitions for words. If we don't, then the question "appropriate behavior according to whom in what situation" is just as troubling as "meaning according to whom in what situation." We cannot avoid relativism by converting it to objective propositions about behavior, and thus must deal in some other way with the problem.

The Problem of Representation

The other problem lies in the assumption that we can build formal structures that represent the knowledge and state of a language understander. In going from a standard deductive system to a structure-dependent formalism like KRL, we still maintain the basic idea of representing the relevant knowledge in formal structures that can be set down according to our understanding of linguistics, psychology, and computation. The question of whether human knowledge can be represented in formal structures has been a major concern for a number of philosophers. Dreyfus (1979) has been the most active critic of artificial intelligence from this perspective, drawing on the philosophy of Heidegger (1962).[18]

For a long time I found the arguments rather incomprehensible, seeing the position that knowledge was not representable as equivalent to the belief that the human nervous system could not operate according to deterministic principles. But Maturana, starting by viewing the nervous system as a mechanistic system, argued in ways that were disturbingly similar. One of the most challenging of Maturana's views is his dogmatic insistence that cognition is not based on the manipulation of mental models or representations of the world. For someone trained in AI (or in cognitive science generally, as illustrated by the other papers in this volume) it is hard to understand what other kind of explanation there could be.

Maturana sees much of the discussion of representation as exhibiting a serious error of confusing "phenomenic domains." Anything we choose to describe as a system can be described in different domains,[19] each with its relevant pheomena. For example, we can look at a TV screen and see an array of luminescent dots excited by a moving electron beam, or we can see a comedian telling jokes. We can talk coherently about what we see in either domain, but cannot combine them meaningfully. Maturana argues that in describing cognition we often fail to carefully distinguish the relevant domains. The error takes the form:

1. A scientist observes some recurrent pattern of interactions of an organism.
2. He or she devises some formal representation (for example a set of generative rules or a "schema") that characterizes the regularities.

[18]For a discussion of the issues from within AI, see Barr (1980).

[19]This use of the word "domain" follows Maturana. It is somewhat different from the more common use in AI, where the "domain" of a particular program is something like "blocks," "airline reservations," or "blood infections."

3. The organism is assumed to ''have'' the representation, in order to be able to exhibit the regularities.

4. (Depending on the particular sub-field) The scientist looks for experiments that will demonstrate the presence of the representation, or designs a computer program using it to see whether the behavior can be generated by the program.

The error is in the reification of the representation at step 3. Working from basic biological examples, Maturana points to many phenomena that *for an observer* can be described in terms of representation, but that can also be understood as the activity of a structure-determined system with no mechanism corresponding to a representation. As a simple example, we might watch a baby successfully getting milk from its mother's nipple and argue that it has a ''representation'' of the relevant anatomy, or of the activity of feeding. On the other hand, we might note that there is a reflex that causes it to react to a touch on the cheek by turning its head in that direction, and another that triggers sucking when something touches its mouth. From the viewpoint of effective behavior, it has a ''correct representation,'' but it would be fruitless to look for neurophysiological mechanisms that correspond to reasoning that uses facts about breasts or milk.[20]

Maturana argues that there is a ''domain of description'' in which it is appropriate to talk about the correspondence between effective behavior and the structure of the environment or ''medium'' in which it takes place, but that we must not confuse this kind of description with the description of the causal mechanisms operating to produce it. In saying that a representation is ''present in the nervous system,'' we are indulging in misplaced concreteness and can easily be led into fruitless quests for the corresponding mechanisms. Whereas the point is obvious for reflexive behavior (which can certainly be quite complex, as pointed out by the animal ethologists), he sees it as central to our understanding of all behavior, including complex cognitive and linguistic activities.

After an initial scepticism (of the ''How could it be anything but . . .'' variety), I thought about how this view might be directly applied to the problems of language understanding. There is a good deal of confusion of domains apparent in the work on ''schemas,'' ''scripts,'' and ''frames.'' Some kind of regularity is observed in text patterns, or the ability to answer certain kinds of questions given text. The cognitive researcher builds a formal representation of this pattern, and often builds some kind of program that uses it to produce minor variants on the observed behavior. The resulting claim is that a person must ''have'' the script or schema and use it explicitly (perhaps not consciously) in carrying out the process.

[20]Geschwind (this volume) exhibits this kind of reification in most direct form: ''. . . the cat who has never seen a mouse attacked will bite through the nape of the neck, thus adopting the ''best strategy'' for immobilizing the prey. These findings suggest the surprising conclusion that a ''model'' of the nape must be present in the nervous system . . .''

My own discussion of discourse (Winograd, 1977a) carried this representational view to its logical extreme. It gives examples of many different dimensions of discourse patterning, referring to them as kinds of "schemas." "Each speaker of a language possesses a large and rather diverse set of schemas dealing with the process of natural language communication. The understanding of these schemas will form the core of a science of discourse." I still feel that the kinds of phenomena that were pointed out and categorized were interesting and important, but dressing up the observations in the language of schemas did little or nothing to sharpen or develop them. A direct implementation of the purported schemas as representation structures in a computer program would have been uninteresting. It would have the flavor of much of the work we see, in which a program "plays back" the schemas or scripts put into it, but in doing so it does not provide any insight into what happens in those cases that don't closely match exactly one of the hypothesized schemas. *The schemas correspond to classes of external behavior, which may not correlate in any straightforward way to the components of the internal mechanism (either physical or functional).*

It was also interesting that the same questions could be raised with respect to computers. In other work (Winograd 1979b) I have been concerned with the problem of languages and programming environments for developing complex computer systems. The appropriate level of description for explaining a system to another person often includes terms that do not correspond to any mechanism in the program. If I say of a program "It has the goal of minimizing the number of jobs on the waiting queue," there is unlikely to be a "goal structure" somewhere in memory or a "problem solving" mechanism that uses strategies to achieve specified goals. There may be dozens or even hundreds of places throughout the code where specific actions are taken, the net effect of which is being described. In the case of computer systems (as opposed to naturally evolving biological systems) the goal can be more appropriately thought of as existing in the specification that was given to the people who programmed it. The situation would be more parallel to that of a living mind if the system had simply "survived" because a collection of changes led to a particular behavior pattern without conscious intention by programmers. But in any case, there is an important lesson in the fact that there are important regularities in the "descriptive domain" that *do not* correspond to mechanisms in the program.

Returning to the problems of language understanding, we can see what the appropriate domain is for talking about context. In traditional linguistics, the context of a sentence is made up of the sentences preceding and following it. In the AI model, as described in Figure 2 above, we assume that context can be understood as a set of cognitive structures within the speaker and hearer. Some of these structures are records (or analyses) of other sentences, but others are things like a "topic structure" representing what the discourse is about, a "script" that is being applied, and a "focus list" of things recently mentioned or thought about. Taking Maturana's examples seriously, we are led to question whether these descriptive notions can appropriately be used as a guide for building or analyzing mechanisms. Perhaps some of the difficulties mentioned in section 3 result from an attempt to characterize regularities in the wrong domain. We need to ask, then, just what the relevant domain might be.

7. UNDERSTANDING IN A DOMAIN OF ACTION

Four Domains for Understanding Language

In getting to this point we have described language in three different phenomenic domains. The assumptions central to a given domain form a major element in the generation of a "paradigm" in the sense of Kuhn (1962). However, it is not a simple matter of choosing the "right" domain. For any field of inquiry, there can be several relevant domains of regularity. In focussing on one domain as central we are led to ask certain questions and pay attention to certain phenomena. For any choice, there are some phenomena that become more easily describable, and others that become more obscure. The three domains we have discussed so far are:

> *The domain of linguistic structure.* This is the domain of traditional linguistics. One looks for regularities in the patterning of structural elements (phonemes, words, phrases, sentences, etc.) in utterances and text. As mentioned above, most of the work on the larger-scale structure of discourse is in this domain, even when it is reformulated in terms of "schemas."

> *The domain of correspondence between linguistic structures and the world.* In this domain, one is concerned with regularities in the correspondence between the structures of linguistic objects and the states of affairs in the world that those objects describe. Much of the current work in the philosophy of language is an attempt to formalize this correspondence. Much of the AI work on natural language has had this orientation as well.

> *The domain of cognitive processes.*[21] In this domain the relevant regularities are not in the linguistic structures themselves, or their correspondence to a world, but in the cognitive structures and processes of a person (or machine) that generates or interprets them. This is the domain explored in much of cognitive psychology and artificial intelligence.

My current work is moving in the direction of a fourth domain for understanding language:

> *The domain of human action and interaction.* In this domain the relevant regularities are in the network of actions and interactions within a human society. An utterance is a linguistic *act* that has consequences for the participants, leading to other immediate actions and to commitments for future action.

---

[21]This view is used as a basis for a comprehensive description in a textbook entitled *Language as a Cognitive Process* (Winograd, forthcoming) and is contrasted with the first two views in Winograd (1977b).

This domain has been explored under the rubric of *speech acts*. The work of Austin (1962) and Searle (1970, 1975) has shown that utterances can be understood as acts rather than as representations. In giving a command or making a promise, a person is not uttering a sentence whose meaning lies in whether it does or does not correspond truthfully to the world. The speaker is entering into an interaction pattern, playing a certain role, committing both speaker and hearer to future actions, some linguistic and others not. In this domain the relevant question about an utterance is "What is the speaker doing?" Understanding is connected with the ability to recognize what the speaker is doing and to participate in the appropriate pattern of actions.

My first reaction on being urged to look at this domain was "Oh, just speech acts." I had been familiar with the basic ideas of speech acts for quite a while and viewed them as a kind of add-on to the central theory of language. In the paper on discourse discussed above they were described, true to form, as a collection of "speech act schemas" that were among the cognitive structures of a speaker or hearer. The challenge, though, was to see what it meant to look at language as a whole from the perspective of speech acts—as action rather than structure or the result of a cognitive process.

This was a difficult shift of view, but one with interesting consequences. It is perhaps easiest if we begin by looking at one of the most often described speech acts, that of *promising*. If someone asks me to come to a meeting tomorrow and I respond "I'll be there," I am performing a speech act[22] that is quite different from describing a state of affairs in the world or making a prediction about future states of affairs. By virtue of the utterance, I am entering into a commitment. It is not relevant to ask whether the promise is "true" or "false," but rather whether it is appropriate, or, to use Austin's term, "felicitous."

An essential thing about speech acts is that they always occur in a social context, with a background implied by that context. If I find out tomorrow that the meeting has been moved to Katmandu and don't show up, I can justifiably argue with you that I haven't broken my promise. What I really meant was "Assuming it is held as scheduled. . . ." On the other hand, if the meeting is moved to an adjacent room, and I know it but don't show up, you are justified in arguing that I have broken my promise, and that the "Katmandu excuse" doesn't apply. This kind of argumentation can be pursued back and forth indefinitely, and forms a part of the network of potential actions related to a promise. The legal system provides a regular mechanism for exactly this kind of interaction.

---

[22]As Searle points out, we can talk about a speech act as being a promise even though it does not use any explicit illocutionary verb, such as "promise" or "assure." Technically, it is said that the utterance has "promise" as its "illocutionary force."

Statements as Speech Acts Initiating Commitment

In the basic works on speech acts, there is a separation between the propositional content of an utterance and its illocutionary force. The fact that my utterance is a promise is its illocutionary force. The fact that it involves my attendance at a particular meeting at a particular time is its propositional content. In further pursuing the connection between meaning and speech acts, it is possible to view more of meaning (including what has been seen as propositional content) in the domain of action, rather than the domain of correspondence with the world.

Consider the following dialog:

A: I'm thirsty.

B: There's some water in the refrigerator.

A: Where? I don't see it.

B: In the cells of the eggplant.

A claims that B's first response was a lie (or "misleading"), whereas B contends that everything he said was literally true. Most work in semantics (including artificial intelligence) can be seen as providing formal grounds to support B. But there is an important sense in which a theory of "meaning" needs to deal with the grounds for A's complaint. In making the statement "There's some water in the refrigerator" B is doing something more than stating an abstract objective fact.

At first, it seems like it might be possible to expand on the definition of "water." Perhaps there is a "sense" of the word that means "water in its liquid phase in a sufficient quantity to act as a fluid," and the statement about water is ambiguous in whether it refers to this sense or to a sense dealing purely with chemical composition. But this doesn't help us in dealing with some other possible responses of B to the initial request:

B: There's no water in the refrigerator, but there's some lemonade.

B: There's a bottle of water in the refrigerator, with a little lemon in it to cover up the taste of the rust from the pipes.

In the first case, the presence of lemon in the water is taken as making it not "water." In the second, the lemon (perhaps the same quantity) is considered irrelevant. The difference lies in a background of assumptions the speaker has about the hearer's purposes and experience. After any amount of fiddling with the definition, one can always come up with a new context (e.g., what if the person were doing a science experiment or checking for sources of humidity), in which the acceptability of the statement "There is water" would not be accounted for by the definition. Every speech act occurs in a context, with a background understood by speaker and hearer. There are "felicity conditions" that depend on mutual knowledge and intentions. The speaker is responsible for things he can anticipate that the hearer will infer from what he says, not just its abstract correspondence with the state of affairs.

What happens, then, if we try to understand the problem of "truth" in the terms of social action and commitment? In making a statement I am doing something like making a promise—committing myself to acting in appropriate ways in the future. In this case, there is a different kind of satisfaction condition. There is no specific action that I am bound to, but there is a structure of potential dialog that we could enter into in the face of a "breakdown." If I say "There is water in the refrigerator" and you can't find any, I am committed to give you an account. Either we agree that I was wrong, or we discuss the assumed background ("I assumed we were talking about something to drink." "I assumed we were talking about chemical composition").

There are several reasons why this shift of viewpoint is potentially advantageous:

It lets us deal with what happens when we actually make statements. Formal approaches to meaning often take as their model the language of mathematics, in which it is generally assumed that the truth of a statement can be determined without reference to outside context or situation.[23] But in real language, we rarely if ever make a statement that could not be construed as having a literal meaning we don't intend. If I say "snow is white" you can point to the murky grey polluted stuff at our feet. I reply "I meant pure snow," and you respond "You didn't say so, and anyway no snow is absolutely pure." It is an edifying exercise to look at the statements we make both in our writing and our everyday conversation and see how few of them can even apparently be judged true or false without an appeal to an unstated background.

It shifts us out of the objective/subjective dichotomy. In the previous section we saw a dilemma arising from trying to identify the "meaning" of a word or utterance. By assuming it had an objective meaning independent of a particular speaker/hearer situation, we banished many aspects of meaning that play a central role in language. But in assuming that meaning is defined in terms of effect on a particular individual in a situation, we lose the sense that meaning can be the same across individuals and situations. In moving to the domain of interactions (rather than that of objective truth correspondence or cognitive process), we are directing attention to the interactional situation in which something is uttered. We draw generalizations across these situations (and their potential for continued conversation) rather than across objective correspondence or mental states.

It places central emphasis on the potential for further articulation of unstated background. By looking at statements as language acts analogous to promises, we bring into prominence the fact that human action always occurs in an unarticulated background. When I promise to do something, it goes without saying that the commitment is relative to a large number of assumptions about the rest of our world continuing as expected. The same properties carry over to language acts. Sociologists working in "ethnomethodology"[24] have explored the problems in recognizing our background

---

[23]In fact, as pointed out by Lakatos (1976), this is not really the case even in mathematics.
[24]For example, Garfinkel (1967).

assumptions. We can never make the background fully explicit, but we can study the nature of the dialog by which people come to a consensus about things that were previously in the background.

8. WHITHER FROM HERE?

Having turned to a different "phenomenic domain" we must raise the question of methodology. How does one proceed in day to day work? My own answer to this question includes both constructive and interpretive activities:

Developing Theories and Formalisms

Just as the structural formalisms of linguistics and the deductive formalisms of predicate calculus were developed to provide a language for description in their respective domains, we need an appropriate "calculus of language acts" if we want to develop detailed theories of language interaction. There will be several parts of such a theory:

1. *Illocutionary logic.* The basic groundwork of speech act theory includes an analysis of the different kinds of illocutionary points and the structure of the felicity conditions associated with them. Searle (1975) proposes a universal taxonomy of five basic illocutionary points, further developed by Searle and vanDerVeken (in press). This analysis can serve as a starting point for understanding the structure of larger composite patterns made up of the basic acts. For example an "offer-negotiation-acceptance" sequence is a standardly observed pattern made up of individual "commissives" and "requests." The formal tools for describing the "syntax" of such patterns may be quite different from those used in traditional linguistics, since they must take into account the passage of time (e.g., not overtly responding to an invitation constitutes a kind of response).

2. *Taxonomy of linguistic grounding.* In order to carry out the suggested program of viewing the truthfulness of statements in the domain of interaction, we need a "logic of argument," where "argument" stands for the kind of elucidation of background assumptions discussed above. When I make a statement, I am making a commitment to provide some kind of "grounding" in case of a "breakdown." This grounding is in the form of another speech act (also in a situational context) that will satisfy the hearer that the objection is met. There appear to be three basic kinds of grounding: experiential, formal, and social.

> *Experiential:* If asked to justify the statement "Snow is white" I may give a set of instructions ("Go outside and look!") such that a person who follows them will be led to concur on the basis of experience. The methodology of science is designed to provide this kind of grounding for all empirical statements. Maturana (in press) points out that the "objectivity" of science derives from the assumption that for any observation, one can provide instructions that if followed by a "standard observer" will lead him or her to the same conclusion. This does not necessarily mean that the result is observer free, simply that it is anticipated to be uniform for all potential observers.

Formal: Deductive logic is based on the playing of a kind of "language game" in which a set of basic rules are taken for granted, and argument proceeds as a series of moves constrained by those rules. For example, if I expect you to believe that all Swedes are blonde and that Sven is a redhead, then I can use a particular series of moves to provide grounding for the statement that Sven is not Swedish. Of course, this depends on the grounding of the statements used in the process—one can recursively demand grounding for each of them. Under this category fall most of the issues that have been discussed in formal semantics,[25] but with a different emphasis. The focus is not on their coherence as a mathematical abstraction, but on the way they play a role in the logic of conversation.

Social: Much of what we say in conversation is based neither on experience nor logic, but on other conversations. We believe that water is H_2O and that Napoleon was the Emperor of France not because we have relevant experience but because someone told us. One possible form of grounding is to "pass the buck"—to argue that whoever made the statement could have provided grounding. This is also recursive, but we assume that the buck stops somewhere. Of course this need not be so (as illustrated by the development of ideologies in societies), but this is not relevant to its role in the dynamics of conversation.

Just as one can develop taxonomies and structural analyses of illocutionary points, it is important to develop a precise analysis of these structures of argumentation. There are many ways in which such a logic will parallel standard formal logic, and others in which it will not. In particular, it seems that the role of analogy and metaphor will be much more central when the focus is on patterns of argumentation between individuals with a shared background rather than on deductive inference from axioms.

In thinking about these problems it is interesting to look at the structure of reasoning done by lawyers rather than mathematicians. The lawyer is not guided by a formal theory of proof that can be used mechanically to establish the validity of a conclusion. Instead, he or she attempts to anticipate the objections that could be raised (by another person in a particular context) and to prepare justifications that can overcome the objections. Those justifications are in turn based on statements that may themselves need other justifications, *ad infinitum.* Superficially, there is an analogy to the hierarchical structure of theorems based on simpler theorems in mathematics, but there is a deep fundamental difference. The legal brief does not "ground out" on unquestionable axions. Instead it rests on suppositions that the lawyer assumes are part of the basic background (experiential, social, etc.) and hence will not be called into question. Of course this is only an anticipation, and there are mechanisms in court for going deeper into the logic of any statement in the form of an adversary dialog.

3. *Theory of reasoning as triggered by breaking-down.* Going one step further, we need to inquire into the relationship between argumentation and reasoning. The classical understanding is that reasoning proceeds by logical

---

[25]Hintikka (1976) uses the notion of games in his development of deductive logic, including modal logic.

deductive steps, and argumentation is a laying-out of the steps for someone else to follow. The orientation provided here is almost the reverse—reasoning is a form of arguing with yourself, and the justification for a step is that it (temporarily, at least) quiets objections to some statement. The motivation for going farther is that something that previously seemed obvious (either on examination or because it had never been examined) has broken down. Starting with the analyses of philosophers like Heidegger (1962) we can look for a "logic of breaking down" that applies not only to linguistic conversations, but to our non-verbal interactions and understanding.

There are interesting ways in which its characteristics (of breakdowns leading to questions to a certain depth, still within an implicit background) are parallel to those of systems using resource dependent reasoning. Perhaps the mechanisms of systems like KRL can be usefully reinterpreted as representing a logic of argument, rather than a logic of cognitive processing. The issues raised in these systems (such as default knowledge, meta-description, and partial matching) have intriguing connections to problems of background and representation. It would be presumptuous to see the existing formalism as an "answer," but it provides a starting point for exploring the interaction between implicit background, formal structures, and patterns of conversation and justification.

Understanding Existing Systems and Designing New Ones

Computer Systems. Much of cognitive science has been both stimulated by and directed towards the construction of computer programs that behave "intelligently." Hundreds of books and articles have been written on how computer systems will soon become prevalent in every arena of life. The question asked of the cognitive scientist is: "What kind of theories do we need in order to build intelligent systems we can use?"

The prevalent view is that in AI we design "expert systems" that can stand as surrogates for a person doing some job. From a viewpoint of human interaction we see the computer's role differently It is not a surrogate expert, but an intermediary—a sophisticated medium of communication. A group of people (typically including both computer specialists and experts in the subject domain) build a program incorporating a formal representation of their beliefs. The computer communicates their statements to users of the system, typically doing some combinations and rearrangements along the way. The fact that these combinations may involve complex deductive logic, heuristic rule application or statistical analysis does not alter the basic structure of communicative acts.

A person writing a program (or contributing to its "knowledge base") does so within a background of assumptions about how the program will be used and who will be interpreting its responses. Part of this can be made explicit in documentation, but part is an implicit background of what can be "normally understood." Except for systems operating within strongly constrained domains, there inevitably comes a time when the system "breaks down" because it is being used in a way that does not fit the assumptions. This is true not only of "expert systems," but of computer programs in all areas. Many of the biggest failures of mundane computer systems (management systems, inventory systems, etc.) have come not because the system failed to do what the designers specified, but because the assumptions underlying that specification were not appropriate for the situation in which the program was used. This will become even more the case as we build systems that are more flexible—that allow the user to develop new modes of interaction in the course of using the program, rather than staying within a fixed set of alternatives.

Of course, to the degree that system builders can anticipate areas of potential breakdown, they can make explicit statements in advance, which the computer can convey (again perhaps with complex recombination) through an "explanation system."[26] Some existing programs incorporate explanation facilities that move in this direction, but they are able to deal with only a limited range of the potential dialogs of explanation. There is always a limit set by what has been made explicit, and always the potential of breakdowns that call for moving beyond this limit.

If we see the machine as an intermediary, it is clear that the commitment (in the sense discussed above in viewing truth in the context of speech acts) is made by those who produce the system. A dialog must be carried on with the people who performed the original speech acts, or those to whom they have delegated the responsibility. In the absence of this perspective it becomes easy to make the dangerous mistake of interpreting the machine as making commitments, and losing the sense that some person or group of people has responsibility for what it does. We need theories that can help in understanding the properties of dialogs in which a person tries to elucidate the background assumptions that may have led to a breakdown. In designing the computer system the focus is shifted from the problem of "How do we make sure it always gives the right answer?" to "What is the best kind of organization for figuring out when and where things are going wrong?"

Medical diagnosis programs provide a good example. Imagine a program written by a team of computer specialists, working with a group of medical experts. It is installed by the administration of a hospital and used by a member of the medical house staff in choosing a treatment. If the diagnosis was wrong and the patient is harmed, who is responsible? The problem may not be one of wrong medical knowledge, but rather one of background assumptions. An answer that is correct in one context may be inappropriate in another. For example, if the program was written with ambulatory patients in mind, it might not be

<hr/>

[26]Winograd (1979a) discusses the importance of developing systems of this type.

appropriate for a chronic bedridden invalid who shows very different symptom patterns. How can the user of the system systematically find out what the relevant assumptions are? If we do not develop theories that help us to cope with these issues, the systems will be useless or worse.

I also believe that there are potential new directions in the design of computer languages in which these issues will play a prominent role. The writing of a program is a communication between one programmer and another. The understanding of existing programs is one of the most important and difficult things we do, and future systems will need to be oriented primarily towards aiding in this understanding. The issues of language and understanding that have been at the heart of this paper will be at the heart of those systems.[27]

Management. Another practical area that looks to cognitive science for a theoretical base is management. There is a significant overlap of concepts, as illustrated by terms like "problem solving," "decision making," and "heuristic strategy." Of course this is no accident. Herbert Simon, one of the founders of cognitive science, is best known for his work on organizational decision making. The management and decision metaphor has played a large role in shaping artificial intelligence from the earliest days.

My own experience is not in this area, but my work with Fernando Flores (who has been a cabinet minister in the Chilean government) has pointed out concerns that are parallel to those arising in the study of language. The view of management as problem solving and decision making suffers from the same problems of background and context. In looking at the role of a manager as optimizing some value by choosing among alternatives for action, we are in the same position as in looking at the understanding of a word as choosing among a set of formal definitions. The hard part is understanding how the alternatives relevant to a given context come into being. The critical act of problem solving in the recognition of the problem.

Again, this is not a new insight. Management specialists (including Simon) have at times pointed out the essential role of "problem acquisition" as a prerequisite to "problem solving." The practical wisdom of management recognizes the importance of the role a manager plays in continually creating the "problem space" in which he or she operates. But the theories provided by cognitive science and artificial intelligence have little to say about this process of creation. To a large extent, a problem is created by the linguistic acts in which it is identified and categorized. Of course, some situation exists previous to the formulation, but its structure as a problem (which constrains the space of possible solutions) is generated by the commitment of those who talk about it.

Once again we cannot look to simple notions of truth and deduction. The "energy crisis" was not created by specific acts of the oil companies, the Arabs,

---

[27]Winograd (1979b) discusses these issues in a more technical vein.

or the American consumer, but by those with the power to create consensus who looked at a long-term situation and determined it to be a crisis. The relevant question is not whether it is "true" or "false" that there is a crisis, but what commitments are entailed (for speaker and hearer) by the speech acts that created it.

Education. A third area where cognitive theories play a central role is in education. To a large extent our current educational practice has grown from experience with no theory at all, or with a hodgepodge of theories borrowed from behaviorism, structuralism, and various kinds of interpersonal psychology. There have been attempts to attract educators to a theory based on work in artificial intelligence, emphasizing how human thought can be described in terms of concepts such as "algorithm," "heuristic," and "bug." Researchers like Papert (1972) point out that in teaching children subject material, we are also "teaching children thinking." In providing instructions for how to go about particular tasks we are also providing models for how to go about tasks in general. By being conscious of this "meta-teaching" and by applying the best theories we can of thought and language, we can provide a more consistent and effective educational environment.

Again, the questions we choose to look at depend on the domain we see as central. If we concentrate on cognitive processing, students will learn to think in that domain. Faced, for example, with a breakdown in some kind of interpersonal situation, they will ask "What is the bug in my model of the other person?" Starting from an orientation toward the structure of interaction, the question becomes "What do we do to make explicit the assumptions that led to the breakdown?" The emphasis is on the nature of the continuing interaction, rather than on the cognitive structure of the participants. No one orientation is good for everything, and the purpose of an educational system should be to give students experience with the broadest possible range. There is a significant place for understanding language and thought in terms of social interaction.

9. CONCLUSION

Those who are familiar with the philosophical discussion about artificial intelligence will have noticed that many of the ideas and sources discussed here (such as the incompleteness of formal representation, Heidegger's notion of background, etc.) are among those cited by critics like Dreyfus (1979), who deny the possibility of developing any formalization of human thought and knowledge. A conclusion one might draw is that having brought these questions to light, we can only proceed by abandoning formal cognitive science and our attempts to program computers to do things we consider "intelligent."

It should be clear from the previous section that this is not my conclusion. I am not advocating (or planning) the abandonment of the scientific study of cognition, but trying to better understand what we are doing, and refocusing my efforts in the light of that understanding. However, it could be argued that the path described in this paper is one leading away from the paradigm of cognitive science. Even granting that an orientation towards language as social action is interesting and useful, it is arguable that it is not "cognitive science"—that it represents a turning away from the domain of "cognitive processing" (or, as it is often called, "information processing"). In some ways this observation is valid, but in others it is misleading.

It is important to recognize what we are doing we apply words like "cognitive" or "science" to a particular enterprise or approach. In our writing, teaching, and interactions with people (both in the field and outside), we are performing speech acts that give those words meaning. Different orientations lead to different practical suggestions, to different ways of interpreting and acting. As has been pointed out in the philosophy of science, the importance of a paradigm may not lie so much in the answers it provides as in the questions it leads one to consider, and a paradigm (like a crisis) is created by a web of interlinked speech acts.

Some day in the future there may be a field called "cognitive science" whose boundaries are defined by a narrow common approach and domain, just as there are fields of "anatomy," "physiology," and "pathology" dealing with the physical structures and functioning of the human body in their own domains. This narrowly defined cognitive science would deal with those aspects of language, thought, and action that are best understood in the domain of information processing. At the moment though, this is not the case. As indicated by this volume and the nascent professional society it represents, "cognitive science" is a broad rubric, intended to include anyone who is concerned with phenomena related to mind. I believe that the kinds of issues I have been led to in looking at language are relevant to a broad segment of cognitive science as generally interpreted, and a serious consideration of them may call into question many of the assumptions at the heart of our current understanding.

ACKNOWLEDGMENTS

My thinking about language has been developed through interactions with a number of people, as chronicled in the paper. I am particularly indebted to Fernando Flores for continually introducing new vistas. It was in conversations with Danny Bobrow and Brian Smith that the ideas of KRL emerged, and work on KRL has involved many other people. Coversations with Don Norman led to some of the original thinking about memory structure. Henry Thompson, Rich Fikes, David Levy, Mitch Model, Paul Martin, Jonathan King, and Wendy Lehnert have all contributed to the ideas and implementations. In addition to Bobrow, Flores, Levy, and Thompson, the Berkeley discussions mentioned at the beginning of section 5 included Hubert Dreyfus, John Searle, and Stephen White. Danny Bobrow, Fernando Flores, David Levy, and David Lowe provided insightful comments on an earlier draft of this paper.

REFERENCES

Austin, J. L. *How to do things with words*. Cambridge, Mass.: Harvard University Press, 1962.

Barr, A. The representation hypothesis. (Stanford HPP-Memo, HPP-80-1, Dept. of Computer Science 1980).

Bobrow, D. G., & Winograd, T. An overview of KRL, a knowledge representation language. *Cognitive Science,* 1977, *1,* 3–46.

Bobrow, D. G., & Winograd, T. KRL: Another perspective. *Cognitive Science,* 1979, *3,* pp. 29–42.

Dreyfus, H. *What computers can't do: A critique of artificial reason.* (2nd Ed.) San Francisco: Freeman, 1979.

Feigenbaum, E., & Feldman, J. *Computers and thought.* New York: McGraw Hill, 1963.

Fillmore, C. An alternative to checklist theories of meaning. In Cogen et al. (Eds.), *Proceedings of the First Annual Meeting of the Berkeley Linguistics Society.* University of California, Berkeley, 1975.

Flores, C. F., & Winograd, T. *Understanding cognition as understanding.* Norwood, N.J.: Ablex Publishing Corporation, in press.

Fodor, J. A. Tom Swift and his procedural grandmother. *Cognition,* 1978, *6,* pp. 229–247.

Fodor, J. A. Methodological solipsism as a research strategy in psychology. *Brain and Behavioral Sciences,* forthcoming.

Gadamer, H-G. *Philosophical hermeneutics.* Translated by David E. Linge. Berkeley: University of California Press, 1976.

Garfinkel, H. What is ethnomethodology? In H. Garfinkel (Ed.), *Studies in Ethnomethodology.* Englewood Cliffs, N.J.: Prentice–Hall, 1967.

Geschwind, N. Neurological knowledge and complex behaviors. *Cognitive Science,* 1980, *4,* pp. 185–193.

Grosz, B. J. Focusing and description in natural language dialogues. In A. K. Joshi, I. A. Sag, & B. L. Webber (Eds.), *Elements of discourse understanding.* Cambridge: Cambridge University Press, 1980.

Heidegger, M. *Being and time.* New York: Harper & Row, 1962.

Hintikka, J. Quantifiers in logic and quantifiers in natural languages. In S. Korner (Ed.), *Philosophy of Logic.* Berkeley, Calif: University of California Press, 1976.

Hobbs, J. R. Resolving pronoun references. *Lingua,* 1978, *44,* 311–338.

Katz, J. J., & Fodor, J. A. The structure of a semantic theory. In J. Fodor & J. Katz, (Eds.), *The Structure of Language.* Englewood Cliffs, N.J.: Prentice–Hall, 1964.

Kuhn, T. *The structure of scientific revolutions.* Chicago: Ill.: University of Chicago Press, 1962.

Labov, W. The boundaries of words and their meanings. In C–J. N. Bailey & R. Shuy (Eds.), *New ways of analyzing variation in English.* Washington, D.C.: Georgetown University, 1973.

Lakatos, I. *Proofs and refutations.* Cambridge, Mass.: Cambridge University Press, 1976.

Lakoff, G. & Johnson, M. The metaphorical structure of the human conceptual system. *Cognitive Science,* 1980, *4,* pp. 195–208.

Lighthill, Sir. J. *Artificial intelligence: A general survey.* London: Science Research Council, 1973.

Maturana, H. R. Biology of language. In R. W. Rieber (Ed.), *The neuropsychology of language.* New York: Plenum Press, 1977.

Minsky, M. *Semantic information processing.* Cambridge, Mass.: MIT Press, 1967.

Minsky, M. A framework for representing knowledge. In P. Winston, (Ed.), *The psychology of computer vision.* New York: McGraw-Hill, 1975.

Minsky, M. K-Lines: A theory of memory. *Cognitive Science,* 1980, *4,* pp. 117–133.

Norman, D. A. Twelve issues for Cognitive Science. *Cognitive Science,* 1980, *4,* pp. 1–32.

Palmer, R. E. *Hermeneutics: Interpretation theory in Schleiermacher, Dilthey, Heidegger and Gadamer.* Evanston, Ill.: Northwestern University Press, 1969.

Papert, S. Teaching children thinking. *Mathematics Teaching: The Bulletin of the Association of Mathematics* No. 58, Spring, 1972.

Rosch, E. Cognitive representations of semantic categories. *Journal of Experimental Psychology: General*, 1975, *104*, pp. 192–233.

Schank, R. & Abelson, R. *Scripts, plans, goals, and understanding*. Hillsdale, N.J.: Lawrence Erlbaum Associates, 1975.

Schank, R. C. Language and memory. *Cognitive Science*, 1980, *4*, pp. 243–284.

Searle, J. *Speech Arts*. Cambridge, Mass.: Cambridge University Press, 1970.

Searle, J. A taxonomy of illocutionary acts. In K. Gunderson (Ed.), *Language, mind, and knowledge: Minnesota studies in the philosophy of science*, Vol. XI. Minneapolis, Minn.: University of Minnesota Press, 1975.

Searle, J. R. The intentionality of intention and action. *Cognitive Science*, 1980, *4*, 47–70.

Turing, A. M. Computing machinery and the mind. *Mind: A Quarterly Review of Psychology and Philosophy*, 1950.

Winograd, T. *Procedures as a Representation for Data in a Computer Program for Understanding Natural Language*. MAC-TR-84, MIT Project MAC, 1971.

Winograd, T. *Understanding natural language*. New York: Academic Press, 1972.

Winograd, T. A process model of language understanding. In R. C. Schank & K. M. Colby (Eds.), *Computer models of thought and language*. San Francisco, Calif.: W. H. Freeman, 1973.

Winograd, T. When will computers understand people? *Psychology Today*, 1974, *7*, pp. 73–79. (a)

Winograd, T. Five lectures on artificial intelligence, PIPS-R. No. 5, Electrotechnical Laboratory, Tokyo, Japan, 1974. Reprinted in A. Zampolli (Ed.), *Linguistic structures processing*. North Holland, 1977. (b)

Winograd, T. Frame representations and the procedural–declarative controversy. In D. Bobrow & A. Collins (Eds.), *Representation and understanding: Studies in Cognitive Science*. New York: Academic Press, 1975.

Winograd, T. Towards a procedural understanding of semantics. *Revue Internationale de Philosophie*, 1976, *3*, pp. 117–118.

Winograd, T. A framework for understanding discourse. In M. Just & P. Carpenter (Eds.), *Cognitive processes in comprehension*. Hillsdale, N.J.: Lawrence Erlbaum Associates, 1977. (a)

Winograd, T. On some contested suppositions of generative linguistics about the scientific study of language. *Cognition*, 1977, *5*, pp. 151–179. (b)

Winograd, T. On primitives, prototypes, and other semantic anomalies. *Proceedings from Theoretical Issues in Natural Language Processing II*. University of Illinois at Champaign–Urbana, 25–32, 1978.

Winograd, T. Towards convivial computing. In M. L. Dertouzos & J. Moses (Eds.), *The computer age: A twenty-year view*. Cambridge, Mass.: MIT Press, 1979. (a)

Winograd, T. Beyond Programming languages. *Communications of the ACM*, 1979, *22*, 391–401. (b)

Winograd, T. Extended inference modes in computer reasoning systems. *Artificial Intelligence*.

Winograd, T. *Language as a cognitive process*. Reading, Mass.: Addison–Wesley, (in preparation).

11

Twelve Issues
for Cognitive Science

DONALD A. NORMAN

University of California, San Diego

HUMAN INFORMATION PROCESSING:
THE CONVENTIONAL VIEW

When I first began the study of psychology, I was interested in mechanisms. The task seemed straightforward enough—difficult, yes, but well defined. The human is an animate being, functioning in the environment. The human has certain biological facets, physical facets, intellectual facets. The basic conceptualization went like this: Intellectual processes are the result of the operation of several separable systems: sensory-perceptual systems, central processing (thought), memory, and response output (motor control). Sensory transducers feed a steady stream of information about the environment to some central processing structures where that information is analyzed, interpreted and fed to a response system which controls body movements and speech sounds.

Considerations of this sort led to the view—the reasonably well accepted view in psychology—of the human as composed of separable subsystems of information processing mechanisms: perceptual systems (including pattern recognition), motor or output systems, memory systems, and systems for internal reasoning and deduction, which includes thought, problem solving, and language. A summary of the components and a rough sketch of their interactions is shown in Figure 1, which might be considered to be a modern updating of the conventional flow chart of the human information processing system. The figure summarizes what is known today about the "Pure Cognitive System," the system built around pure cognitive functioning, with a physical symbol system as its central component.

Different workers might put more weight on one aspect of this system than

265

on another, but on the whole, this has come to be a fairly well accepted view of things. I will not review for you the history of this and other approaches to the study of the human information processing system, but I will discuss some aspects of it. Basically, I believe that although this view is accurate, it is but one of many possible views. Taken alone, this view is both inadequate and misleading.

In recent years I have become more and more dissatisfied with the conventional view of information processing. The source of the dissatisfaction was not obvious: each of the components of Figure 1 seemed reasonable, and although one might (and did) argue about the details, the powerful arguments for physical symbol systems seemed persuasive. The problem seemed to be in the lack of consideration of other aspects of human behavior, of interaction with other people and with the environment, of the influence of the history of the person, or even the culture, and of the lack of consideration of the special problems and issues confronting an animate organism that must survive as both an individual and as a species, so that intellectual functioning might perhaps be placed in a proper perspective. These considerations have accumulated until they finally have forced themselves upon me. The human is a physical symbol system, yes, with a component of pure cognition describable by mechanisms of the sort illustrated in Figure 1. But the human is more: The human is an animate organism, with a biological basis and an evolutionary and cultural history. Moreover, the human is a social animal, interacting with others, with the environment, and with itself. The core disciplines of cognitive science have tended to ignore these aspects of behavior. The results have been considerable progress on some fronts, but sterility overall, for the organism we are analyzing is conceived as pure intellect, communicating with one another in logical dialogue, perceiving, remembering, thinking where appropriate, reasoning its way through the well-formed problems that are encountered in the day. Alas, that description does not fit actual behavior.

These objections are not novel. They are raised in one way or another by other contributors to these proceedings. Simon reminded us that behavior is always relative to the environment, so in the study of human behavior we are really studying social behavior. I agree, but feel he did not go far enough: there is more to interaction than social interaction. Geschwind reminded us of our biological origins, with emotional systems playing a central role, not just in overall behavior, but perhaps even in such "pure" cognitive functions as memory. We have wired-in, specialized sybsystems for doing what might seem to be general processes, such as recognizing faces. Johnson-Laird and Lakoff reminded us that thought may not proceed smoothly through logical constructions, but may instead rely upon metaphorical modeling of the current situation as an instance of a past experience, so that experience colors thought in fundamental ways. And Winograd argued for a much richer analysis of our history and our social and cultural interactions as a prelude to the understanding of language.

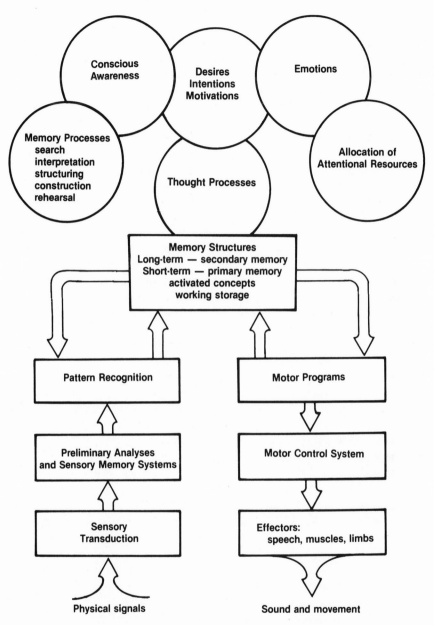

Figure 1. A modern version of the conventional flow chart of the human information processing system. The basic components are a series of processing mechanisms that take in information about the environment, perform general central processing operations, and control motor output. The central processing is complex, with various sources of knowledge interacting with one another, controlled by an as-yet little understood processing structure which allows for some simultaneous operation, self awareness, consciousness of some of the processes. The stuff in the central part of the figure is sufficiently vague as to allow for a large number of interpretations of its nature.

I expand upon these arguments, for although I sympathize with them, I do not think that even they went far enough. Each of the papers of these proceedings presents one point of view, each view appropriate for some aspect of intelligent behavior. I wish to take yet another view, one that attempts to put the others into proper perspective. Let me illustrate by several examples. One is a brief description of an airplane accident, another the view of classroom behavior. These two examples are followed by some general discussion of human functioning and then by a re-evaluation of the role of pure cognition. I conclude that there is more to human intelligence than the pure cognitive system, and that a science of Cognition cannot afford to ignore these other aspects.

Tenerife

In March of 1977, two Boeing 747 airliners collided on a runway at Tenerife, in the Canary Islands. The crash killed 582 people. What caused the accident? No single factor. The crash resulted from a complex interaction of events, including problems of attentional focus, the effects of expectation upon language understanding that combined with an inability to communicate effectively over a technically limited communication channel when there were major difficulties in language (although all involved were speaking English), the subtle effects of differences of social structure among the participants, the effects of stress, economic responsibilities and social and cultural factors upon decision making. All in all, it is a fascinating—if horrifying—story for Cognitive Science.

A View of the Classroom

Consider the classroom situation, especially the early grades of school. The teacher has a point to make, a body of information to get across. This aspect of teaching has been receiving considerable attention in recent years. The teacher must construct a mental model of student knowledge, match the model of the student with that of the desired endpoint, determine some strategy for presenting the information not yet currently held by the students, and go forth and teach. Figure 2 shows a possible model of the teacher. Don't worry about the details, just think of the model as an attempt to summarize how the teacher determines the appropriate way to transmit the topic matter to the class.

The individual students must themselves be represented by models similar to that of Figure 2, except complementary in that they respond to the new information about the topic matter and construct mental memory structures to accommodate them. Each student has some knowledge and as the student interacts with the teacher, the student knowledge is altered and enriched in appropriate ways. If questioned by the teacher, the student can apply the new knowledge in order to answer the query, thereby providing feedback to the teacher about the state of learning.

Alas, anyone who has actually taught in a classroom (especially an elementary school classroom) knows that this description provides only the most idealistic view of the real behavior. Some of the description is appropriate, but there is much more happening. In some classrooms, it would be difficult to find any evidence that teaching—in the sense just described—was ever taking place. The students are in a social setting, interacting with one another, acutely aware of each other and of the overall classroom behavior. Individual students tailor their behavior for the other students to some degree, sometimes entirely for the other students. The behavior of the teacher and the individual students is responsive to the events of the classroom, but the classroom events are the results of the combination of behaviors of the teachers and the students.

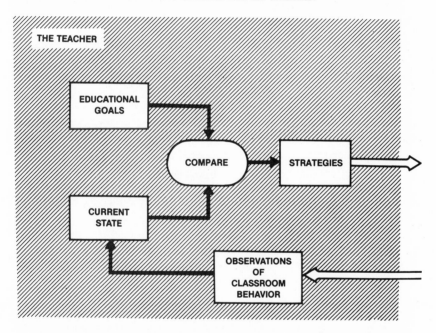

Figure 2. An information processing model of the teacher. Starting with educational goals, the teacher compares those goals with the current state of classroom behavior and knowledge and uses an instructional strategy appropriate to the situation. The teacher continually monitors classroom behavior and modifies the instructional strategy, or the knowledge being taught accordingly. This is a feedback model of instruction. The "current state" implies, among other things, a model of student knowledge and behavior. This model of a teacher is common to modern instructional theory (including my own). It is probably necessary, but by itself, it fails to be useful in the prediction of classroom behavior.

Cybernetics and Behavior. Cybernetics. A term connoting engineering models of servomechanism systems, the sort of systems one would expect for motor control, or for homeostatic body functioning. Why do I introduce it here?

I use the term "cybernetics" to mean a feedback system, one in which the operation of the system depends upon interaction with the environment. This is what Norbert Weiner meant when he coined the term. The concept has been lost from most of cognitive studies, in part because of the lack of study of output and of performance (more on this later). Without output, there is no feedback. Without global views of functioning, the question of the role of feedback does not arise.

Much social interaction can be viewed as a cybernetic system. Each person is responsive to the environment. Each person is a human information processing system, consisting of something like the components of Figure 1, each behaving something like the model of the teacher presented in Figure 2. But the overall behavior is the result of all the participants, and the participants, in turn, respond to the total behavior. The overall view is something like Figure 3—a view that works for both the classroom and for the Tenerife situation as well.

Suppose we are interested in classroom instruction. In this case we need to understand classroom interaction, the classroom behavior. We must take a view that is something like that shown in Figure 3. We need to understand the several different interactive themes that are simultaneously active within the classroom: the social interactions among the students, the sociolinguistics of their language use, the status differences among the students and between students and teacher. These all color the use of language and participation. Even the seating pattern and room arrangement will turn out to matter.

Obviously one also needs to know of the motives that drive the teacher, the lesson that is to be taught, the time constraints that must be obeyed, the kind of classroom interaction the teacher desires, and the kind that the teacher will tolerate.

Now, if one wishes to understand the particular responses of the teacher or of an individual child to a particular classroom event, then it is going to be necessary to have an information processing view of the person, somewhat of the form of Figure 2. But the model is only going to be useful if it is coupled with an understanding of the several simultaneous (and possibly conflicting) goals and motivations of the various participants.

My point is not an indictment of any particular approach to the study of learning and teaching. On the contrary, it is a statement that all approaches are necessary. The information processing psychologist who studies the transfer of knowledge from teacher to student is contributing some understanding of the classroom situation. The person who studies the sociological influences upon the students' behavior and their tolerance to classroom discipline is also contributing some understanding, of an entirely different kind. My argument is that the situation is not going to be understood until all these different points of view are combined, for the overall classroom behavior is a result of all these forces, no one more fundamental than another.

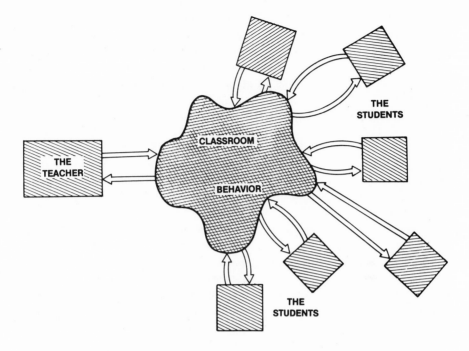

Figure 3. The classroom behavior is the result of a combination of interactions. Each student responds to the behavior of the classroom, as well as to the internal goals of satisfying other students, the teacher, and self needs. So too with the teacher. The teacher and students are all modeled by something akin to Figure 2, but understanding of their behavior requires understanding of the entire interaction. The classroom is a system of individual cybernetic actors. (This basic picture of interaction applies to a variety of situations in addition to the classroom. Only the labels need be changed.)

How Much Does Cognitive Science Know?

I am struck by how little is known about so much of cognition. The crash at Tenerife and the interactions of the classroom are but two examples of the complex interactions of cognitive factors that can play important roles in our lives. But there are much simpler examples.

Memory. I have studied memory for years, yet am unable to answer even simple questions about the use of memory in everyday life. Mental activity. The study of thought processes has concentrated upon logical, systematic behavior, one step at a time. What about the processing deeply buried within the subconscious where it can go on without awareness for hours, days (months?).

Slips, Freudian and Otherwise. People make slips of the tongue, slips of action. Some are undoubtedly easy to explain: confusions, lack of knowledge, or obvious sources of the error. But others require much more subtle analyses, involving the nature of memory and retrieval, activation and stress, or conflicting simultaneous thoughts. Freud had a theory, one that I suspect is much more appropriate than Cognitive Scientists tend to give credit today. At least Freud did worry about the relationships among emotions, conscious and subconscious events (we would say ''processing''), and how the subconscious is manifested in behavior.

Performance. Consider the highly skilled typist, producing over 100 words per minute, about 10 keystrokes per second. Or the professional pianist playing 25 notes per second in a Chopin Nocturne. Motor skills are fascinating aspects of our behavior, little understood, little studied (in comparison with, say, language). How does one hit a baseball that is travelling at great speed, or steer a speeding automobile through narrow spaces, or control a large crane, making precise movements at the end of a boom a hundred meters long with controls that seem to have little relevance to the actions being performed?

Language. If you think we understand language, well, how about real language, the language between two people in casual conversation? By the rules of formal language, such language is often ungrammatical and it should be unintelligible. Indeed, as an inveterate eavesdropper on the conversations of strangers (in the name of Science, of course), I can attest that one-minute fragments of other people's conversations are unintelligible and remarkably free of content. The conversants would not agree. They have established sufficient bonds that they can relax the normal constraints of language. Gesture, timing, intonation can carry as much weight as the formal content of the words. This observation is not meant to be a surprise: We are all aware of the phenomenon. But not as scientists: we do not understand how.

You will not be surprised if I tell you that we understand little of the interactions of social groups, or of society, or of cultures, especially of the mechanisms of that interaction. You might be surprised if I claim that these factors play a large role in everyday behavior, even in performance on our abstract tasks within the laboratory. Perhaps one reason that our theories of the separable components of information processing say so little about real world activities is the neglect of social and cultural factors, among other things.

One goal of this paper is to convince you that the study of cognition requires the consideration of all these different aspects of the entire system, including the parts that are both internal and external to the cognizer. (By ''internal,'' I mean the knowledge, the processing mechanisms, the rules, strategies, and control mechanisms. By ''external'' I mean the environment, the society, culture, and the interaction of all these with one another.) Of course no one can study everything all at the same time, but I argue that we cannot ignore these things either, else the individual pieces that we study in such detail will not fit together in the absence of some thought about the whole.

ON THE DIFFERENCES BETWEEN ANIMATE AND ARTIFICIAL COGNITIVE SYSTEMS

Intelligence, thought, cognition—these are central topics in the study of Cognitive Science. So let us start by considering the elements of a cognitive system. Suppose we concentrate on the intellectual functioning—what are the essential elements of a cognitive system? Let me go through the arguments of the necessary components, starting with a reasonably traditional view (I will end quite differently). The basic picture of the human information processing structure, in its modern format, has been presented as Figure 1.

Now consider, if you will, an intelligent artificial system, one that might be the goal of your favorite robotologist. What does an artificial system need? Obviously there are several possible answers. If we consider only the *Pure Cognitive System* (henceforth, PCS), then we see obvious differences in structure between natural and artificial systems, between electronics and biology. Nerve cells convey their signals through electrical potentials, by chemical transmission. They are affected by biological chemicals (hormones, nutritive fluids, transmitter substances). And natural systems have wiring diagrams that are not yet understood, that seem to be adaptive, that have billions of interconnections. But despite the obvious differences, there are no obvious differences at the level of functional mechanisms. Presumably, the biological system has memory structures, perceptual structures, and so on, and in principle, if we wish to and knew enough we could build artificial systems whose operations mimicked the biological ones. We would need to learn a considerable amount more than we currently know about the functioning of such a system, but the "in principle" point is what is critical for those of us who pursue the study of psychological mechanisms.

But wait. The difference between natural and artificial devices is not simply that they are constructed of different stuff; their basic functions differ. Humans survive, get nourishment from the environment, protect themselves against physical insult, form families and societies, reproduce themselves and protect and educate the young. Much of this is handled with the aid of biological structures that I will call the *Regulatory System* (RS). Consider how the RS interacts with the cognitive system—something like Figure 4 emerges.

Consider the implications of Figure 4. (Yes, even such a simple diagram does have implications.) Dangerous situations require immediate attention, immediate response. If potential danger is to be discovered quickly, there must be continual monitoring of possible sources of evidence. Moreover, when danger is detected, then the organism must be alerted to the problem and it must allocate sufficient resources to deal with it. It is easy to understand how this might be done when dealing with things like changes in body states, such as temperature,

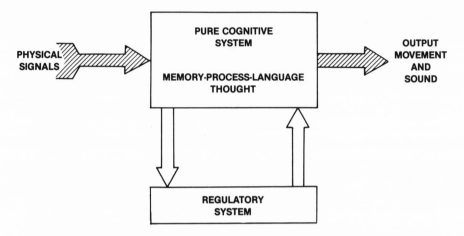

Figure 4. To the Pure Cognitive System of Figure 1 we must add the properties of the Regulatory System. In this view of things, the Cognitive System dominates. This view is an obvious one, but probably wrong.

blood sugar level or fatigue. Environmental situations that lead to pain or otherwise send sensory signals that can be monitored are also easy to understand with the framework shown in Figure 4.

The issues are not so simple when we consider how to respond to events that must be interpreted: dangerous heights, the sight of a wild tiger, fire, the sound of an explosion, or the airline pilot's announcement that two engines have failed. For these events, perception, knowledge, and language must be called into play—essentially, all the mechanisms of the Pure Cognitive System. But these interpretations must operate with immediacy, interrupting whatever primary task was going on. The problem here is that it takes the cognitive system to do the interpretation for the maintenance system, thereby allowing the maintenance system to interrupt the cognitive system. It can't work.

We need to rethink the organization implied in Figure 4: maybe the PCS is not the pinnacle of human functioning. It is comforting to think so, that the focal point is PCS, with the RS serving to maintain both the body and the PCS. This egotistical point of view is especially nice for intellectuals, but it doesn't hold up. It is always dangerous to invent and then to rely on biological principles and evolutionary causation, but it is also useful. Did the evolutionary sequence that produced superior cognitive systems do so to permit professors to exist, to publish, to hold conferences? One suspects not, that the regulatory system was first, that the cognitive system grew out of the requirements of that system. To determine that a limb should be withdrawn from a painful stimulus did not require much cognition: to avoid the situation in the first place did.

The point is simply that the functions and the requirements of animate systems include the problem of survival, and that this problem requires a regulatory system of considerable complexity, one in which considerable cognitive power is required. And so, the cognitive system is apt to be the servant of the regulatory system, not the other way around, as shown in Figure 5. Emotional systems might very well be an interplay between the two, so that perceptual analysis (done by the PCS) might at times cause the RS to create the necessary emotional arousal to alert the PCS.

If the RS dominates, with the cognitive system its servant, interesting implications follow. Perhaps PCS is a myth, with intellectual thought an outgrowth of the use of biological function for purposes somewhat foreign to the original need. Cognitive systems might be the result of the generally increasing demands of the regulatory system for an intelligent component. Perhaps when the cognitive side reached some critical mass, it then possessed sufficient computational power to have its own existence and to establish its own goals and functions. But only afterwards, grafted on, if you will, to the functions of supporting one's own life.

What about emotions? Are they superfluous to cognitive functioning? Most of us—and I include myself in the "us"—would prefer to believe this. Contemporary theories of cognitive functioning—no matter the discipline—seem to be theories of pure reason. Emotions have to do with something else, perhaps an evolutionary carry over from an earlier time when the demands upon human functioning were different. Well, the novelist, the playwright, the clinical psychologist and psychiatrist know differently. If I am correct in my assertion that the cognitive system is subservient to the regulatory system, with pure cognition an artificial situation grafted on to a biological organism, then emotions play a critical role in behavior.

A summary of these arguments about the nature of cognitive systems in general and of animate cognitive systems in particular is presented in Table 1. I believe that we should reconsider the functioning of human processing. Some things will not change: our observations and theories will still apply. But I suspect some aspects will change in fundamental ways. I cannot now tell you what will change and what will not: we must wait and see.

SOME ISSUES FOR COGNITIVE SCIENCE

The arguments of the preceding pages suggest that we must broaden the issues considered by the discipline of Cognitive Science. In fact, twelve major issues attract my attention. These twelve are neither independent of one another nor equal in importance. I do claim, however, that these twelve are among a core group of issues along which we must progress if our field is to make substantive advances.

I believe in the value of multiple philosophies, multiple viewpoints, multiple approaches to common issues. I believe a virtue of Cognitive Science is that it

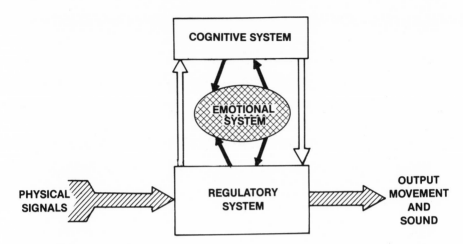

Figure 5. The Regulatory System is here given primacy over the Pure Cognitive System. Compare
with Figure 4: the basic format is the same, except that sensory inputs and motor outputs now leave and
enter RS rather than PCS. An emotional system stands between. And the relative sizes of the boxes that
symbolize the systems have been changed to mark the change in emphasis.

brings together heretofore disparate disciplines to work on common themes. My
reason for discussing these twelve issues is the hope that I can focus some efforts
upon them. I introduce and discuss these issues from my own perspective, which
is primarily that of a psychologist interested in the workings of the mind. I treat
the twelve briefly. My intention is to raise them, not discuss them in detail: that is
done elsewhere. Alternative points of view are possible, welcome, and necessary.

Issues Are Not Levels

The issues are topic matters that are to be studied. They are not the names of
disciplines nor prescriptions for methods of study. Each issue should be addressed from different directions, yielding different levels of explanation.

When we come to describe the mechanisms of cognition, the explanations
should be couched at several different levels. The psychologist talks of functional
mechanisms and of behavior, the neuroscientist talks of cells and neural systems.
The anthropologist and the sociologist each have their levels of analysis. Linguists, philosophers, and computer scientists each view cognition from their
special perspectives, each different, yet complementary. I believe that the complete science must have all of these different levels represented. We need to
know about the neurological and biological basis for animate cognitive systems,
about the mathematical and philosophical basis for cognitive systems, about the

TABLE 1
Essential Elements of Cognitive Systems:
In General, and in Animate Organisms

All Cognitive Systems

All cognitive systems, animate and artificial, must have the following:
   A way of receiving information about the world: receptors
   A way of performing actions upon the world: motor control
   Cognitive processes, which include:
      a means of interpreting and identifying information received by the receptors
      a means of controlling the actions to be performed
      a means of guiding the allocation of cognitive resources when more needs to be done than can
         immediately be done (this can be derived from the fact that a finite system must have
         finite resources)
      a memory for the history of actions and experiences
   These cognitive processes imply that:
      because resources are finite, there will be times when more is being attempted than can be
         accomplished; some means of resource allocation (attention) will be required
      because there will be synchronization problems with events in the environment and internal events,
         buffer (short-term) memories are required
      There must be basic operations, an interpreter, and some feedback mechanisms that can observe
         the effect of operations upon the world and change accordingly
      There must be some way to devise plans and then to monitor their operation; this requires levels of
         knowledge—meta-knowledge
      For intelligent interaction, there must be a model of the environment, of one's self, and of others
      There must be learning, changing one's behavior and knowledge in fundamental ways (as opposed
         to simple adaptation), and this will probably require a system capable of inferring
         causality, inter-relations among concepts and events, and self-observation

---

Animate Systems

   A major difference between animate and inanimate systems is that an animate system maintains
itself, protects itself, regulates its own operation, and reproduces itself. A newly born organism requires
considerable physical, biological, and educational maturation, which takes place through a protracted
time course of infancy, childhood, and adulthood. The organism at birth differs from adulthood:
      It is smaller, both physically and in the amount of its cognitive (neural) structure;
      It has less knowledge;
      Its regulatory system is not fully developed.
   An animate system must survive, which means it must be alert for unexpected occurrences: its
regulatory and cognitive systems must interact. The regulatory system is a homeostatic system, designed to
maintain life. It must interact with the cognitive system, for interpretations are required of the situation and
actions are required to maintain homeostasis, comfort, and safety.
   An animate system has goals, desires, purposes. The system is motivated to perform some activities. There must be a means of selecting "interesting" and goal-related tasks from among those that
could possibly be done, controlling the amount of effort devoted to that task, and scheduling the initiation
and termination of the various activities. Long term goals and issues related to survival receive dominance,
although the mechanisms for accomplishing these may not be part of the self-awareness of the organism.

---

mechanistic basis for artificial systems. But that is not the point of this paper. The issues I discuss are not statements about the philosophy or level of approach. Rather they are issues, or problem areas, that should be considered.

The Twelve Issues

I give you the following issues:

Belief systems	Emotion	Learning	Performance
Consciousness	Interaction	Memory	Skill
Development	Language	Perception	Thought

"What a strange list," you must be thinking. Not what you expected. Emotion? Skill? On the same level as language and memory? Aren't learning and memory and skill and performance all the same, or at least highly related? What about motivation, or representation, or whatever your favorite topic? Wait, I will clarify some of the problems (though not all). Remember, these 12 issues are ones that I see as key to the development of a science of cognition. Not all are recognized by everyone as being relevant. Not all are thought to be important. Some are well studied, but not normally thought to be a part of cognition. Some issues are seen as simply subsets of others. I disagree: all are essential.

A BRIEF TOUR OF THE TWELVE ISSUES

Belief Systems

I start with Belief Systems, accidentally the first in my alphabetized list of issues, but deserving of primacy under other criteria as well. For belief systems mark the merger of the traditional domain of cognitive science—the study of knowledge—with the domains of those who study real world interaction of humans—the anthropologists, the social psychologists and the sociologists. This issue could perhaps more easily be called "knowledge," or perhaps, "world knowledge." I do not use these labels in order to emphasize the merger of several different classes of knowledge, including culture, belief, and world knowledge of several sorts. The basic concept here is that we acquire a lot of knowledge over our lifetime which then colors our interactions with others, with the environment, and even our internal processing. A major component of anthropology and sociology is concerned with the examination of these belief structures.

Cultural knowledge is that special subset of general knowledge that is passed on from generation to generation, taught in the family, or in the schools, or (more commonly) not so much taught as experienced. Styles of dress, social interaction, rankings of social groups, interaction patterns including conversational (discourse) rules, social deference, and other patterns are included here. The physical shape of the environment is altered through culture. The style of buildings, paths, transportation—our technology.

The belief systems go beyond obvious cultural interactions, however. They carry over to such things as rules for memory and thought. You will come to believe these statements more the more you believe that thought and memory are done through reference to real world experience. Suppose that logical inference is normally done by setting up a mental model of a concrete analogy to the problem, using experience to guide the solution of that concrete analogy, then interpreting the result for the problem at hand. If this is the case, then belief systems are of critical importance in determining the basis for much of thought.

Similar statements can be made about memory, perception, problem solving, the interpretation of texts and the conduct of dialogs, legal negotiations, and so on, and on, and on. Many of you are familiar with delusional belief systems that result from mental abnormalities (paranoia being the most fashionable to discuss, for it seems most directly tied to the development of a rich, delusional system, self consistent in its own way, but a great danger to the possessor).

So, belief systems are important, both as interesting items of study in their own right but also as important determiners of much of the rest of cognitive behavior. At the moment, the tools for formal analysis of such structures are just being developed. There is much talk among cognitive anthropologists and sociologists of scripts and schemas, of story grammars, and representational issues. I have an obvious interest in this direction of work, having myself urged the importance of the study of representation and the utility of the study of structured memory units (schemas). The major issue, though, is not yet the one of representation. Rather, we must first lay out the development of the problem itself, examine the nature of belief systems in general, and determine what the implications are for cognitive behavior. My brief excursions into this area have left me impressed with how much my own hidden belief structures influence my "pure" logical inference, memory processes, and social interactions. I suspect that we will find that more of our behavior is thus determined, not less.

Consciousness

"Everyone knows what attention is." So said William James in 1890, and so too have I said repeatedly in my courses and lectures on attention. But the statement is false, quite false. We really do not know about attention, to a large extent because we do not know about consciousness. Studies of attention have restricted themselves to a small segment of the phenomena of which James wrote:

> It is the taking possession of the mind, in clear and vivid form, of one out of what seems several simultaneously possible objects or trains of thought. Focalization, concentration, of consciousness are of its essence. It implies withdrawal from some things in order to deal effectively with others (James, 1890, Vol. I., p. 403–404).

Consciousness, under which I include the issues of conscious and subconscious thought, the problem of self awareness, attention, the control structures of cognition, the formation of intentions. Here too are such issues as the phenomenological states of awareness, states of consciousness. Hypnosis: a powerful force, potentially a powerful tool for the investigation of consciousness, but little understood, not sufficiently well explored.

It should not be necessary to talk about consciousness to a group concerned with cognition. But consciousness is a peculiar stepchild of our discipline, agreed to be important, but little explored in research or theory. There are legitimate reasons for the relative neglect. This is a most difficult topic, one for which it is very difficult to get the hard, sensible evidence that experimental disciplines require. We have little idea of the real nature of consciousness, of the functions it might serve, of the nature of the subconscious. We are just beginning to get a glimmer of the phenomenology of consciousness, of different states of awareness and different phenomenological experiences (though most of this comes from nontraditional sources).

It is exactly the description given in the quote from James that we do not understand, cannot understand until we come to a better appreciation of the working of the mind, of the several simultaneous trains of thought that can occur, of the differences between conscious and subconscious processing, and of what it means to focus upon one train of thought to the exclusion of others. What—who—does the focussing, what happens to those other trains of thought as they are excluded? (Some, I am certain continue silently, unheeded, as subconscious processes that may later interrupt to again force conscious attention to themselves.) And what does it mean to have *conscious attention*? Can there be attention that is not conscious? What—who—experiences the result of conscious attentional processes?

Some of these issues seem to result directly from the properties of an animate cognitive organism. An animate organism can not afford the luxury of concentrating entirely upon a problem until it has been completed. Animate organisms must be multiple-minded, data-driven by environmental events, ever ready to capitalize on the accidents of the world, or to avoid the unexpected dangerous spots. The tasks we assign ourselves to do are often long and complex ones, things which we are incapable of completing at one sitting. We have finite cognitive resources and these must be deployed in some manner that is effective. We can't be entirely data-driven, else the steady flow of information from the sensory system would completely occupy our attention: we must be able to exclude the excludable, to concentrate upon that which is most important (or interesting) at the moment.

Subconscious processing seems essential to functioning. Whatever the special properties of consciousness, they are not needed by all mental processes. (Elsewhere I have argued that consciousness is important for the formation of intentions, the monitoring of their performance, and that it is needed only where the actions to be performed are not routine and well established.) More on this in the section on skills.

Glimpses into the role of conscious and subconscious processing can come from several sources. Hypnotic experiences offer one method, and they can be performed with some rigor in the experimental laboratory. Experiences of sub-conscious problem-solving or memory retrieval are often experienced and talked about, and there is some possibility that they too can be explored experimentally. Studies of attention are, of course, another possible route, one that has been under active exploration. And there are the errors that people make, slips of the tongue, slips of action, another source of information about subconscious pro-cesses and their relationship to conscious ones, to thoughts and motives and intentions. Experiential literature is relevant too, although it must be approached with caution, separating out the description of the experience from the interpreta-tion of that experience, something the experiencer may not be able to do as well as an external observer.

Development

A child is not a small sized-adult, simply lacking in experience, in physical development, and in knowledge, waiting for its head to be filled with the mindstuff of an adult. As adults, we have a wide range of skills, enormous amounts of detailed, specialized knowledge, well established belief systems. We are not just more than children, we are different.

The study of development is well established, of course, hardly in need of suggestions or advice. (Although the studies concentrate upon the years just after birth, with little exploration of adolescence, adulthood, or aging). But in the study of adult cognition there seems to be the implicit assumption that once we come to understand adults, children will simply be seen to be at various stages along the pathway towards the adult. Perhaps. But perhaps also that the complex-ity and experience of the adult will forever mask some properties. Automatic behavior masks the underlying structure, pushing things beneath the conscious surface to the inaccessibility of subconscious processes. Well established belief and knowledge systems mask their content.

Much of cognitive behavior could be studied best through the developmen-tal cycle, with the history of the development leading to better understanding of the adult. Animate organisms take very long times to reach adulthood: the human is learning new concepts throughout the entire life span. Language learning goes on through the late teenage years, and vocabulary learning never ceases. We are fundamentally organisms that learn, that develop over time. By ignoring this aspect of behavior and concentrating on the static phases we may miss the keys to understanding.

Emotion

And what is the role of emotion in the study of cognition? We leave it to the poet, the playwright, the novelist. As people, we delight in art and in music. We fight, get angered, have joy, grief, happiness. But as students of mental events, we are ignorant of why, how.

Emotion. Is it a leftover of a primitive alerting system, or is it a sophisticated set of states reaching its highest pinnacle in the human? Earlier I argued in the direction of the latter point of view. Now, I simply remind you of the issue. The study of emotion is an important field, with important findings and implications for the study of cognition. We cannot ignore our biological heritage, ignore our emotional states. Geschwind, in his paper, reminds us of the fundamental role that emotion plays in biological organisms, and of the close relationship between the neurological structures thought to be important for emotion and those thought to be important for memory. Indeed, there is some experimental evidence for state-induced memory retrieval, so that we remember best events whose emotional content matches our current state: sad events are best remembered while sad, happy ones while happy. Geschwind suggested that some neurological control structures have dual activations, one from below—from the emotions—one from above—the intellect. We smile, cry, and laugh from emotional signals: our attempt to mimic these acts from intellectual desires or upon receipt of a verbal command to do so recreates neither the true emotion, nor the same motor actions. An observer can often tell which behavior is real, which synthetic.

Interaction

Human beings are social organisms. Our intelligence does not operate in isolation, but rather in conjunction. We interact with others, we transmit knowledge through cultures.

We supplement our intelligence with social interaction, by our use of the environment, through the construction of artifacts: reading and writing (and paper, pen, printing press); machine transportation; communication methods that operate over distance (signalling devices, mail services, tele- graph, phone, vision); machines for commerce, for other essentials of life; and machines for computation. The interactions that result become a fundamental aspect of our behavior. In some sense our intelligence has become partially externalized, contained in the artifacts as much as in our head. (''I don't need to know that,'' we say, ''I just need to know . . .''—choose one: ''who to ask,'' ''where to look,'' ''where to go to find out,'' ''that it is known.'')

My major concern here is social interactions, but the issues of interaction share properties, whether it be with person, society, machine. We need to have mental models of the people (and things) with which we interact, for communication depends strongly upon mutual use of shared knowledge, shared understandings. Without a good model of the digital-chronograph-stopwatch-calendar-timer-watch, remembering which buttons to push for what is a hopeless task. With a good mental model (''good'' does not mean the ''true'' model, just a consistent one), the buttons make sense and the use is facilitated. Without a good mental model of our conversational partners, the conversation does not make progress. ''Where is the empire state building?'' The answer depends upon why the question was asked, in what part of the world it was asked, and how much the questioner needs to know.

Much of the study of cognitive processes has been the study of the isolated person. Much of the study of interactive groups has been of the dynamics of the situation, or of the behavioral aspects of the group. To my knowledge, little has been done to combine these efforts, to examine the individual cognitive processes as they are used within interactive settings. But, because the normal mode for the human is to interact, the studies of memory and language and problem solving and decision making in isolation address only one part of the mechanisms of human cognition.

The earlier section on "Cybernetics and Behavior" was intended to introduce the importance of the consideration of interaction, and so I pass on to the next issue.

Language and Perception

I include these two issues to remind us that they exist, to dispel any illusion that I have forgotten them. But I do not wish to discuss either language or perception, primarily because they are of such central importance that they have already received sufficient emphasis. Actually, the emphasis is itself a problem. There is a tendency to identify the study of Cognitive Science with the study of these two topics (and within perception, with visual perception). I believe this to be mistaken, a view that is both wrong and unfortunate. Even language and perception themselves are complex topics, with many different aspects of cognition interwoven together. Like all of the issues within Cognitive Science, these different aspects support one another, enriching the performance of one domain through the knowledge and characteristics of the other domains. I do not believe we can solve the problems of interpretation of language and of perception until we have made substantive progress on the other 10 issues of cognitive science.

Learning

Learning. Recognized by many as a key issue. Still eluding us. In the early days of psychology and in the construction of artificial devices for intelligent behavior, learning was the core topic of study. Machines were constructed that were to learn through their interactions, perhaps to acquire broad, general intelligence as a result. Psychologists developed global theories of human and animal behavior, often built around such fundamental learning principles as "the law of effect" or "associative properties of learning and memory." It all has come to nought. Today, the study of learning is not considered a central part of either psychology or artificial intelligence. Why? Perhaps because the understanding of learning requires knowing about problems of representation, of input (perception), of output (performance), and of thought and inference. It is only recently that we began to understand these issues with appropriate depth.

We spend much of our lifetimes learning: in a sense, we learn from everything we do. If learning is not yet understood, it is because there is more to it than the simple accumulation of knowledge. Accumulation is indeed one form of learning, but there are other things that must be done. One fundamental mode of learning is that of restructuring one's knowledge, reformulating the very basis of understanding of some topic as a result of new concepts and new experiences. Then there is the tuning of behavior, the fine sharpening of adequate skills and understanding to that of the expert, smooth, efficient, effortless.

There has been remarkably little study of learning—real learning, the learning of complex topics, the learning that takes months, even years to accomplish. Elsewhere I have estimated that experts at a task may spend 5,000 hours acquiring their skills: that is not such a long time; it is 2½ years of full-time study, 40 hours a week, 50 weeks a year. Not much time to become a professional tennis player, or computer programmer, or linguist. What goes on during that time? Whatever it is, it is slow, continuous. No magic dose of knowledge in the form of pill or lecture. Just a lot of slow, continual exposure to the topic, probably accompanied by several bouts of restructuring of the underlying mental representations, reconceptualizations of the concepts, plus many hours of accumulation of large quantities of facts.

The relative importance of learning is well understood and often stated. We know how important learning is for the child, and how important the developmental sequence from child to adult. Most of us are professional educators. Surprise, then, that so little is known about learning (and so little about the complement, teaching). And in this case, the lack is, in part, from lack of trying. People talk fondly of computer programs that will start with some fundamentals and acquire all the knowledge needed by some natural sequence of learning, experiencing the environment in which it must function. Very little effort gets spent at studying what it would take to accomplish this, perhaps because there is implicit realization that the task is harder than it might seem. Perhaps the sober realization that a newborn infant takes 25 years to become a fledgling professional, perhaps 5,000 hours of practice and training after the fundamentals have been acquired. Who wants a computer program that can't perform well for the first 25 years of fulltime running (or even for the first 5,000 hours—try explaining that to the government funding agency or the University faculty committee, especially when the first few attempts don't even learn after those periods). And so the study and understanding of the learning process remains at a miniscule level. Pity.

Memory

Do not be impressed by all that is presumably known about the psychology of memory. Less is known than you might think.

Research on the properties of memory has several important functions, some obvious, some not so obvious. For one, it must be obvious that human memory is central to human cognition, and that in general, memory systems are central to cognitive systems (that PCS again). But the complexities of retrieval from a very large memory store are not well appreciated. In Computer Science, the real difficulties of memory retrieval have not yet been faced.

How does one find the information required to answer a question when the form of the question was not anticipated at the time of acquiring the information? Not possible with artificial systems today, a commonplace occurrence with people. And how is the desired information recognized once it is found if it wasn't known in the first place? If I seek the name of a long-lost colleague and retrieve the name Isaac Newton, how do I reject that as the name I seek when I do not know the sought-for name? This example provides its own clue to the solution, but the general case is not so simple. How do we remember stories, events, experiences? More to the point, how do we retrieve them when least we expect them?

Memory has some other puzzles. We recognize the meanings of words in tenths of seconds (as in reading), yet may take hours or days to retrieve one of those words when we seek it for use in a sentence. And what is it that keeps the memory search going for those hours or days, while conscious thought proceeds in other directions, when the need for the word may have long passed? Current events bring to mind previous experiences, not always in any obvious fashion. It is a well accepted statement that memory is associative, that memory structures are organized into some form: networks, concepts, prototypes, basic levels, schemas, frames, units, scripts. How? We need to understand the representation of knowledge, including the process that operate upon the representation. What is motor memory like, or image, or spatial information?

Associations among memory concepts have the immediate suggestion that somehow there is the equivalent of wires interconnecting memory structures. A little thought indicates that the notion of wires (neurons) simply will not do. That implies much too much knowledge of the wire (or its biological equivalent) that is to snake its way among the already existing stuff to the spot some distance away that might correspond to the new stuff (hold with me for the moment the belief that memories are stored in places). Alternatives to wires are not easy to find, the major candidate being numbered, labelled places (don't worry about numbers: just realize that each place must have a unique name). Then, the association between two memory structures is done by giving each one the unique name of the other, trusting to the existence of some clever machinery that can get from one place to another if only it has this name. This problem—I call it the "address problem"—is fundamental to the organization of any large scale associative memory. Bobrow and I have suggested that memory access is by means of "descriptions" of the items sought, our attempt to overcome the address problem. In these meetings, Minsky proposes an alternative view, one that says there are indeed wires (nerves) between associated memory structures, and that the problems of physical interconnection thereby create severe practical constraints on the sorts of things that can get related to one another.

But wait a minute. Why is it that I assume that memories are stored in places. Can't they be distributed in space? (Remember the hologram.) They can. Essentially there are two different classes of memory structures: place memories (the sort I have just described) and additive memories, memory structures which superimpose particular memories on top of one another, relying on various schemes to extract the relevant information. Additive memories include holograms, so-called "associative memories," and perceptrons (and its modern descendants). These memories offer, for free, content-addressable storage and retrieval, but pose their own host of problems. There has not yet been sufficient research on additive memory structures.

And finally, but of great importance, there are the functional properties of the memory system that have received some attention. Short-term (primary memory) working memory, activations in memory. Then there are various uses of memory: strategies for organizing, strategies for retrieval, rehearsal, the repeating over and over again of an item in temporary memory in order to maintain it while—while what?—while other operations can get done on it, I suppose. Is there one temporary memory? Many? Any? How is stuff represented in permanent memory, in working memory? Images? Propositions? I stop. I could go on indefinitely, but these issues are well known.

Performance

Performance, too long neglected, now just starting to receive its due attention. The problem of output, of performance, of motor control. The human hand is a marvelously complex instrument, with 27 bones, controlled by over 40 muscles (most of the muscles being in the forearm, connected to the fingers through an intricate set of tendons). The high-speed typist or musician moves the fingers with intervals of less than 100 msec., fingers simultaneously moving in different directions for different targets, with different time schedules for their time of tapping the target key (or string). Interesting errors arise in these high-speed operations, errors indicative of control structures: the doubling error in typing in which the wrong letter of a word is doubled, as when "look" becomes "lokk"; the alternation error, similar in spirit to the double in which "these" might become "thses"; the transposition error, in which two neighboring letters exchange positions so that "music" gets typed as "muisc," almost always occurring across hands as if the difficulty resulted from a synchronization problem between the hands, hardly ever within hands. And once mis-synchronized, the hands can continue, smoothly, wrongly, as in my transformation of "artificial" into "aritifical" in the typing of the draft of this paper, each "i" coming one position early. The control process for going from perception of rough draft to the rapid movement of the fingers that produces the final copy is immense, involving synchronization of looking, perception, reading, motor programming, and feedback.

Consider handwriting, simple on the surface, complex in the details. A set of orthogonal muscle control systems, with intricate timing relationships (50 msec timing pulses, so some say). Handwriting can be thought of at many levels: organization of the ideas, determination of the words, physical organization of the words on the page, control of the letters, with individual motions of various sorts—micro motion to make the individual letters, macro motion to shift the palm across the page (the movement occurring only at orthographically determined locations), the global motion to place the hand on the page or move it when returning to a new line or adjusting the placement of words on the page. Each level controlled, perhaps, by different parts of the cognitive system, for the control of the precise timing signals that create the letter segments would seem to be a different problem than determining during what part of the word the palm may shift, which is in turn different from the backup required to dot the i's, cross the t's, or the large shift required when, say, deciding to set things off indented with a large gap from the preceding line.

The motor control programs are non-trivial in character, their set up being as much a cognitive function as is reading, or perceiving, or talking. They take time—longer with longer or more complex motor sequences. They can be interfered with by simultaneous acts. They require long periods of training.

With all the muscles to control, with so many degrees of freedom possible because of the numerous joints and the flexibility of the body, the computation of the proper motion of each antagonist muscle pair seems beyond possibility. It probably is. Bernstein (1967), the Soviet investigator of motion, argued for complexes of motor control, systems in which one controls ratios and higher level parameters, the local computation available at the spinal cord and lower taking care of the local translations into muscle commands.

Huge hunks of the brain are devoted to motor control. The cerebellum, a marvelous device, seems dedicated to the function, as is the motor cortex. With so much of the brain dedicated to motor control, it seems unthinkable that this issue should be divorced from the study of higher mental processes. The sensory systems and the motor control systems are intimately linked, closely related neurologically. Probably closely linked psychologically.

The problems of performance are real, they require understanding of computational issues of considerable sophistication, and they interact with perceptual and thought processes in fundamental ways. It is possible to argue that much of our knowledge of the world resides in our knowledge of the procedures that interact with the world, that the perceptual-cognitive-motor schemas are unitary memory constructs, and the separation of one from the others destroys the whole.

Skill

Skill? Why is not skill the same as learning, or performance, or memory? Isn't skill simply expert performance?

Skill. A combination of learning and performance. But more than that, perhaps a fundamental aspect of human cognition. Suppose that our biological heritage developed by means of specialized subsystems for specialized behavior. Maybe skills are independent pockets of knowledge, with independent knowledge sources, computational resources, even independent brain and body structures. Maybe, maybe not. As usual, I suspect the truth is somewhere in–between: we are neither general purpose computational devices, all knowledge and abilities being treated alike, nor are we highly specialized subsystems, each independent of the rest. In fact, let me call separate skills "separable," as opposed to "independent." We cannot ignore the specialization of function of an evolving biological creature, and so the issue of whether we have separable skills is an important one, with major implications for theories of human cognition.

Skills, specialized subsystems of knowledge and of performance. The expert at a task performs differently than the non-expert: the statement is correct, but misses the essence of the difference. The expert performer is qualitatively and quantitatively different than the non-expert. Bartlett, in his book on thinking, stated that a major difference between expert and non-expert performance was timing. Experts had lots of time. They did their tasks easily, smoothly, without apparent effort, and with plenty of excess time. The expert tennis player is there before the ball. The expert pilot flies "ahead of the plane." The difficult looks simple. The non-expert is always scurrying, barely able to cope, rushing from this to that. With the non-expert, the difficult task looks difficult.

There are other differences, differences in perspective. Consider what happens when you first learn to drive an automobile. The instructions you receive emphasize the actions and the mechanics: hold the steering wheel this way, synchronize foot (for clutch) and hand (for gearshift) that way. As you progress, the point of view changes. Now you are turning the wheel, not moving your hands clockwise. Then you are turning the car, later you are entering that driveway. Eventually, when a truly expert driver, you drive to the bank, go shopping. The differences in the qualitative feeling of the performance are great. At the expert level, you may no longer be aware of all the subsidiary operations that you perform: you look at the driveway, form the intention to enter, and the car obediently follows suit. Driving the car becomes as natural as walking, the car becoming as much a part of the body's controlled appendages as the limbs.

Thought

It is hardly necessary to state that the study of cognition should include the study of thought. The concern, though is not that thought should be included, it is with how the inclusion should go. You may have thought we know a lot about thought. I claim not: what we do know is important, but primarily restricted to that part of the thought process available to conscious awareness—and as long as we lack knowledge of consciousness, we will lack a complete understanding of the role of conscious thought.

A question to be debated seriously is how much thought can be studied in isolation, as if it were a pure, abstract activity, divorced from special knowledge or special mechanisms. The mathematics of thought does indeed have this character, and as that mathematics has been used for models of human thought, it has tended to yield the vision of the human as a general purpose computational device.

But what if we are not so general, if our thought processes are designed for world interaction, with mental models of experiences being the major reasoning method, with limited ability to hold formal constructions in mind while we perform abstract operations upon them. I believe that too much emphasis has been given to possible formal properties of human reasoning, not enough to informal, experiential based models of reasoning. Take care, though, with this argument. I agree with Newell that we must have some class of a general physical symbol system as a basis for much of cognition. We may be specialized, but we can also be general, learning new abilities, reasoning through novel situations, planning. Still, the strategy used may be to model experiences, to use the properties of spatial arrays to aid our computations, perhaps by using wired-in, specialized spatial knowledge. So I agree with Johnson-Laird, too.

The environment plays an important role in thought. We solve some problems by imagining the environment, solve others by using the environment. Micronesian navigators evidently use the outrigger of their canoe as a sort of analog computer which, when coupled with star positions and rate of passage of water past the canoe, can be used to aid precise navigation for hundreds of miles, out of sight of land much of the way (Hutchins, 1979). We use external aids ourselves, such as pencils, papers, drawings, even the placement of objects on a table. The computer is, in some sense, an artificial extension of our intellect, invented by humans to extend human thought processes. Just as we no longer need to master the art of memory because of the ease of writing, and just as we may no longer need to master arithmetic because of the availability of the calculator, or calligraphy because of the typewriter, we may perhaps forego some forms of thought once small portable computers become commonplace. (Hopefully, thus freeing ourselves for higher levels of thought processes.) Here is not the place for social commentary on these changes, just notice of the heavy dependence our culture places on technological aids to thought processes.

AFTERTHOUGHTS

Is There a Thirteenth Issue? "You left out an issue," my readers rush to tell me, "why do you not have X?" The answer to some extent must be arbitrary. The division of Cognitive Science into 12 issues is idiosyncratic. My list is meant to cover the important principles and phenomena, to be those things that must be included in the study of cognition. The important point, therefore, is not whether my divisions are correct, but whether I have complete coverage. Have I left out anything? Among the various suggestions I have received, one stands out: motivation.

Motivation, the Thirteenth Issue? What makes something interesting? Why do I sometimes watch a television show when I pass by an active set, even when I do not wish to? ("Turn off that TV set," I tell my son, as I walk into the living room, sit down beside him, and watch for 30 minutes, muttering to myself all the while.) For years I studied learning, concerned about the proper way to present material to improve a student's understanding. I studied many things, including proper organizational structure of the material, various instructional strategies, the making of detailed models of teacher, of student, and of topic matter. Yet none of these variables seemed to be as powerful as the one I did not study: changing the motivation of the student. Why is it that we do some tasks easily, readily, while others, seemingly no different, repel us, requiring huge amounts of self discipline to start, and then to finish? Interest and motivation seem intimately linked, the issues seemingly more complex than can be provided by simple analysis of missing knowledge structures or recourse to concepts such as the overall goals of a person. Note too that the desire to do something is not the same as being motivated to do that thing: I may want to do something, but find it difficult to force myself to do it. I may wish not to do something else, yet find it difficult to stop myself. I am reminded of the distinction Geschwind has made between laughing or crying to a verbal command or to internal signals, the one is difficult or impossible, the other natural and easy.

The arguments for motivation were pointed out to me by Craig Will, one of my graduate students who read an early draft of the paper. Motivation can make the difference between learning or not, decent performance or not, what one attends to, what acts one does. Once, it was a leading topic in psychology, although oftentimes linked to emotion: "Motivation and Emotion," one chapter of a textbook on Human Information Processing is called. Will was persuasive. Is motivation a thirteenth issue?

I think not. I believe motivation to result from a combination of things, from one's fundamental knowledge and goal structures, partially from emotional variables, and partially from decisions about the application of mental resources. Hence, the phenomena of motivation come from various aspects of several issues: Belief Systems, Emotion, and Consciousness. Moreover, and more important, I am not convinced that there is a single phenomenon of motivation (if there is, it should indeed be afforded the special status of an issue). Rather, I believe it to be a complex of things, some biological, some cultural, some emotional, some the result of conscious goals and intentions, others subconscious. Motivation is indeed important, worthy of serious study, and a major determiner of our behavior. I believe, however, that it is a derived issue, composed of different aspects of the others.

The Environmental System and Cultural Knowledge

One early reader of this paper, Michael Cole, suggested that I did not give proper consideration to the role of environment, especially in its role in development. It was his view that my treatment was not satisfactory, that I ". . . need badly to consider the ES, the Environmental System, consisting of physical and social parts, that is an equal partner in giving shape to the super-system comprised of RS and PCS" (The Regulatory System and the Pure Cognitive System). In part, Cole argued that I could make a much stronger case for:

> . . . the relevance of evolutionary neuroscience, developmental psychology, and cognitive anthropology. Why? Because the mature system that encompasses RS and PCS must develop through a series of interactions between RS and ES (the Regulatory and the Environmental Systems). The PCS should be seen as an evolving adaptation. Where does culture enter? At some point it becomes a part of ES, one with an external source of memory over generations to supplant the "memory" built in by evolution. The Cognitive System does some work on the Environmental System too, so the current environment is always the product of Regulatory—Environmental—Cognitive System interaction.

The discussion with Cole continued for several days. The behavior of people is shaped by their environment, we both agreed, and a good deal of one's cultural knowledge is the shared strategies that develop for the use of environment. We change the environment through our technological developments and our science, literature, and mathematics. The culture provides us with cultural transformers, and amplifiers, tools that expand our mental abilities. Cole argued that:

> What culturally organized knowledge does is to carry a lot of information for us. An extreme way to talk about it is that the information is in the environment, not in the head, so a lot of the processing that experiments require to be done in the head can be, and is, short-circuited in real life. . . . One issue is how to describe cognition as an interaction between head and world where some of the thought power resides in each locus.

The comments are complete enough to be self-contained. Where they are not, where, for example, the manner in which we use environmental information is unclear, the field is unclear. A major task for Cognitive Science.

IMPLICATIONS FOR COGNITIVE SCIENCE

The fact that I can write such a paper, ask such questions, complain with some reasonable specificity, is a positive sign about the emergence of a new discipline. It is a sign of progress that things are sufficiently well understood that the list of non-understood topics can be prepared.

What are the implications for research? In part, my suggestions are going to be received with displeasure. Am I suggesting that everyone become everyone, each person an expert in all other disciplines, all issues? No. I do not believe that productive research, the sort that leads to solid advances in understanding, comes about when efforts are spread apart too thinly over too wide a range. I believe in depth-first research, in concentration upon the minute details of the problem.

But detailed, narrowly-based research should not take place within a vacuum. The choice of the area in which to make the detailed, deep probes must be selected with thought and care to the eventual product of the research. My argument is for goal directed, conceptually based research planning, leading to careful selection of topics, then plunging as deeply as possible into the tangled web of specific problems that exist within any area of concentration. Then, let the results drive the investigation, so that the studies become the driving force for further research: ye olde standard combination of top-down and bottom-up processing, both conceptually driven and data-driven.

But the research efforts should cease now and then for pause and reflection. Where is the work leading to? Are the tangled problems worthy of further effort, or do they simply lead further from the goal? Without such broad reconsiderations there is a tendency in all domains of research to be captured by the problem of the year, by the race among competing research groups to untangle the theory problems that seem to be holding up current progress. The danger is that in the fun of the race, in the excitement of overcoming technical difficulties, one may forge off in directions of little concern to anyone. For me to urge the need to step back and resurvey the direction of research is not particularly novel (although perhaps it cannot be stated too often). But I am also urging a particular way in which to stand off, a particular set of issues to reconsider each time the overview is made.

I believe in the decomposition of difficult problems into smaller, nearly independent issues—what Simon has called the nearly decomposable problems. We make progress by picking the right size problem, the one we can handle with today's knowledge. I would be doing a disservice were I to convince too many of you to become generalists, biting off more than can be chewed, or swallowed, or digested, even if the bites were from the correct things. I urge the philosophy of nearly decomposable systems, but global considerations of the sort I discuss here are necessary in order to determine the right decomposition.

The major results of my concerns should probably be in the education of new researchers, education at the advanced levels. It is here that I think my points best made, for it is within the education of ourselves and our students that the wider implications and wider aspects of our field ought to be acknowledged, discussed, considered. I would certainly not want my 12 issues to become 12 examination questions or 12 reading lists. I wish Cognitive Science to be recognized as a complex interaction among different issues of concern, an interaction that will not be properly understood until all the parts are understood, with no part independent of the others, the whole requiring the parts, and the parts the whole.

REFERENCES

I avoided references in the text, for the purpose of the paper was to convey the spirit of the argument, not the technical details of each issue. Here I attempt to make up for that lack, citing key references for points discussed within the paper. On most of the issues of this paper I will not give references. Many of the areas are well known, well studied, and for me to select one or two references would do little good. I will present references to material that has heavily influenced me or to things I think are important but not well enough known. This set of references is not meant to be an exhaustive listing of the critical works in Cognitive Science. It is a personal listing of works that I have found useful along with citations for key ideas discussed in this paper.

A view of the classroom relevant to my discussion—and in part the source of my ideas—comes from the work of Mehan and his colleagues: Mehan (1978, 1979). The report on the Tenerife crash comes from Roitsch, Babcock, and Edmunds (1979).

I restrict myself to two references on consciousness. I take this opportunity to refer to my own "Slips of the mind" (Norman, 1979), a paper that addresses some of the issues of conscious and subconscious control, and gives a reading list on these topics (including Freud, and the rather extensive literature on Slips of the Tongue and Spoonerisms). Second, I recommend Hilgard's (1977) treatment of hypnosis.

I am not expert enough in belief systems to give definitive references. Moreover, some of the work I do know of has only been reported to me verbally. But I recommend Berlin and Kay (1969) on color terms, Berlin (1978) on ethnobiological classification, Cole and Scribner (1974) on culture and thought, Cole, Sharp, and Lave (1976) on the cognitive consequences of education, D'Andrade (1976) on beliefs about illness, and Rosch (1978) on the principles of categorization. Abelson has long been studying belief systems from the point of view of social psychology, including the construction of simulation models of people's belief structures (see Abelson, 1973).

Emotion is a field with an extensive literature. The book that has had the major influence on me is *Mind and emotion*, by George Mandler (1975). This book gives an explicit treatment of the relationship between emotion and cognition from within the framework of human information processing. My discussion of the subservience of the cognitive system to the emotional and regulatory system had its origin here (and from my discussions with Mandler).

Memory has a large literature, and I will therefore avoid citing any of it.

But several non-traditional sources seem important to mention. One new book that contains extensive discussions of neglected areas is Kihlstrom and Evan's (1979) *Functional disorders of memory*. Here are discussions of anomalies, amnesias, aging, dreaming, state-dependent memory, motivated forgetting, and repression. There are other treatments of most of these topics, but nowhere are they all so conveniently gathered together: an important collection of topics that ought also to be important, but that have been largely ignored in the cognitive psychology of memory.

Kohonen (1977) provides one treatment of associative (additive) memories, as does Anderson, Silverstein, Ritz, and Jones (1977). The book edited by Hinton and Anderson (in preparation) will treat many aspects of additive memories.

Performance and skill have a few simple references I can point you at. I have already mentioned the Soviet investigator Bernstein (1967), and his works provide an important foundation. Stelmach's (1978) collection provides a valuable place to start for the psychological literature. Gallistel (1980) gives an interesting and important review of the neurological work in this area. Other sources exist.

Abelson, R. P. The structure of belief systems. In R. C. Schank & K. Colby (Eds.), *Computer models of thought and language*. San Francisco: Freeman, 1973.

Anderson, J. A., Silverstein, J. W., Ritz, S. A., & Jones, R. S. Distinctive features, categorical perception, and probability learning: Some applications of a neural model. *Psychological Review*, 1977, *84*, 413–451.

Berlin, B. Ethnobiological classification. In E. Rosch & B. B. Lloyd (Eds.), *Cognition and categorization*. Hillsdale, New Jersey: Larry Erlbaum Associates, 1978.

Berlin, B., & Kay, P. *Basic color terms: Their universality and evolution*. Berkeley: University of California Press, 1969.

Bernstein, N. *The co-ordination and regulation of movements*. New York: Pergamon Press, 1967.

Cole, M., & Scribner, S. *Culture and thought*. New York: Wiley, 1974.

Cole, M., Sharp, D. W., & Lave, C. The cognitive consequences of education. *The Urban Review*, 1976, *9*, 218–233.

D'Andrade, R. G. A propositional analysis of U.S. American beliefs about illness. In K. H. Basso & H. A. Selby (Eds.), *Meaning in anthropology*. Albuquerque: University of New Mexico Press, 1976.

Gallistel, R. *The organization of action*. Hillsdale, N. J.: Lawrence Erlbaum Associates, 1980.

Hilgard, E. R. *Divided consciousness: Multiple controls in human thought and action*. New York: Wiley, 1977.

Hinton, G. E., & Anderson, J. A. (Eds.), *Parallel models of associative memory*. Hillsdale, N.J.: Lawrence Erlbaum Associates, 1981.

Hutchins, E. Conceptual structures in pre-literate navigation. Unpublished manuscript. La Jolla, California: Program in Cognitive Science, University of California, San Diego, 1979.

Kihlstrom, J. F. & Evans, F. J. (Eds.), *Functional disorders of memory*. Hillsdale, N. J.: Lawrence Erlbaum Associates, 1979.

Kohonen, T. *Associative memory: A system-theoretic approach*. Berlin: Springer-Verlag, 1977.

James, W. *Principles of psychology*. New York: Holt, 1890. (Reprinted New York: Dover, 1950.)

Mandler, G. *Mind and emotion*. New York: Wiley, 1975.

Mehan, H. Structuring school structure. *Harvard Educational Review*, 1978, *48(1)*, 32–64.

Mehan, H. *Learning lessons*. Cambridge, Mass.: Harvard University Press, 1979.

Norman, D. A., *Slips of the mind and an outline for a theory of action*. (CHIP technical report 88). LaJolla, California: Center for Human Information Processing, the University of California, San Diego; La Jolla, CA. 92093, 1979.

Norman, D. A. *Human learning and memory*. New York: Scientific American, 1980 (in press).

Roitsch, P. A., Babcock, G. L., & Edmunds, W. W. *Human factors report on the Tenerife accident. Aircraft accident report: Pan American World Airways, Boeing 747, N737 AP: KLM Royal Dutch Airlines, Boeing 747, PH-BUF; Tenerife, Canary Islands, March 27, 1977.* Washington: Air Line Pilots Association, 1979. (Actual report is not dated.)

Rosch, E. Principles of categorization. In E. Rosch & B. B. Lloyd (Eds.), *Cognition and categorization*. Hillsdale, New Jersey: Larry Erlbaum Associates, 1978.

Stelmach, G. E. (Ed.), *Information processing in motor control and learning*. New York: Academic Press, 1978.

ACKNOWLEDGMENTS

This paper is the direct result of the interactions within our Cognitive Science Program. Two major seminars, each lasting for the entire academic year, served as the testing ground for many of these ideas, the source for others. One was our "Cognitive Science Seminar," a course held primarily for our visiting scholars in the Program, but including local faculty, graduate students, and visitors. (The major contributors were Dave Rumelhart, Bob Buhr, Larry Carleton, Geoff Hinton, Ed Hutchins, Ian Moar, Chris Riesbeck, and Len Talmy. Jim Anderson and Mike Maratsos joined us at the end of the year.) The other seminar was a faculty meeting, organized by Mike Cole, with fierce and useful interchanges among Aaron Cicourel, Mike Cole, Roy D'Andrade, George Mandler, Jean Mandler, Bud Mehan, and Dave Rumelhart. Thus, the section on the relationship between the regulatory and the pure cognitive systems originated in (and was modified by) the Cognitive Science Seminar, while the section on the cybernetic view of the classroom resulted from the faculty seminar's consideration of the studies of Mehan and Cole. The support for all of this was provided by a grant from the Alfred P. Sloan Foundation.

Several people have made useful comments on a draft of this paper, especially Craig Will and Mike Cole. I have incorporated their comments at relevant spots in the paper (Will on motivation, Cole on culture).

Although research results are not presented in this paper, various research projects over the years have helped develop these views. Research on learning (and memory) was supported by a contract from the Office of Naval Research and the Advanced Research Projects Agency, monitored by ONR under contract N00014-76-C-0628, NR 154-387. Research on motor performance was supported by ONR under contract N00014-79-C-0323, NR 157-437. Research on pilot errors and applied human information processing was supported by DARPA and monitored by ONR under contract N00014-79-C-0515, NR 157-434. Support was also provided by grant MH-15828 from the National Institutes of Mental Health to the Center for Human Information Processing.

Author Index

Adams, N., 119, *146*
Allport, D. A., *84*
Ashby, W. R., 42, *84*
Austin, G. A., 13, *24*

Barr, A., *262*
Bartlett, R., 115, *144*
Baylor, G. W., 168, 174, *187*
Begg, I., 152, 153, *187*
Berlin, B., 148, *187*, 293, *294*
Beth, E. W., 159, *187*
Bethell-Fox, C. E., 182, *189*
Birnbaum, L., *146*
Black, J. B., 119, 120, *144*
Black, M., 81, *84*
Bledsoe, W. W., 160, *187*
Bloomfield, D., 31, *35*
Bobrow, D. G., 241, *262*
Boger, R. S., 160, *187*
Boole, G., *187*
Bower, G. H., 119, 120, *144*, 148, 167, 168, 174, *187*
Braine, M. D. S., 160, *187*
Brainerd, W. S., 51, 52, *84*
Brooks, L., 167, *187*
Bruner, J. S., 13, *24*
Buchanan, B. G., 20, *24*
Bugelski, B. R., 168, *187*
Buneman, O. P., *100*
Butterfield, E. C., 40, *85*
Byrne, B., 167, *187*

Cameron, S., 42, *85*
Carbonell, J. G., 107, 116, 118, *144, 145*
Carnap, R., 162, *187*
Carroll, 113, *144*
Ceraso, J., 153, *187*
Chapman, I. J., 154, *187*
Chapman, J. P., 154, *187*
Chase, W. G., 169, *187*
Chisholm, R. M., 211, *230*
Chomsky, N., 13, *25*, 164, 173, *187, 189*
Church, A., 52, *84*
Clark, H., 40, *84*
Clark, H. H., 161, 162, 169, *187*
Clark, E., 40, *84*
Clark, E. U., 161, 162, *187*

Clarke, A. C., *100*
Cohen, M. R., 160, *187*
Colby, K. M., *144*
Cole, M., 293, *294*
Collins, A. M., 161, *187*
Cooper, L. A., 167, *187*
Courtois, P. J., 18, *25*
Craik, K., 149, *188*
Crick, F., *84*
Cullingford, R. E., 115, 116, *144*

Danto, A., 224, *230*
Davidson, D., 227, 228, *230*
Davies, D. J. M., 165, 173, *188*
DeJong, G. F., 107, 116, *144*
deMowbray, J., 162, 182, *189*
Dennett, D. C., *188*
Denny, J. P., 152, 153, *187*
Derksen, J. A., 83, *85*
Doyle, J., *100*
Dresher, B. E., 119, *144*
Dreyfus, H., 248, *262*
Duda, W. L., *25*

Ehrlich, K., 180, *188*
Erickson, J. R., 153, *188*

Falk, G., 148, *188*
Feigenbaum, E., *262*
Feinberg, J., 224, *230*
Feldman, J., *262*
Feynman, R. P., 40, *84*
Fillmore, C., 108, *144, 262*
Fillmore, C. J., 148, *188*, 200, *206*
Flores, C. F., *262*
Flynn, J. P., 31, 33, *35*
Fodor, J. A., 106, *145*, 158, 161, 173, 174, 179, *188, 189, 262*
Fodor, J. D., 161, 173, 174, 179, *188*
Fujimura, O., 33, *35*
Funt, B. U., 169, *188*

Gadamer, H-G., 246, *262*
Galaburda, A. M., 34, *35*
Galanter, E., 173, *189*
Galton, F., 167, *188*
Garfinkel, H., *262*

Garnham, A., 183, *189*
Garrett, M. F., *188*
Gelernter, H., 169, *188*
Gershman, A. V., 107, *145*
Geschwind, N., 33, *35*, 76, *84*, *262*
Gibbs, G., 162, 182, *189*
Goldman, N., 114, *146*
Goldstein, G. D., 42, *85*
Goodnow, J. J., 13, *24*
Grosz, B. J., *262*
Guyote, M. J., 154, *188*

Haibt, L. H., *25*
Hampshire, S., *230*
Hayes, J. R., 20, *25*, 167, *188*
Hayes-Roth, F., 82, *85*
Hays, D. G., 106, *144*
Hebb, D. O., *100*
Heidegger, M., 248, 257, *262*
Hemphill, L. G., 112, *144*
Henneman, W. H., 160, *187*
Hewitt, C., 83, *84*, 174, *188*
Hintikka, J., 79, 158, *84*, 174, *188*, *262*
Hobbs, J. R., *262*
Holland, J. H., *25*
Holyoak, K. J., 167, *188*
Hopcroft, J. E., 63, *84*
Hornstein, N., *144*
Hume, D., *188*

Inhelder, B., *188*
Isard, S. D., 165, 173, *188*

Jacobi, G. T., 42, *85*
Jenkins, J. J., *144*
Johnson, M., 198, 199, 201, *206*, *262*
Johnson-Laird, P. N., 153, 155, 156, 158, 159, 162, 165, 173, 180, 182, 183, *188*, *189*
Jones, R. S., *294*

Kamp, H., *189*
Kaplan, D., *189*
Karttunen, L., 182, *189*
Katz, J., 109, *144*
Katz, J. J., 161, 162, *189*, *262*
Kay, P., 148, *187*
Kemper, T. L., *35*
Kieras, D., 168, *189*
Kintsch, W., 162, 174, 179, *189*
Klein, S., *145*
Kneale, M., 160, *189*
Kneale, W., 160, *189*
Kosslyn, S. M., 167, 168, *189*
Kripke, S., 79, *84*
Kuhn, T., 251, *262*
Kuo, Z. Y., 31, *35*

Labov, W., *262*
Lachman, J. L., 40, *85*
Lachman, R., 40, *85*
Lakatos, I., *262*
Lakoff, G., 81, *85*, 148, *189*, 198, 199, 201, *206*, 247, *262*
Lamb, S. M., 106, *145*
Lardweber, L. H., 51, 52, *84*
Langley, P., 20, *25*
Lebowitz, M., *146*
Legrenzi, P., 153, *189*
Leighton, R. B., *84*
Leirer, V. O., 154, *190*
LeMay, M., *35*
Lewis, D., *189*
Lighthill, Sir J., 234, *262*
Lindsay, P. H., 40, *85*
Longuet-Higgins, H. C., *100*
Lyons, J., 162, *189*

MacDonnell, M. F., 33, *35*
Mani, K., 180, *188*
Marr, D., *100*, 148, 176, *189*
Martin, E., *189*
Maturana, H. R., 244, 246, 248, 249, *262*
Mazzocco, A., 153, *189*
Meehan, J., 115, *145*
Mehler, J., 106, *145*
Miller, G., 176, *189*
Miller, G. A., 13, *25*, 161, 164, 165, 173, 179, *189*
Minsky, M., 51, 52, *85*, 95, 97, 98, *100*, 107, 139, *145*, 178, *189*, 200, *206*, 241, *262*
Mitchell, T. M., 20, *24*
Montague, R., 173, *189*
Mooers, C. E., *100*
Moran, T. P., 168, 174, *189*
Mountcastle, V., *100*
Moyer, R. S., 167, *190*

Nagel, E., *187*
Nagel, R., 160, 162, 174, *189*
Neisser, V., 40, *85*
Neves, D. A., 20, *25*
Nilsson, N. J., 19, *25*, 74, *85*
Nishihara, H. K., 148, 176, *189*
Norman, D. A., 40, *85*, 148, 161, 169, *190*, 200, *206*, 240, *262*, 293, *295*

Orasanu, J., 182, *190*
Osherson, D., 159, *190*

Paivio, A., 167, 168, *190*
Palmer, R. E., *262*
Palmer, S. E., *85*, 168, 169, 174, *190*
Papert, S., 97, *100*, 260, *262*
Penfield, W., 217, *230*
Piaget, J., *188*

Pomerantz, J. R., 168, *189*
Pribram, K., 179, *189*
Provitera, A., 153, *187*
Putnam, H., 148, *190*
Pylyshyn, Z. W., 168, 169, *190*

Quillian, R., 110, *145*

Reiter, R., 160, *190*
Revlin, R., 154, *190*
Revlis, R., 154, *190*
Rips, L. J., 161, *191*
Ritz, S. A., *294*
Roberts, L. G., 176, *190*
Robinson, J. A., *190*
Rochester, N., 25
Roncato, S., 153, *189*
Rosch, E., 148, *190*, *263*
Rumelhart, D. E., 40, *85*, 148, 161, 169, 174,
    183, *190*, 200, *206*
Sasanuma, S., 33, *35*
Newel, A., 13, 14, *25*, 38, 40, 43, 71, 76, 82,
    85
Rieger, C., 114, *145*, *146*
Riesbech, C. K., 107, 114, *145*, *146*
Rulifson, J. F., 83, *85*

Sands, M., *84*
Saporta, S., *144*
Schank, R. C., 106, 107, 108, 109, 111, 112,
    113, 114, 115, 116, 120, 133, 143, *145*,
    146, 161, *190*, 200, *206*, *263*
Scott, D., 176, *190*
Schorr, D., 120, *146*
Searle, J., 252, 255, *263*
Searle, J. R., *230*, *263*
Sells, S. B., 152, *190*, *191*
Shephard, R. N., 167, 168, *190*
Shoben, E. J., 161, *191*

Silverstein, J. W., *294*
Simon, H. A., 13, 15, 18, 20, 23, *25*, 38, 40,
    43, 71, *85*, 175, *190*
Sloman, A., 168, *191*
Smith, E. E., 119, *146*, 161, *191*
Stalnaker, R. C., *191*
Steedman, M. J., 153, 156, 158, 160, *189*
Stenning, K., 182, *191*
Sternberg, R. J., 154, *188*, *191*
Störring, G., *191*
Strachey, C., 176, *190*

Tealer, L., 106, *145*, *146*
Turing, A. M., *263*
Turner, M. E., 154, *191*
Turner, T. J., 119, 120, *144*

Ullman, J. D., 63, *84*

Waldinger, R. J., 83, *85*
Wasman, M., 31, *35*
Waterman, D. A., 21, *25*, 82, *85*
Weber, S., *146*
Weisbrantz, L., 218, *230*
Wilensky, R., 107, 115, 116, 118, *146*
Willshaw, P. J., *100*
Wilson, E. O., 23, *25*, 42, *85*
Winograd, T., 119, *146*, *191*, 234, 237, 239,
    250, *262*, *263*
Winston, P., *85*, *100*
Wittgenstein, L., 148, *191*, 215, *230*
Woods, W. A., 165, 173, *191*
Woodworth, R. S., 152, *191*
Wykes, T., *191*

Yerkes, R. M., 31, *35*
Yovits, M. C., 42, *85*

Subject Index

Action, 209, 251
    spontaneous, 212
    without intention, 212
Acts, 110
Adaptation, 28
Adaptive systems, 15
Address problem, 94–95, 102, 285
Agents, 7, 88–90
AM, 20
Animate Systems, 277
    cognitive, 273
Architecture, 76, 102
Artificial cognitive systems, 273
Associations, 285
Associative memories, 286, 294
Atmosphere hypothesis, 152, 153
Attention, 34, 279
Automatic action, 212

BACON, 20
Beliefs, 112–113, 208
Belief systems, 278, 293
Brain, 28

Conscious control, 293
Causality, 114
Classroom, 268
Cognitive processes, 251
Cognitive science, 1, 27
    definition, 1, 144, 147, 186, 261
    metaphors, 205
Cognitive systems, 277
Conversation, 200
Church's thesis, 52
Circuit level, 75
Computability, 51
Computer metaphor, 38
Computer systems, 257
Conceptual dependency, 106, 116–117
Conditional operators, 67
Conditions of satisfaction, 208, 214
Consciousness, 279
Conflict resolution, 97
Control, 102
Crossbar problem, 94, 102
Cross-cancellation principle, 97
Cultural knowledge, 278, 291
Cybernetics, 49, 268

Decomposition, 161
Decompositional semantics, 184
Denotation, 58
Designation, 58
Development, 281
Device level, 75
Dispositions, 88, 91, 101
Dissociations, 33
Domains, 249
    for understanding language, 251

Education, 260, 268, 293
Emotion, 33, 88, 101, 208, 275, 281–282, 293
Entailments, of metaphor, 195
Environmental system, 291
Ethnomethodology, 254
Evolution, 23
Expectations, 107
Experience of acting, 217
Experiential Gestalts, 199
Expert systems, 257
Explicit knowledge, 99
Expression, 44

Fear, 208
Feedback, 101, 269–270
Figural effect, 150
Forgetting, 103
FRAN, 148
Frame, 102, 139, 249

General computation, 32
Goals, 74, 115, 118

HAM, 148
Hermeneutics, 244–245
Hierarchical structures, 18
Hope, 208
Human action, 251
Human information processing, 265

Idea, 196
Illocutionary logic, 255
Images, 167–172
Inference, 109–111, 118, 150
Innate systems, 31
Intelligence, 72
Intelligent systems, 14

Intention, 10, 111, 207
  as cause, 223
  of action and perception, 217
  of seeing, remembering and acting, 219
  of usual experience, 214
Intentional objects, 208
Interaction, 251, 282
Interlingual representation, 106
Interpretation, 60
Interpretor control structure, 48
Invariants in artificial phenomena, 15

Kana and Kanjii, 33
K-Knowledge, 96
K-Lines, 12
  principles, 93–94
K-nodes, 92–93, 95–96
Knowledge, 79
Knowledge-tree, 95
K-pyramid, 91
K-recursion principle, 94
KRL, 241

Language, 272, 283
Language understanding, 237
  model, 233, 236
Learning, 19, 95, 98, 103, 283
  not present, 31
Level-band principle, 93–94
Levels of descriptions, 176
Linguistic grounding, 255
Linguistic structure, 251
LNR, 148
Logical inference, 8
Logic of breaking down, 257

Management, 259
MARGIE, 114
Meaning, 161, 239
  postulates, 162, 184
Medical diagnosis, 258
Memory, 270, 284, 293–294
  event, 121
  intentional, 122
  situational, 122
Memory address problem, 94–95
Memory form, 242
Memory Organization Packets, 126, 135, 138, 142
Mental model, 9, 149, 161
  vs propositional, 174, 184
METADENDRAL, 20
Meta-knowledge, 242
Metaphor, 9
  consistency of, 198
  definition, 193
Mimicry, 169

Mind, 72, 88
  constraints on, 41
Model structure, 159
MOP's (see Memory Organization Packets)
Motor control, 287

Naming, 58
Nearly decomposable systems, 18
Natural reasoning, 241
Neural net, 101
Noncomputable functions, 51
Nonmonotonic logic, 241

Objectivity, 247
Ontological metaphors, 194
Orientational metaphors, 193

P-agents, 92
Parallel processes, 17
Perception, 283
Performance, 277, 286, 294
Phenomenal properties, 218
Physical symbol system, 6
  Hypothesis, 72
  universality of, 71
Plans, 117
P-nets, 91
P-pyramid, 80, 95
Pragmatics, 172
Prepositional relationships, 108
Pre-understanding, 245
Primitive, 243
Procedural representation, 235
Procedural semantics, 165
Processor level, 75
Production systems, 17, 82
Program level, 75
Promising, 252
Propositional representations, 167–172
  vs mental models, 174, 184
Prototype, 148, 243
Psychological mode, 208
Purposive systems, 50

Quote, 68

Rationality, 73, 83
Reasoning, 184, 243, 256
Recursion principle, 94
Reference, 58
Referential continuity, 183
Reflexive behavior, 249
Reinforcement, 98
Reminding, 90, 127–128, 131
Representation, 78, 88, 101, 172, 209, 248
  Gestalt structure, 200
Resource dependent reasoning, 257
Resource limited reasoning, 241–243

Schemas, 246, 249, 279
Scripts, 115–116, 120, 123, 138, 142, 249
Self-awareness, 99
Self description, 243
Selfreferential intentions, 213
Semantic elements, 161
Semantic primitives, 161
Serial processes, 17
Short term memory, 91
SHRDLU, 119, 232, 254
Skill, 287–288, 294
Slips, 272, 293
Social interaction, 282
Society of Mind, 88, 101
Spatial inference, 178
Specialized systems, 32
Speech acts, 252
Structural metaphors, 195
Subconscious control, 293
Subjectivity, 247
Syllogisms, 150
Syllogistic inference, 8
Symbol, 39
Symbol processing system, 3
Symbol structures, 44

Symbol system, 16, *38*
   example of, 44
System levels, 74

Tacit knowledge, 99
Teaching, 293
Tenerife, 268, 293
Themes, 118
Thought, 288
Trans, 109
Translation of language, 106
Triggering process, 247
Turing machines, 53
Turing test, 247

UNDERSTAND, 20
Understanding, 128, 251
Universality, 49
   of symbol systems, 71

War, 200
Wired-in mechanisms, 4, 31
Word definition, 238
Working memory, 17